Who's Who in Stuart Britain

being the fifth volume in the
Who's Who in British History series

C. P. HILL

SHEPHEARD-WALWYN

© 1988 C. P. Hill
All rights reserved
First published as *Who's Who in History* Vol. III
by Basil Blackwell, 1965

Revised and enlarged edition first published 1988
by Shepheard-Walwyn (Publishers) Ltd
Suite 34, 26 Charing Cross Road, London WC2H 0DH

British Library Cataloguing in Publication Data

Hill, C. P. (Charles Peter), *1914 -*
    Who's Who in Stuart Britain. — 2nd ed.,
    Rev. and enl. — (Who's Who in British History)
    1. Great Britain, 1603-1714. Biographies.
    Collections
    I. Title   II. Hill, C. P. (Charles Peter),
    1914-   England 1603-1714   III. Series
    941.06′092′2

ISBN 0-85683-075-5

Typesetting by Alacrity Phototypesetters, Banwell Castle,
Weston-super-Mare, Avon.

Printed in Great Britain by A. Wheaton & Co., Ltd., Exeter

CONTENTS

GENERAL INTRODUCTION

The original volumes in the series *Who's Who in History* were well received by readers who responded favourably to the claim of the late C. R. N. Routh, general editor of the series, that there was a need for a work of reference which should present the latest findings of scholarship in the form of short biographical essays. Published by Basil Blackwell in five volumes, the series covered British history from the earliest times to 1837. It was designed to please several kinds of reader: the 'general reader', the browser who might find it hard to resist the temptation to go from one character to another, and, of course, the student of all ages. Each author sought in his own way to convey more than the bare facts of his subject's life, to place him in the context of his age and to evoke what was distinctive in his character and achievement. At the same time, by using a broadly chronological rather than alphabetical sequence, and by grouping together similar classes of people, each volume provided a portrait of the age. Presenting history in biographical form, it complemented the conventional textbook.

Since the publication of the first volumes of the series in the early sixties the continuing work of research has brought new facts to light and has led to some important revaluations. In particular the late mediaeval period, a hitherto somewhat neglected field, has been thoroughly studied. There has also been intense controversy about certain aspects of Tudor and Stuart history. There is plainly a need for fuller treatment of the mediaeval period than was allowed for in the original series, in which the late W. O. Hassall's volume covered the years 55 B.C. to 1485 A.D. The time seems also to be ripe for a reassessment of some Tudor and Stuart figures. Meanwhile the continued requests of teachers and students for the series to be reprinted encourages the authors of the new series to think that there will be a warm response to a fuller and more comprehensive *Who's Who* which will eventually include the nineteenth and early twentieth centuries. They are therefore grateful to Shepheard-Walwyn for the opportunity to present the new, enlarged *Who's Who*.

Following Volume I, devoted to the Roman and Anglo-Saxon period, two further books cover the Middle Ages. The Tudor volume, by the late C. R. Routh, has been extensively revised by Dr. Peter Holmes. Peter Hill and I have revised for re-publication our own volumes on the Stuart and Georgian periods. Between Edward I's conquest of Wales and the Act of Union which joined England and Scotland in 1707, the authors' prime concern has been England, with Scotsmen and Irishmen figuring only if they happened in any way to be prominent in English history. In the eighteenth century Scotsmen come into the picture, in the nineteenth Irishmen, in their own right, as inhabitants of Great Britain. It is hoped that full justice will be done to Scotsmen and Irishmen – and indeed to some early Welshmen – in subsequent volumes devoted to the history of those countries. When the series is complete, we believe that it will provide a comprehensive work of reference which will stand the test of time. At a time when so much historical writing is necessarily becoming more technical, more abstract, or simply more specialised, when textbooks seem so often to have little room to spare for the men and women who are the life and soul of the past, there is a place for a history of our country which is composed of the lives of those who helped make it what it was, and is. In contributing to this history the authors can be said to have taken heed of the stern warning of Trevor Roper's inaugural lecture at Oxford in 1957 against 'the removal of humane studies into a specialisation so remote that they cease to have that lay interest which is their sole ultimate justification'.

The hard pressed examinee often needs an essay which puts an important life into perspective. From necessarily brief accounts he may learn valuable lessons in proportion, concision and relevance. We hope that he will be tempted to find out more and so have added, wherever possible, the titles of books for further reading. Mindful of his needs, we have not however confined our attention to those who have left their mark on church and state. The man who invented the umbrella, the archbishop who shot a gamekeeper, a successful highwayman and an unsuccessful admiral find their place among the great and good. Nor have we eschewed anecdote or turned a blind eye to folly or foible: it is not the authors' view that history which is instructive cannot also be entertaining.

With the development of a secure and civilised society, the range of characters becomes richer, their achievements more diverse. Besides the soldiers, politicians and churchmen who dominate the mediaeval scene there are merchants, inventors, industrialists; more scholars, lawyers, artists; explorers and colonial pioneers. More is known about more people and the task of selection becomes ever harder. Throughout, whether looking at the mediaeval warrior, the Elizabethan seaman, the Stuart radical or the eighteenth century entrepreneur, the authors have been guided by the criterion of excellence. To record the achievements of those few who have had the chance to excel and who have left a name behind them is not to denigrate the unremarkable or unremarked for whom there was no opportunity to shine or chronicler at hand to describe what they made or did. It is not to deny that a Neville or a Pelham might have died obscure if he had not been born to high estate. It is to offer, for the instruction and inspiration of a generation which has been led too often to believe that individuals count for little in the face of the forces which shape economy and society, the conviction that a country is as remarkable as the individuals of which it is composed. In these pages there will be found examples of heroism, genius, and altruism; of self-seeking and squalor. There will be little that is ordinary. It is therefore the hope of the authors that there will be little that is dull.

GEOFFREY TREASURE
Harrow

INTRODUCTION TO SECOND EDITION

A second edition has provided an opportunity to make a number of changes in this book, including some additional lives. Errors have been corrected and emphases revised where appropriate. I have made numerous alterations and additions in the suggestions for further reading, in an attempt to keep close to the substantial output of serious historical writing on Stuart England which the last twenty years have brought. For the work of such scholars as Christopher Hill, Ivan Roots, John Kenyon, Geoffrey Holmes, and Conrad Russell has done and is still doing much to make us revise our views of significant aspects and developments of the period and has begun to condition the biographical writing. Many readers will want no doubt to turn from reading biography to other seventeenth century historical reading. They will find an excellent bibliography of the period by J. S. Morrill in his 'Seventeenth Century Britain 1603–1714' in *Critical Bibliographies in Modern History*, vol. 2, 1980.

Mr. Geoffrey Treasure, who has followed the late Mr. C. R. N. Routh as general editor of the series to which this volume belongs, and Mr. Anthony Werner of the publishers have provided me with encouragement as well as guidance. I have been much helped in various ways – critical, informative and constructive by my wife, Joan; by Dr. Prys Morgan of the University College of Swansea and by Professor Ian Cowan of the University of Glasgow; above all by Professor Ivan Roots of the University of Exeter, who has lent me books and given most generously of his time, his friendly advice, and his profound understanding of Seventeenth Century England. My old friend, John Wright, has supported the project throughout.

C. P. HILL
Starcross, Exeter, 1986

Publishers' Note
The author sadly died before the book was published. The publishers wish to thank his widow, Joan Hill, Professor Ivan Roots, Sarah E. Jones and Donald Leech for their help in the final stages of publication. Their thanks are due to Judith Prendergast of the National Portrait Gallery in London for assistance in selecting the illustrations.

INTRODUCTION TO FIRST EDITION

This third volume of *Who's Who in History* * covers English History from 1603 to 1714. As in the first two volumes, the entries are arranged in broadly chronological order, with some occasional variation to meet special circumstances; in particular, the great majority of the scientists are grouped together. Most of the men and women who appear in these pages were English, yet it would plainly be nonsensical to define 'English' strictly in a period when three of England's five Kings were foreign-born. Therefore Scots like Montrose and Lauderdale, Irishmen like Ormonde and Swift, and Welshmen like Bishop Williams have their place here, and so too have men from the European mainland, like Van Dyck, Samuel Hartlib and Bentinck, who made their home in this country and contributed in various ways to the changing pattern of seventeenth-century English life.

Any selection of the sort made in the books of this series is necessarily personal and subjective. Clearly there are many seventeenth-century figures whom no author can omit; but beyond them lies a great group of men and women, all of them interesting and in some sense significant, among whom choices have to be made if the book is to be of tolerable length. What I have tried to do here is to provide a selection of biographies which does rough justice to the importance of their subjects both in the Stuart period itself and in the minds of later generations, and which at the same time is reasonably representative of a wide range of English activities in the seventeenth century. The central emphasis is political, for here in the conflict between Crown and Parliament the Englishman still finds the great theme of that age. Yet the century itself did not interpret politics narrowly. Most notably, Englishmen found it impossible to disentangle religion and politics in what was by any standards a profoundly religious age, and there are many names in this book which illustrate the extraordinary diversity of religious experience and expression of that time. In the natural sciences the seventeenth century was the seminal period of English history. In some other human activities – for example, in political theory, in the practice alike of revolution and of generalship, in architecture and antiquarianism, in the writing of blank verse and of pamphlets – the period from 1603 to 1714 may fairly claim to be regarded as a golden age in this country. I have attempted to give fair space to all these, as well as to such other matters as

*Basil Blackwell, 1965.

economic development, music and painting, colonization and privateering, in the belief that only in this way can a series of biographies reveal both the flow and the flavour of a period.

The limitations of biography are obvious enough. Yet the seventeenth century itself, as Clarendon, the greatest of its historians, showed, was not unwilling to examine even contemporary history in a strongly biographical form. Much recent original work on this period has tended to concentrate upon analysis, or even upon the identification, of groups, like the gentry, the merchants, the Puritans, or political parties. By this process scholars have immensely deepened and widened our understanding, and not least our understanding of the social forces which moved individuals great as well as small in such crises as those of 1642 and 1688. Yet it may well be that the non-specialist reader will find his most rewarding and fruitful introduction to this age in a wide-ranging approach which is biographical in detail and chronological in form. It is in this belief, as well as in the hope that the book may serve as a useful and interesting work of reference, that I have written this volume in the series.

The seventeenth century is the age of 'the character', and offers a peculiar abundance and variety of source material to the biographer. I have drawn heavily upon Clarendon and Aubrey, Pepys and Evelyn, Anthony à Wood and Burnet, to mention the more famous names; I have modernized spelling and punctuation only where this has seemed to make meaning clearer. I have not hesitated, particularly in the longer political biographies, to offer my own interpretation of career and action, for it seems to me quite impossible to avoid doing so, especially when discussing men who lived through a period of revolution.

Nobody who writes, however modestly, about the past can weigh his immense debt to others in any exact scales; but I am deeply aware of my dependence on the many distinguished historians who have made this period their own. It has attracted more than its share of great scholars and fine writers. Macaulay, Gardiner, Firth (whose remarkable series of articles in the *Dictionary of National Biography* remain invaluable) and G. M. Trevelyan provided between them a commanding account of this period. It was upon this account that my generation was brought up: I still recall the excitement with which, as a sixth form boy, I read Trevelyan's volumes on *England under Queen Anne* when they first appeared. Later historians, often starting from a very different standpoint, more analytical in their approach, exploiting new material with fresh techniques, have added to and in several ways transformed our picture of Stuart England. To name only three, I should like to acknowledge my debt to the studies and insights of Mr. David Ogg, Professor Christopher Hill and Professor J. P. Kenyon.

Where possible I have added at the end of each biography the title of a book or article to which a reader who wishes to investigate the particular subject further may go for greater detail. It has not been invariably possible, for an appropriate book does not always exist, and here the reader must turn to the *Dictionary of National Biography*. For reasons of space I have usually mentioned one book only, and in its choice I have borne in mind considerations both of scholarship and of accessibility to the general reader; occasionally, where the importance of the subject or the range of books available made it desirable, I have given more than one. The general books, as for example Professor Christopher Hill's *The Century of Revolution*, customarily provide a carefully-considered short list of books and articles on special topics.

I am grateful to many people for assistance of various kinds in the preparation of this book. Among them are the librarians and staffs of the Roborough Library in the University of Exeter, the Cornwall County Library at Truro, the Borough Libraries at Penzance and Falmouth, and the Library of Friends House in London. Mr. F. W. Scott, Headmaster of Stockport Grammar School, Professor Christopher Lloyd of the Royal Naval College, Greenwich, Mr. R. C. Latham of Royal Holloway College, Mr. Desmond Gregory, and Mr. Vincent Waite have kindly answered detailed queries. My old friends Mr. and Mrs. T. P. Swann have helped me greatly, by the loan of books, by much wise advice, and by most hospitable encouragement. My colleagues Dr. H. J. J. Winter and Mr. D. G. Tahta, and Mrs. Marie Yemm, have given me the benefit of specialist knowledge in the articles on scientists and mathematicians. Above all, Professor A. H. Woolrych of the University of Lancaster has read every biography in typescript, saved me from numerous errors of fact and emphasis, and made many suggestions of improvements in detail. I am very deeply indebted to him. The editor of this series, Mr. C. R. N. Routh, has been extraordinarily tolerant, has provided me with valuable detailed material for several of the biographies, and has given most generously of his time and scholarship in connection with the illustrations. Mr. Kingsley Adams has kindly put his expert knowledge of English portrait painting at my service. Mr. John Cutforth of the publishers has been very patient and helpful, not least about the musicians. My wife has made it possible for me to devote time to this book, and has done a considerable amount of typing.

C. P. HILL
Exeter
November, 1964

LIST OF ILLUSTRATIONS

The author and publisher wish to express their grateful thanks to the owners of the portraits listed below for permission to reproduce them in this book. Unless otherwise stated they are from the collection of the National Portrait Gallery in London.

THE STUARTS

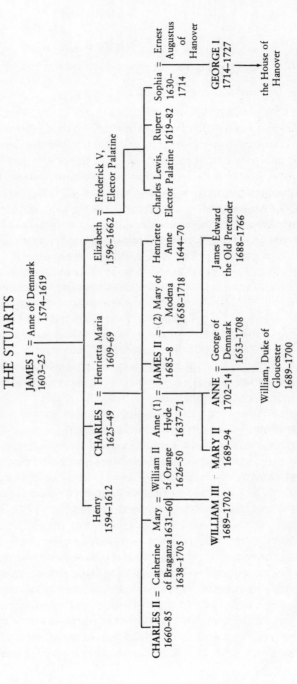

NOTE.— *English monarchs are in bold capitals and the dates beneath them are those of their reigns. For all other persons the dates given are those of their lives.*

xiv

WHO'S WHO IN STUART BRITAIN

JAMES I (1566–1625), who ascended the English throne in 1603, had been James VI of Scotland since he was one year old, crowned by the nobles who had deposed his mother, Mary, Queen of Scots. In view of the enormous difficulties that faced him in Scotland — his long minority, Mary's intrigues and efforts to recover power, the plots and counter-plots of turbulent nobles, the challenge of the Scottish Kirk to the monarchy, the poverty of crown and country — James had done well to hold his throne, to increase royal authority and to impose some degree of order on the country. Ever since his mother's execution in 1587 he had looked forward eagerly to the English throne, and when the news of Elizabeth's death reached him in 1603 he set off without delay to claim his inheritance. He was enthusiastically welcomed. Nobles, officials and office-seekers, courtiers and flatterers sped northwards to escort their new King to London; great crowds of the common people, out of simple loyalty and curiosity, blocked the country roads and pressed upon the royal cavalcade. For all the devotion to Gloriana, it was good to have a King again. Popular relief at the peacefulness of his accession, after a generation of apprehension about what would happen when Elizabeth died, redounded to James's credit; and he made a good first impression on nobles and courtiers.

His popularity did not last. James I is difficult to assess; perhaps more than many characters of the past, he is a victim of the historian's knowledge of later events, for we tend to see his reign as a prologue to the catastrophe of Charles I. Nor can we easily expect normality of him; before he was a year old, his father had been murdered, his mother had married the murderer, and he had seen her for the last time; his boyhood was a weird blend of flattery and Presbyterian sermons, self-indulgence and the terror of being kidnapped or assassinated. He was a precocious child, apt at languages, with a retentive memory, intelligent far above the average; he became a learned man, shrewd and pedantic rather than original, yet certainly the most learned of English kings. His writings were prolific, the most interesting being *The Trew Law of Free Monarchies* (1598) which expounded his ideas on kingship and the duty of

1

James I, c.1621
(Artist: Daniel Mytens)

subjects; *Basilikon Doron* (1599), a book of instruction for his son, Henry; and some short treatises such as *Daemonologie* (1597), dealing with witchcraft, and his vigorous *Counterblaste to Tobacco* (1604). He came to the English throne a man of thirty-six, 'an old, experienced King, needing no lessons', as he told the Commons; and the flattery he received in his first months in England (as Bishop Montague put it, 'God hath given us a Solomon') blinded him to the truth about himself and about his new country.

Physically unprepossessing, with spindly legs and a tongue over-big for his mouth, which made him an undignified eater; a heavy drinker, who tended to get drunk more often as he grew older; dirty in habits (he washed rarely) and slovenly in dress; uncouth in speech, often to English ears unintelligible in his broad Scots; fond of bawdy jokes even beyond the generous taste of his age; frequently homely, to say the least, in his language (as soon after his accession, when, his courtiers having told him the crowds came of love to see him, he cried 'God's wounds! I will pull down my breeches and they shall also see my arse', or at Hampton Court Conference in 1604, when he 'wished those who would take away the surplice might want linen for their own breeches'); terrified of assassination and wearing dagger-proof doublets — he was neither superficially attractive nor dignified.

But these were relatively small things, though much magnified by the contrast with James's high opinion of himself. There were more serious defects, pointed out by his mother's envoy, Fontenoy, in 1584, who observed, 'he does estimate correctly his poverty and insignificance but is over-confident of his strength and scornful of other princes; his love for favourites is indiscreet and wilful and takes no account of the wishes of his people; he is too lazy and indifferent about affairs, too given to pleasure, allowing all business to be conducted by others. Such things are excusable at his age [James was then eighteen], yet I fear they may become habitual'. The next forty years proved the accuracy of this analysis. James's laziness was demonstrated in a lifelong passion for hunting, for which he was ready to set aside all affairs of state and which led to a roaming, restless life for the court and to inefficient 'government by corres-pondence'. He relished being a King but neglected the business of governing. His love for favourites (the homosexuality which was surely the consequence of his extraordinary childhood) led to his pathetic and drooling affection first for Robert Carr, and then for George Villiers, Duke of Buckingham. The use Buckingham made of the power which James's passion gave him did great harm to the realm and exacerbated relations between Crown and Parliament. Above all, there was his colossal vanity. Fed by the extravagant flattery characteristic of the age, it made him regard the welcome he received in 1603 as a tribute to his own wisdom and goodness. The Hampton Court Conference (1604) was an opportunity to display his theological expertise. The House of Commons was a body to be lectured on the art of government, the European world a stage on which he would demonstrate his power as a peacemaker. The most obvious outlet for his vanity came in his interpretation of the doctrine of the Divine Right of Kings. In his words, 'Kings are not only God's lieutenants upon earth and sit upon God's throne, but even by God himself they are called gods'. Perhaps his most outrageous expression of it was his defence to the Council in 1617 of his relations with Buckingham, when he said, 'I wish to speak in my own behalf and not to have it to be thought a defect, for Jesus Christ did the same and therefore I cannot be blamed. Christ had his John, and I have my George.'

James had been an effective King of Scotland, the most successful of all its Stuart rulers. Perhaps this very success unfitted him for the different problems he met in England. On some of these his judgment was badly wrong. The poverty of Scotland prepared him to believe England and the English crown far richer than they were, and the hectoring manners of the Scottish Presbyterian clergy made him suspicious of the real moderation of English Puritans early in his reign. He could not see why so many Englishmen regarded his foreign policy as pro-Spanish rather than enlightened. From the start he misunderstood the function of the Commons and misjudged the temper of its members. Yet in some ways the first decade of his reign did not go ill. He crossed the Commons over several matters, and relations were bad when he dissolved his first Parliament in 1611; but on the most immediately important problem, the right to levy extra-parliamentary taxes by 'Impositions', the judges had decided in his favour. His chief and wisest minister, Robert Cecil, Earl of Salisbury, had managed by 1610 to get the Crown's debts down to the figure at which Elizabeth had left them. James had made peace with Spain in 1604; and whatever the long-term consequences of the Hampton Court Conference, the Canons of that same year were an effective damper on clerical puritanism for the time being. A generation later English churchmen would look back on James I's time as a period of scholarship and moderation, free from violent dispute and symbolised by the Authorised Version of the Bible (1611).

The middle years of the reign brought a deterioration in the King's relations with the 'political nation', illustrated by the futility of the Addled Parliament (1614). In part this was the result of factors outside James's control, like the deaths in 1612 of Salisbury and of the heir to the throne, Prince Henry, and the outbreak in Germany in 1618 of the Thirty Years' War. These too were the years of the favourites, of Somerset to 1615 and of Buckingham thereafter; of the influence of Gondomar, Spanish ambassador from 1613; and of the execution of Sir Walter Raleigh in 1618. The King himself was in physical decline by the time he was fifty (1616), with recurrent arthritis and gout; after the Queen's death in 1619 he was desperately ill with nephritis. He grew even less willing to deal with the routine of government, and fell into what was occasionally maudlin dependence on Buckingham, upon whom he showered titles, offices, wealth, opportunities of patronage, and political responsibility.

Yet both his physical decline and its effects upon policy — particularly upon foreign policy — can be exaggerated. Thus from 1618 to 1624 James resisted pressure for war against Spain on behalf of his son-in-law Frederick of the Palatinate; when the Parliament of 1621 demanded war, he dissolved it and tore out of the Commons Journal the page recording their protestation. Although after the foolhardy and futile journey of 'his two sweet boys' to woo the Infanta in Madrid in 1623 he changed his policy, he made it plain that he was ready to send troops to the Low Countries to restore the Palatinate but not to fight Spain at sea.

When James I died in 1625 he left to his son a legacy whose most obviously dangerous element was an arrogant and hated favourite. The old king had fallen out with parliaments, had mismanaged his finances, and had disappointed those who wanted him to lead a Protestant crusade in Europe. Yet he 'was still ruling over a united country' *. External peace, a working union with Scotland, a

* Conrad Russell, *Parliament and English Politics, 1621–1629*, 1979, p.420.

national Church which enjoyed the confidence of the vast majority of his English subjects — all these must be set to his credit. The crisis which developed in the next reign — and within its first five years — reflected the policies of a new and more active king, and the changing response of a Commons at once more fearful and bolder. They must not distort our assessment of the first Stuart ruler of England.

D. H. Willson, *King James VI and I*, 1956.
R. Ashton, *James I by his contemporaries*, 1959.
S. J. Houston, *James I*, 1973.
Jenny Wormald, 'James VI and I: Two Kings or One?', *History*, June 1983.

ANNE OF DENMARK (1574–1619), Queen Consort of James I, was the second daughter of Frederick II of Denmark, and married James in 1589. Attractive with golden hair, high-spirited, frivolous and empty-headed, she meddled rather ineffectually in Scottish politics and quarrelled a good deal with James. In the 1590s she was converted to Roman Catholicism, a fact somewhat embarrassing to James when he became King of England. She had expensive tastes in clothes and jewels and loved elaborate masques, which added a good deal to the costs of the court and diminished its reputation. She had little in common with James, and they did not live together after about 1606; Anne resided mainly at Denmark House. Her political influence in England was negligible, although she promoted the project of a Spanish marriage for Prince Henry. After some years of ill-health she died of dropsy in 1619.

HENRY, PRINCE OF WALES (1594–1612) was the eldest son of James I and Anne of Denmark. His death from typhoid fever at the age of eighteen and the course of events in his brother Charles's reign led men at the time and later to exaggerate his virtues. Yet there is no doubt that he possessed qualities which both James I and Charles I lacked. An athletic young man, much given to martial exercises, he enjoyed tilting in the ring and was keenly interested in naval matters. Dignified, serious-minded, a patron of scientists, he despised the favourite, Robert Carr, and was openly critical of the unseemly manners of his father's court. He was a friend of Raleigh,

Henry, Prince of Wales, c.1610
(Artist: Robert Peake)

who wrote a eulogy of him at the end of the first part of his *History of the World,* and is said to have remarked that only his father could keep such a bird in a cage. Already before his death he had shown signs of ambition and of a real independence of outlook, and it is difficult not to compare him with the young Henry V two centuries earlier.

Roy Strong, *Henry Prince of Wales and the Lost Renaissance*, 1986.

PRINCESS ELIZABETH (1596–1662), Queen of Bohemia, the eldest daughter of Anne of Denmark and James I, was born at Dunfermline and baptized in Holyrood. Her later sufferings no doubt inclined both contemporaries and historians to be romantically generous in their treatment of her, but there is no doubt that she was a gay and beautiful girl who grew into a courageous and lively woman, and that she enjoyed a popularity among the English people granted to none of the male Stuarts except possibly her brother Henry. In addition to her own attractive qualities, her athletic energy, and her high spirits, she symbolized causes which neither her father nor her brother Charles always appeared to represent; she was a Protestant heroine, and she was named after the great queen. Her marriage in 1613 to Frederick the Elector Palatine of the Rhine was celebrated with lavish ceremonies, popular enthusiasm, and, among other things, a sham battle on the Thames costing £9,000 and a rather inadequate *Epithalamium* by John Donne. It marked the beginning of nearly half a century of exile, tribulation and frugality for the bride.

In 1618 Frederick, a rash man with little political judgment, accepted as Protestant champion the throne of Bohemia, and in 1619 Elizabeth was crowned Queen in Prague. His action precipitated the Thirty Years' War and within two years he had lost Bohemia and the Palatinate alike, and 'the Winter Queen' was a refugee in Holland. There, until she came back to England in 1661, she spent the rest of her days, living often in great poverty, dependent on irregular grants from Holland and England, and perpetually in frustrated hopes. Frederick, to whom she bore thirteen children, died in 1632 without recovering his lands. Their eldest son was drowned in 1629, and Charles Louis, the next in line, who eventually regained half his German territories in 1648, was a cynical and surly man whose relations with his mother were often bad. His support of the Parliamentarians in the English Civil War embarrassed Elizabeth, whose favourite son, Rupert, was Charles I's most distinguished soldier. Three of her children, including her gifted eldest daughter,

Princess Elizabeth
(Artist: Unknown)

joined the Church of Rome, with her disapproval. Maurice, another of her favourite children, disappeared at sea in 1652. Elizabeth herself, autocratic, managing, voluble, impulsive, was not always easy to get on with. Yet her impoverished court, largely through her continuing vitality and vigour of spirit, remained a centre of attraction throughout her long exile.

Carola Oman, *Elizabeth of Bohemia*, 1964 ed.
The Letters of Elizabeth, Queen of Bohemia, ed. L. M. Baker, 1953.

ARABELLA STUART (1575-1615) was in the last years of Elizabeth I's reign next after James VI of Scotland in succession to the English throne. Her father, the Earl of Lennox, younger brother of James's father, Darnley, was, through the female line, grandson of Margaret Tudor by her second husband the Earl of Angus. Her claim was slight by comparison with that of James, but his apprehensiveness, always exaggerated, was stimulated by the facts that Arabella was English-born and that the common law forbade aliens, Scots included, to inherit land in England. To make matters worse, Arabella fell in love with William Seymour, grandson of Lady Catherine Grey, heiress to the throne through the Suffolk line under Henry VIII's will, which had disinherited Margaret Tudor. Arabella herself was harmless enough, and James in the early months of his reign sensibly ignored the talk which linked her name with the alleged plotting of Cobham and Raleigh. Until 1609 he treated her kindly, though parsimoniously. Then he imprisoned her when it was rumoured that she was about to marry Seymour. Early in 1610 the couple declared solemnly to the Council that they would not marry without James's consent, and they were restored to favour. But that July their long patience snapped, and they married secretly. Inevitably the news reached the King, and they were imprisoned separately. Seymour escaped and got away to Ostend. Arabella, too, escaped, but was recaptured off a French ship in the Channel. James locked her in the Tower, where the unhappy woman went out of her mind and died in 1615.

ROBERT CECIL, 1st EARL OF SALISBURY (1563-1612), first minister of James I, was born at Westminster, second son of Elizabeth's great minister, Lord Burghley. Frail, very short, with a twisted back, he was educated privately before going to St. John's, Cambridge. Like Chatham two centuries later, Burghley gave to a gifted younger son the affection and the particular upbringing he denied to a stupid heir, and Robert Cecil was trained for statesmanship. He entered the Commons in 1584 as member for Westminster, and from about 1590 he was in effect Secretary of State without holding the office. But he owed more to his own genius than to his father's patronage. A contemporary of Essex, Raleigh, and Francis Bacon, he could not have succeeded in the polished savagery of Elizabethan politics without extraordinary qualities. Cecil had a clear mind, courage, eloquence as well as subtlety, and his father's immense capacity for loyalty. His physical inheritance compelled him to caution, prudence and industry. These were the qualities his royal mistress approved, and they gave him victory in his prolonged contest with the imperious and selfish Essex. Elizabeth made him Secretary of State in 1596, while Essex was at Cadiz; old Burghley died in 1598, and in the next year the Queen appointed Cecil to succeed him as Master of the Wards, while Essex was away in Ireland. In 1601 came Essex's rebellion and execution, the final triumph of Cecil, who, to his credit, seems to have done his best to save his rival from self-destruction.

Characteristically and wisely, Cecil, though entirely loyal to Elizabeth, opened a secret correspondence with the King of Scotland as a new reign drew near. The ease of James I's accession owed much to his management. His reward, besides the Earldom of Salisbury (1605), was power until he died nine years later. Although he did not receive the principal office of state, the Lord Treasurership, until 1608, Cecil was the mainspring of English government from 1603 to 1612. He negotiated the peace with Spain in 1604, guided James through the perils of the Gunpowder Plot in 1605, extended the impositions through a new book of rates in 1608, and attempted to stabilize financial relations between Crown and Commons by negotiating the Great Contract in 1610. Judgment, nerve and toil contributed both to his hold upon power and to a measure of success which no other minister of the Stuarts was to enjoy for half a century. He was grossly overworked: while James I idled, talked, and hunted, his 'little beagle' Cecil laboured incessantly upon the affairs and correspondence of state. Nor did the King make his task simpler. Royal extravagance made nonsense of Cecil's financial policy, and it was the King's demand for more that wrecked the Great Contract; while royal loquacity and dogmatism did much to undermine Cecil's judicious management of Parliament. Moreover, in the last year of Cecil's life, when he was ill and weary, James turned against him and began to lean upon his new-found favourite, Robert Carr.

Robert Cecil died in May 1612. He was unpopular with contemporaries, who thought him corrupt and crooked, and later historians have condemned him as a sublime mediocrity, quoting with approval Bacon's barbed judgment, made to James I, that, 'I do think he was no fit counsellor to make your affairs better; but yet he was fit to have kept them from growing worse'. Certainly Cecil was an able administrator rather than a creative statesman; and his political formula was the Elizabethan one which was no longer sufficient. Nevertheless, he was the vital link between Elizabethan and Stuart government. Moreover, it was a major achievement under the Stuarts to keep royal affairs from growing worse, and the disorders that followed, in finance, administration and foreign policy, during the second half of James's reign, are a measure of the consequences of Cecil's death. As James I's biographer has put it, 'he was a servant far nobler and more able than James deserved'. * To later generations Cecil has left as a majestic legacy one of the great mansions of England, Hatfield House, begun during his lifetime though not completed until after his death.

Joel Hurstfield, 'Robert Cecil', *History Today,* May 1957, pp. 279-89.
Algernon Cecil, *A Life of Robert Cecil,* 1915.

CATESBY, ROBERT (1573–1605), leader of the Gunpowder Plot, was born at Lapworth in Warwickshire of a recusant family which had paid for their faith in fines and imprisonment. Strong and handsome, Catesby grew into a reckless extremist, brooding upon the sufferings of Catholics, his temper sharpened perhaps by the economic difficulties of the midlands of the 1590s. In 1593 he inherited a substantial estate at Chastleton in Oxfordshire, but in 1601 he came out for Essex, and had to sell his lands to pay his fines. When the hopes of relief raised by James I's accession faded, Catesby was the prime mover in the plan to blow up the entire government. He left London on 2 November 1605, to raise a revolt in the west midlands; hunted down after the arrest of Fawkes and the exposure

* D. H. Willson, *James VI and I,* 1956, p. 177.

of the plot, he died fighting at Holbeche in Staffordshire, an image
of the Virgin in his hand.

GUY FAWKES (1570–1605), the best-remembered figure of
English seventeenth-century history, nevertheless remains both mysterious and subject to inaccurate statements. He was not a Spaniard,
but a Yorkshireman; nor was he born a Catholic, for he was the son
of a lawyer employed by the church courts in the city of York, and he
was baptized an Anglican in St. Michael-le-Belfry there. But Yorkshire remained one of the strongholds of the old faith in the latter
part of Elizabeth's reign and the ideological issue was more keenly
felt there than in southern England. When his father died, his mother
married again, and her second husband was a Catholic. Probably
most important of all, Guy Fawkes went to St. Peter's School in
York, and the evidence strongly suggests that he imbibed Catholicism here; John Pullen, then Headmaster of St. Peter's, was later
suspected of being a Jesuit, and no fewer than four of Fawkes's
fellow-conspirators in the Gunpowder Plot itself were among his
contemporaries at the school. Whatever the reason, Guy Fawkes was
converted to Catholicism, and in 1591 he sold his property in York
and went off to join the Spanish army fighting in the Netherlands.
He proved himself a capable soldier, winning distinction at the siege
of Calais in 1596. His devotion to Catholicism was fanatical, and
his overriding purpose in life was to restore Papal supremacy in
England. Like many exiles he was wildly optimistic, exaggerating
the strength of Catholicism in England, and in the last years of
Elizabeth's reign he was involved in various plots and schemes,
notably that devised by Sir William Stanley, the commander of the
English Catholic troops in the Netherlands. In 1603 he went to
Madrid to try to persuade Philip III to take advantage of the
opportunity provided by the death of Elizabeth and the accession of
James I.

   The story of the Gunpowder Plot itself is familiar enough.
Fawkes's part in it was not simply that of a tough and fearless subordinate who knew how to dig tunnels and could be utterly trusted to
undertake the most perilous part of the enterprise. Well known since
boyhood to several of the conspirators, an experienced soldier
dedicated to the Catholic faith, as deluded as Catesby about the
chances of success, he provided a useful link with the projected help

from Spain. When the moment of discovery came, Fawkes, alias 'John Johnson, servant of Mr. Percy', was resolute in his terrible purpose; and he withstood the brutalities of the torture courageously. He was put to death in the February after the plot.

S.M. Toyne, 'Guy Fawkes and the Powder Plot', *History Today*, November 1951, pp. 16-24.
Philip Caraman, *Henry Garnet, 1555-1606, and the Gunpowder Plot*, 1964.

ROBERT CARR, EARL OF SOMERSET (1586–1645), favourite of James I, was a Scot of the border nobility from Roxburghshire. Flaxen-haired and handsome, tall and strong in body, he was a good athlete; he was also stupid, arrogant and weak in character. In 1607 he was deliberately brought before James's eyes by his fellow Scotman, James Hay, who wanted to shore up his own influence over the King. A happy accident assisted the scheme, for Carr's horse threw him in the tiltyard and broke his leg while James was watching. The King's passion was captivated at once. The royal physician was commanded to attend Carr, and James spent hours at the sick-bed. Henceforward, until the arrival of George Villiers seven years later, the relationship between the two men dominated the King's personal life. The direct effect of Carr upon policy was far less than that of his successor, for he had fewer wits and less political ambition than Villiers. Moreover, James was still a man of energy, and the wise and powerful influence of Robert Cecil continued until his death in 1612. Yet the Carr affair added nothing to the seemliness of the court, and Carr soon became the centre of, and profiteer by, a considerable traffic in honours and jobs with its accompanying intrigue and faction. It seemed wise of Carr to lean for advice upon his clever friend, Sir Thomas Overbury.

In 1609 James gave Carr the manor of Sherborne, the much-loved property of the imprisoned Sir Walter Raleigh, and in 1611 created him Viscount Rochester. By now he had fallen in love with the shameless Frances Howard, Countess of Essex, and in 1612 they decided to obtain a divorce from the Earl. 1613 marked the peak of Carr's career. James appointed a divorce commission and applied outrageous pressure to the bishops who were among its members to decide in favour of the Countess, on the ground that Essex was bewitched and impotent towards her. Carr, created Earl of Somerset, married Frances Howard in high ceremony in the last days of December. There had only been one serious difficulty — Overbury, who had opposed the marriage because he foresaw the loss of his influence over Carr. The Howards persuaded James to put him in the Tower because of the insolent manner in which he refused an embassy in Russia, and took care to keep him there while the divorce commission was sitting. Carr merely pretended to Overbury that he was doing his best to get him released; but Frances Howard, without Carr's knowledge, set out to have Overbury poisoned, and eventually succeeded. There were suspicious rumours about his death, but these died away, and the crime remained unexposed for two years.

In 1614 Somerset was appointed Lord Chamberlain. But a syndicate of the Howards' enemies discovered another handsome young man; George Villiers, later Duke of Buckingham, was introduced at Court and won James's favour, and Somerset's power began to wane. In 1615 he had a serious quarrel with the King. More important, the tales about Overbury's death grew again and enough circumstantial evidence appeared to warrant Somerset's enemies going to the King who, prudently and to his credit, ordered a full inquiry. As a result, Somerset and his wife were put on trial before the House of Lords in 1616. They were found guilty, condemned to death, and pardoned by the King. Kept in the Tower until 1621, they were then released to live in retirement in the country. Their love for each other did not survive the trial. The Countess died in 1632, Somerset himself not until 1645.

William McElwee, *The Murder of Sir Thomas Overbury*, 1952.

SIR THOMAS OVERBURY (1581–1613), victim of the greatest scandal of James I's court, was the son of a landowner of Bourton-on-the-Hill in Gloucestershire. Educated at The Queen's College, Oxford, and the Middle Temple, he was a good-looking, tall young man with some literary talent and an abundant natural vanity. He served in the office of the Secretary of State under Robert Cecil, who sent him to travel in France and the Low Countries; but his rise to high influence, and his doom, came through his connection with Robert Carr, later Earl of Somerset. He had first got to know Carr, a younger man than himself, and a less intelligent one, on a visit to Edinburgh in 1601, and when Carr suddenly became the favourite of James I 1607 it was to Overbury he turned as friend and confidant. As the King's devotion to Carr increased, so Overbury grew in power and in wealth as 'the man behind the favourite'. A natural careerist, he was appointed Server to the King and he became the channel through which those who wanted to use Carr's influence had to apply. He seems to have become insufferable in behaviour and generally unpopular — in the words of Bishop Goodman, 'a very witty gentleman, but truly very insolent'. In 1611 he was involved in a quarrel with the Queen (who the year before had cried out on seeing Carr and Overbury strolling outside her window, 'There goes Carr and his governor') and had to flee to Paris to avoid the Tower, but was allowed to return because Carr was unable to handle the business of state without him.

The comedy of Overbury turned to melodrama when Carr fell in love with Frances, Countess of Essex. Overbury encouraged the affair, but opposed it when in 1612 the lovers decided to open the way to marriage by divorcing Frances from her husband, for he feared the replacement of his own influence over Carr by that of the Howard family to which Lady Essex belonged. As a result he incurred the hostility of the Howards, headed by the Earl of Northampton, who got Overbury put into the Tower after he had declined to go as an ambassador to Russia, and kept there while the divorce proceedings began. Lady Essex then decided to poison him, and this she finally achieved, after some ineffectual attempts, by getting sublimate of mercury put into an enema administered to him. This sordid crime was kept dark for two years, during which time Carr, created Earl of Somerset, married Lady Essex, released from her husband after divorce proceedings which James did his best to facilitate. The revelation of the truth ruined the Somersets and lowered even further the shoddy reputation of the Court of James I. The murder and the discovery gave to the literary works of the victim — notably his poem 'The Wife' and his essays 'The Characters' — a publicity and a fame which, on their merits, they scarcely deserved; indeed, writers of the eminence of Donne and Sir Henry Wotton found it worthwhile having their poems published with those of Overbury in order to get into print.

William McElwee, *The Murder of Sir Thomas Overbury*, 1952.

GEORGE VILLIERS, 1st DUKE OF BUCKINGHAM (1592–1628), royal favourite, was the younger son by a second marriage of a knight from Brookesby in Leicestershire. Tall, well-proportioned, handsome, he was sent by his mother to France to master the courtly accomplishments of riding, dancing and duelling, and soon after his return he first met King James, at Apethorpe in 1614. The King's passions were roused at once. He was beginning to tire of Carr, and a group of courtiers, notably Archbishop Abbot, deliberately backed the new young man. The appointment of Villiers as a Gentleman of the Bedchamber in the spring of 1615 began an ascent, which in Clarendon's phrase, 'was so quick, that it seemed rather a flight than a growth'. James showered titles and estates upon him, making him Master of the Horse and a Viscount in 1616, an Earl in 1617, Master of the Wardrobe in 1617. With honours went political authority. Carr had been ruined in 1616 through the Overbury murder and the Howards were removed from power in 1618. Within four years of the Apethorpe meeting Buckingham, at twenty-six, had become the principal figure in the land, and for the next ten years he was the virtual ruler of England.

Buckingham had more than physical beauty and athletic skill to commend him. He had courage, charm and affability, he learned to dispatch business quickly, and his management of James and Charles showed both adroitness and a real loyalty. No doubt it was very much to his interest to suffer patiently James's petting and pawing of his 'Sweet Steenie', and the manner in which he pretended to return the King's love is as nauseating as it was skilful. In the circumstances his conquest, after an initial outburst of jealousy, of the friendship of the decorous Charles and the latter's deep devotion to him are remarkable phenomena. Nor did he lack political talent. Whereas Carr had been a nincompoop dependent on Overbury's brains, Buckingham recognized both the need for financial reform and the ability of Cranfield to undertake it. Nevertheless, his rise and regime did irreparable damage to the relations between the Stuarts and their subjects. The roots of his greatness were tainted: he could never cease to be an upstart whose authority was founded upon his physical attractions for a drooling monarch, and he provides the classical example of 'the favourite' in modern English history. Moreover, the most obvious use he made of his power was to build up a network of nepotism and clientage, with his worthless

George Villiers, 1st Duke of Buckingham c.1616
(Artist: attrib. William Larkin)

relatives in high office. Fortified by the extension of monopolies and
the sale of honours, such a system merely drove the country gentry
away from sympathy with the crown. As Christopher Hill has said,
'the monopolization of patronage by Buckingham did much to cause
the division between court and country, the split in the ruling class,
which made possible the Civil War'. * In the process he enriched
himself on a gigantic scale, for his motive was as much profit as
power. Buckingham was neither statesman nor competent administrator. Young, inexperienced, the spoiled darling of fortune, arrogantly confident of his ability to rule, he was — as Clarendon points
out in a distinctly generous assessment — unable through the very
nature of his role to obtain the wise advice which he needed. The
events of his years of power revealed that his 'policy' was merely an
unhappy mixture of opportunism and selfishness. Above all, he
proved hopelessly incapable of understanding and of managing the
revolutionary force of his time, the opposition in the House of
Commons.

The removal of the Howards and the employment of Cranfield as
Lord Treasurer promised well. The realities emerged when the
Parliament of 1621, for which Buckingham had made no adequate
preparation, attacked the monopolists, among whom the favourite's
two brothers were prominent. The Lords were notably hostile to the
upstart family, and Buckingham sacrificed the monopolists. He was
happy to see Bacon become a scapegoat and happier still when James
dissolved Parliament in his fury at the 'Protestation' of the Commons. In foreign policy at this time Buckingham, gaining power as
the King aged, warmly supported the Spanish marriage project and
hobnobbed with the Spanish ambassador Gondomar. When in 1623
Prince Charles produced his hare-brained scheme of going incognito
to Madrid and returning with the Infanta as his bride, Buckingham
helped persuade the reluctant James to let them go. He deeply
offended the Spaniards by his careless manner and bad temper; yet he
appears to have realised the folly of the whole enterprise more
quickly than Charles. The two returned, as Tawney put it, 'in the
mood of the disappointed suitor who demonstrates the depth of his
devotion by cutting the ungrateful loved one's throat'. * * Cashing in
on the national joy over the fiasco in Madrid, he demanded war with

*Christopher Hill, *The Century of Revolution*, 1961, p.71.
* *R.H. Tawney, *Business and Politics under James I*, 1958, p.235.

Spain, in a short-lived agreement with the Commons. This entailed the sacrifice of Cranfield, who opposed the war and had already offended Buckingham by making it plain that his economies would not halt when they reached the Villiers family. When Cranfield was impeached, James, in a flash of wisdom from his dotage, cried out, 'By God, Steenie, you are a fool and will shortly repent this folly and will find that in this fit of popularity you are making a rod with which you will be scourged yourself'.

The old man died in March 1625. Buckingham's domination of the new King was complete, perhaps because he appealed to an underlying romanticism in Charles's complex personality. The results were two scandalously unsuccessful foreign wars and a gulf, never to be crossed, between Charles and the Commons. The war with Spain brought two disasters in 1625, both very largely the result of Buckingham's incompetent management. In March, Mansfeld's expedition withered away at Ostend, without ever encountering the enemy, and in October the attack on Cadiz collapsed in neglect, cowardice and drunkenness. Parliament, meeting in the summer and denied an explanation of foreign policy, refused supply and was promptly dissolved when it showed signs of attacking Buckingham. Worse was to follow. Charles's French marriage (May 1625), itself a fatal fruit of Buckingham's policy, led first to the employment of English seamen against the Protestant strong-hold of La Rochelle and then, through the breakdown of its terms, to a war with France. There were other and more important causes, notably mutual seizures of merchant shipping in the Channel and Buckingham's own behaviour in negotiations in Paris. Arrogantly offended that Richelieu declined to fall in with his plans for a joint attack upon Spain, he took revenge by making love to Louis XIII's Queen, Anne of Austria. Meanwhile at home the second Parliament of the reign (1626) had under Eliot's leadership launched an open attack upon Buckingham and demanded his impeachment. Charles saved his friend by dissolving the Houses, having again failed to get a grant.

Against this background of disunity and mismanagement the French war began in 1627. Buckingham in person led an expedition of 8,000 men to the Isle of Rhé to relieve the Huguenots besieged in La Rochelle. He showed bravery and energy, but the enterprise was a total failure. The troops were untrained and ill-provided, the naval planning was lamentably inefficient, and he returned to Portsmouth with half his force destroyed. A further expedition to Rhé later in the year under the Earl of Denbigh also achieved nothing, and Buckingham advised Charles to summon a third Parliament in March 1628. The Commons, under the more moderate leadership of Coke and Wentworth, turned first to broader grievances and produced the Petition of Right, which Charles reluctantly accepted in June. But then, whipped up once more by Eliot, they drew up a remonstrance against the favourite, and Charles prorogued them at once. Buckingham went down to Portsmouth to prepare a third expedition to La Rochelle, and there in August he was assassinated by John Felton. The London crowds cheered the news. Certainly his murder removed an obstacle to good relations between Crown and Parliament, for no man did more to misdirect the Stuarts. Yet the manner of his death, and the popular rejoicing, could not fail to sear the mind of a King whose politics were so much a matter of personal emotion.

Roger Lockyer, *Buckingham*, 1981.

JOHN FELTON (1595?–1628), assassin, was a soldier from a Suffolk gentry family. He had taken part in Buckingham's two unsuccessful expeditions, to Cadiz in 1625 and the Isle of Rhé in 1627, and nursed a grievance against the Duke for his failure to get command of a company and for arrears of pay. In 1628 he read the Commons' remonstrance against Buckingham and decided that it was his duty to rid the country of him. He borrowed money from his mother, left instructions at a London church that he should be prayed for on the following Sunday, bought a dagger for tenpence, and walked to Portsmouth where the favourite was supervising preparations for the Rochelle expedition. There he mixed with the crowd in Buckingham's house in the High Street, and got near enough to stab him over the heart. Buckingham died almost at once. Felton, who was hanged at Tyburn, was regarded as a popular hero, the 'David' who had slain 'Goliath', and celebrated in ballads, poems and health-drinking.

SIR EDWARD COKE (1552–1634), champion of the Common Law, was born at Mileham in Norfolk, son of a barrister, member of a family solidly established among the Norfolk gentry. Educated at

Sir Edward Coke
(Artist: eng. by Michael van der Gucht)

Norwich Grammar School, Trinity College, Cambridge, and Clifford's Inn, he was admitted to the Inner Temple in 1572 and became a barrister in 1578. Recorder of Coventry and Norwich in 1586, M.P. for Aldeburgh in 1589, Recorder of London and Solicitor-

General in 1592, M.P. for Norfolk and Speaker of the Commons in 1593, Coke was a distinguished figure of Elizabethan England when the last decade of the Queen's reign began. He owed his rise in part to the patronage of Burghley, yet in the main to his abilities and his thrustfulness. Tall and handsome, possessing a forceful mind, a remarkable memory and immense industry, Coke had the advocate's gift of speech and the frank ambition of the men of his age for posts that brought both money and honour. So in 1594 he was appointed Attorney-General, beating Essex's candidate, Francis Bacon, in the race — a victory that brought him the task of leading for the Crown against Essex and Southampton after the former's rising in 1600, against Raleigh at the beginning of a new reign in 1603, and against the Gunpowder plotters in 1605.

His reward for such eminent service to the state was promotion by James I to the Chief Justiceship of the Common Pleas in 1606. The advocate became the judge, viewing the law from a different angle. In 1607 Coke condemned the *ex-officio* oath used in the Court of High Commission, and issued writs of prohibition against the ecclesiastical courts, and in 1610 he ruled against the creation of offences by royal proclamations — decisions which brought sharp conflict with a King whose vision of the prerogative was wider than that of Coke. But the deaths in 1612 of Robert Cecil, the Lord Treasurer and Coke's ally in the Privy Council, and in 1613 of Chief Justice Fleming of King's Bench, opened the way to a scheme engineered by Francis Bacon. Coke was moved from Common Pleas to King's Bench, a promotion he could not refuse to a place in which it was hoped he would be more pliable; Bacon himself became Attorney-General. For two years James I had no trouble with Coke. Then in 1615, over the case of Peacham, an elderly Puritan parson from Somerset accused of treason on the strength of rough notes for a sermon, Coke stood out against the King's wish to obtain the judges' opinions before trial. He yielded in the end — though the opinion he gave was against the Crown. But before long he was in jurisdictional conflict with, and issuing writs of *praemunire* against, the Court of Chancery —   the Court, in the words of Bacon, now in growing favour with the King, 'of your majesty's absolute power'. And in 1616 he defied the King's instructions to stop procedure in the Case of Commendams, which involved the right of the Crown to present benefices to be held *in commendam*, i.e. by deputy in the absence of the regular incumbent. Such actions were inevitably intolerable to James, even without Bacon's constant zeal against his rival, and in November 1616 Coke was dismissed from the office of Lord Chief Justice. It was said in London that 'Four Ps have overthrown and put him down, that is Pride, Prohibitions, Praemunire, and Prerogative'. In the spring of 1617 Bacon became Lord Chancellor.

Coke did not remain wholly out of favour for long: his abilities were valuable to the state, and James, unlike his son Charles, did not bear malice. He was readmitted to the Privy Council in 1617, and was elected to the Commons of 1621, a Crown nominee for the Cornish borough of Liskeard, but he became the leader of the opposition to the royal policies, prominent — no doubt with strong personal satisfaction — in the impeachment of Bacon, denouncing monopolies, the friendship with Spain and the increase of papists. It was at Coke's proposal that the Protestation of December 1621 was drafted, claiming that 'the liberties, franchises, privileges and jurisdictions of Parliament are the ancient and undoubted birthright and inheritance of the subjects of England', and that Parliament 'hath and of right ought to have freedom of speech' to discuss the defence of the realm and the Church of England. James, dissolving Parliament, imprisoned its leaders: Coke, most severely treated of all, was in the Tower for nearly seven months. But he reappeared as M.P. for Coventry in the last Parliament of James, backing the war with Spain, and for Norfolk in the first of Charles, in which he denounced Buckingham's mismanagement of the Navy. Excluded from that of 1626 by being pricked as Sheriff of Buckinghamshire, he could only support its impeachment of the royal favourite from afar. But he was back in the Commons in 1628, this time for Buckinghamshire, and in this, his last, Parliament led them in drafting the Petition of Right. He lived on until 1634, dying at his great house at Stoke Poges — while the agents of Charles ransacked his desk and library there and his rooms in the Temple for seditious documents.

Coke married twice. His first wife, Bridget Paston, mother of seven children, died in 1598. His second marriage, in that same year, to the beautiful and wealthy widow Lady Elizabeth Hatton, for whom Bacon was an unsuccessful suitor, was a disaster for Coke and the source of gossip and scandal for the rest of his days. He was forty-

six; Lady Elizabeth was twenty, gay, wilful, dedicated to fashion
and society as Coke was to the law. There were endless disputes over
property and, most sensationally, over the marriage planned for
their only child, Frances, with Coke breaking into a mansion with a
band of retainers to remove her from her mother's control; there
were cases before the Privy Council; and ultimately Lady Elizabeth
Hatton lived apart — seeing Coke only when she needed his professional advice in her litigation with others!

There is a sense in which Coke seems to have lived three careers,
not one, and these not easy to reconcile with one another. The
Attorney-General who savaged Raleigh so ruthlessly on behalf of the
Crown does not seem to merge readily into the Lord Chief Justice
who so strictly interpreted the Crown's prerogative, or to merge at
all into the Commons' leader who used precedent as a means of
invading royal authority. It is clear enough that Coke's outlook in
some ways changed during an unusually long political lifetime. The
world of Buckingham was, after all, very different from that of
Burghley, and lawyers are notoriously realistic in their politics. Yet
it may be that the explanation of Coke's career lies not so much in
adaptability of even in a growing and genuine devotion to Parliamentary 'Liberties', in the sense in which the seventeenth century
used that word, as in the fact that Coke was an Elizabethan, the last
of the great Elizabethans, a man already past fifty when the Queen
died. The consistency which Coke's political career seems to lack
was not one of the Elizabethan virtues. The ambition, the vigour and
the zest for life and work, the buoyancy to which James I pointed in
his remark, 'Throw this man where you will, and he falls upon his
legs', the patriotism which Coke expressed in his attacks upon both
Raleigh and Buckingham — these were indeed Elizabethan qualities.

In one respect he was unique. He has remained by common
consent the peculiar champion of the English Common Law, the
man in whom, in Maitland's phrase, 'the common law took flesh'.
This role of Coke in English history was reflected in his own
lifetime, in the dispute he conducted with Francis Bacon over the
relative jurisdictions of Common Law Courts and Chancery, the
legal aspect of the constitutional conflict of the seventeenth century.
For us it has become embodied in his literary legacy, the written
work which so long remained at the centre of legal studies and
training in the Anglo-Saxon world — Coke's *Reports* in thirteen

volumes (the first eleven published 1600-15, the last two not until 1650-59), and *Coke on Littleton* and the other three *Institutes of the Laws of England* (published 1628-44). The *Reports*, which Coke began when he was a law student, contained the records of some forty years of law cases, and became a unique and authoritative record of precedent in English law courts. The *Institutes* attempted to provide a comprehensive survey of English law, beginning with a commentary upon the land-law expounded by the fifteenth-century judge, Littleton. Taken together, *Reports* and *Institutes* have given Coke a greater influence than any other single Englishman over the shaping and growth of the Common Law.

C.D. Bowen, *The Lion and the Throne: The Life and Times of Sir Edward Coke*, 1957.
S.D. White, *Sir Edward Coke and the Grievances of the Commonwealth*, 1979.

FRANCIS BACON, 1st BARON VERULAM and VISCOUNT ST. ALBAN (1561–1626), philosopher of science, essayist and Lord Chancellor, was born in York House in the Strand, the son of Sir Nicholas Bacon, Elizabeth I's Lord Keeper. The Queen admired his precocity; he went up to Trinity College, Cambridge, at twelve, and it was there that, in his secretary Rawley's words, 'he first fell into the dislike of the philosophy of Aristotle', because of the 'unfruitfulness' of Greek philosophy. He entered Gray's Inn, but spent the years 1576–9 in France, under the care of the English Ambassador. Recalled on the sudden death of his father, he never went out of England again. He turned to the law as a profession, and in 1584 he entered Parliament for Melcombe Regis.

Francis Bacon was unusually gifted, with the finest intellect of any Englishman of his day. He was also well connected, for Burghley was his uncle by marriage. Yet his career made little headway in Elizabeth's reign. Macaulay believed that this was because Burghley saw Bacon as a potential threat to the success of his own favourite son, Robert Cecil, and Bacon himself in later years spoke harshly of both the Cecils. There were other reasons. The brilliant child of a dominant Puritan mother, Bacon suffered from a deep-rooted uncertainty and displayed to the world a blend of conceit and

Francis Bacon, 1st Baron Verulam and Viscount St. Alban
(Artist: Unknown)

servility which could scarcely fail to provoke hostility. For all his
early wisdom, his gentleness, his tolerance, there were elements in his
complex personality which did not appeal to all men. His 'delicate,
lively hazel eye' was, so William Harvey told John Aubrey, 'like the
eye of a viper'. Nor did he ever learn to handle men easily, while his
relations with women were necessarily affected by the homosexual
feelings which led him, both in his bachelor days as a rising lawyer
and in the time of his magnificence under James, to surround himself
with young male servants.

Certainly Queen Elizabeth in the 1590s made her distrust of
Bacon clear. There were at least two valid political grounds for it.
The first was Bacon's unusually ill-judged speech to the Parliament
of 1593, in which he attacked the subsidy proposals, saying, 'we are
here to search the wounds of the realm and not to skin them over'.
For this he was forbidden the Court. The second, more serious in the
context of the age, was his attachment to the rising star of Essex,
formed when Bacon realized there was little to be got from the
Cecils. Essex characteristically tried to drive Elizabeth into appointing Bacon Attorney-General in 1594. When the Queen denied him
this, on the reasonable grounds of Bacon's relative youth (Coke, who
was appointed, was nine years older) and inexperience of the law,
Essex pressed for the Solicitorship-General for Bacon in 1595. This
too she refused. And the friendship with Essex ended in disaster and
shame. Essex made a substantial gift of land to Bacon, which the
latter afterwards sold to pay off his debts. Bacon, the older as well as
the wiser man, gave Essex much good advice, warning him to seek
civil power rather than military and not to accept the government of
Ireland, and trying to reconcile him with the Queen. But by the time
Essex plunged into the rebellion of 1601, Bacon had abandoned him.
He was one of the counsel for the prosecution at Essex's trial for
treason, and after the execution he produced at Elizabeth's command a propagandist *Declaration of the Practices and Treasons* of
Essex and his supporters.

The new reign in 1603 brought a change of fortunes for Bacon. He
was knighted — like some six hundred others — in its first year. In
1607 he became Solicitor-General, in 1613 Attorney-General. The
death of Robert Cecil (1612) removed an obstacle. His influence
with, and usefulness to, the King grew, as was revealed by James's
employment of him to persuade Coke, now Lord Chief Justice, to

give a private opinion in Peacham's Case (1615). He shared the King's high view of the royal prerogative and his limited opinion of the functions of Parliament. In 1617 he became Lord Keeper and the following year reached the climax of his authority and ambition as Lord Chancellor. Even the chronic need for money, and that inability to handle it which in 1598 had brought him temporary imprisonment for debt, was stayed, and he lived in superb and elegant style both at York House and at his country mansion of Gorhambury at St. Albans. Yet real power eluded him: this belonged to the favourite Buckingham, whom Bacon sedulously flattered. Ironically it was his connection with Buckingham which led to Bacon's sudden fall in 1621. The Commons, after attacking Buckingham and other holders of patents for monopolies, turned their attention to Bacon, who had drafted some of the patents, and he was impeached for accepting bribes from suitors at his court. He admitted his guilt and was dismissed from office, sent to the Tower and fined £40,000. Released after a day or two, he retired in disgrace to Gorhambury, where he devoted most of his time to writing, before his death in 1626.

As a politician Bacon was not successful, nor was he an attractive failure. As a stateman his vision was clear and in certain ways forward-looking, as, for example, in his support for James's project of union with Scotland; yet on the great issue of his age, that of sovereignty, he lent his support to the authoritarianism which England was to overthrow in the coming decades. As a lawyer he was not specially distinguished: he saw the law primarily as a profitable career, and his views on the role of law in the state were conditioned by his belief in prerogative, which led him to regard judges, in his famous phrase, as 'lions, but yet lions under the throne'. As a writer, on subjects other than science, he has won fame by his works — his finely-chiselled *Essays*, ten of which were published as early as 1579, and which he himself regarded 'as the recreations of my other studies'; and his *History of Henry VII*, written after his fall, and in its force a measure of the continuing strength of Bacon's mind.

But it is above all as a philosopher of science that Bacon has commanded the attention of posterity. In *The Advancement of Learning* (1605) and the *Novum Organum* (1620) he put forward a great plea, and something of a plan, for the reorganization of scientific method. Knowledge, instead of concerning itself with 'cobwebs of learning, admirable for the fineness of thread and work, but of no substance or profit', should be sought 'to the benefit and use of men'. Science should copy the mechanical arts and be 'founded on nature and the light of experience'. Above all, the scientist must experiment. Truth will be found by the method of induction, based upon experiment: here, as displayed in the *Novum Organum*, is the new scientific method to replace the outworn logic of Aristotle. Bacon was not himself a scientist. He bothered little about what contemporary experimental scientists like Galileo and Gilbert were doing, and he gave little credit to such theoretical science as the Copernican astronomy. His own attitude to experiments was naively impatient, although it is unjust to imply that he believed in random experimentation; he saw the need for planning, as his utopian exercise *New Atlantis* (*c.* 1617) demonstrated, and also sensed the possibilities of co-operative research. Men have often read into the Baconian philosophy of science more than can properly be found there; for example, they have tended to exaggerate Bacon's own vision of the use of science in improving the material welfare of mankind. 'The relief of man's estate' was not for Bacon the sole end of knowledge. Nevertheless, when every qualification is made, Bacon's work was a major achievement of the English mind, and one whose consequences were immeasurably great, even though not until the second half of the seventeenth century did men really begin to accept them. Not only did he give science 'an incomparable advertisement, by associating with it his personal prestige, his "Elizabethan" glamour, and his great literary power'. * He turned men's minds to the study of the physical properties of matter, he insisted on the separation of scientific study from religious truth, and above all he compelled men to weigh knowledge in new scales. Bacon was the author of an intellectual revolution.

T. B. Macaulay, 'Francis Bacon', *Critical and Historical Essays*, 1837.
Paolo Rossi, *Francis Bacon: From Magic to Science*, 1968.
Christopher Hill, *Intellectual Origins of the English Revolution*, 1965, pp. 85-130.

* Basil Willey, *The Seventeenth-Century Background*, 1962 ed., p. 31.

LIONEL CRANFIELD, EARL OF MIDDLESEX (1575–1645), the most successful of James I's finance ministers, was the younger son of a London merchant, a mercer engaged in the export trade. Educated in the Mercers' school, St. Paul's, and apprenticed in 1590 to Richard Sheppard who traded in textiles and other goods with Northern Europe, in 1597 he was admitted a member of the Mercers' Company and set up in business on his own as a cloth exporter; he married Sheppard's daughter in 1599 (and later had to provide his father-in-law with a job). Cranfield did well in the export business, selling fine cloth to the Netherlands and coarser material in Germany, and dabbling occasionally in other commodities including pepper, dyewood, grain and guns. As with many contemporary merchants, his profits were the basis of widespread speculation — in customs-farming, in deals in Crown lands, in moneylending — and by 1613 Cranfield was a rich man, a merchant financier highly respected in the City for his acumen. In that year, with Henry Howard, Earl of Northampton, then Lord Privy Seal, as his patron, he was appointed Surveyor-General of the Customs. In the role of expert called in from the business world to advise the government on trade, Cranfield increased the royal income from customs by £30,000 a year by the autumn of 1615, and put forward a scheme (rejected by the King) for reorganizing the tariff system. In the next six years he was the leading spirit in a programme of retrenchment affecting a wide range of government departments, notably the Household, the Navy and the Wardrobe; in 1619 he was appointed Master of the Court of Wards and increased its average receipts by one quarter within the next six years. These achievements, though modest in face of James I's financial difficulties and extravagance, were useful. As M.P. for Arundel, he was the leading business expert in the Parliament of 1621; and late in that year he was appointed Lord Treasurer, becoming Earl of Middlesex in 1622. For the next three years he attempted a policy of strict economy, believing that this would rescue the King in a way acceptable to the classes represented in Parliament. He cut pensions and fees, tightened up the terms of the customs-farmers, compelled the payment of debts due to the Crown, and began to tackle the problem of encroachment on the royal forests. But the task was hopeless. James too readily yielded to the courtiers' demands despite Cranfield's efforts to prevent any grants being made without his own consent.

Buckingham, for a time his patron (Cranfield married as his second wife in 1620, Anne Brett, a kinswoman of the favourite) grew cool as he realized that Cranfield meant economy to touch even the highest; and he turned violently against the Lord Treasurer in 1624 when the latter opposed his new policy of war with Spain. The Commons, too, also wanting war and therefore in brief harmony with Buckingham, were hostile to Cranfield, who had offended many by his truculence of manner in the House. Courtiers thought him an upstart; Bishop Williams called him 'a man *plebeius*, creeping into so many offices, where there are so many worthy and learned noblemen'. And Cranfield had given hostages to fortune by amassing much wealth and land while in office. In 1624 he was impeached, and found guilty of 'bribery, extortion, oppression, wrong and deceipt'; fined £50,000 (most of this was remitted) and sent briefly to the Tower. Although he lived on in comfortable circumstances until 1645 (Parliamentary troops searched his house for arms in 1644) and although Charles I wrote once or twice for advice (and ignored it), Cranfield was never employed by the Crown again. The most apt comment is that of Sir John Eliot in 1626 — 'Middlesex had merited well of the King, and had done him that service that few had ever done'.

R.H. Tawney, *Business and Politics under James I — Lionel Cranfield as Merchant and Minister*, 1958.
Meama Prestwich, *Cranfield, Politics and Profits under the Early Stuarts*, 1966.

SIR ARTHUR INGRAM, (1565–1642) was a company promoter and moneylender whose career throws light on the management of public finance in the reigns of the first two Stuarts. The son of a Yorkshireman well established as a London merchant in the later years of Elizabeth's reign, he took over from his father about 1600. He moved rapidly into the customs service, with its opportunities of pickings and certainty of patronage, and soon became a controller of the Port of London. Thereafter his enterprises were manifold — including the management of customs farms, the sale of prize goods, of licences, and of Crown lands, monopolies of dyewoods and of starch-making — and to all of them he brought acumen, unscrupulousness, a ruthless appetite for profit and a

staggering self-righteousness. He benefited substantially from a long
partnership with Cranfield, yet avoided serious damage when the
latter fell. To courtiers he became invaluable both as a 'contact
man' and a source of ready cash, and in 1615 he was asked to
produce a memorandum on fiscal policy for the government. He
seems to have been extraordinarily unpopular, and his unsuccessful
attempt to secure the office of Cofferer of the Royal Household
provoked an uproar throughout the department. Before this he had
bought the post of Secretary to the Council of the North, and
although his devotion to its duties was little more than minimal, he
spent much of the later part of his life in Yorkshire. Here he invested
his profits in land and built houses for himself and his sons, in York,
at Sheriff Hutton and, most notably, at Temple Newsam. In the
1630s he was the leading citizen of York, founding Bootham
Hospital. His business activities at this stage included the organization of the production of alum (in which he lost substantially), the
farming of recusancy fines, and the management of various financial
enterprises for his fellow-Yorkshireman Thomas Wentworth with
whom, scarcely surprisingly, he eventually quarrelled. He sat in a
succession of parliaments from 1610 onwards; somewhat Puritan in
his religious outlook, he had by the time of his death in 1642 moved
cautiously but clearly to the side of the opposition in the Commons.

A. F. Upton, *Sir Arthur Ingram*, 1961.

RICHARD BANCROFT (1544–1610), Archbishop of Canterbury, was born at Farnworth in Lancashire and went from the local
grammar school to Christ's College, Cambridge. An outspoken anti-
Puritan during his teaching career at Cambridge, he became a
member of Whitgift's High Commission. In 1589 he denounced the
'Martinists' in a savage sermon at Paul's Cross, and he helped detect
the printers of the Marprelate libels. Whitgift made him his chaplain
in 1592, and he rapidly became the Archbishop's right-hand man. As
Bishop of London from 1597 his influence was great, and he was the
obvious successor to the primacy in 1604. To Clarendon, looking
back over half a century of trouble and disaster for the Church,
Bancroft was the great archbishop; his 'never enough to be lamented
death' opened the way to disorder and difficulty. This may be a
generous verdict, even if it is clear that his successor Abbot was a

mediocrity in comparison. Certainly Bancroft was a strong man in his own right as well as the wearer of the mantle of Whitgift. It was characteristic that he should call out pikemen in 1601 to scatter Essex's rebels at Ludgate. He was above all an administrator, who halted the alienation of church property and attempted to discipline the Church. In 1604 as one of the representatives of the hierarchy at Hampton Court he took a tough and violent line against the Puritans. His Book of Canons of the same year, to which all ministers had to subscribe in the terms of the *ex animo* oath, enforced acceptance of each of the Thirty-Nine Articles and compelled the wearing of cope and surplice and kneeling at communion, thus driving a number of Puritan clergy out of their livings. It was Bancroft rather than James who 'harried them out of the land', and Bancroft, the enemy of compromise, who sabotaged such agreement as had been reached at Hampton Court. Moreover, the new Canons brought dispute with the common lawyers, alarmed at a possible extension of jurisdiction by the ecclesiastical courts. Bancroft had no hesitation about engaging his foes. Such vigour, attractive in retrospect to one who had seen the sectaries in power, had its perils. No doubt Bancroft was successful for the short term in checking clerical Puritanism. Yet his actions in connection with Hampton Court effectively stimulated the growth of lay Puritanism in the House of Commons, a force far more dangerous, as Laud was to learn.

S. B. Babbage, *Puritanism and Richard Bancroft*, 1962.

LANCELOT ANDREWES (1555–1626), was born at Barking, the son of a merchant, and educated at Coopers School and at Merchant Taylors under Richard Mulcaster. Going up to Pembroke Hall, Cambridge, he became the most distinguished theological scholar of his day, and Fellow and Master of the college. Twice he refused bishoprics from Elizabeth, declining to alienate lands as a condition of entry to the see. In 1601 he became Dean of Westminster, and in 1605 James I made him Bishop of Chichester; in 1609 he went to Ely; in 1619 to Winchester. It had been widely expected that he would succeed Bancroft at Canterbury. Among the bishops of James I, 'those worldly, courtly, talented, place-hunting *dilettanti*, the ornamental betrayers of the Church', * Andrewes

* H. R. Trevor-Roper, *Historical Essays* (1957), p. 145.

shines out in many ways as the great exception. Perhaps, indeed, this was why James preferred Abbot, usually more malleable — except in the Essex divorce, where Andrewes was much more compliant — and certainly more humdrum. For Andrewes was celebrated for the austerity and industry of his life as well as for his simplicity, charity and modesty. He was a scholar of immense patristic learning, profoundly read in sacred literature and skilled in ancient languages; the most eminent of the divines commissioned to produce the Authorized Version of the Bible, he took a large share in the translation of the Old Testament. He conducted a vigorous and celebrated controversy on the temporal power of the Papacy with the Roman Catholic Cardinal Bellarmine, at a remarkable level of style and erudition. His kindness and generosity, both to eminent foreign visitors like Isaac Casaubon and to the poor, the needy and the criminal at home, were famous in his own day. He was an outstanding preacher whose influence on contemporaries was great, and the author of books of devotions, especially his *Preces*, which solaced and aided generations of Anglicans after his time. As a churchman he belonged to the Arminian school, stressing the worth of ritual and the value of decency and orderliness in the conduct of services, and upholding the divine origins of royal authority in church and state (and of tithes). Unquestionably he was the most distinguished and attractive of the Jacobean bishops, and it is clear that the Catholic tradition in the Church of England owes a good deal to him — more perhaps than to Laud, whose rigidity and extremism endangered the values in which both men believed. On the other hand, it is impossible not to note his almost total silence upon the political issues of his day. Here his practical subservience to the Crown was complete.

P. A. Welsby, *Lancelot Andrewes* (1555–1626), 1958.
T. S. Eliot, 'Lancelot Andrewes', in *Selected Essays*, 1953.

GEORGE ABBOT (1562–1633), Archbishop of Canterbury, was born at Guildford, the son of a clothworker, and educated at Guildford Grammar School and Balliol. He had a distinguished career at Oxford as theologian (his lectures on the Book of Jonah were particularly celebrated) and preacher; in 1597 he became Master of University College and in 1600 Vice-Chancellor, in which capacity he is said once to have sent one hundred and forty undergraduates to prison for sitting with their hats on in his presence at St. Mary's. His religious opinions were firmly, though moderately, Puritan, and among the dons whose views he attacked was William Laud of St. John's. In 1608 he became chaplain to the Earl of Dunbar, then favourite of James I; he went with the King to Scotland in that same year and played an important part in the reintroduction of episcopacy there, and he gained further favour by writing a pamphlet praising the King's role in the Gowrie Plot. These activities brought extraordinarily swift preferment — the see of Lichfield in 1609, London in 1610, and Canterbury itself in 1611. The last promotion was unexpected, not least by Abbot himself, for James was not sympathetic to men of Puritan views, and there was an obvious candidate in Lancelot Andrewes. It may be that James sensed that the latter's verdict on his private life would be the more censorious; and Abbot had shown that he did not find Calvinist theology incompatible with adulation of the monarch.

To succeed the disciplinarian Bancroft could not be easy, and to serve James I would have tested a Dunstan. Abbot found himself involved in the intrigues of a disreputable court, and the deaths in 1612 of Prince Henry and Salisbury removed almost at once his two strongest allies. He was anti-Catholic, anti-Arminian and anti-Spanish, and these opinions brought him into conflict with the favourite Carr and with the powerful Howard faction. He soon quarrelled with James, first over the King's unsuccessful attempt to convert to his own uses the fortune left by the merchant Thomas Sutton for the foundation of the Charterhouse School, and secondly and more seriously over the Countess of Essex's divorce. Abbot's opposition, even though it was eventually overruled, earned him the violent hostility of Carr, her new husband, and to counteract this Abbot introduced George Villiers, later Duke of Buckingham, to the court. Within a short time the remedy was to prove worse than the disease, and Abbot was a principal opponent of Buckingham's Spanish marriage project. In the Church the Arminians gained ground, winning the support of the favourite; and since much of the dispute at this stage concerned episcopal authority, Abbot as a Puritan bishop was in a false position. Then came a bitter stroke of ill luck. In 1621 Abbot, out hunting, aimed his crossbow at a buck and shot and killed Lord Zouch's gamekeeper instead. He was profoundly distressed, while his enemies seized the opportunity to attack him. A group of bishops-elect, one of them Laud, declined to be consecrated by a homicidal prelate; and although Abbot was formally pardoned the episode clouded the rest of his career. The accession of Charles I in 1625 could only make his position even more difficult, for the new king was entirely committed to the Arminians. When Abbot declined to approve for publication Robert Sibthorp's sermon supporting the forced loan, he was suspended (1627) and his powers were taken over by a commission headed by Laud. Although he was restored to favour after the death of Buckingham his authority could never be very great. Yet his survival until 1633 hindered the full introduction of Laudian uniformity.

P. A. Welsby, *George Abbot* (1562–1633), 1962.

SIR ROBERT COTTON (1571–1631), member of a Huntingdonshire gentry family, was educated at Westminster School when William Camden, author of *Britannia*, was its Master, and at Jesus College, Cambridge. He helped Camden found the Society of Antiquaries, and at seventeen decided to devote himself to historical studies, starting to collect appropriate materials for this purpose. So began the creation of what became the most celebrated of English scholarly libraries. His collection, for the most part in manuscript, grew almost daily, by purchase, gift, and loan (and even, occasionally, theft). It was widely used by scholars, lawyers, M.P.s, state officials, heralds, and churchmen. Lord Treasurer Cranfield borrowed the accounts of Henry VII's finance minister Dudley, and Ben Jonson classical plays. In 1622 Cotton moved from Blackfriars to a house in Westminster next to the House of Commons. His wish at this time to give the library to the nation was frustrated by the opposition of the royal favourite, Buckingham; and not until the beginning of the eighteenth century did the Cottonian Library become national property, uniting in 1753 with the Sloane Collection to form the British Museum.

Cotton's lasting fame rests upon his library, which in his own day was a research centre uniquely valuable to scholars, especially to students of the English past. But this is only part of the picture of the man, for he was also active in court and parliament. Client and adviser in the early years of James I's reign to Henry Howard, Earl of

Northampton, Cotton was knowledgeable in matters of law and trade as well as of learning. As Knight of the Shire for Huntingdon in the Commons of 1604–11, he and his library provided an invaluable quarry of precedents for his fellow-members. But the death of his patron in 1614 was a turning-point in Cotton's career. He now became a client of the royal favourite Robert Carr, Earl of Somerset, who that December married Northampton's great-niece Frances Howard. Cotton thus found himself involved in the Overbury murder case. In this unsavoury affair he seems to have given his patron bad advice, and to have tampered with evidence by forging false dates on letters; he suffered a spell of imprisonment in consequence. Moreover the fall of Somerset opened the way for the rise of George Villiers (Buckingham), with whom Cotton appears never to have got on good terms. From 1618, now a client of Thomas Howard, Earl of Arundel, he was a member of the peace party who opposed Buckingham's warlike policies during the mid-1620s. On friendly terms with Sir John Eliot, he was active behind the scenes in the discussions which led to the Petition of Right in 1628. But the assassination of Buckingham that August transformed the political scene, and Cotton fell victim to the purge of the favourite enemies which soon followed. In 1629 he was imprisoned, and his library closed by government order. Although he was soon set free, the library remained shut, and in 1631 Cotton died, his end hastened by these events.

Sir Robert Cotton was certainly a great collector and librarian. But neither as politician nor historian does he come near the front rank. Yet perhaps the most interesting aspect of his life is his view of history as directly relevant to contemporary political issues. This involved not merely the provision of precedents, for example from Magna Carta, appropriate to negotiations between Crown and Commons; or the custom of following such writers as Guicciardini and Machiavelli in finding models of wisdom and virtue, folly and vice, in the annals of Rome. Cotton made altogether sharper use of the English past, most notably in his *History of Henry the Third*, published in 1627. This tells of a king who, having let himself be guided by corrupt favourites, turned them out, reformed his court, and set out to re-establish his leadership of an united people The message was plain, and it is scarcely surprising that Buckingham, who twice previously had sought to have the library closed, had

Cotton haled before the Council after the book's publication. In Cotton's view the essential role of historical scholarship was to work towards and help maintain unity within the realm — and this in the 1620s meant to restore that harmony between sovereign and subjects which he believed had distinguished the great days of Elizabethan England in which he had grown up.

Kevin Sharpe, *Sir Robert Cotton, 1586–1631: History and Politics in Early Modern England*, 1979.

SIR THOMAS BODLEY (1545–1613), was born in Exeter and spent part of his childhood in Geneva whither his family migrated during the Marian persecution. Returning on Elizabeth's accession, he went to Magdalen College, Oxford; he became something of a Hebrew scholar and a Fellow of Merton. An accomplished linguist, he travelled widely, and although he was for a time M.P. for Plymouth and for St. Germans, he served Elizabeth's government as a diplomat in Denmark, in France and then (1589–96) in the exasperating post of permanent resident in the United Netherlands. His lasting fame, however, rested not upon this but upon the great library which he founded and endowed in the University of Oxford, work to which he devoted the last period of his life. Beginning with the modest ambition to restore Duke Humphrey's library, Bodley quickly widened his vision, winning a good deal of help from donations and gaining the support of James I when he came to the throne. The new library opened in 1603 with 2,000 volumes (by 1620 there were 16,000). In 1604 letters patent were issued to confer upon it the title 'Bodleian', in 1605 the first catalogue was compiled, and in 1620 the Stationers' Company consented to give the library a copy of every book printed. When Bodley died in 1613 he made the University of Oxford his chief legatee. He lies buried in Merton College chapel.

A. B. Wormald and C. D. Wright, *The English Library before* 1700, 1958.

WILLIAM HERBERT, 3rd EARL OF PEMBROKE (1580–1630), owner of Wilton House and the richest of James I's subjects, played various roles in the life of his era. As courtier and politician (he was Lord Chamberlain from 1615 to 1628) he was an opponent of the Howards and, consistently though somewhat ineffectually, anti-Spanish. This attitude to foreign policy reflected his concern for overseas trade and colonization; he helped to found the Virginia Company, he was a member of the Council of New England, and he was interested in Bermuda and in the East India Company. He was a munificent patron, in Aubrey's words 'the greatest Maecenas to learned Men of any Peer of his time; or since': among the beneficiaries of his wealth were Massinger, Ben Jonson and Inigo Jones. Speculation has identified him with the 'Mr. W. H.' of Shakespeare's Sonnets; certainly in 1623 the First Folio of Shakespeare's plays was dedicated to him and his brother Philip. The University of Oxford made him its Chancellor in 1617; Pembroke College, incorporated in 1624, took its name from him, and in 1629 he presented the famous Baroccio collection of Greek manuscripts to the Bodleian Library. Appropriately enough, Clarendon, one of his successors as Chancellor, described Pembroke in one of the most agreeable of his character-studies. He speaks of him as 'the most universally loved and esteemed of any man of that age', and as 'of a pleasant and facetious humour and a disposition affable, generous, and magnificent'. Pembroke had, perhaps, shown some sign of this tendency as a young man in Elizabeth's reign, when he had got one of the Queen's maids-of-honour, Mary Fitton, with child, and been sent to the Fleet. Clarendon suggests that its cause was 'want of domestic content and delight ... for he paid much too dear for his wife's fortune, by taking her person into the bargain'. What Clarendon calls 'excessive indulgences' may have contributed to his death on his fiftieth birthday, 'of an apoplexy, after a full and cheerful supper'. In Aubrey's words, "twas thought, had he not been suddenly snatched away by Death (to the grief of all learned, and good men) that he would have been a great benefactor to Pembroke College in Oxford; whereas there remains only from him a great piece of Plate, that he gave there'.

EDWARD ALLEYN (1566–1626), was already celebrated as an actor by his middle twenties. A member of the Lord Admiral's Company, he played the hero in Marlowe's *Tamburlaine* and

Doctor Faustus as well as Orlando in Green's *Orland-Furioso*, and Ben Jonson praised him highly. He was also a very astute business man as an actor manager, making a considerable fortune out of the Fortune Theatre which he built and out of his position as Master of the Royal Game of bulls, bears and mastiffs. He married wisely, for his first wife was the step-daughter of Philip Henslowe, with whom he went into partnership in the theatrical business. Alleyn, unlike the great majority of his fellow-actors, was a considerable and respected figure among the upper class of his time. Yet what has established Alleyn's lasting historical fame is the use to which he put his fortune. In 1605 he began buying the Manor of Dulwich and in 1614 he held the whole estate. A year before this he had started to build a school there; a chapel was consecrated in 1616, and in 1619 there took place the formal foundation of the College of God's Gift, now generally known as Dulwich College.

G. L. Hosking, *The Life and Times of Edward Alleyn*, 1951.

BEN JONSON (1572–1637), playwright and poet, was by his own account of Scottish border ancestry, the posthumous son of a minister. Schooled at Westminster, he worked as a bricklayer for his stepfather, fought as a mercenary in the Netherlands, and made an unhappy marriage before he began in 1597 to work for Henslowe's company as actor and playwright. He killed a fellow-actor in a duel and turned Catholic during his imprisonment; he abjured Rome twelve years later. His first play, *Every Man in His Humour*, produced in 1598, established his reputation, and it was followed by a succession of others over the next thirty years, of which *Sejanus* (1603), *Volpone* (1606), *The Silent Woman* (1609), *The Alchemist* (1610), and *Bartholomew Fair* (1614) are the best known. From 1605 to 1630 Jonson, with Inigo Jones designing the settings, delighted the Court with a series of masques, and apart from a brief imprisonment for libelling the Scots he was in high favour with James I, who in 1616 gave him a pension as 'King's poet'. In 1618 he travelled to Scotland and stayed for some time with the poet William Drummond of Hawthornden. The death of James and the accession of a new King whose tastes were notably different made Jonson's fortunes less certain. Illness overtook him in the later

1620s; his play, *The New Inn* (1629), failed badly; and after his quarrel with Inigo Jones in 1631 he produced no more masques at Court. He died in 1637 and was buried in Westminster Abbey. His fellow-poets honoured his memory in a collection of verse entitled *Jonsonus Virbius*. The famous inscription on his tombstone, 'O Rare Ben Jonson', was, according to Aubrey, 'done at the charge of Jack Young, afterwards knighted, who, walking there when the grave was covering, gave the fellow eighteen pence to cut it'.

Drummond of Hawthornden painted an unattractive portrait of Jonson at the age of forty-six, saying, 'He is a great lover and praiser of himself, a contemner and scorner of others; given rather to lose a friend than a jest, jealous of every word and action of those about him (especially after drink, which is one of the elements in which he liveth)'. Big, noisy, quarrelsome, generous, Jonson was certainly a man of extraordinary range, and he dominated the literary life of London for an unusually long time. This was not simply a measure of the variety of his writings, of the lyrics, the epigrams, the splendid blank verse passages. It was first and foremost a reflection of personality. At the Mermaid Tavern in the first years of the seventeenth century he was the central figure of the famous meetings of writers, the scene of the combats of wit between Jonson and Shakespeare described by Fuller in his *Worthies*, and in their later years he was laying down the law to a circle of younger men, 'the tribe of Ben', at the Sun, the Devil, and elsewhere. But his range of friends was by no means confined to young writers in taverns. It included men of such varied brilliance as Donne and Selden, Bacon and Clarendon, the last of whom spoke of Jonson's 'extraordinary kindness for Mr. Hyde, till he found he betook himself to business, which he believed ought never to be preferred before his company'; and he enjoyed the country-house patronage of aristocrats like the Sidneys, the Earl of Pembroke, and the Duke of Newcastle. His own remarkable and uneven genius was no doubt self-made. The classical learning he displayed so lavishly in his plays was the product of omnivorous reading in his younger days rather than of his formal education. Yet in many ways — in his self-assertiveness and yearning for supremacy, his zest for life, his blend of coarseness and delicacy, honesty and scandal, erudition and vulgarity — Jonson was peculiarly representative of Jacobean England, or at least of that part of it which was untouched by Puritanism.

C.H. Herford and P. Simpson, eds., *Ben Jonson: Works*, 1925–52, Vols. I and II (*The Man and His Work*).

J. Palmer, *Ben Jonson*, 1934.

INIGO JONES (1573–1652), designer and architect, was a Londoner, the son of a Smithfield clothworker. We know little about the first thirty years of his life. Before 1603 he had been to Italy and learned the draughtsmanship which marked him above his contemporaries. He went there again, in the company of the Earl of Arundel, in 1613-14, visited Rome, read the writings of Palladio and compared the master's drawings of classical buildings with the originals. Jones's copy of Palladio still exists, with his annotations: it symbolizes the injection of classical antiquity into English architecture in 1615, the year in which he began seriously to practise. Hithero he had been predominantly concerned with designing stage sets, machines and costumes for the masques which James I's Queen, Anne of Denmark, enjoyed so much. From 1605 until they quarrelled in 1631 Ben Jonson and Inigo Jones presented at Court a series of elaborate shows, and Jones continued as designer until the masques ceased in 1640. He introduced the proscenium arch and such devices as moving shutters, rotating columns and possibly a revolving platform, and his career is of original importance in the history of the English stage.

In 1615 he became Surveyor of the King's Works, and thenceforward until the outbreak of the Civil War he gave most of his time to the supervision and extension of royal buildings. Much of what he did has been pulled down, and some — for example, the proposed immense reconstruction of Whitehall — never got further than the drawings. Among the buildings which survive, revealing the Palladian imprint which Inigo Jones brought to English architecture — and the English feeling which he imparted to Palladian — are the Queen's House at Greenwich, begun in 1617 and finished in 1635; the Banqueting House at Whitehall (1619–22), with its superb proportion; and Marlborough House chapel (1623-7). Jones was also responsible for the layout of the piazza at Covent Garden, an early, if modest, example of town-planning, and for St. Paul's Church there, built like a Roman temple; and he was involved in the plans for the rehabilitation of old St. Paul's Cathedral. It is significant that he did little for private patrons (though perhaps no

Inigo Jones
(Artist: after etching by Robert van Voerst after Sir Anthony van Dyck)

English architect has had so many scores of buildings incorrectly attributed to him). This was partly because as Surveyor he necessarily spent much of his time on routine jobs of maintenance; partly, no doubt, because of the insularity of some of the nobility; yet partly also, it has been suggested, because 'a style backed by the prestige of the Crown and the genius of Jones failed to gain the approval of the country as a whole' in a period when 'the Court was increasingly isolated'. * Certainly Inigo Jones's fortunes were tied to those of the Court. He left London in 1642, and in 1645 was among the Royalists besieged in Basing House, when he was captured and 'carried away in a blanket, having lost his clothes'. He was fined and had to compound for his lands. Yet he found a wealthy Puritan patron, for in the last years of his life he was working for the 4th Earl of Pembroke in the rebuilding and decorating of Wilton House. He died at Somerset House in 1652.

John Summerson, *Inigo Jones*, 1966.

JOHN DONNE (1572–1631), poet and preacher, was a Londoner, the son of a well-to-do ironmonger of Welsh extraction whose Catholic wife brought the child up in her own faith. Educated at Hart Hall, Oxford, and at Lincoln's Inn, he was a fashionable young 'wit' in the last decade of Elizabethan England, and a good many of his love poems, the *Songs and Sonets*, belong to this period. He went with Essex to Cadiz in 1596 and on the Islands Voyage in the following year, and in 1598 he became secretary to Sir Thomas Egerton, the Lord Keeper. But in 1601 he wrecked his chances of a secular career by eloping with Ann More, niece of Lady Egerton. The girl's father had Donne put in the Fleet Prison, and Egerton dismissed him. For the next few years he lived on the charity of his wife's relatives and friends, and it was at this time that he turned from the earlier erotic verse to the first of his *Divine Poems* and to meditations in prose. He had departed from Catholicism before 1600, yet he remained unwilling to yield to the pressure of friends that he should take Anglican orders, and not until 1615 was he ordained. Donne preached his first surviving sermon to the Queen in April of that year. He became Reader in Divinity to the benchers of Lincoln's Inn in 1616, and from 1621 until his death ten years later he was Dean of St. Paul's. In Izaac Walton's charming words, 'in his penitential years, viewing some of those pieces that had been loosely (God knows too loosely) scattered in his youth, he wish't they had

*E. Mercer, 'The Houses of the Gentry', *Past and Present*, No. 5, May 1954, p. 27.

been abortive, or so short liv'd that his own eyes had witnessed their funerals'. He continued to write poetry, including 'many Divine sonnets, and other high, holy, and harmonious composures'. But his public reputation now rested mainly upon his sermons, many of which were printed, and he was generally regarded as the finest preacher in the country. The chief of the 'metaphysical poets', as Dryden called them, in some ways strongly medieval in outlook, Donne exercised a powerful influence upon younger poets for a generation after his death.

E. Gosse, *Life and Letters of John Donne*, 2 vols., 1899.

JOHN BULL (*c.* 1562–1628), musician, probably came from a Somerset family and was born at Wellow. A pupil of William Blitheman in the chapel of Queen Elizabeth, he was appointed organist of Hereford Cathedral in 1582, and after his master's death in 1591 he was in effect organist at the Chapel Royal. From 1596 to 1607 he was the first Professor of Music at Gresham College, receiving special permission to lecture in English and not in Latin. For over twenty years he served the Crown in various ways as a musician. In 1611, for example, he was the first of Prince Henry's musicians, and in 1613 he composed an anthem for the marriage of Princess Elizabeth. But in that year he departed abroad, perhaps because, like Byrd, he was a Catholic, although the official line was that he had fled to escape prosecution for fornication and other moral offences. Bull went to the Spanish Netherlands, and from 1617 he was organist at Antwerp Cathedral, where he was buried when he died in 1628. He was apparently a remarkable executant both upon the virginals and upon the organ, and for posterity his fame has rested mainly upon his compositions for these instruments, as, for example, his 'Queen Elizabeth's Pavane' for the virginals. He also wrote many anthems as well as works for viols, and it seems not unlikely that the actual air of the National Anthem derives from a keyboard tune by this composer.

Musica Britannica, XIV (John Bull, Keyboard Music: I), 1960 (esp. pp. xxi–xxv).
Percy Scholes, *God Save the Queen*, 1954.

ORLANDO GIBBONS (1538–1625) musician, born at Oxford, was taken to Cambridge as a child, and became a member of King's College choir. His talents as an executant on the organ and virginals appeared early, and in 1605 he became organist of the Chapel Royal, a post he held for twenty years until his death from apoplexy in 1625. In 1623 he was also appointed organist of Westminster Abbey. Gibbons, a Protestant, was prominent in the varied musical activities of James I's Court and received a succession of grants from the King. He left some forty compositions for keyboard and several for strings, and he wrote many madrigals and motets, the best-known being 'The Silver Swan'. Yet his historical reputation has rested mainly upon his church music, and particularly upon his numerous anthems, of which 'The Record of John' is perhaps the most popular. Gibbons was the youngest of the great group of late Elizabethan musicians, and his work, notably in his use of polyphony in some of his finest anthems, revealed in musical terms a trend towards the ceremonial associated with Arminianism and with Rome.

E. H. Fellowes, *Orlando Gibbons and his Family: the last of the Tudor School of Musicians*, 1952.

JOHN NAPIER (1550–1617), inventor of logarithms, was a Scottish laird, born at Merchiston Castle near Edinburgh and educated at St. Andrew's. He seems to have travelled abroad for some years before settling on the family estates. Napier was a man of tough practical mind, and of a varied genius, unusual among the Scots gentry of James VI's time. A firm Calvinist, in 1594 he published *A Plain Discovery of the Whole Revelation of St. John*, a very successful piece of anti-papal propaganda. An inventive landowner, he obtained a patent in 1597 for a device, based upon a hydraulic screw, to check flooding in coalpits; and about the same time he sent Francis Bacon's elder brother a detailed project for making new weapons of war, including great mirrors as burningglasses and a musket-proof metal chariot. An amateur mathematician, even more of an amateur than Englishmen like Wallis and Barrow fifty years later, Napier made use of a set of rods, known as 'Napier's Bones', to work out sums, and commended an arrangement of metal plates in a box which served as a kind of calculating machine. But what brought him immediate and lasting fame was a highly utilitarian mathematical discovery, the development of the theory of logarithms, which he expounded after twenty years' work in his *Mirifici Logarithmorum* of 1614. Their rapid adoption — in an age which for purposes of astronomy and navigation, taxation and banking, was growing increasingly in need of easier methods of calculation — was largely the work of a Cambridge mathematician, Henry Briggs, who proposed 10 as the base and worked out elaborately detailed tables.

E. W. Hobson, *John Napier*, 1914.
W. Brownlie Hendry, 'John Napier of Merchiston, *History Today*', April 1967.

   SIR THOMAS ROE (1581?–1644), diplomat and explorer, born of merchant stock at Low Leyton in Essex and educated at Magdalen College, Oxford, a young courtier in the last years of Elizabeth's reign, was knighted in 1605. An Elizabethan in his versatility, charm, conversational powers and Protestant nationalism, he was sent by Henry, Prince of Wales, to search for gold between the Amazon and the Orinoco in 1610–11. Roe advocated the formation of a West Indian Company; went as ambassador to the Mogul Emperor for the East India Company (1615–18) and won leave for Englishmen to travel for trade in his dominions; served as political adviser to Elizabeth, Queen of Bohemia, and as Chancellor of the Order of the Garter; and collected precious manuscripts and coins for the University of Oxford. His embassies on behalf of the Crown took him to Turkey (1621–8), to Poland and Sweden, where Gustavus Adolphus presented him with £2,500 (1629–30), and to Hamburg and the Empire (1638–40). Roe hoped in 1632 to be appointed Secretary of State, and his qualities would have lent distinction to that office. But he stood for an anti-Catholic foreign policy, directed mainly against the Habsburgs, and this old-fashioned attitude did not appeal to his friend Laud, who threw his influence on the side of Windebank instead. Nor did Laud show much sympathy for the project of the Scotsman John Durie, whom Roe backed, advocating the unification of all Protestant churches.

M. J. Brown, *The Life of Sir Thomas Roe, Itinerant Ambassador*, 1970.

THOMAS MUN (1571–1641), economist, was the son of a London mercer. Mun went into trade early, particularly with the Levant and the Italian cities, and became a prosperous merchant. He was chosen a member of the committee of the East India Comapny in 1615, and his first book, published in 1621, was a defence of the company against the charge that they exported too much specie in order to pay for their imports of luxuries. His second and most famous book, *England's Treasure by Foreign Trade*, was probably written before 1630 but was not published until 1664. In this he generalized the theme behind his earlier work, and laid down the doctrine of the 'balance of trade', a doctrine whose fulfilment required us 'to sell more to strangers yearly than we consume of theirs in value', i.e., to ensure that the balance was tilted in our favour. Mun, whose own business success lent much weight to his theorizing, wrote in an age when foreign trade was growing rapidly in importance, and was felt to add mightily to the strength and reputation of the country, and he was the first considerable exponent in England of what came to be known as the 'mercantile' system of political economy.

JOHN SMITH (1580–1631), effective founder of Virginia, was the son of a tenant-farmer of Willoughby in Lincolnshire. He was twenty-seven when he sailed to Virginia, and before that date he had already had a lifetime's adventures, even if we may trust only parts of his own account. According to this, he had sailed to Italy with a party of pilgrims from France, been thrown overboard as a Huguenot and rescued by a pirate; fought for the Emperor in Styria and killed three Turkish champions in single combat; been captured, sold into slavery and taken to Constantinople and Varna; killed his cruel master, made his way to Morocco, and reached home on an English naval vessel. By 1606 he was active in forming the Virginia Company, and in 1607 he was one of the one hundred and twenty men who set out to the promised land. Arrested during the voyage on a charge of conspiracy, he was found to be one of the councillors named in sealed orders to manage the affairs of the colony, and was soon released. This was as well, for the evidence suggests that without Smith's leadership the colony would have collapsed through the idleness and faction of many of the settlers. By his resourceful direction and personal exertions, in building Jamestown, farming, dealing with the Indians and exploring, John Smith set Virginia on its feet during the rather over two years that he spent there as a young man. The most famous tale about him — that he was captured by hostile Indians and condemned to have his brains beaten out with clubs, but released on the intervention of Pocohontas, the young daughter of the chief Powhatan — is not well-authenticated, yet it is not inherently improbable. In two voyages in 1608 he explored the coasts of Chesapeake Bay and sailed up the Potomac and Rappahannock rivers. For the best part of a year (1608–9) Smith was president of the colony, and conditions improved substantially. His *A True Relation*, the first printed description of Virginia, was taken to England in manuscript in 1608, and its publication was of propagandist value; while his *Map of Virginia with a Description of the Country*, published at Oxford in 1612, was remarkably accurate and was still in use in the late nineteenth century. Smith himself set sail for England in 1609 after being injured in an accident. Although he actively encouraged colonization and took part in voyages to New England, he never returned to Virginia.

Philip L. Barbour, *The Three Worlds of Captain John Smith*, 1964.

WILLIAM BRADFORD (1590–1657), Pilgrim Father, came from yeoman origins in south Yorkshire. Converted to Brownism, he migrated to Holland, reaching Leyden in 1609, and was one of the leaders among those who sailed in the *Mayflower* in 1620. In 1621 he was chosen by his fellow-pilgrims to succeed John Carver as governor of the new colony, and he held this office for the rest of his life apart from one or two occasions when he did not choose to stand for election. The tiny Plymouth colony owed much to Bradford's energy, wisdom and adaptability, and to the good relations which, on the whole, he maintained with the Indians. Bradford was a man of culture, with Greek as well as Latin, and he found time to write extensively, compiling diaries in addition to treatises in theology. His most important work was *The History of Plymouth Plantation*, 1620–47, a remarkable book which is the main source of information about the early struggles of the pilgrims.

William Bradford, *Of Plymouth Plantation*, ed. S.E. Morison, 1952.

CHARLES I (1600–49), who ascended the throne in 1625, was the second son of James I and Anne of Denmark, becoming heir in 1612 on the death of his elder brother Henry. James — vain, overbearing, disreputable — and Anne — frivolous, shallow, often spiteful — were scarcely ideal parents, nor did they get on well with one another. It seems certain that Charles learned as a child, in self-defence, the reticence and the habit of dissimulation which he displayed as King. He was a delicate boy, with a speech impediment which lasted throughout life, but he became a good horseman, and he shared his father's enthusiasm for hunting. He grew up a virtuous, sensitive and godly young man, withdrawn yet with a capacity for deep affection which found its outlet about 1618 in his friendship, after initial quarrels, with James's favourite, Buckingham. This friendship was cemented by the hare-brained escapade of 1623, when the two young men went incognito to Madrid to win the hand of the Spanish Infanta for Charles and came back thirsting for war with Spain. In 1625 Charles married Henrietta Maria of France, a girl of sixteen. The marriage was a success, after early storms which ended when Charles sent the Queen's French attendants packing. Charles became a devoted husband and father, whose standards of family and court life were high and dignified, in contrast to the coarseness and scandals of the previous reign. Yet it was unfortunate for the country, and tragic for himself, that the two people to whom Charles gave his full trust and affection were politically disastrous — the one an arrogant monopolist of patronage, the other a devout Roman Catholic, both highly unpopular.

Charles was ill-equipped to face the problems of his inheritance. He lacked his father's intellectual ability and quickness of wit; a good deal of his devotion to principle masked slowness and stupidity. He attracted immense loyalty, more perhaps to the monarchy than to himself, but failed miserably in its use; there was bitter experience behind Archbishop Laud's verdict on his master — 'a mild and gracious prince who knew not how to be, or be made, great'. His mind was inflexible, lacking that ultimate readiness to compromise which had contributed to James's success in Scotland. In defeat he turned readily to evasion, as his attitude to the Petition of Right was to show early in his reign. In victory he was unfeeling, as the Eliot case revealed; as even Clarendon observed, Charles I 'was not in his nature bountiful'. In his religion Charles grew up an

Charles I
(Artist: Edward Bower, 1649)

unswerving Anglican of the Arminian school, and in his political beliefs he inherited to the full James's view of Divine Right, saying in 1628, 'I must avow that I owe the account of my actions to God alone'. In an age when religious and political beliefs were inseparable this was a natural combination. But it set him from the very start against a powerful and growing group of his subjects, those members of the landed and mercantile class who were adopting Puritan opinions and who had made clear in his father's reign their intention of using the House of Commons to press their policies. The causes of the English Revolution of the seventeenth century go far deeper than the clash between Charles I and his Parliaments; in a real sense Charles, merely because he was King, was a King caught in the toils, a victim of circumstances. Nevertheless, his beliefs and conduct did much to direct the course of events, to produce an armed conflict and to prevent a negotiated settlement after the fighting.

His troubles began at once. The first Parliament of his reign, called in 1625 to grant money, offered about one-seventh of what was needed, proposed to grant tonnage and poundage for one year only instead of — as was customary — for life, attacked the writings of a leading Arminian (Dr. Montagu), criticized foreign policy, and began to oppose Buckingham. Charles dissolved Parliament. He was to call two more in the first four years of his reign, and then, of deliberate policy, to rule without one for eleven years. The Commons' hostility from 1625 to 1629 ranged over a wide field: the expeditions (to Cadiz in 1625 and the Isle of Rhé in 1627) which Buckingham so mismanaged, the power of the favourite, Charles's attempts at unparliamentary taxation (notably the Forced Loan of 1626), his arbitrary imprisonment of those who refused the loan, the use of billeting and martial law, Arminianism (Montagu was made Bishop of Chichester in 1628), the failure of the government to enforce the laws against Roman Catholics. The central cause of trouble at this stage, the 'grievance of grievances', was the power of Buckingham; Charles had to dissolve the second Parliament to save him after the Commons had impeached him. But Buckingham's assassination in 1628 did not heal the breach. The King was embittered at the popular rejoicing over the murder. The Commons of the third Parliament, elected in an outburst of feeling against the court, compelled Charles to accept the Petition of Right, condemning unparliamentary taxation, arbitrary imprisonment, martial law and billeting. In its second session they went on to attack the King's continued illegal collection of tonnage and poundage and the appointment of Arminians to high places in the Church. The session ended with the famous scene in which, while the Speaker was held down in his chair to forestall Charles's intended adjournment of the house, the Commons passed the Three Resolutions against those who brought in innovation in religion 'or by favour or countenance seem to extend or introduce Popery or Arminianism' and against those who advised and those who paid 'the subsidies of tonnage and poundage, not being granted by Parliament'. In all these episodes, not merely in the last one, the Commons were being revolutionary, demanding, in effect, an extension of their power into fields hitherto denied to them, notably foreign policy, the Church, and the appointment of ministers.

It is scarcely surprising that Charles in 1629 determined to manage without calling parliament; but it was an unhappy decision, for the so-called 'Eleven Years' Tyranny' provided a fresh crop of grievances. The various expedients used to raise money — distraint of knighthood, forest fines, fines for enclosure, and above all Ship Money — offended the propertied class. Ship Money in particular, and the pressure placed upon the judges, opened the way to royal absolutism. In religion the Arminians, with their leader Laud at Canterbury from 1633, were given their head. The suppression of Puritan lectureships, the enforcement of uniformity in ritual, the use of Star Chamber against pamphleteers, were signs of episcopal absolutism. And taken in conjunction with the open Romanism of the Queen's circle at court and the offer of a cardinal's hat to Laud, they smelt of Popery. A feeble and vaguely pro-Spanish foreign policy offended patriotic Englishmen. The one achievement of the regime was peace. It was destroyed by a major strategic blunder, the decision of Charles and Laud to impose the English prayer book upon Scotland. The Scots rose in rebellion, and Charles had no effective forces with which to crush them. Strafford, the ablest of the King's servants, whose change from the Commons to the King's side had been Charles's one solid gain in the early years of his reign, was recalled from Ireland too late to be of use; and Charles was in 1640 forced to make a truce with the Scots and to recall parliament. The 'Short Parliament' refused to grant supply without redress of grievances, and Charles dissolved it. The truce expired, the Scots occupied Northumberland and Durham, and the King had to summon another Parliament.

With the meeting of this, the 'Long Parliament', in November 1640, Charles I's effective authority as King of England was at an end. He had united the property-owning class against him, and for most of the next twelve months he faced a House of Commons where only a small minority of members supported his policy. He was forced to accept a series of constitutional changes — the destruction of Star Chamber and other prerogative courts, the abolition of Ship Money, forest fines and distraint of knighthood, the ending of unparliamentary taxation, a Triennial Act to prevent an interval of more than three years between Parliaments, an Act forbidding the dissolution of the present Parliament without its own consent. His greatest servants were sacrificed: Strafford went to the block, Laud to the Tower (and to the block in 1645). But circumstances and a division in the ranks of his opponents came to his aid. There was a conservative reaction in the summer of 1641. Proposals to abolish episcopacy 'root and branch' split the Commons majority on a religious issue; a rebellion and massacres in Ireland raised the central constitutional issue of the revolution. For an army would be required to quell the Irish; to entrust this to Charles was to invite him to use it to destroy Parliament, to do otherwise was to say decisively that the Crown was no longer sovereign. On both the religious and constitutional issues raised in 1641 nearly half the Commons were ready to support the King. The Grand Remonstrance, the appeal to the nation by Pym and the parliamentary party, was carried by only 159 votes to 148 in November 1641. Charles, with the tide of opinion swinging in his favour, chose to turn to the policy which had won only short-lived success in the 1620s. In January 1642 he came in person with troops to the Commons in an attempt to arrest Pym and four other leading members. War was not far off. Within a week Charles left London, and after futile negotiations war broke out in the summer.

In 1642 Charles was no trained soldier — any more than Cromwell — although he would fight bravely, not least in the decisive disaster at Naseby. Parliament's control of the wealth of London and the South-East, the Scottish alliance of 1643 and the military genius of Cromwell tilted the scales against the King; and in the first year of war, when he held the strategic initiative, he failed to take advantage of it. After 1643 he was unable effectively to control the Royalist commanders in the north and west, or to prevent his forces disintegrating in defeat. The splendid achievements of Montrose in Scotland were neglected; Charles's negotiations with the Irish, conducted without sincerity on his side, did more harm than good to his cause. Yet when in May 1646, with his armies totally defeated, he surrendered to the Scots, he was still in a position of great strength. For few men at this stage wanted to destroy him or the monarchy; moreover, there were obvious rifts to exploit between the Army and Parliament. It was here that Charles's utter lack of political judgment was fatal to him. He seems to have believed that sooner or later his foes would fall out and that he would then recover his power unimpaired; he would gain by temporizing and by duplicity what he had lost in war. Negotiating with the Scots and Parliament, he delayed decisions so long that the Scots early in 1647 handed him over to Parliament. The Army, mistrusting Parliament's plans to disband many of the troops without sufficient arrears of pay and to impose Presbyterianism, seized him; and in August put forward their own scheme, the Heads of the Proposals. Once again Charles dragged out negotiations; in November he escaped to Carisbrooke in the Isle of Wight, and in December signed the secret Engagement with his supporters in Scotland, providing for a Scottish invasion to restore him to the throne and to establish Presbyterianism for three years. This precipitated the Second Civil War in 1648. The Army, already restive and distrustful, went to battle determined to call to account 'Charles Stuart, that man of blood'. Cromwell's victory at Preston in August 1648 destroyed the Scottish army. Parliament was still for negotiation; but early in December Colonel Pride purged the Commons of the Presbyterian members, leaving the 'Rump', the Independent minority, the servants of the Council of Officers. In January 1649 a special court was set up to try the King; he refused to accept its jurisdiction. On 30 January he was executed outside the Banqueting Hall of the Palace of Whitehall.

In his life Charles I had been an inept and untrustworthy King; in his death he proved himself to be a man of outstanding dignity and courage. Like many of his subjects on both sides in the Civil War, he died for the principles in which he believed. His principles were not those upon which a constitutional monarchy could have been founded. In his few words from the scaffold he said he 'did not believe the happiness of people lay in sharing government, subject and sovereign being clean different'. The Church of England, to which he was devoted with a sincerity many of his Puritan subjects refused to credit, has found in him one of her martyrs; Falmouth and Tunbridge Wells have their churches of King Charles the Martyr. The book *Eikon Basilike*, written by John Gauden but at the time proclaimed as the King's own work, and published a few days after the execution, was an extraordinarily influential propagandist defence of his policies and faith; it went through thirty-six editions in a year, and did much to hearten Royalists during the eleven years of the republic.

Charles I will always remain a subject of controversy in politics and religion. As a patron of the arts, no English king can compare with him. As Professor Trevor-Roper has put it: 'His Court was the last Renaissance court in Europe, and himself perhaps the greatest royal patron that art has ever found.' He loved masques and plays and poetry. He spent lavishly on the masters, Titian, Raphael, Mantegna among them, and built up a superb collection, four hundred pieces of sculpture and one thousand four hundred paintings, which the Commonwealth sold off. He employed Van Dyck to paint him, and Inigo Jones to build for him. Above all, he employed Rubens to decorate the Banqueting Hall in the palace of Whitehall.

King Charles I, (Historical Association Pamphlet, G.11), 1949.
J. P. Kenyon, *The Stuarts*, 1958, pp. 73–111.
C. V. Wedgwood, *The Trial of Charles I*, 1964.
Pauline Gregg, *King Charles I*, 1981.
Charles Carlton, *Charles I: The Personal Monarch*, 1983.

HENRIETTA MARIA (1609–69), most important of the wives of the Stuarts, was born at the Louvre, the youngest daughter of Henry IV of France and Marie de' Medici. Married at fifteen to Charles I, a solemn prig of twenty-four who was preoccupied with his friendship with Buckingham, she was deprived of her French attendants and endured three miserable years until the murder of the favourite turned Charles's devotion to her. Thereafter they enjoyed a married happiness rare among the monarchs of seventeenth-century Europe and marred only by what was in Henrietta's eyes her husband's extraordinary attachment to his Anglican heresy. Vivacious rather than beautiful, with a quick though superficial mind

Henrietta Maria c.1632–5
(Artist: after Sir Anthony van Dyck)

and strong prejudices, she was more forceful than Charles and during the 1630s her ascendancy grew. Her love of dancing, masques and music made Whitehall and Hampton Court centres of fashion and gaiety, and she gathered round her a circle of poets and playwrights, young officers and elegant courtiers. This offended Puritans, yet was of no great political significance at this stage. It was her Romanism which was disastrous, and which gives Henrietta Maria her peculiar place in the downfall of the Stuart monarchy. Mass was said more or less openly in her chapel at Somerset House; Jesuits and Capuchins, confessors and papal agents were numerous and influential; conversions were fashionable and flaunted. No single facet of Charles I's rule did him more harm with his people, exhibited as it was in the heart of his Puritan capital.

With the breach between Crown and Parliament after 1640 the Queen began to play a direct part in royal policy, and her influence undoubtedly pushed the King towards intransigence and violence. She encouraged the Army plots and pressed Charles to arrest the Five Members; during his absence in Scotland in 1641 she was the heart of opposition to the Commons; and she was fertile in schemes for foreign intervention, by the Dutch, the French, the Duke of Lorraine, and the Pope. Puritan and Parliamentarian opinion against her rose to fury after the Irish Rebellion, known as 'the Queen's Rebellion', because she was widely believed to have fomented and authorized it. In 1642 she left for Holland to raise munitions, cash and, if possible, troops for the Royalist cause, and her attitude after the fighting began was expressed in a phrase she once wrote to Charles: 'Do not suffer your army to be disbanded, or any peace to be made, till this Parliament be ended'. She came back in 1643, landing at Bridlington while Parliamentarian ships were firing on the town, and the Commons paid her the compliment of voting her impeachment. Henrietta displayed spirit and energy in rousing Royalist enthusiasm, nick-naming herself 'the She Majesty Generalissima', but she also intrigued freely against Rupert, while the policies she continued to advocate, for example, those of calling in the French and of raising an Irish army, were not likely to commend Charles to his people.

In 1644, as the Royalist armies failed, she escaped from Falmouth to France, where she pawned her jewels and tried to enlist Mazarin's aid, and she watched from exile the deepening tragedy of her husband's cause and life. Naturally she encouraged the negotiations with the Irish Catholics; she also urged him to take the Covenant, for one heresy differed little from another in her eyes. France remained her home throughout the Interregnum, and she bought the Château of Colombes near Paris. She found solace in the loyal companionship of Henry Jermyn, one of the gay courtiers of the 1630s and now her Chamberlain, but there is no convincing evidence of the truth of contemporary rumours that they were married. Her relations with her two eldest sons were not easy: Charles, though affectionate, firmly rebuffed her efforts to dictate the composition of her council and allowed her no influence upon policy, and James broke from her apron-strings to go and fight in Flanders. There was serious trouble over her attempt to convert her youngest son, Henry, Duke of Gloucester, to Catholicism. She disliked Edward Hyde as much for his parvenu origins as for the moderation of his policy, and she returned to England at the Restoration determined to undo the marriage of his daughter Anne to James. Unsuccessful in this and in her efforts to make Charles II marry a wife of her choice, she made her peace with the Hydes, and remained in England until her return to France in 1665. Four years later she died at Colombes.

Gavin Bone, *Henrietta Maria, Queen of Cavaliers*, 1972.
Elizabeth Hamilton, *Henrietta Maria*, 1976.

JOHN DIGBY, 1st EARL OF BRISTOL (1580–1653), diplomatist, came from a gentry family of Coleshill in Warwickshire and was educated at Magdalen College, Oxford. His good looks won James I's favour: he was knighted in 1607 and sent in 1611 as ambassador to Madrid, spending the greater part of the next twelve years there. Bristol (he was given his Earldom in 1622) was a moderate, committed to peace with Spain yet not to subservience, who believed in the possibilities of a Spanish match, regarding it as a means of bridging the religious gulf in early seventeenth-century Europe. So he tried hard to negotiate the marriage of Charles and the Infanta between 1614 and 1618, and again after 1621, when he shared his master's belief that an agreement with Spain might persuade the Habsburg Emperor to restore James's son-in-law, Frederick, to the Palatinate. The sudden arrival of Charles and Buckingham in Madrid in 1623 to conduct the wooing in person angered Bristol, not surprisingly, and he was rash and honest enough to report to James what the Spaniards thought of Buckingham. This cost him Charles's favour for life. On his return to England in 1624 he was put under house arrest. Charles at his accession struck him off the Privy Council, and in 1626, fearing revelations about Buckingham's conduct, sent him to the Tower and denied him a summons to the Parliament. The Lords, offended by this treatment of a peer, eventually got him released in 1628. It is scarcely surprising that Bristol opposed the Crown over the Petition of Right.

Bristol took no part in public affairs in the eleven years after 1629, but lived quietly on his estate at Sherborne, Raleigh's former property, which he had acquired after the fall of Carr. In the crisis from 1640 he began as a leading opponent of the Crown, but was gradually alienated from the Parliamentarians by what Clarendon calls 'their unwarrantable violences'. He became, like Hyde himself, a constitutional Royalist, and in 1642 he joined the King. By his conduct at this time he offended the opposition as deeply as he had angered Charles in the 1620s, and after his surrender to Fairfax at the capitulation of Exeter in 1646 he was sent into exile. Bristol died at Paris in 1653. Clarendon notes that 'though he was a man of great parts, and a wise man, yet he had been for the most part single, and by himself, in business'. His career may illustrate the unhappy fate of the moderate and non-partisan in times of revolution.

MONTAGUE, RICHARD (1577–1641), controversialist and bishop, was the son of a vicar of Dorney in Buckinghamshire; educated at Eton and King's College, Cambridge, he became a Fellow of both and in 1617 was appointed a Canon of Windsor. A considerable scholar, he was ready to defend — with a sarcastic pen — the Church of England against both Catholics and Puritans. His views were Arminian, and before the end of James I's reign his sermons had been attacked by the Puritans. In 1625 he wrote, *Appello Caesarem*, condemning Puritanism and Popery alike. The Commons committed him to custody; released on bail, he was made a royal chaplain by Charles I. Next year the Commons put in a petition that the book should be publicly burned and its author punished. Characteristically, Charles made him Bishop of Chichester in 1628, and here he remained until his translation to Norwich ten years later, a firm disciplinarian on the Laudian pattern. In the 1630s Montague was concerned in the tentative negotiations with the Pope for reunion. He died in 1641 shortly after the Long Parliament had set up a commission to consider his offences.

JOHN WILLIAMS OF CONWAY (1582–1650), Archbishop of York and the most distinguished Welshman of the seventeenth century, came from an ancient North Welsh family. Educated at Ruthin Grammar School and St. John's College, Cambridge, of which he became a Fellow, Williams, an able scholar, fluent and witty in speech, politician rather than spiritual leader, accumulated a series of benefices, thanks largely to the patronage of Lord Ellesmere, before he hitched his wagon to Buckingham's star and became in 1620 Dean of Westminster, and in 1621 Bishop of Lincoln. Prudence rather than principle impelled him to decline consecration by Archbishop Abbot after the latter's unfortunate homicide. In 1621 also he was appointed Lord Keeper, and he held this office for the remainder of James I's reign. Shrewd and moderate in outlook even if he was an unblushing careerist, he gave Buckingham good advice, not always accepted; he told him to abandon the monopolists, and he was against the Spanish war. Characteristically, James I liked and appreciated Williams, just as he distrusted Laud.

Things were different after 1625. Neither the worldliness nor the moderation of Williams appealed to Charles I, and his opposition to war with Spain had lost him Buckingham's patronage. He was dismissed from the office of Lord Keeper, forbidden (even though he was Dean of Westminster) to take part in the coronation, and ordered to withdraw to his diocese. These were bitter blows, but Williams was neither broken nor abashed. In 1625 and 1628 he supported the policies of the Commons. Secure in his power in his great diocese, the largest in England, which he regarded almost as a feudal appanage; a pluralist who had amassed wealth by impropriations and who held rectories, prebends and the Deanery of Westminster as well as Lincoln; he lived in high state in his palace at Buckden, building, planting and enclosing, patronising scholars like Selden, entertaining and providing musical festivities at which he displayed his native gifts as a singer. From moderation, or independence, or perhaps lack of any real concern, Williams, in Professor Trevor-Roper's words, 'behaved throughout his career as if no differences in religious principles existed'. * Such an attitude may have had wisdom in it for the bishop of a diocese which in the 1630s

*H.R. Trevor-Roper, *Archbishop Laud*, 1962 ed., p. 54.

contained a great many active Puritans, but it was anathema to Laud, a personal enemy since the days when they had clashed for Buckingham's patronage. There was a brush over Laud's effort to turn the communion table into an altar at the east end, and Williams licensed an anonymous book, really his own work, *The Holy Table, Name and Thing*, which took a moderate line. Yet Laud was clearly determined to crush Williams, and eventually he succeeded. From 1628 onwards a series of charges, ranging from revealing Privy Council secrets to favouring Puritans in his diocese, was brought in the Star Chamber. Williams, relying on friends at court, bribed witnesses to give false evidence and so played into Laud's hands. In 1637 he was fined £10,000, suspended from carrying out his episcopal functions, and sent to the Tower where he preferred to stay rather than accept exile to a Welsh or Irish bishopric. A second Star Chamber case, based on correspondence with the headmaster of Westminster School in which the latter called Laud 'a little meddling hocus-pocus', brought upon Williams a further fine of £8,000.

The coming of the Long Parliament reversed fortunes: Williams was released from the Tower in 1640, and Laud sent into it a few months later. Williams continued to take an independent line over religion, attempting to solve the problem of episcopacy by regulating the authority of bishops. Characteristically he advised the King to sign the attainder of Strafford in 1641 on the ground that he must distinguish between his private conscience which told him to refuse and his public conscience which required him to sign in order to avert further bloodshed. Later the same year Charles made Williams, Archbishop of York, a barren gesture of moderation. Bishops were out of favour. In December, Williams and some of his brethren going to Parliament had to be rescued from riotous apprentices, and when he and eleven other members of the bench formally protested that acts passed by the Lords in their absence were null and void, the Commons impeached them and the Lords sent them to the Tower.

When war broke out Williams went to York and joined Charles. Later he departed to North Wales and fortified Conway Castle for the King. There he quarrelled with the Royalist military leaders, maintaining that their proceedings were damaging the interests of his people of North Wales. When in 1645 the Royalist commander Sir John Owen dispossessed him of the castle, he came to terms with the Parliamentarians and shortly before his death in 1646 assisted them in reducing it. This astute and resourceful Welshman blended calculating ambition and genuine moderation in a remarkable career. Playing the part of a prince of the Church before both Laudian agents and Puritan sectaries, he spent £1,000 a year in charity in his diocese and left benefactions on a princely scale, including libraries to Westminster School, Lincoln College, Oxford, and St. John's College, Cambridge, scholarships at Westminster and Fellowships at St. John's.

B. Dew Roberts, *Mitre and Musket*, 1938.

JOHN PRESTON (1587–1628), Puritan divine, the son of a 'decayed' Northamptonshire gentleman farmer, was educated at Northampton Grammar School and King's and Queens' Colleges, Cambridge, becoming a Fellow of the latter. He contemplated a diplomatic career, but after hearing an evangelical sermon by John Cotton in 1611 devoted himself to Calvinist divinity. Able, witty, highly effective as a tutor and lecturer, he quickly became a leading Puritan. In 1615 he distinguished himself when James I visited Cambridge by an ingenious argument for the view that dogs can reason. Some years later he gained the favour of Buckingham whose influence got him appointed in 1621 as a chaplain to Prince Charles and in 1622, aided by Preston's own flair for academic intrigue, election as Master of Emmanuel, a notably Puritan college. For some years Preston, who in 1621 had written a paper against the Spanish marriage project, was a leading figure in a scheme to win the favourite's support for an anti-Spanish foreign policy and a plan of church reform at home, involving the confiscation of the lands of deans and chapters, which would be financially profitable to the Crown. Buckingham took the idea seriously; war with Spain broke out — because of the fiasco of Charles and Buckingham's visit to Madrid — in 1624; and Preston for a time seemed on the verge of great political influence. But the death of James I and the accession of the Arminian Charles transformed the situation. Laud was predominant in ecclesiastical affairs, and Puritan reforms were condemned. Preston lost Buckingham's favour and for the short remainder of his life (he died from tuberculosis in 1628) supported the Parliamentary opposition to the favourite. He was prominent in setting up the Feoffees for Impropriations (1625-6) who purchased advowsons and impropriate tithes in order to instal Puritans in livings and lectureships. Yet his true historical importance lies neither in this nor in his abortive political project, but in the long-term consequences of his preaching. As Preacher at Lincoln's Inn from 1622 until his death, he had in his congregation many who were to be prominent on the Parliamentary side in future. His sermons, posthumously published, were of continuing and inspiring influence in spreading the covenant theology, that central and explosive doctrine of seventeenth-century Puritanism. Few men did more than John Preston to toughen the King's opponents for the struggle.

Irvonwy Morgan, *Prince Charles's Puritan Chaplain*, 1957.
Christopher Hill, *Puritanism and Revolution*, 1958, pp. 239-74.

SIR JOHN ELIOT (1592-1632), the leading figure in the Commons opposition to royal policies in the first three Parliaments of Charles I, belonged to the Cornish landed gentry. Born at Cuddenbeak, St. Germans, he was educated at Blundell's School, Tiverton, and at Exeter College, Oxford. In 1609, just before his father died, he married Radigund Gedy, heiress of a rising Cornish family. By the time of his own death Eliot was the owner of substantial property in Devon and Cornwall, including the borough of St. Germans; it included also the lovely Tudor house of Port Eliot, formerly an Augustinian priory, although he himself seems to have lived little in it, remaining rather at Cuddenbeak. He sat in the second and fourth parliaments of James I and the first three of Charles I, at first for the boroughs of St. Germans and Newport, and then — a mark of his increased authority and wealth — as Knight of the Shire for Cornwall. He was knighted in 1618, and made Vice-Admiral of Devon (a useful rather than an honorary post in those days of maritime hostility to Spain) in 1622. Both these things he owed to Buckingham, then Lord Admiral, whose client he was; and although in the Parliament of 1624 he attacked monopolies and impositions, he remained loyal to the favourite, demanding war with Spain and joining in the attack on Cranfield. It was in the next

Sir John Eliot
(Artist: Unknown)

year and the next reign that he began to have doubts of Buckingham's competence; and what he saw at Plymouth that autumn of
the pathetic remnants of the disastrous Cadiz expedition — 'Yesterday', he wrote, 'fell down here seven in the streets' — turned Eliot

from a 'courtier' into the chief Parliamentary opponent of the favourite. He launched his attack in 1626; he did not yet name Buckingham, but it was clear enough whom he was attacking when he cried 'Our honour is ruined, our ships are sunk, our men perished, not by the sword, not by an enemy, not by chance, but apparently discerned beforehand out of strong predictions, by those we trust, by that pretended care and thrift that makes all our misfortunes'. The impeachment of the favourite followed, with Eliot bitterly denouncing his former patron, whom he compared with Sejanus. The King sent Eliot to the Tower and saved Buckingham by dissolving Parliament. Eliot was again imprisoned in 1627 for refusing to contribute to the Forced Loan. In Charles's third Parliament he denounced the loan, claiming 'Upon this dispute not alone our lands and goods are engaged, but all that we call ours. These rights, these privileges, which made our fathers freemen, are in question.' He played a leading role in the events which brought about the Petition of Right (1628), clashing with Wentworth on the part which the Commons should play in government. The climax of his career of opposition came in 1629, when he drew up the Three Resolutions of the Commons, on Arminianism and Tonnage and Poundage, which were read while the Speaker was held down in his chair so that the House could not be adjourned. For this Charles sent Eliot and eight others to the Tower. Three of the nine, Eliot, William Strode and Benjamin Valentine, who were tried by the King's Bench and sentenced to be imprisoned during the King's pleasure, refused to buy their freedom by acknowledging their offence. Strode and Valentine were each to spend ten years in prison; Eliot, not a robust man, contracted consumption and died in the Tower in 1632. To his son's request that he might take Eliot's body back to Cornwall for burial Charles replied, 'Let Sir John Eliot's body be buried in the church of that parish where he died'.

To his contemporaries Sir John Eliot was the greatest orator of his time. He was a pioneer in parliamentary oratory. Sensitive, emotional, impetuous, he created for himself and for them an idealized picture of the Commons. He was a bad tactician, as was shown in his handling of relations with the Lords during the debates of 1628; temperamentally averse to compromise, he was no doubt partially responsible by his actions for Charles I's decision not to call Parliament for eleven years. After 1629, far more after 1632, he became a martyr, the role in which later generations of Englishmen have known him. Eliot was not a selfless man: there was financial sharp practice in his record. Yet his refusal to yield to Charles was an act of high courage and principle and of obstinate loyalty to his vision of the Commons, the more remarkable in view of the treatise *De Iure Maiestatis*, which he wrote in the Tower and which contains a theoretical defence of kingship. Not until 1667 in the Cavalier Parliament of Charles II was the sentence upon Eliot declared illegal, 'against the freedom of privileges of Parliament'. That such a Parliament could make such a declaration is a measure of the success of the constitutional revolution in which Eliot had been a prime mover.

Harold Hulme, *The Life of Sir John Eliot*, 1957.

THOMAS WENTWORTH, 1st EARL OF STRAFFORD (1593–1641), the most formidable of the ministers of the Stuarts, was born in London, the son of a wealthy Yorkshire landowner. He spent most of his youth in Yorkshire; his education was that customary to his class — the Inner Temple and St. John's, Cambridge, to Court at eighteen, a tour of France (1611–13). In 1614 his father died, leaving him the heir to considerable property around Gawthorp and Woodhouse in the West Riding, and to heavy responsibilities (there were nine younger children). Although the same year 1614 saw Wentworth's first election to the House of Commons, as member for Yorkshire in the Addled Parliament, he passed most of the next few years in administering his estates, increasing their profits and establishing his authority in the West Riding. But he was early ambitious to use his talents in national affairs, going often to London and winning useful friends at Court like Archbishop Abbot, Sir George Calvert, the Secretary of State, and the rather shady financier, Sir Arthur Ingram. His opportunity came in the 1620s in the clashes of the Stuart Kings and their Parliaments — at first as an opponent of the Court. He sat in four of the five Parliaments of the 1620s, three times for Yorkshire and once (1624) for Pontefract. First prominent in 1621 as a moderate critic of royal policy, he was sufficiently important for the King deliberately to exclude him from the Parliament of 1626 by picking

Thomas Wentworth, 1st Earl of Strafford, c.1636
(Artist: after Sir Anthony van Dyck)

him as Sheriff of Yorkshire. In 1627 he was one of those who refused
to pay the Forced Loan, and he was briefly imprisoned in the
Marshalsea; and for some weeks in 1628 he was the effective leader
of opposition in the Commons, hoping that the Commons' grant of

supply and the King's redress of grievances would 'go hand in hand as one joint and continued act'; and supporting Sir Edward Coke's project for the Petition of Right.

Then in the summer of 1628, he changed sides; he accepted a barony and became President of the Council of the North, the principal agent of the royal prerogative beyond the Trent. For this he was at his trial a few years later to be attacked as an apostate, and Macaulay would dub him 'the lost Archangel, the Satan of the Apostasy'. But in 1628 the gulf between Court and Commons was not yet so deep. Wentworth had always been restrained in his opposition, far different in outlook from the extremer Eliot; and there were practical arguments, appealing strongly to a man of his cast of mind, for the view that the old Elizabethan harmony between Crown and Parliament had now failed, and that until it could be restored only the Crown had the authority and the instruments to govern. Moreover, Wentworth was deeply ambitious, conscious of his powers and impatient to exercise them; and there was in him something of the harsh violence of the seventeenth-century north country in which he grew up. As Lord President he ruled the North in authoritarian fashion for some five years from the fine house at York, enforcing the Poor Law, upholding the prerogative powers of the Council, and humiliating northern magnates who resisted its edicts.

In 1633 he went to Ireland as Lord Deputy, drawn partly by 'the personal profit to be gained from the place', partly by the challenge that wretched and barbaric land offered to his own abilities and to the King's authority. Given full powers, and, on almost all occasions, full support from Whitehall, he 'ruled Ireland like a king', as one contemporary put it. In six years he reorganized the finances, the army and navy, the law courts; tackled the immensely complex land problem, brought new men and new vigour to the Protestant Church; increased the revenue from the customs, began industrial projects, checked pirates; in all, he gave Ireland a brief spell of relative prosperity and more efficient administration. For the most part his policies were not novel. Plantations continued, he treated the Irish woollen industry as harshly as his predecessors had done, his vaunted linen project was a short-lived private monopoly which seems to have done more harm than good, the customs farm was on traditional lines. But he made himself felt as his predecessors had not, for he had more power and he used it more thoroughly and more brutally — thus creating a host of enemies throughout the land who were ready to turn upon him when he fell. There were two great changes. His financial policy was highly effective, so that no subsidy was needed from England; and he pursued among the Irish Protestants the Laudian policy of enforcing discipline upon the clergy and resuming ecclesiastical lands from the laity. His very success in these two directions, finance and religion, with its threats to the security of landed and mercantile property as well as to the beliefs of Puritan Ulstermen, aroused widespread discontent among the influential classes in Ireland — and contributed much to the fear which his name began to arouse in England. What made him the more hated was that he himself became 'monstrous' rich by such normal incidents of patronage as selling offices and taking over the bulk of the customs farm himself, while at the same time denouncing with a blend of harshness and moral superiority other men's financial intrigues. In 1639 his income from Irish sources was £13,000 a year, enough to make him one of the richest of Charles I's subjects. Finally, his rule in Ireland, intensely personal, left nothing permanent behind. By the middle of 1641, on the eve of the Ulster rising, his policies had utterly collapsed.

In 1629 he was appointed a member of the Privy Council; but he contributed little to the government of England in the 1630s. Partly this was through his absence in Ireland, yet mainly because he never had the entire trust of a King who was more than half afraid of the ruthlessness of Wentworth's methods. His main contact with English policy was indirect, through his correspondence with William Laud, appointed Archbishop of Canterbury in 1633. A deep friendship arose between the two, both by temperament authoritarian men of action, and from it emerged an attitude towards government to which they gave the name of 'Thorough' — an unsparing emphasis on loyalty to the Crown and on individual responsibility among the King's servants, combined with a relentless inquiry into abuses and a merciless crushing of opponents. Such an attitude was too far-reaching for Charles I and his courtiers. Yet when in 1638–9 the whole fabric of his government was threatened by the Scottish revolt against Laud's ecclesiastical policy, it was to Wentworth that the King turned for help, with the famous message ending, 'Come when you will, ye shall be welcome to your assured friend, Charles R'.

It was too late; the task was beyond the abilities and even the resolution of Wentworth — and it led straight to his own ruin. He came at once, to be given the earldom (of Strafford) he had long craved. He advised Charles to call a Parliament, and when this, the Short Parliament (1640), declined to grant the supplies the King wanted until its accumulated grievances were dealt with, it was Strafford who took command of such forces as could be put in the field against the Scots. The position was hopeless; the King's army, in Strafford's own words, was 'altogether necessitous and unprovided of all necessaries'. The Scottish army occupied Northumberland and Durham, Charles was compelled to come to terms at Ripon, and to summon another Parliament. Strafford, with high courage and perhaps believing even now in his ability to master the Commons, turned southward to continue serving his King — and to face the certain prospect of a demand for his own death; 'I am tomorrow to London with more danger beset, I believe, than ever man went with out of Yorkshire'. There had already been demonstrations against him by London mobs. Pym and the Parliamentary leaders saw him as the greatest single peril to their cause. Clouds of witnesses, the accumulated enemies of eleven years of stern rule in the North and in Ireland, were ready to rise against him. So, when the Long Parliament met in November 1640, the first action of the Commons was the resolution to impeach Strafford of high treason The trial before the Lords opened in March 1641. Strafford rebutted his accusers with great dexterity, and the impeachment, resting mainly on the charge that he had proposed to bring an Irish army to subdue England, seemed likely to break down. So a group of members in the Commons turned to the ruthless procedure of attainder, and carried a majority of their fellows with them in an atmosphere embittered by panic rumours of army plots against Parliament. The Lords passed the attainder under pressure from violent crowds. Charles, who had but lately promised Strafford that he should not suffer in life, honour, or fortune — although Strafford had, in a letter of high nobility, absolved him from that promise — eventually yielded and signed the act for fear of an attack by the mob on his palace and his family. On 12 May a vast crowd, which some put as great as 200,000, saw Strafford beheaded on Tower Hill. No execution in English history has been greeted with greater public rejoicing.

Few Englishmen, even of the seventeenth century, have had a more ambiguous fame than Strafford; few, perhaps, have been so over-rated both by their friends and by their enemies. Certainly, for all his courage and his idealistic devotion to the service of an unworthy King — for Strafford may be regarded as the most eminent of the many victims of Charles I — he had great faults and notable defects. 'Nature', said one contemporary, 'hath not given him generally a personal affability'; he was harsh, arrogant, domineering, vindictive, excessively sensitive both to praise and to criticism. He was highly strung and moody, frequently laid low by a variety of illnesses many of which must have been nervous in their origins; he desperately needed personal sympathy (he married three times, and the death of his second wife, Arabella Holles, in a premature confinement in 1631 was a shattering blow), and his intimate friends were few, though deeply loyal. In an age when politics were intensely personal he had a disastrous capacity for making enemies. This was the more serious in a man who tended to identify government with administration, and who so readily found the only solution to public problems in action by himself or by those loyal supporters whom he appointed to office, like his lifelong friends George Radcliffe and Christopher Wandesford, whom he made members of the Irish Council. His ambition was immense and plain. Nor was it for power only; he pursued energetically, and sometimes unscrupulously, the wealth in land and in cash which the seventeenth century saw as the necessary foundation and façade for political power and place. His Irish proconsulate yielded him a fortune as well as producing real, if temporary, benefits for many of his subjects. And his severity towards those who used government office to feather their own nests tended to blind him — though not his opponents — to his own not dissimilar activities. Strafford laid himself open to the charge that the laws he administered and the standards which he proclaimed did not always apply to himself; and this was an important element in the almost universal climate of hostility that brought about his fall.

Any assessment of Strafford's political career and of his place in English history is dominated by the fact that he chose what proved to be the losing side in the great political conflict of his age — in the central political conflict of modern British history. His belief in paternal government by the Crown was essentially Elizabethan. In so far as it rested upon a harmony between the Crown and a Parliament representing the property-owning class it was out of date, disproved by the facts of political life in the 1620s and 1630s, by the personality of Charles I and by the revolutionary claims of the gentry who made up the House of Commons. At its highest Strafford's vision of government — like Strafford's character at its best — was a noble one, embracing justice as well as order and security, and extending these benefits to the community as a whole, to poor as well as rich, to the backward north as well as to the more settled south, to Irish as well as to English. Yet this is not the whole tale. The ideal could not be separated from the methods used to achieve it; Strafford was 'Black Tom Tyrant', the terrible exemplar of Stuart rule. It is Strafford's tragedy that he is perhaps the only great man in English history whose overwhelming impact on his fellow countrymen was simply to make them fear him. This was what lay behind the calculations of Pym and the hysteria of the mob in 1641; this was what inspired alike the terrible comment of Oliver St. John, arguing the case for the attainder before the Lords, that 'it was never accounted either cruelty or foul play to knock foxes and wolves on the head . . . because they be beasts of prey', and the blunt phrase of Essex, 'stone dead hath no fellow'.

C.V. Wedgwood, *Thomas Wentworth, First Earl of Strafford*, 1961.
H. F. Kearney, *Strafford in Ireland*, 1959.

WILLIAM LAUD (1573–1644), Charles I's ecclesiastical champion, was born at Reading, the son of a clothier. From Reading Grammar School he went in 1589 to St. John's College, Oxford, of which he was successively scholar, Fellow and (1611) President. Whether or not the long years that he spent as a don unfitted him for a courtier's life, as many writers from Sir Philip Warwick onwards have implied, it was certainly at Oxford that he developed the vehement anti-Puritanism that was his most obvious characteristic when he became a prince of the Church. In the first years of the seventeenth century the Arminian tide was beginning to flow at Oxford, not least at St. John's, the college of Campion and other recusants a generation before. So it is perhaps not surprising that in 1603 we find Laud, as Proctor, involved in a doctrinal brush with

William Laud c.1636
(Artist: after Sir Anthony van Dyck)

the Vice-Chancellor, the Puritan George Abbot. Promotion in the wider world came to Laud through a leading Arminian, Richard Neile, Bishop of Rochester, to whom he became chaplain in 1608. Neile got him appointed a royal chaplain in 1611, yet not until ten years later did Laud get a bishopric. In the interval he had become

Dean of Gloucester (1615) and signalled his arrival by having the communion table moved from the centre of the cathedral to the chancel and converted into an altar. His slow advance reflected the hostility of Abbot who in 1611 had succeeded Bancroft as Archbishop of Canterbury, and — perhaps even more — the doubts of James I about Laud, expressed in the famous comment 'he hath a restless spirit, and cannot see when matters are well, but loves to toss and change and bring things to a pitch of reformation floating in his own brain'. Neile moved upwards in preferment, to Lincoln and then (1617) to Durham, and the Arminians grew stronger and more claimant. But it was attachment to a patron at once far stronger and less reputable than Neile, the King's favourite, Buckingham, that gained for Laud the bishopric of St. David's in 1621. He paid two visits to this remote and poor see during the six years for which he held it.

The death of James I in 1625 and the accession of Charles was as decisive in the career of Laud as in the history of the English constitution. To a King who distrusted him there succeeded one whose ideas on doctrine and church government were in entire harmony with his own — and one, moreover, who was to prove as naive politically as Laud himself. It was Laud who preached the sermon, in terms stressing the divine origins of royal authority, at the opening of Charles's first Parliament in 1625; Laud who supplied Buckingham with lists of Arminian churchmen to promote and Puritans to hold back; Laud who became the director of the King's ecclesiastical policy. In 1627 he became Bishop of Bath and Wells (which he never visited), and in 1629 of London. His rise was assisted by the troubles of Abbot, who had been suspended from office in 1627 for his opposition to Charles's arbitrary policy. Laud was one of the commission of five bishops appointed to carry out the Archbishop's duties, and although Abbot recovered favour with the King, Laud was now evidently the dominant figure in the Church of England. When Abbot eventually died in 1633 Charles greeted Laud with the words 'My Lord's Grace of Canterbury, you are very welcome'. He remained Archbishop until he was executed in 1645, although he achieved little after the outbreak of the Scottish Wars in 1639, and for the last three and a half years of his life he was a prisoner, almost forgotten, in the Tower.

Laud was an unattractive man. Red-faced, short, harsh of speech, bad-tempered, fussy, humourless, he was little liked by contemporaries, whatever their religious opinions. Courtiers thought him a low-born upstart and found him something of a vulgarian. Clarendon, whose verdict is friendly and who pays generous tribute to Laud's courage, draws attention to his vindictiveness. His relations with women were never easy, and he did not win the Queen's trust. Dedicated to his task of restoring the Church of England to greatness, temperamentally welcoming the routine and details of business, Laud had little time and less capacity for affability. His devotion to the policy of 'Thorough' — a policy which was quite unrealistic in the atmosphere of the Stuart Court — ensured him enemies among those who administered the law as well as among those who suffered from it. Laud's mind was blinkered and unimaginative. His defects were not those of the authoritarian who loved power for its own sake. He enforced formality and pomp because he believed them appropriate to the Church and the episcopal order to which he belonged, not to satisfy his own love of authority; indeed, he was personally austere to the point of meanness. His narrowness was entirely that of a man who cannot understand why others sincerely differ from him. As to his unimaginativeness, Clarendon's comment goes deep. 'He was a man of great parts, and very exemplary virtues, allayed and discredited by some unpopular natural infirmities; the greatest of which was (besides a hasty, sharp way of expressing himself), that he believed innocence of heart, and integrity of manners, was a guard strong enough to secure any man in his voyage through this world.'

For Laud was an idealist with a closed mind. His ideal was reactionary, the restoration of the Church in England to its medieval power and status, subject only to the authority of King instead of Pope. It was a response to the challenge of Puritanism; 'with Laud the forces of conservatism found their most determined leader'. * So his activities in the years after 1629 ranged over an immense field. As Bishop of London he cleared the gossips and businessmen out of St. Paul's and set Inigo Jones to begin the restoration of the fabric; suppressed Puritan preachers and lectureships; and in the Instructions to Bishops (which Charles compelled Abbot to send out) required bishops to reside in their sees and not to lease their lands,

* Christopher Hill, *Economic Problems of the Church* (1956), p. 339.

and to tackle the problem of Puritan lecturers throughout their dioceses. From Canterbury after 1633 he launched his Metropolitical Visitation of his province, in effect an inquisition into every detail of church life — conduct of services, state of buildings, vestments, sermons, behaviour of the clergy — whose purposes included the imposition of Arminian orthodoxy and the restoration of uniformity in externals. Throughout his time at Canterbury he tried strenuously to raise clerical incomes by the recovery of impropriated tithes and other church property. His attacks upon Puritan propagandists — like the punishment of Prynne, Bastwick and Burton — were merely the most spectacular incidents of his policy.

Laud, who joined the Privy Council in 1627, was no politician, yet the attainment of his ideals in the Church depended wholly on royal authority; moreover, he became deeply involved in the secular policies of the 'thirties. He was prominent — not least by his severity — in Star Chamber as well as upon its ecclesiastical counterpart, High Commission. When Portland died in 1635 Laud was the main figure in the Commission which took over the Treasury, until he got his own nominee, Bishop Juxon, appointed in 1636. For a time he was head of a junto for foreign affairs. His friendship and alliance with Strafford necessarily involved him in politics, for he saw himself as the champion of Strafford's Irish policy — and of 'Thorough' in general — against the 'Lady Mora', the procrastination and corruption of the courtiers. And the problem of Romanism became a political issue also. Laud, who had engaged in a celebrated controversy with the Jesuit Fisher in the last years of James's reign (and apparently thereby rescued Buckingham for Anglicanism), was as hostile to Rome as to Calvinism; but he was in a difficult plight, for Henrietta Maria made the Court the effective hub of English Romanism. The offer of a cardinal's hat, made immediately upon Abbot's death in 1633, helped to strengthen the widespread Puritan suspicion that Laud himself was a papist.

When the non-parliamentary regime collapsed in 1639–40 Laud's power and policy vanished. He resisted the inevitable recall of Parliament as long as he could, for he was essentially an authoritarian; as Trevor-Roper puts it, 'Laud had a natural antipathy to discussion'. Indeed, his church policy had contributed much to the unpopularity and to the failure of the regime. Arminianism smelt of

Popery; the attempt to recover church lands and income threatened property-owners; Laudian episcopacy was inextricably committed to arbitrary government, to Star Chamber and Ship Money and the other features of the regime. So the power of the hierarchy was destroyed, and Laud himself was packed off to the Tower, to remain in cold storage until he went to the block early in 1645. When in 1660 Anglicanism came into its own again, it was an Anglicanism very different, politically and constitutionally if not ceremonially, from that which Laud would have imposed. It was compelled to acknowledge the existence of organized dissent; and it was firmly subordinated not only to the central government but to the gentry in the countryside. Only in Oxford did William Laud's work survive. There the lectureship in Arabic in which he installed Edward Pococke (1636), the new Statutes which he gave to the University, and — most notable of all — the superb Canterbury Quadrangle with which he endowed St. John's have provided a lasting memorial.

H.R. Trevor-Roper, *Archbishop Laud* (1573–1645), second ed., 1962.
Kevin Sharpe, 'Archbishop Laud', *History Today*, August 1983.

RICHARD WESTON, 1st EARL OF PORTLAND (1577–1635), came from an Essex family of Catholic traditions and was educated at Trinity College, Cambridge. As a courtier and holder of minor office he showed competence in business; James I made him Chancellor of the Exchequer in 1621, and Charles I, Lord High Treasurer in 1628. A crypto-Catholic and pro-Spanish in sympathy, he favoured the peace policy which enabled Charles I to dispense with Parliament, and he was the main figure behind the fiscal devices adopted after 1629. For this as well as for personal reasons he was quite exceptionally unpopular. Clarendon praised the adroitness with which he 'did swim in these troubled and boisterous waters' in the days of Buckingham's supremacy, but for the rest denounced him in one of the most savage of all his studies as 'a man of big looks, and of a mean and abject spirit'. What angered men most was that while Portland demanded high taxes and economy from others, he engrossed lands and money for himself: twice the King paid his debts, amounting to £40,000, and also gave him Chute

Forest in Hampshire into the bargain. Laud condemned him as 'Lady Mora', the very model of delay and sloth.

M. V. C. Alexander, *Charles I's Lord Treasurer*, 1975.

Portland must not be confused with RICHARD WESTON (1591–1651), the agricultural reformer from Sutton in Surrey, Roman Catholic and Royalist, who fled to Flanders during the Civil War. He experimented with new rotations, including turnips and clover, and while in exile wrote a *Discourse of Husbandry used in Brabant and Flanders*, published in 1650. He also used locks to improve the navigation of the Rivery Wey between Guildford and Weybridge.

FRANCIS, BARON COTTINGTON (1579–1652), came from an old-established family of clothiers and small landowners near Bruton in Somerset. Through the patronage of Robert Cecil he became an English agent in Spain where he lived for much of James I's reign. After Prince Charles's futile visit to Madrid in 1623 Cottington, who was consistently pro-Spanish and had opposed the enterprise even though he took part in it, lost Buckingham's favour. Only after the murder of the latter was he admitted a Privy Councillor (1628). It was Cottington who negotiated the Treaty of Madrid (1630) ending the war with Spain, and he was made a baron in 1631. With the backing of the Lord Treasurer Portland, Cottington as Chancellor of the Exchequer from 1629 was a hard-working administrator and a leading member of the royal councils during the eleven years of non-parliamentary rule. Shrewd and bland, he used his sharp wit at the expense of the humourless Laud; so on Portland's death in 1635 Laud got Bishop Juxon, not Cottington, appointed Lord Treasurer. Cottington solaced himself with a strict and profitable Mastership of the Court of Wards (1635–41) and with the estates this position enabled him to buy at low prices.

But the coming of Long Parliament inevitably put him at risk, and in May 1641 he resigned both the Exchequer and the Wards, and retired to his house at Fonthill Gifford in Wiltshire. Driven from there by Parliamentary forces in 1643, he joined the King at Oxford. After signing the royalist capitulation of 1646 he went abroad, and eventually settled in Spain, dying at Valladolid in 1652. In the words of C. H. Firth, Cottington's 'religious history was indeed somewhat remarkable'. He was said, truthfully or not, to have been converted to Roman Catholicism during a serious illness in 1623; despite outward conformity to Anglicanism in the 1630s he was widely regarded as a crypto-Catholic; and he openly embraced Catholicism some years before his death. Clarendon pays tribute to his even temper and sense of humour, but says 'his greatest fault was, that he could dissemble, and make men believe that he loved them very well, when he cared not for them'.

Martin Havran, *Caroline Courtier: The Life of Lord Cottington*, 1973.

WILLIAM JUXON (1582–1663), Archbishop of Canterbury, was born at Chichester and educated at Merchant Taylors School and St. John's College, Oxford, where he studied civil law. President of St. John's from 1621 to 1632, he owed much to the friendship and patronage of his predecessor, Laud, whose ecclesiastical views he shared and upheld when in 1632 he became Bishop of Hereford and in 1633 of London. But where Laud was harsh and rude, Juxon was meek and gentle in manner, and contrived to manage his Puritan diocese without arousing widespread enmity. His appointment as Lord Treasurer in 1636 caused surprise and resentment, because he was an ecclesiastic and clearly Laud's nominee. Inexperienced in politics, he was at least refreshingly honest and industrious. And in Philip Warwick's words, 'so well he demeaned himself through his whole seven years' employment, that neither as Bishop or Treasurer, came there any one accusation against him in that last Parliament 1640, whose ears were opened, nay itching after such complaints'. A humble, unambitious man, he was left in peace at Fulham. In the years after 1646 he was in frequent attendance on the King, and ministered to him on the scaffold. During the Commonwealth he retired to his house at Little Compton in the Cotswolds, conducted Anglican services at Chastleton Manor, and spent much of his time hunting, for which he had a passion. Once when his hounds, said to be the finest pack in England, disrupted a Puritan meeting at Chipping Norton there was a complaint to Cromwell, who brushed it aside, saying that Juxon should enjoy his hunting so long as he did not disturb the government. He was the obvious choice for Canterbury at the Restoration, but he was already an ailing man; he took no real part in the work of the Savoy Conference, and died in 1663. As Bulstrode Whitelocke put it, Juxon 'was a person of great parts and temper, and had as much command of his temper as of his hounds. He was full of ingenuity and meekness, not apt to give offence to any, and willing to do good to all.'

Thomas A. Mason, *Serving God and Mammon, William Juxon 1582–1663*, 1985.

ENDYMION PORTER (1587–1649), courtier, born of Gloucestershire gentry but with a Spanish grandmother, was brought up in Spain and became a page in the household of the statesman Olivares. In England as a young man he took service with Buckingham, was employed in the Spanish marriage bargaining, and accompanied Prince Charles and the favourite to Madrid in 1623. After the war with Spain he took part in the peace negotiations which led to the treaty of 1630. During the next ten years 'Dim' Porter was perhaps the most intimate confidant of the King, whose cultivated enthusiasm for art and literature he shared, and whose great collection of paintings he helped to build up. Yet, as C.H. Firth put it, 'Porter's rewards more than kept pace with his services'. Besides generous payment for his diplomatic activities and his pension as Groom of the Bedchamber he drew fees as collector of fines in the Star Chamber and surveyor of petty customs in the Port of London; got long leases of land at low rentals and shares in such monopolies as soap and white writing paper; and was a member of Sir William Courteen's Association to break into the East India trade. His wife was a Catholic, notorious for her proselytising activities. When the Long Parliament met Porter was elected for Droitwich. He was one of the courageous minority who voted against Strafford's attainder, and the Commons later named him as one of the eleven delinquents they were not prepared to pardon. He was certainly involved in the Army Plots against Parliament, and was suspected of having instigated the Irish Rebellion. During the First Civil War he was with Charles at Oxford, and in 1645 he escaped abroad, first to France and then to the Spanish Netherlands. He returned to England in 1649 and compounded for his estate, but died later that year. The client of Buckingham and the loyal and trustworthy friend and servant of Charles I, Endymion Porter,

wirepuller, monopolist and patron of the arts, with his Catholic
wife and Spanish sympathies, personified many of the grievances
and suspicions which Puritan Englishmen harboured against their
second Stuart King.

Gervas Huxley, *Endymion Porter*, 1959.
The article in *D.N.B.* is by C.H. Firth.

SIR KENELM DIGBY (1603–65), virtuoso, son of the Gunpowder plotter, Sir Everard Digby, of Gayhurst in Buckinghamshire,
brought up as a Roman Catholic, was sent to Gloucester Hall (now
Worcester College) at Oxford. As a young man he travelled widely:
he was in Madrid when Charles and Buckingham arrived in 1623,
came home with them, and was knighted within three weeks, at a
ceremony in which James I nearly poked his eye out with the
sword. * In 1625 he married Venetia Stanley, a remarkable beauty
who was the mistress of the Earl of Dorset, and in 1628 as the
commander of an English squadron, piratical rather than naval in
composition, he won brief though barren fame by capturing three
French ships in the harbour of Scanderoon (Alexandretta). After the
sudden death of his wife in 1633 he fell into a melancholy and retired
to Gresham College, where he diverted his mind with chemistry. His
temporary abandonment of Rome for Anglicanism at this time did
not last long.

As a recusant he was distrusted by the Long Parliament, and in
1641 he departed to Paris, where he killed an opponent in a duel.
Although he returned to England several times, he spent most of the
years 1642–60 abroad. In the 1640s he was Chancellor to Henrietta
Maria, and it was in this capacity that he had a celebrated row with
Pope Innocent X. Deeply shocked, like most Englishmen, by the
execution of Charles I, he nevertheless made his peace with the
Council of State of the republic, and struck up a personal friendship
with Cromwell. It seems likely that Digby helped to arrange the
Anglo-French alliance of the 1650s, but he did not obtain from
Oliver the toleration he hoped for English Catholics. Settling in
England after the Restoration, he was a founding member of the

* See Sir Walter Scott's *The Fortunes of Nigel*.

W.S.B.—D

Royal Society. He died in 1665. The tomb beneath which he and his wife lay was destroyed next year by the Fire of London.

His epitaph ran:

> Under this tomb the matchless Digby lies,
> Digby the Great, the Valiant and the Wise,
> The Age's Wonder for His Noble Parts,
> Skilled in Six Tongues, and Learn'd in All the Arts.

Aubrey says he 'was held to be the most accomplished Cavalier of his time'. A handsome giant of a man, he had extraordinary talents. Dancer, philosopher, duellist, scientist, sea-captain, diplomat, writer, talker, cook, theologian, libertine, he dazzled his contemporaries; and he was notably courageous and kind-hearted. Yet the evidence also suggested that he was a mountebank (Evelyn's word for him) and startlingly credulous. Aubrey says 'that had he been dropt out of the clouds in any part of the world, he would have made himself respected'; yet he enjoys adding 'But the Jesuits spake spitefully, and said 'twas true, but then he must not stay there above six weeks'. Kenelm Digby's positive achievement was quite unworthy of his abilities, mainly because he was incapable of completing any tasks which he began. As a scientist, for all his genuine friendships with such men as Descartes, he was by the standards of his day a mediocre amateur, and the greatest British practitioners, like Boyle and Newton, thought very little of him. As an amateur doctor, his reputation rested upon his 'Powder of Sympathy', a 'cure' which was to be applied not to the wound but to the weapon which had caused it: it was, in fact, powdered vitriol. It is perhaps not surprising that the physician Henry Stubbe called him 'the very Pliny of our age for lying'.

R. T. Petersson, *Sir Kenelm Digby*, 1956.

SIR JOHN SUCKLING (1609–41), Cavalier poet, born at Twickenham in Middlesex, son of James I's future Secretary of State was educated at Trinity College, Cambridge. Inheriting his father's considerable estates in 1627, he travelled abroad and fought for Gustavus Adolphus. In the 1630s he was prominent among the younger courtiers. Aubrey describes him as 'famous at Court for his ready sparkling wit' and as 'the greatest gallant of his time, and the greatest Gamester'; credits him with the invention of cribbage; but adds, 'he sent his cards to all Gameing places in the country, which were marked with private marks of his; he got twenty thousand pounds by this way'. Suckling wrote several plays which were performed at Court, a good deal of facile, cynical and licentious verse, and a savage piece of satire about his contemporaries, *The Session of the Poets*. When the Bishops' Wars broke out Suckling used the remnants of his fortune to raise a troop of horse for the King. He dressed them splendidly in white doublets and scarlet breeches, coats, hats, and feathers and gave them battle-axes, but they did not distinguish themselves in any other way. In 1641 he was involved in the Army Plot and fled to Paris, where he soon died in poverty, either of the pox or, according to Aubrey, by poisoning himself.

SIR ANTHONY VAN DYCK (1599–1641), painter, son of a prosperous Antwerp mercer, first came to England in 1620 and spent some months in the service of James I. From 1621 to 1632 he was on the continent, mostly in Italy and Flanders. Yet he kept in touch with England during this time, and in 1632 Charles I appointed him 'Principal Painter in ordinary to their Majesties', with a pension of £200 per annum, a knighthood, and a studio in Blackfriars. He spent almost all the remaining nine years of his life in England, producing his remarkable series of royal portraits and a large number of other masterpieces, many of them splendid portraits of the aristocracy. We know relatively little of the organization of the studio, save that he employed Flemish assistants who must have been responsible for the many replicas of his work which contemporaries demanded: its output was certainly very great. A man of distinguished bearing and courtly manners, an artist whose brilliant technique was established and international reputation secure before he settled in England, Van Dyck treated his patrons as his equals and shed a distinctive lustre upon the court of Charles I. A pupil of Rubens, deeply influenced by Titian and the Venetians, he owed nothing to England in his development as an artist. Yet his influence upon English history was immense, in two ways. In the field of art itself, Van Dyck virtually created the pattern and the formulae within which English portrait-painting developed and functioned during the next two centuries. In that of historical understanding, he has exerted an imponderable influence upon our judgment of the Stuarts and of the

Cavaliers. Certainly his portraits of the Stuarts flattered them as individuals. More significantly, he was, in the words of Ellis Waterhouse, used by Charles I 'as a propagandist in the cause of absolutism'. Over the centuries no man, except perhaps Charles I himself on the scaffold, has been a more successful champion of the Stuart cause than Van Dyck.

A.P. Oppé, 'Sir Anthony Van Dyck in England', *Burlington Magazine*, lxxix (1941), pp. 186–90.

WILLIAM DOBSON (1610–46), portrait-painter, came from a St. Albans' family: his father was Master of the Alienation Office and, if Aubrey is to be believed, spent his estate upon women, with the result that 'necessity forced his son Will Dobson to be the most excellent painter that England hath yet bred'. A pupil of Francis Cleyn, he owed a good deal, indirectly, to the Venetian school, and curiously little to Van Dyck. From 1642 until the Royalist surrender he was with the court at Oxford, and most of the fifty-odd portraits which are known display the Cavaliers. Before the fighting Van Dyck had flattered the Stuarts and over-stated their case in his paintings. Dobson, in the years of war and defeat, was a more truthful as well as a more intellectual artist, and revealed the doubts and inner conflicts of his sitters. His most celebrated picture, 'Charles II as Prince of Wales' (in the Scottish National Portrait Gallery at Edinburgh), shows a painter whose aim was higher than that of any Englishman before Hogarth. He did not long outlast the environment in which he made his name, dying in poverty in London before 1646 was out.

HENRY LAWES (1596–1662), musician, born at Dinton in Wiltshire, was associated with the Chapel Royal in various capacities from 1626 onwards, losing his official posts during the years of the Civil Wars and Interregnum and recovering them at the Restoration. Contemporaries thought very highly of him both as singer and as composer. In 1633 he wrote the music for Thomas Carew's masque *Coelum Britannicum*, and in 1634 for *Comus*, which he seems to have suggested to Milton and in the first performance of which at Ludlow he played the part of Attendant Spirit. Lawes also set the verse of Herrick and other Caroline poets to music. He published several books of songs and wrote a number of anthems, notably 'Zadok the Priest', composed for the coronation of Charles II. Perhaps no single Englishman did as much as Lawes to establish traditional modes and rules for the setting of his native language to music, and in this sense he did much to make the achievements of Purcell possible.

W.M. Evans, *Henry Lawes*, 1941.

WILLIAM HARVEY (1578–1657), discoverer of the circulation of the blood, was born at Folkestone, son of a prosperous merchant, and educated at King's School, Canterbury, and Caius College, Cambridge. From there he went to Padua to study under the eminent anatomist Fabricius of Aquapendente, who for some years had been discussing in his lectures the valves in the veins. Returning to England in 1602, Harvey practised in London, where he was appointed Physician to St. Bartholomew's Hospital in 1609. In 1618 he became Physician Extraordinary to James I, and thenceforward he was closely connected with the Court. Thus in the 1630s we find him travelling to Scotland in the train of Charles I and, as a member of Arundel's mission to the Emperor, buying paintings in Italy for the King. When the Civil War began Harvey followed Charles I, and he was present at the battle of Edgehill in 1642, where the Prince Charles and James were entrusted to his care. Aubrey records that Harvey told him that 'he withdrew with them under a hedge, and took out of his pocket a book and read; but he had not read very long before a Bullet of a great Gun grazed on the ground near him, which made him remove his station'. Charles rewarded Harvey's loyalty by making him Warden of Merton at Oxford, and at Merton he stayed until the surrender of the city to Parliament in 1646. He seems to have spent the remainder of his days in retirement until his death at Roehampton in 1657. Aubrey, who knew him 'right well' in his later years, gives an impression of an old man with a pithy wit, 'wont to say that man was but a great, mischievous Baboon'. He also observed that 'all his Profession would allow him to be an excellent Anatomist, but I never heard of any that admired his Therapeutic way'.

It was as an anatomist that Harvey made his great intellectual achievement. The discovery of the circulation of the blood was

William Harvey c.1627
(Artist: Unknown)

announced in the book he published when he was fifty, *De Motu Cordis* (1628). In 1615 Harvey had been elected Lumleian lecturer to the Royal College of Physicians, a life appointment, and the manuscript notes for his early lectures show that by 1618 he was clearly stating his new doctrine, which was firmly based upon experimental evidence, provided by Harvey's use of dissection and

the vivisection of cold-blooded animals. His theory, an admirable
example of the new natural philosophy of the seventeenth century,
was warmly approved by the scientists who met at Gresham College
in the 1640s. But it met much opposition from the doctors, and it
seems to have had little influence upon medical practice during the
century. Even Harvey went on using bleeding as a 'cure'.

Louis Chauvois, *William Harvey*, 1957.
Sir Geoffrey Keynes, *The Life of William Harvey*, 1966.

HENRY MORSE (1595–1645), born at Broome near the
Suffolk-Norfolk border, entered Corpus Christi College, Cambridge, in 1612, and two years later fled to the English seminary at
Douai, where he was received into the Church of Rome. Henceforward, as novice, priest and Jesuit, he dedicated his life to his faith,
partly on the Continent (he spent five and a half years at the English
College in Rome), partly on a series of missions to his native
country. His experiences were typical enough — the escapes from
pursuivants and informers, the hourly peril sharpened by the growing Puritanism of the age, the administration of the sacraments to
loyal Catholic households, the imprisonments, the strengthening of
faith by constant spiritual exercises. What makes Morse's story
peculiarly attractive is his devotion to the poor and sick and his
universal charity, qualities which found their noblest expression in
the years 1633–7 when he served as Catholic priest in the poor parish
of St. Giles-in-the-Fields. In 1635–6 London suffered from a severe
visitation of the plague. Morse, nursing the sick, administering the
sacraments to the dying, visiting Protestant and Catholic poor alike,
organizing financial help from country Catholics and from Queen
Henrietta Maria and her co-religionists at Court, was heroic and
untiring in his work. He also made numerous converts, and this led
to his arrest and trial at the Old Bailey. A pardon from the King, at
the Queen's instigation, saved him on this occasion. But so zealous a
missionary was unlikely to survive, particularly in the Civil War
years. After further adventures and exile, he fell into Parliamentarian hands near Newcastle-upon-Tyne late in 1644, and he
was hanged at Tyburn in 1645.

Philip Caraman, *Henry Morse, Priest of the Plague*, 1957.

NICHOLAS FERRAR (1592-1637), was the son of a well-to-do London merchant and was educated at Clare Hall, Cambridge. He travelled abroad for five years for his health; took a leading part in the affairs of the Virginia Company; became an M.P.; and then withdrew from public life, to devote the remainder of his days to religion. Laud ordained him deacon in 1626, and he established a religious community at Little Gidding in Huntingdonshire. The 'protestant nunnery', as it was called, consisted of some thirty persons, many of them members of the Ferrar family. It was semi-monastic, keeping the canonical hours of praise and prayer, but it was not celibate. Its members provided a school and hospital for the neighbourhood and practised bookbinding. Nicholas Ferrar died in 1637. A pamphlet, *The Arminian Nunnery*, denounced Little Gidding in 1641, but the community managed to survive, even in Puritan Huntingdonshire, until 1647.

J.H. Shorthouse's novel, *John Inglesant*, 1800.
A.L. Maycock, *Nicholas Ferrar of Little Gidding*, 1938.

GEORGE HERBERT (1593-1633), poet and parish priest, born in Montgomery Castle of the famous Marcher landowning family, was educated at Westminster and at Trinity College, Cambridge. He was a man of great gifts, a considerable scholar, a friend of Francis Bacon and John Donne, and an accomplished musician. As Public Orator to the University of Cambridge (1619-27), he could expect high preferment. Instead, afflicted by a sense of insufficiency, by Christian standards, of the life he was leading, and influenced by Nicholas Ferrar, he was ordained deacon in 1626. From 1630 to his early death in 1633 he was Rector of Bemerton in Wiltshire, and Izaak Walton has described in his *Life* the saintliness of a man whom he regarded as the model for a parish priest. Herbert himself wrote a kind of practical manual to guide the country clergyman, *A Priest to the Temple* (published in 1652). His fame as a poet rests upon his serene *Sacred Poems* published by Nicholas Ferrar after his death.

A.G. Hyde, *George Herbert and His Times*, 1906.
M. Bottrall, *George Herbert*, 1954.

RICHARD CRASHAW (1613?–1649), poet, was a Londoner, the son of a Puritan parson. Educated at Charterhouse and Pembroke Hall, Cambridge, he became a Fellow of Peterhouse in 1636. Crashaw was a gifted linguist, a fine draughtsman, and a man of deep piety. In the later 1630s, influenced by Nicholas Ferrar, he moved far away from the Puritanism of his upbringing. There was no room for a scholar of Crashaw's views in Cambridge after the Civil War had begun. Peterhouse Chapel was ransacked in 1643 and the Fellows were required to swear to the Solemn League and Covenant. Crashaw refused and was expelled in 1644. He made his way overseas, first to Paris and then to Italy. Probably in 1645, he became a Catholic, and at the time of his death in 1649 he held a minor benefice in the Cathedral at Loretto. The most distinguished of the 'metaphysical' poets after Donne, Crashaw wrote relatively little, most of his poetry being first published in 1646. Much of his inspiration was Italian — as, for example, in the hymns to Saint Teresa — and the intensity behind his passionate, intricate and sometimes humourless writing was deeply Catholic.

ROBERT HERRICK (1591–1674), poet, was the son of a London goldsmith who died within a year of the child's birth. Herrick probably went to school at Westminster, and then served six years' apprenticeship with his uncle, also a goldsmith, before going to St. John's and Trinity Hall at Cambridge. A cheerful and sociable person, Herrick listened to Ben Jonson in the London taverns of the 1620s before becoming in 1629 the incumbent of Dean Prior, a village near Ashburton in Devon. Here he remained until the Puritans ejected him in 1647, and hither he returned from 1662 until his death in 1674. He spent the intervening years in London, dependent on charity and living rather as a layman than as a clergyman. In 1648 he published some 1,200 poems in his *Hesperides*. The book was a failure, and in effect Herrick's poetry had to wait for rediscovery in the 1820s. Herrick complained of the isolation at Dean Prior and welcomed the chance to return to his old haunts in London. Yet he wrote much of his best verse in the country and nearly all of it about the countryside. For all his conscientious classicism, his epigrammatic form and his imitations of Horace, Herrick was very different from his contemporaries among the Royalist poets. Whereas they were either courtiers or 'metaphysicals' and occasionally both, Herrick described the life of seventeenth-century country folk, their customs, beliefs and legends.

JOHN WINTRHOP (1588–1649), Puritan colonist, came from a mercantile and landed family in Suffolk, where he inherited the manor of Groton. Educated at Trinity College, Cambridge, Winthrop was a man of natural force of character and firmness of judgment who exemplified Puritan piety at its sternest. He was one of many, especially in East Anglia, who for religious reasons grew dissatisfied with Stuart rule in the 1620s, believing that 'evil times are coming when the church must fly to the wilderness', and in 1629 he made up his mind to sail to North America. Shrewd enough to take the lead in compelling the Massachusetts Bay Company to transfer in advance political authority to those who actually settled in the colony, he was one of the handful of its members who sailed with about a thousand others of Puritan persuasion in 1630. As first Governor of the Massachusetts Bay Colony, Winthrop played the main role in its establishment in the area centred upon Charlestown and Boston. He was primarily responsible for the decision of 1631 whereby full citizenship — i.e. the right to be a freeman and to vote at meetings of the governing body of the colony — was to be limited to church members, and for the expulsion of Roger Williams and Anne Hutchinson, with their heretical opinions, from Massachusetts. Frequently re-elected to the governorship, Winthrop probably did more than any other single individual to give Massachusetts, and thereby new England as a whole, its peculiar pattern of narrow orthodoxy, by embodying Puritan beliefs in the laws and constitution of the colony. Like many of the early New Englanders, Winthrop was a good scholar with a strong belief in education. Harvard College was founded during his time, and he himself kept a journal which has been a valuable source for historians.
E. S. Morgan, *The Puritan Dilemma: The Story of John Winthrop*, 1958.

ROGER WILLIAMS (1604?–83), champion of religious liberty, probably London-born, the protégé of Sir Edward Coke, was educated at Charterhouse and Pembroke College, Cambridge. He became a Puritan preacher and migrated to Massachusetts in 1630. There he quickly came into conflict with the Governor and the controlling body of freemen over the two beliefs which he was to champion for the remaining fifty years of his life — that the individual had the right to worship in whatever way he wished without any interference by the established church, and that the state had no right to interfere in matters of conscience. Expelled from Massachusetts, he moved into the Narrangansett country to the south and in 1636 founded the settlement of Providence. Rhode Island, the colony which developed round this nucleus, offered toleration to men and women of all faiths. In 1643–4 Williams visited England and secured from the Parliamentarians a charter for the colonists. About the same time he wrote *The Bloudy Tenent of Persecution for Cause of Conscience*, a vigorous demand for religious liberty. The view that 'it is the will and command of God, that ... the most Paganish, Jewish, Turkish or Antichristian consciences and worships' be permitted was acceptable to few in England in 1644, and the month after Williams set sail for Providence again Parliament ordered his book to be burned by the common hangman. He paid one more visit to England in 1651–4, and devoted the rest of his long life to the well being of Rhode Island. Roger Williams, whose friends in England included Milton, Henry Vane the Younger and Hugh Peter, was in some ways a disputatious man, apt to provoke hostility. His historical achievement, in which he was a pioneer among Puritans, was to push the Puritan belief in the individual conscience to its logical conclusion of complete religious liberty, and to found in the tough yet favourable circumstances of seventeenth-century North America a colony based upon this.

J. Ernst, *Roger Williams*, 1932.
S. H. Brockunier, *The Irrepressible Democrat, Roger Williams*, 1940.

WILLIAM PRYNNE, (1600–69), Puritan pamphleteer, born at Swainswick near Bath, the son of a gentleman-farmer, was educated at Bath Grammar School and Oriel College, Oxford, and became a member of Lincoln's Inn. Much influenced by the sermons of John Preston, he began his career as a pamphleteer in the Puritan cause in 1626. Altogether he wrote some 200 pamphlets and books, and according to Anthony Wood, writing just after Prynne's death, there

William Prynne
(Artist: Unknown)

were thirty-six volumes of his works at Lincoln's Inn. Prynne was always prolix and often scurrilous; many of his earlier writings were directed against 'externals' which offended Puritans, like long hair, bowing in church, and the drinking of toasts, and the most cele-brated of his writings, *Histriomastix* (1633), was an assault as abusive as it was learned, over one thousand pages long, on the stage and everything associated with it, and on many things rather tenuously associated with it, such as organs, paintings in church and May-day festivities. Published at a time when Henrietta Maria was about to take part in a play and containing in the index the item 'women actors notorious whores', it brought Prynne into the Tower and before the Star Chamber, where he was condemned to the pillory, the cropping of both ears, life imprisonment and a fine of £5,000. Prynne retaliated with a series of pamphlets against the Bishops in general and Laud in particular for which in 1637, in company with Henry Burton and John Bastwick, he was once more brought before the Star Chamber, and once more condemned to the loss of both ears (or what was left of them) in the pillory, life imprisonment and a fine of £5,000, in addition to being branded 'S.L.' (for Seditious Libeller; Prynne's version was Stigmata Laudis) on his cheeks. The savage sentences made Prynne a popular martyr; handkerchiefs were dipped in blood from his ears, and his journey to imprisonment in Caernarvon Castle (whence he was later moved to Mount Orgueil in Jersey) was a triumph.

Released in 1640, he became a prosecutor for the Parliament and conducted proceedings against Laud with malicious relish. But he soon found himself in opposition again, pouring out his writings against the Army, the Independents, the execution of the King, the extreme claims of the Presbyterian ministers, and Oliver Cromwell (whom he compared with Richard III). Not surprisingly, he was a victim of Pride's Purge in 1648, and in prison once more from 1650–3. In 1659–60 he was strongly in favour of the return of the monarchy, and in February 1660 he was prominent among the secluded members who re-entered the Commons. Charles II made him Keeper of the Records in the Tower. The Clarendon Code brought him out against the Bishops once more, and Pepys records him as 'every day so bitter against them in his discourse in the House'.

Aubrey speaks of Prynne's 'strange Saturnine complexion' and quotes Wren's remark that he had 'the countenance of a witch', and calls him 'a learned man, of immense reading, but is much blamed for his unfaithfull quotations'. Pepys' friend Finch described him as 'a man of mighty labour and reading and memory, but the worst judge of matters, or laying together of what he hath read, in the world', a verdict which Pepys did not believe. Anthony à Wood, more authoritatively, noted that most scholars thought Prynne's works rather 'rhapsodical and confused than in any way polite or concise'. Maitland paid tribute to his work in calendaring the records in the last years of his life. Sheer persistence, in antiquarianism as in controversy, was Prynne's greatest quality, as the epitaph Aubrey quotes suggests:

> Here Lyes Will. Prinne
> Bencher of Lyncoln's Inne
> Who went through thick and thin
> Alwaies out and alwaies in.

William Lamont, *Marginal Prynne*, 1963.

JOHN BASTWICK (1593–1654), born at Writtle in Essex and for a short time a student at Emmanuel College, Cambridge, served in the Dutch army, took a doctorate of medicine at Padua and practised at Colchester. In the 1630s he began writing Puritan tracts, at first in Latin to suggest that their target was merely the Church of Rome; in 1637 he turned to the vernacular and published *The Litany of Dr. John Bastwick*, a considerable piece of scurrility, directed mainly against the Bishops, whom he condemned as enemies of God, the Tail of the Beast, depicting them in a series of lurid anecdotes as gluttonous, lecherous, brutal and arrogant. This brought him before the star Chamber, in company with Henry Burton (1578–1648), a Puritan clergyman who had been denouncing Laud as a papist for twelve years, and the lawyer William Prynne, whose punishment three years earlier had not stopped him from publishing further Pamphlets against the Laudian Bishops. The court sentenced all three men to stand in the pillory at Westminster and have their ears cut off, to pay a fine of £5,000 each, and to suffer life imprisonment. The execution of the punishment produced a wild popular demonstration of sympathy, and their journeys to their places of imprisonment were triumphant progresses. Bastwick was ultimately imprisoned on St. Mary's in the Scilly Isles, whence he was freed in 1640. He fought on the Parliamentarian side in the Civil War, and wrote further tracts, this time for the Presbyterians against the Independents.

THOMAS EDWARDS (1599–1647), was a graduate of Queens' College who achieved notoriety at Cambridge and the nickname of 'Young Luther' by his preaching. He was attacked by Laud for his Puritanism, and was a prominent Presbyterian preacher in the 1640s. His fame rests principally upon his publication of 1646, *Gangraena, or a Catalogue and Discovery of many Errors, Heresies, Blasphemies and pernicious Practices of the Sectaries of this time*, a virulent and malevolent work against the Independents and religious toleration. It ran into a second edition at once and provoked many answers, including tracts by Lilburne and Walwyn. Edwards retaliated with *A fresh and further Discovery*, etc., which produced further replies, which he answered with a third instalment. In face of the outcry which this caused he deemed it wise to retire to Holland, where he died soon after his arrival.

T. Edwards, *Gangraena (1646)*, reprinted Exeter 1977 (see Introduction)

LUCIUS CARY, 2nd VISCOUNT FALKLAND (1610–43), was born at Burford in Oxfordshire. His mother, a gifted linguist and a convert to Roman Catholicism, was one of the most brilliant and formidable women of the century; his father was Strafford's predecessor as Lord Deputy in Ireland, and Falkland was educated at Trinity College, Dublin. In 1625 he inherited from his maternal grandmother the estate of Great Tew, near Burford. He angered his father by marrying for love, and sought military service under the Dutch Republic, but soon came back to England, and to country life at Great Tew. Here there grew around him a circle of friends, cultured and deeply humane like Falkland himself, men and women of whom Edward Hyde and Chillingworth were perhaps the most distinguished; a circle whose members were seeking a way through the religious and political controversies of the 1630s, neither Laudian nor Puritan, believing in reason and tolerance and free discussion. Withdrawn from the court and from the contemporary conflict, the Great Tew circle found in the sincere and modest Falkland a host who combined charm, honesty and wide intellectual interests. Yet Great Tew could not escape the central issue of the day. In 1639 Falkland served under Essex in the First Bishops' War, and in 1640 he was chosen M.P. for Newport, Isle of Wight, in both the Short and the Long Parliaments. At first he was against the Court. He disliked the intolerance of Laud and, like his friend Hyde, he spoke and voted against Strafford. Then, shocked by what seemed to him the unconstitutional objectives and the rabble-rousing methods of Pym and his followers, he turned away from the Parliamentary cause, and in 1642, urged on by Hyde, he reluctantly took office as Charles's Secretary of State. The outbreak of war filled him with sadness, and despondency took hold of him as the struggle intensified. Clarendon tells how 'sitting among his friends, often, after a deep silence and frequent sighs, (Falkland) would, with a shrill and sad accent, ingeminate the word Peace, Peace'. In 1643 he sought death in vain at the siege of Gloucester. He found it later that year in the first battle of Newbury, riding at a gap in a hedge which he knew to be covered by enemy musketeers.

The manner of his death has earned Falkland immortality. So too has the splendid prose in which Clarendon enshrined the memory of his friend: if the *History of the Rebellion* had a hero, it could only be Falkland. In his life he achieved little. He was an ineffectual Secretary of State, he offered no solution to the great political dilemma of his time, he left no writing of lasting distinction. He is the classical 'moderate' of English history, his ideals shattered and his life destroyed as he is forced to choose between the extremes. No doubt there was something unreal about Great Tew in the midst of the English Revolution. 'To examine and refine those grosser propositions, which laziness and consent made current in vulgar conversation', in Clarendon's dignified phrase, was perhaps an academic exercise while Laud and the Puritans were fighting for English souls. Yet this is less than fair to Falkland, who appears in the pages of Clarendon as something more than a rare and gentle spirit who hated war. The legacy of the Great Tew circle lay in their deeply civilized belief that the claims of religion and politics can be tested by reason in free and tolerant discussion. Falkland, at the heart of the circle, embodied in real measure the integrity, courage, and kindness which alone make civilised progress possible.

Irene Coltman, *Private Men and Public Causes*, 1962.

K. B. Murdock, *The Sun at Noon*, 1939.

J. A. R. Marriott, *Life and Times of Lucius Cary, Viscount Falkland*, 1907.

WILLIAM CHILLINGWORTH (1602–44), theologian, was the son of a well-to-do Oxford brewer. William Laud was his godfather. He was a scholar and Fellow (1628) of Trinity College, Oxford, and quickly won a reputation as a controversialist against the Jesuits. Attracted by the Roman doctrine of infallibility, he was converted to Catholicism and went to Douai in 1630; but there he had doubts, and returned to Oxford and declared himself a Protestant once more in 1634. (Aubrey says unkindly that the authorities at Douai 'made him the porter, so he stole over and came to Trinity College again'). Yet he declined to accept the Thirty-nine Articles. After further disputes with the Jesuits, he went to live at the home of Lord Falkland at Great Tew, and in 1638 he published — after submitting it to leading Anglican theologians — his masterpiece, *The Religion of Protestants a Safe Way of Salvation*, a book which defends in lofty and elegant language the right of free inquiry, as the central principle of Protestantism. Chillingworth was attacked from all sides, by Puritans, Jesuits and high Anglicans; yet Laud, tolerant in doctrine if not in ritual, was sympathetic. Eventually he accepted the Articles and became Chancellor of Salisbury. In the Civil War, after writing on the King's behalf against the Scots, he joined the Royal Army and was present at the siege of Gloucester — apparently with a military device of his invention, in Clarendon's words 'an engine that should move so lightly, as to be a breastwork in all encounters and assaults in the field'. Later in the same year, a sick man, he was taken prisoner at Arundel Castle, and he died at Chichester in 1644. Chillingworth, an intellectual of fine and delicate mind, found himself, like other members of the Great Tew group, out of accord with the violent enthusiasms and absolute religious systems of the time of Charles I. His reliance upon reason as the ultimate interpreter of the scriptures and his emphasis on the logical necessity of toleration in the search for truth had an increasing appeal in later years. *The Religion of Protestants*, reprinted eight times between the Restoration and the middle of the eighteenth century, did as much as any work in its own field to lay the foundations of the Age of Reason in England.

Irene Coltman, *Private Men and Public Causes*, 1962, pp. 152-7.

EDWARD HYDE, 1st EARL OF CLARENDON (1609–74), the greatest of the Royalists, was born of a Wiltshire landed family at Dinton near Salisbury. His father, in Clarendon's words, 'contributed much more to his education than the school did'. At thirteen he went to Magdalen Hall, Oxford, and thence to the Middle Temple, 'entered' by his uncle, Nicholas Hyde, later Chief Justice of the King's Bench. An able young barrister, comfortably off after his father's death in 1632, by his own account something of a snob and a good deal of a prig, Hyde won the favour of Archbishop Laud; yet he was also a member of the liberal circle at Great Tew which included Falkland and Chillingworth, and a friend as well as admirer of such different men as Ben Jonson and John Selden. He had no enthusiasm for Charles I's Court, and a strong distrust of the attitude of the government towards the common law. When Parliament met in 1640, Hyde (M.P. for Wootton Bassett in the Short Parliament and for Saltash in the Long) joined the opposition, and was to the fore in the attack on Strafford and in the demolition of the prerogative courts. Essentially a moderate, he broke with Pym and the later leaders of the rebellion when they proposed to exclude bishops from the Lords; a champion of the rule of law, he opposed what he saw as the revolutionary demands of the Grand Remonstrance and helped to draw up the King's reply. Moreover, he distrusted profoundly Pym's use of the mob as a political force. He became the effective Royalist leader in the Commons, yet a leader who misjudged the situation, for unlike Pym and the King, he was ready to compromise and thus he believed that a peaceful settlement was possible. Charles did not warn Hyde of his intention to arrest the Five Members.

He joined the King at York in the summer of 1642 and was his chief civilian adviser in the war years. His influence was limited, for he stood for peace by negotiation if reasonable terms could be obtained, and his emphasis upon the necessity of a constitutional monarchy was not acceptable to the extremer Royalists. In 1645 he took part in the abortive negotiations at Uxbridge, and then he went to the west of England as the chief member of the Council of the Prince of Wales, eventually reaching Jersey in 1646, where he began the writing of his *History of the Rebellion*. He rejoined the Prince at the Hague in September 1648. An opponent of the agreement with the Covenanters, he was sent off on a fruitless mission to Madrid

Edward Hyde, 1st Earl of Clarendon
(Artist: after Adriaen Hanneman)

(1650–51). He returned to the exiled court at the end of 1651 and became Charles's principal adviser — shrewd and level-headed yet aloof and often unaccommodating, Anglican in outlook, distrustful of co-operation with Catholics, building up a fund of unpopularity with the younger Royalists in the tensions of a world of *émigrés,* intriguers and spies. In 1657 Charles appointed him Lord Chancellor with what seemed a barren gesture.

But the death of Oliver in 1658 transformed the scene and opened the way to the Restoration, the great achievement of Hyde's statesmanship. He drafted the Declaration of Breda on the lines suggested by Monck, which were in accord with his own moderate and practical approach, and he was on the Royalist side the principal architect of the reintroduction of a constitutional monarchy. He became the chief minister in the new government and was created Earl of Clarendon in 1661. Yet his seven years of office were unsuccessful. He was unlucky in the events of his time: the Plague, the Fire, the barrenness of Catherine of Braganza, the Dutch raid upon the Medway were scarcely Clarendon's fault, but they increased discontent. Rigid, economical, moral, he was out of place at the restored court; and his role as father-in-law of the heir to the throne (the Duke of York married Anne Hyde in 1660) was at best invidious. Yet his political errors did him as much harm as circumstances or personal characteristics. His constitutional formula was old-fashioned, for he neglected the Commons, attempting a kind of conciliar government which was no longer practicable. They warned him by forcing through the ecclesiastical settlement which has come to be known as the Clarendon Code, though it was not on the lines which he wanted, and they repaid him by impeachment in 1667. In foreign affairs he set his country well on the way to becoming a satellite of Louis XIV and allowed economic forces which he did not grasp to involve her in the unsatisfactory Dutch War of 1664–7. By the end of the war Clarendon was the perfect scapegoat, and he was virtually ordered to leave the country. Charles's ingratitude, typical of the Stuarts, was no doubt sharpened by the realization that his successors would be less censorious than the man to whose advice he had had to listen since boyhood. Defended only by his sons and son-in-law, he withdrew to France, and Parliament passed an Act of Banishment condemning him to lifelong exile. He lived on, never ceasing to hope for recall and devoting his time to writing his *Life* and his *History*, until his death at Rouen in 1674.

Clarendon's defects, notably his pride and a lack of imagination which would be labelled as narrow-mindedness in lesser men, became more evident with age. Yet the Stuarts never had a more honourable or a more successful servant. In his own phrase, 'his integrity was ever without blemish, and believed to be above temptation'. His success rested upon his moderation. In the years of defeat and exile he did more than any other man to keep the Stuart cause in touch with political reality. He must share with Monck the credit for the great facts that the Restoration was made by agreement and without foreign arms. In the triumph of 1660 his own record in the early days of the Long Parliament and his lifelong devotion to law provided a guarantee against an arbitrary settlement and ensured that the clock should not be turned back past 1641. As David Ogg has observed, 'it might have been a kinder fate for him and for England had he been withdrawn at the moment of achievement', * before the Cavalier Parliament met in 1661.

Yet posterity owes much to his second exile, for in it he wrote his *Life* and rewrote and completed the *History of the Rebellion*, first printed in 1702–4. Clarendon ranks high among English historians, and among writers of 'contemporary history' in the English language he is without peer. And his greatness as an historian rests upon an unusual combination of qualities. For he is at once a master of the character-study and a luminous analyst of social forces, giving us a full measure of both in a style strong, learned without being polished, and dignified yet never artificial. In his writing as in his political career Clarendon reflects a sane as well as an opulent conservatism, hostile both to the arbitrary and to the 'fanatic' elements in seventeenth-century life.

B.H.G. Wormald, *Clarendon: Politics, Historiography and Religion 1640–1660*, 1951.
R.W. Harris, *Clarendon and the English Revolution*, 1983.
Selections from Clarendon, ed. G. Huehns, 1955.

JOHN PYM (1583–1643), the most effective Parliamentary opponent of the Stuarts, was born at Brymore near Cannington in Somerset, an estate owned by the Pyms since the thirteenth century. He was an infant when his father died and his mother married Anthony Rous of Halton St. Dominic in east Cornwall; thus John Pym was brought up in a Puritan household close to Plymouth in the days of the Armada, close also to the Tavistock estates of the

England in the Reign of Charles II, 1956 ed., Vol. 1, p. 151.

John Pym c.1641
(Artist: after Edward Bower)

Russells, the richest Puritan magnates of the South-West. In 1599 he
went with his step-brother Francis Rous to Broadgates Hall (later
Pembroke College), Oxford, although he took no degree there, and

in 1602 he was admitted to the Middle Temple. Presumably he spent a good deal of his early manhood administering the wide estates he owned in northern Somerset; at some date between 1605 and 1613 he gained profitable — and, in view of his later political activities, useful — government employment as Receiver of Hampshire, Wiltshire and Gloucestershire.

His House of Commons career began in 1621 when he sat for Calne in James I's third Parliament, making his mark as a moderate member of the opposition, yet one who was strongly anti-Spanish and anti-Catholic. He was important enough to be placed under house arrest after the Commons Protestation of 1621. In 1624 he sat for the Russell seat of Tavistock, which he continued to represent in the five more Parliaments of his life. By 1629 he had emerged as one of the leaders of the Commons, a principal figure in the impeachment of Buckingham and in the Petition of Right and a vigorous foe of the Arminian clergymen, Montague and Manwaring; an energetic committee-man and a weighty speaker, yet far more moderate and less prominent than the emotional Eliot, whose martyrdom in 1629 he did not share. In the eleven years of non-parliamentary rule (1629–40) many of the opposition, for motives part commercial and part religious, turned their attention to colonization in the New World: Pym was treasurer of the Providence Island Adventurers and also a grantee of lands in Connecticut. The significance of the Providence Company's activities was greater in domestic history than in the Caribbean. The colony, never very flourishing, was lost to Spain in 1641, but the board meetings of the company, attended by such eminent Puritans as the Earl of Warwick and Viscount Saye and Sele, seem to have been used, particularly at the time of the Ship Money crisis in 1637, to concert opposition to the King's activities.

The year 1640 brought Pym national opportunity and responsibility when Charles I was compelled by the Scottish crisis to summon Parliament; for of the main figures of the Commons of the 1620s Coke and Eliot were dead, Wentworth was now the King's servant, and Pym alone remained. He took his chance and showed his power by a masterly statement of the nation's grievances in the opening debate of the Short Parliament, and thereafter his leadership was assured. The era of 'King Pym' had begun. After the dissolution of the Short Parliament (May) Pym established contact with the Scots, and when the royal failure in the Second Bishops War was evident he was prominent in drawing up the Petition of the Peers (August) which led to the summoning of another Parliament (November). In the election campaign which preceded this Long Parliament, the most celebrated in English history, Pym, in the phrase of Anthony à Wood, 'rode about the country to promote the elections of the puritanical brethren to serve in Parliament', and he was prompt and decisive in action when the Commons met, turning its members' burning sense of misrule into the attack on the apostate Strafford, in Pym's words 'the greatest enemy to the liberties of his country, and the greatest promoter of tyranny, that any age had produced'. Much of his energy in the first session went into the impeachment of Strafford; and when that was clearly breaking down, he rapidly accepted the plan of attainder proposed by others and carried it mercilessly through, taking full advantage of the rumours of army plots and of the tension of the London mob to compel Charles to sign the death warrant. Meanwhile he was prominent in what came to be the lasting constitutional work of the Long Parliament, the series of laws prohibiting arbitrary taxation and destroying the prerogative courts. In these matters Pym acted in harmony with the great majority of the Commons. But the second session brought division, and Pym's course, hitherto set within a traditional interpretation of the constitution, moved into revolutionary directions. The central issues upon which the Commons divided were three. One was religious: Pym moved from acceptance of a limited episcopacy to support for the 'Root and Branch' policy, which would have destroyed the ancient system of church government. The second and third were political. Pym insisted that command of the army — not merely of the force to subdue the Irish rebels — could be entrusted only to men acceptable to Parliament, and this struck at the very heart of royal sovereignty. Further, he demanded that the King should 'employ only such counsellors and ministers as should be approved by his Parliament'. This challenge to royal authority and the established constitution gave Charles a party in the Commons; Pym's appeal to the people, the Grand Remonstrance, with its catalogue of royal misgovernment and its famous demand for the employment of ministers 'as the Parliament may have cause to confide in, without which we cannot give His Majesty ... supplies for the support of his own estate', was carried by a majority of eleven votes only. In January 1642 came Charles's essay at a *coup d'état*, the attempted arrest of the Five Members. Pym and the others (Hampden, Hesilrige, Holles and Strode, together with Lord Mandeville from the Upper House) took refuge in the City, returning to Westminster in triumph a week later. Charles had left his capital the day before. The lines of civil war were being drawn.

The final phase of Pym's career began in January 1642; it was the period in which the Commons' majority turned itself into an executive government, preparing for and conducting a war. Pym was the central figure in this government, responsible for the Militia Ordinance (March 1642), for the Nineteen Propositions (June) which Charles rejected, and for the establishment of the Committee of Safety (July) of fifteen members on which he served. After the fighting began in the summer, his principal contributions to the Parliamentary cause were in finance and in diplomacy. The creation of the excise tax in 1643, so vital to victory, sprang originally out of a proposal by Pym. Even more important were his negotiations with the Scots, for these led in September 1643 to the signature of the Solemn League and Covenant, the treaty which opened the way to Marston Moor and the Parliamentarian capture of the north. It was Pym's final achievement. He died of cancer in December 1643 and was buried in Westminster Abbey.

No Englishman of the seventeenth century left so deep a mark on the development of his country's political life and institutions as John Pym. Pym, not Cromwell, was the architect of revolution and of Parliamentary supremacy. Yet he remains something of a mystery. There are patches of his career of which we know little; of his inner and personal life, unlike that of Cromwell or even of Strafford, we are almost entirely ignorant; and he has not been the subject of a major biography by a modern historian. In his last three years of intense political activity (1640–43) it is difficult to assess Pym's work separately from that of other Parliamentarian leaders. What we do know of him is often unattractive. He appears as a tough, subtle, unscrupulous politician, evidently moved by rancour as well as by fear in his dealings with Strafford, ready enough to whip up the London mob as a weapon against Charles and all who supported him or seemed likely to do so. And there is no doubt truth as well as bitterness in Clarendon's comment that he 'had observed the errors and mistakes in government, and knew well how to make them

appear greater than they were'. Yet the starting-point of any verdict
on Pym's political career must be that he was — like Clarendon
himself — essentially a moderate, in the early 1640s as in the 1620s;
a moderate whose aim was to restore what he believed to be the
Elizabethan constitution in church and state. More logical and a
good deal more ruthless than men like Clarendon, the men whom he
carried with him in his attacks on Strafford, on unparliamentary
taxation and on the prerogative courts, but who recoiled from an
assault on the central citadel of royal supremacy, Pym clearly came
to believe in the autumn of 1641 that the King could no longer be
trusted. It is unlikely that he realized the constitutional implications
that followed from this: for he was firmly in the Parliamentary
tradition which in some measure he created, empirical and opportunist. Carried forward on the swell of a revolutionary tide, Pym
was yet no Robespierre driven by dogma and vanity. He was
throughout his life deeply hostile to Arminianism which, like most
contemporary English gentry, he tended to equate with Popery, and
to its exponents like Montague and Laud, and this was certainly a
powerful — perhaps the decisive — motive in his opposition to a
King whose court seemed thick with Arminians and Catholics. It is
usual to regard him as a Puritan, yet he did not regard himself as one;
he was no sectary, and, indeed, he saw himself as a conservative in
religion, restoring the sound Protestantism of Elizabethan days. As a
practical politician he was outstanding, genuinely 'a great House of
Commons man'; a cogent speaker, sensitive to the moods of the
House and masterly in the marshalling of argument; a superb
tactician in his management of business and an expert in finance;
highly successful in the manipulation of public opinion, creative in
the development of the committee system. Above all, there is the
claim Pym put forward in his speech to the City of London shortly
after the battle of Edgehill: 'We shall pursue the maintenance of
our Liberties, Liberties that may not only be the Laws and
Statutes, but Liberties that may be in practice, and in execution.'
These 'Liberties were the liberties and privileges of a small class
of subjects, in the context of the seventeenth century; Pym and
his supporters were neither democrats not egalitarians in any
sense. Yet their defence — and expansion — of these liberties
in Parliament and through the Civil War became the basis of
parliamentary democracy. The challenge which 'King Pym' threw

down to King Charles is the central fact of English constitutional history.

J.H. Hexter, *The Reigh of King Pym*, 1941.
Anthony Fletcher, *The Outbreak of the English Civil War*, 1981.
Conrad Russell, 'The Parliamentary Career of John Pym, 1621-29' in P.Clark, A.G.R. Smith and N. Tyacke, eds., *The English Commonwealth, 1547-1640*, 1979.

JOHN HAMPDEN (1592-1643), opponent of Charles I, was born in London, the eldest son of a well-to-do Buckinghamshire landowner, and educated at Thame Grammar School, Magdalen College, Oxford, and the Inner Temple. His Commons career began in the stormy Parliament of 1621, and as M.P. for Wendover in the first three Parliaments of Charles I he became a friend of Eliot and a prominent opponent of royal policies. In 1627 he was briefly imprisoned for refusing to pay the forced loan. Like other leading Puritan laymen, he was involved in the 1630s in promoting colonization schemes: we find him concerned in the foundation of Connecticut, as one of the Saybrook patentees. His opposition to the second writ of Ship Money (1635) and the judges' decision for the Crown in the Hampden Case (1637-8) made him a national figure, a symbol of opposition to royal tyranny. In the Short Parliament and again in the Long he sat for Buckinghamshire, and only Pym among his fellow-members has won greater celebrity as a Parliamentarian champion. Inevitably he was one of the Five Members whom the King tried to arrest in 1642. When the fighting began Hampden raised troops in Buckinghamshire and secured the county for Parliament. He showed himself to be a man of decisive action, advocating in 1643 a Parliamentarian attack on the King's headquarters at Oxford, and it was in the course of Rupert's counter-attack against this that he was mortally wounded in a skirmish at Chalgrove Field.

Hampden's particular role in the quarrel between Crown and Parliament has been hard to assess, for the Ship Money episode and his early death gave him a mythical quality which he has never really shaken off. All men, even the Royalists, admitted his fine gifts — his courage, modesty, affability and powers of persuasion. Clarendon speaks of men seeing him in 1640 as 'the pilot that must steer the vessel through the tempests and rocks which threatened it'. The strength of his influence was admirably shown in the fierce debate on the Grand Remonstrance in 1641, when, in Philip Warwick's famous account, 'I thought we had all sat in the valley of the shadow of death; for we, like Joab's and Abner's young men, had catch't at each other's locks, and sheathed our swords in each others bowels, had not the sagacity and great calmness of Mr. Hampden by a short speech prevented it'. Above all he had a reputation for integrity and honesty, which was undoubtedly of great value to his cause. Yet it is possible to share some of the doubts expressed by Clarendon, who speaks of his 'cunning' and of his 'discerning spirit' and attributes much of Hampden's seeming reasonableness to prudence and calculation, and some of his influence to timing rather than to uprightness. Certainly he makes it plain that Hampden's strength in the Commons lay not in oratory but in judicious debating and in the arts of the committee man.

For all his firm devotion to principle, Hampden was a moderate by temperament. He had not joined Eliot in the rowdy scene that closed the Parliament of 1629, he had not been among the most violent against Strafford, he had come slowly to Root and Branch in religion. It seems likely that the episode of the Five Members hardened him against Charles and when war began he was not half-hearted; in Clarendon's words 'when he first drew his sword, he threw away his scabbard'. Yet it is difficult to believe that the great influence he is said to have had over Pym was not exerted for moderation. And his death was a damaging blow to the unity of the King's opponents. For not only had he, in Professor Hexter's words, 'acted as a sort of moral cement for the parliamentary cause'. * His particular qualities, above all his power to conciliate, were precisely those in which the victors of the Civil War showed themselves to be deficient in the later 1640s.

The article in *D. N. B.* is by C. H. Firth.

T. B. Macaulay, 'John Hampden', in *Critical and Historical Essays*, 1843.

C. E. Lucas Phillips, *Cromwell's Captains*, 1938.

---

* J. H. Hexter, *The Reign of King Pym*, 1941, p. 94. The whole passage is illuminating on Hampden.

SIR ARTHUR HESILRIGE or HASELRIG, (*d.* 1661), one of the Five Members, was a Leicestershire baronet who represented the county in both the Short and the Long Parliaments. Aggressively Puritan, he was a henchman first of Pym and then of Cromwell. Ludlow describes him as 'a man of a disobliging carriage, sour and morose of temper, liable to be transported with passion, and to whom liberality seemed to be a vice'. Prominent in Strafford's attainder, he was one of the Five Members, no doubt marked out for arrest by Charles as a champion of Root and Branch and of Parliamentary control of the militia. When war came he formed his own regiment of cuirassiers and put them in red armour; inevitably they became known as 'Lobsters', and they had a very bad time indeed in the Royalist victory of Roundway Down (1643), where their foes rolled them helplessly down the steep chalk slopes. Hesilrige fought bravely at Edgehill and at Lansdown, and in the second Civil War he held the Newcastle area, of which he was Governor, for Parliament. From 1647 to 1653 he was a leader of the Independents in the Commons. He was wise enough to refuse to serve on the court which condemned the King, although he seems to have approved the execution and was a prominent member of the Commonwealth Councils of State. He enjoyed considerable un-popularity through the skill with which he acquired lands and mineral rights for himself in the North-East, among them those of the See of Durham. But he broke with Oliver when the latter expelled the Rump, and henceforward he was an ardent and determined opponent of the Protectorate. In 1659 he had a brief spell of authority with the return of the Rump. There was no room for Hesilrige in the Restoration settlement. He was too stamped with republicanism even though he was not a regicide, and he cannot have accumulated much personal goodwill. So he was imprisoned, al-though Monck's support saved his life, and he died in the Tower in 1661.

The article in *D.N.B.* is by C.H.Firth.

DENZIL, 1st BARON HOLLES (1598–1680), Presbyterian politician and one of the Five Members of 1642, had a political career of remarkable length and consistency. Born at Haughton in Nottinghamshire, second son of the Earl of Clare, he sat in James

I's last House of Commons; fifty years later in the Lords he denounced the absolutism of Charles II. As a young M.P. he joined his brother-in-law Thomas Wentworth in attacking Buckingham. In 1629 he was one of those who held the Speaker in his chair while the Commons passed the Three Resolutions. This cost him a heavy fine and prolonged imprisonment, and embittered him against Charles I: so in the Long Parliament he was a passionate opponent of the Crown — although he took no part in the prosecution of Strafford — and the King's attempt to arrest him in 1642 is understandable. But in the Civil War he soon became an advocate of moderation and leader of the 'peace group' in the Commons, as his fear of radicalism grew. In 1644 he wanted to impeach Cromwell and in 1646 he nearly fought a duel with Ireton; but in 1647 the army impeached him, and next year, on the eve of Pride's Purge, he fled to France. Not until the Protectorate did he come back to England, to live quietly in Dorset. The Restoration brought him back to politics, and gave him a peerage. In 1667 he helped to negotiate the Treaty of Breda with the Dutch. One of the only four peers who opposed the banishment of Clarendon, Holles became once more a critic of royal policy, especially while Danby was in power: he acted in uneasy alliance with Shaftesbury, although he preferred 'Limitations' to 'Exclusion'. Holles, in his lifetime an effective orator and a foe at once of royal tyranny, of radicalism, and of an army-dominated republicanism, became after his death something of a Whig legend.

Patricia Crawford, *Denzil Holles, 1598–1680*, 1979.

WILLIAM LENTHALL (1591–1662), Speaker of the Long Parliament, was a barrister, born at Henley-on-Thames of gentry stock and educated at St. Alban Hall, Oxford, and Lincoln's Inn, who had already done well in his profession and bought country estates (including Burford Abbey from the Falkland family), before entering the Commons in 1640 as member for Woodstock. He is celebrated for his adroit reply to Charles I when the King entered the House with an armed retinue in January 1642 and demanded to know where the Five Members were: 'May it please your Majesty, I have neither eyes to see nor tongue to speak in this place but as this House is pleased to direct me, whose servant I am here; and humbly beg your Majesty's pardon that I cannot give any other answer than this to what your Majesty is pleased to demand of me'. The remainder of his long record as Speaker is not glorious. He sided with Parliament against the King in 1642 and with the Army against the Presbyterians in 1647. He accepted Pride's Purge in 1648 and, although he was not a member of the Court which condemned the King, he showed no reluctance to be the nominal chief magistrate of the Republic. He was turned out with the Rump in 1653, when he put up a token resistance and compelled Harrison to help him down from his chair, but he was back again as Speaker of the first Protectorate Parliament next year. In the Parliament of 1656 Lenthall had a seat but not the Speakership, and was one of those who urged Oliver to take the Crown; yet in 1659 he came back leading the Rump. At the Restoration he backed Monck. But fortune deserted him: he got no seat in the Convention and although his life was secure he was excepted from the Indemnity. A testimonial from Monck saved him from imprisonment, and he returned to his estates at Burford to die in 1662. It was no doubt a measure of his fears for his own safety that he stooped to give evidence against one of the regicides, of words spoken in the Commons.

SIR SIMONDS D'EWES (1602–50), Puritan, antiquary, was born in the parish of Chardstock in Dorset: his father was a Suffolk gentleman and D'Ewes went to school at Bury St. Edmunds, and thence to St. John's, Cambridge, and the Middle Temple. He was comfortably off, marrying well in 1626, and devoted his life to the collection and study of historical records, especially those of Parliament and the law. D'Ewes represented Sudbury (Suffolk) in the Long Parliament and turned against the King in 1642; but he was always a conservative Puritan, and was one of the members purged by Pride in 1648. He died in Suffolk in 1650. Pedantic, austere, long-winded in debate, D'Ewes was zealous both as chronicler of contemporary events and as collector of documents. Later historians of the seventeenth century have made extensive use of his *Diaries* of debates and transactions in the Long Parliament, especially for the years 1643-7, and of his *Autobiography*, while a good deal of our knowledge of the Elizabethan House of Commons rests upon his *Journals of the Parliaments of Elizabeth*, the major work of his life.

His collection of documents was bought by Robert Harley in 1705.

The Autobiography and Correspondence of Sir Simonds D'Ewes, ed.
   J. O. Halliwell, 2 vols., 1845.

JOHN SELDEN (1584–1654), antiquary and conversationalist,
came of Sussex yeoman stock and was educated at Chichester Free
School, Hart Hall, Oxford, and the Inner Temple. Called to the Bar
in 1612, he won even as a young man an immense reputation for his
knowledge of legal records and history, but he practised little. If
Aubrey is to be believed, he found it more profitable to be steward to
the Earl of Kent, whose Countess was his mistress. He took the
Puritan side in politics. In 1617 he was in trouble with the High
Commission for his *History of Tithes*, in which he doubted their
divine sanction. He was an anti-Buckingham M.P. in the 1620s and
was imprisoned in 1629 after the attack on the Speaker. As member
for Oxford University in the Long Parliament he remained in
London after 1642. But it is difficult to discern revolutionary
enthusiasm in Selden, and certainly after the outbreak of civil war he
played little part in politics. To the Assembly of Divines of the
1640s he brought a cool and somewhat cynical scholarship which
can scarcely have pleased zealots of any persuasion: in Aubrey's
phrase, 'he was able to run them all down with his Greek and
Antiquities'. Clarendon speaks of his 'stupendous' learning, and
certainly his range was vast. He wrote authoritatively on duels and
titles, on problems of inheritance and of sea-power. His *Mare
Clausum*, claiming English control of the narrow seas, was published by royal order in 1635. His edition of Eadmer's *Historia
Novorum* (1623) included the first critical essay on Domesday Book
and has remained of value to scholars. He won a European reputation as an orientalist by his treatise *De Deis Syriis* (1617). Yet
Selden was no pedant. His most celebrated memorial is his *Table
Talk*, first published in 1689, for he was an engaging conversationalist, with a dry and agreeable irony, whose intimate friends
ranged from Ben Jonson to Clarendon. The latter 'valued himself
upon nothing more than upon having had Mr. Selden's acquaintance
from the time he was very young'.

OLIVER ST. JOHN (1598?–1673), Parliamentarian, came from the Bedfordshire gentry and was educated at Queens' College, Cambridge, and Lincoln's Inn. He was imprisoned for a short time in 1629 on suspicion of sedition, and Clarendon, who describes him as 'a man reserved, and of a dark and clouded countenance, very proud', says that this embittered him against the court. Other factors brought him into the ranks of the King's enemies: he was a Puritan, he was in the Providence Island Company, and he was connected with Cromwell by marriage. As counsel for Hampden he won fame by his speech in the Ship Money case, and as M.P. for Totnes he was second only to Pym in the opposition in the Long Parliament. His appointment as Solicitor-General in 1641 made no difference. He led the attack on Ship Money and was prominent in the onslaught on Strafford; arguing for attainder, he advocated the overriding of the normal process of law, 'for it was never accounted either cruelty or foul play to knock foxes and wolves on the head... because they be beasts of prey'. After Pym's death St. John and Vane were the joint leaders of the war party in Parliament, successfully plotting against Essex in 1644 and backing Cromwell and the Army in 1647. In 1648 St. John was appointed Chief Justice of the Common Pleas, and from this time onwards he was much less prominent. Whether this was because he disapproved of the proceedings of the Commonwealth or because he was genuinely more concerned about the law than about politics is not wholly clear. Certainly he took no part in the trial of Charles I. Although he approved the expulsion of the Rump, he opposed the Instrument of Government, and in 1657 he tried to persuade Oliver to take the Crown as a constitutional monarch. A hard and fanatical Puritan, yet a lawyer who feared the perils of disorder, he backed Monck in 1660 and accepted the Restoration. Excluded from the Act of Indemnity, he lived in retirement until he went into exile in 1662, dying abroad in 1673.

The *D.N.B.* article is by C.H.Firth.

SIR HENRY VANE the Younger (1613–62), Puritan politician, was born at Debden near Newport in Essex, the son of the elder Sir Henry who later became Comptroller and Treasurer of the royal household. Educated at Westminster and Magdalen Hall,

Oxford, he had, in the words of his speech from the scaffold in 1662, 'been, till he was seventeen years old, a good fellow, but then it pleased God to lay a foundation of grace in his heart'. As his strange book, *The Retired Man's Meditations*, shows, there was something of the mystic in him. In 1635 he went to New England for conscience's sake, and for a year he was Governor of Massachusetts. Then he got involved in the controversy over saving grace provoked by Anne Hutchinson, and in 1637 he sailed back to England. Appointed joint Treasurer of the Navy in 1639 and knighted in 1640, he nevertheless became a follower of Pym and sat in Long Parliament as member for Hull. He played a somewhat unsavoury role in the condemnation of Strafford; discovering in the papers of his father, now Secretary to the Council, the records of the meeting in which Strafford had suggested bringing over the Irish Army to reduce 'this kingdom', he had provided Pym with a copy which served as the basis for impeachment and attainder. Prominent in the war party from 1642, a lucid and persuasive speaker, Vane was the principal English negotiator of the Solemn League and Covenant and for a time a leader of the Commons after Pym's death in 1643. A champion of liberty of conscience, he fell out with the Presbyterian majority in the House. Yet he was no ardent supporter of the Army and, although he was himself left in the Rump, he seems to have disapproved of Pride's Purge in 1648, and he played no part in the King's trial or in the events leading to it.

This did not stop him accepting the Republic. Vane believed in the sovereignty of the people, and saw the Rump as their remaining representative. So from 1649–53 he was a central figure in English government and in the project to perpetuate the power of the Rump. When Cromwell brought in his musketeers to dissolve it in 1653 Vane called out 'It is against morality and common honesty', to which Oliver replied, 'The Lord deliver me from Sir Henry Vane!' He declined to join Barebone's Parliament, and in 1656 wrote the pamphlet *A Healing Question*, opposing secular control of religion and condemning the Protectorate. This led to a brief period of imprisonment. When Oliver died in 1658, Vane joined the soldiers in denouncing Richard and in destroying the Protectorate, and he enjoyed a further spell of power when the Rump was restored in 1659. But the swing to monarchy in 1660 left him, a convinced Republican, without friends. Arrested before the Restoration, he was excluded from the Act of Indemnity on the understanding that Charles would spare his life if he were attainted. Tried in 1662, he chose to defend himself by vindicating parliamentary sovereignty, and the King went back on his word. Pepys saw Vane executed, and noted the courage and the 'humility and gravity' with which he died.

Vane's end was in a sense a measure of the distrust he aroused. Lely's portrait reveals a man self-willed and fanatical, who, for all his wit and fine manners, made enemies too easily and too widely. Clarendon spoke of his 'very profound dissimulation', Richard Baxter of his 'Subtilty'. As J. H. Hexter has put it, Vane 'used men for his secret purposes and then tossed them aside'. * Nevertheless, he stood for two of the great liberal principles of modern English history, parliamentary sovereignty and religious freedom. There is no evidence that he championed either of them with anything but complete sincerity, and it is difficult to deny that he died because of his championship of them.

Roger Howell, 'Henry Vane the Younger and the Politics of Religion', *History Today*, April 1963, pp 275–82.
Violet A. Rowe, *Sir Henry Vane the Younger*, 1970.

HENRY MARTEN (1602–80), wit, Republican and regicide, the son of a distinguished civil lawyer, inherited wide estates in Berkshire. Educated at University College, Oxford, and by travel abroad, he was in Aubrey's phrase 'as far from a Puritan as light from darkness'. Aubrey has a story that 'Henry was in Hyde Park one time when his Majestie was there going to see a Race. The King [Charles I] espied him, and sayd aloud, Let that ugly Rascall be gone out of the Parke, that whore-master, or else I will not see the sport.' Cromwell, too, when he ejected the Rump in 1653, called Marten a 'whore-master'. Elected M.P. for Berkshire in 1640, he was violently anti-Royalist, and one of the earliest Republicans. Clarendon records Marten saying to him at this time (1640-42) : 'I do not think one man wise enough to govern us all'; and in 1643 the House sent him to the Tower for saying that it were better one family were destroyed than many. A brilliant talker with a gift for repartee, the records suggest that he was the wittiest member of a Parliament that

* *The Reign of King Pym*, 1941, p. 147.

badly needed wit but did not always appreciate it. When a godly M.P. moved that all 'profane and unsanctified persons', a category for which the deist wencher Marten was admirably qualified, be expelled, Marten's counter-motion that all fools might be put out likewise, 'and then there would be a thin House', can scarcely have endeared him to his colleagues.

He raised troops for Parliament in both Civil Wars but his part in the fighting was undistinguished. His role in the conflict with the King was that of pamphleteer and speaker. He may have been the author of *A Correction of the Answerer*, a tract of 1646 demanding the condign punishment of Charles, and in 1647 he moved in the Commons for 'no further addresses' to the King, a motion lost by 34 (among them Blake) to 84 (including Cromwell). This year also saw Marten collaborating closely with the Levellers and supporting the Army in its quarrel with Parliament. With the Levellers he shared not only their wish to deal sternly with Charles but also a good deal of their political and social programme. He was probably one of the three authors of the Leveller *Remonstrance of Many Thousand Citizens* (1646) and he certainly had a hand in drafting the democratic constitution, *The Agreement of the People* (1647). Marten was liberal-minded enough to demand (with John Selden) toleration for Roman Catholics, and — though not himself a Leveller — sufficiently radical in social outlook to write in 1648 the tract *England's Troublers Troubled, or the just resolutions of the plain men of England against the rich and mighty,* a satirical onslaught upon the London capitalists. It was about this time too that he told a jury at a trial to put their hats on to show that they, not the men on the bench, were 'the chief Judges in the court'.

Marten sat on the court which tried Charles I, and signed the death-warrant; and a Royalist witness attributed to him the formula on which the court based its authority, 'in the name of the Commons in Parliament assembled and all the good people of England'. After 1649 he was a member of the Council of State and in that year proposed the abolition of imprisonment for debt; one of those who thought that the Rump should perpetuate itself, he broke with Cromwell and was turned out in 1653. During the Protectorate he was out of politics, and seems to have spent some time in prison as a result of the debts he had incurred on the Parliament's behalf in the wars. In 1659 he returned with the Rump. When the Restoration came he was put on trial and defended himself with courage and ability; yet according to Aubrey, his life was spared through a wit similar to his own, Lord Falkland saying, 'Gentlemen, yee talke here of makeing a Sacrifice; it was the old Lawe, all Sacrifices were to be without spott or blemish; and now you are going to make an old Rotten Rascall a Sacrifice'. Marten was imprisoned for life, in the Tower, at Windsor, and finally at Chepstow, where he died. Many Royalists saw him as 'that pernicious Catiline', in the phrase of one of their pamphleteers. Aubrey, more kindly, calls him 'a great and faithful lover of his Country ... a great cultor of Justice, and did always in the House take the part of the oppressed'.

C. M. Williams, 'Henry Marten', in *Puritans and Revolutionaries*, ed. Donald Pennington and Keith Thomas, 1978 (pp. 118-138).

PRINCE RUPERT (1619–82) was born in Prague, the third son of Frederick of the Palatinate and James I's daughter, Elizabeth. His parents were driven out of both Bohemia and the Palatinate soon after his birth, and Rupert spent nearly all his boyhood in Holland, growing into a tall and powerful young man, as impulsive as he was athletic, earning the nickname of Rupert-le-diable. A visit of six months to England in 1636–7 won him the favour of Henrietta Maria and a dashing reputation at court. Inevitably he joined the Dutch Army fighting in the Netherlands and took part in the siege of Breda in 1637. Next year he was captured by the imperialists at Vlotho, and until 1641 he remained a prisoner in Austria. When his release had been negotiated he came to England early in 1642, scenting the prospect of war; and after escorting Henrietta Maria to Holland he returned, to be commissioned in August as General of the Horse in the Royal Army. It was an extraordinary appointment for a man of twenty-three who had spent more years in captivity than on campaign, even though he had put his time to use in studying the theory of war.

Rupert served Charles I with complete loyalty and boundless courage throughout the First Civil War, and he was undoubtedly the ablest soldier in the Royalist armies in England. As a leader of cavalry he was superb, whether in the raids like that round Chalgrove in 1643 or in the charges in battle as at Edgehill and Naseby. He had learned from Gustavus, and Cromwell was in some measure

Prince Rupert c.1670
(Artist: attrib Gerard Honthorst, c. 1641–2)

his pupil. Moreover, he brought to the conduct of the King's war a swiftness of action — as, for example, round Oxford in the autumn of 1642 and on the eve of Marston Moor in 1644 — which was tactically invaluable and which could have served as a tonic and model to a command less rent by faction. How well he mastered the arts of siege and storm he showed in Lancashire in 1644 and at

Leicester in 1645. Nevertheless, for all his qualities he was in some ways disastrously deficient in generalship. Despite his devotion to the Royalist cause, his concentration upon the needs of his own troops was too great. Even as a cavalry commander he failed, as Oliver did not, to retain control of his troops after the charge. Above all, he lacked the comprehensive vision of the great commander, and neither in campaign nor in battle did his grasp compare with that of Fairfax or of Cromwell. He was much handicapped by the indecisiveness of the King and by the chronic obstructionism of such men as Goring, Digby and Wilmot. Yet not all the faults were theirs. Rupert had more than his share of the impatience of youth, and his impatience quickly became contempt. He was a man of prejudices, and he had plenty of charm but very little tact. In the intensely personal structure of the Royalist high command, Rupert's characteristics were more likely to irritate than to inspire, especially since from the very beginning he appeared to owe his high rank to his relationship with the King.

His first encounter in the Civil War was the skirmish at Powicke Bridge in September 1642. Next month after Edgehill he was for driving on to London, and at Brentford on the outskirts we find him leading an infantry charge in an attempt to force a way into the capital. During the first half of 1643 he spent much time extending Royalist control from Oxford over the south and west midlands, and in July he took Bristol for the King. But that September at Newbury — in the first major battle of the war and a decisive turning point in Royalist fortunes — Essex and the trained bands of London apprentices withstood Rupert's cavalry. Moreover, he was already involved in serious quarrels with the Queen as well as with courtier-soldiers like Wilmot. Yet the early months of 1644 brought Royalist successes and showed Rupert at his most brilliant. Moving northwards towards the challenge of the invading Scots, he relieved Newark in March by rapid and masterly manoeuvre, and in early summer he overran Lancashire, slaughtering the defenders of Bolton in one of the few conflicts of the English wars which had the savage flavour of the Thirty Years' War.

His career had reached its peak. In June he moved east and relieved York, surprising his enemies by moving swiftly in from the north. But on 2 July, outnumbered three to two, his army was shattered at Marston Moor. Thereafter the final defeat of the Royalists was delayed more by the mistakes of the Parliamentarians than by the skill of their own generals. Rupert withdrew southwards with the remains of his army. In November he was appointed Commander-in-Chief of the Royal armies, a post which quickly involved him in disputes with Goring and Digby. The spring campaign which he planned for 1645 from his base in the Welsh Marches came to nothing, while the enemy was organizing the instrument of final victory, the New Model Army. At the end of May the Prince won his last victory, compelling the surrender of Leicester; in mid-June came his utter defeat at Naseby. His opponents among the Royalists were ready to make him the scapegoat of the King's disasters, the more so when he argued at this stage for a treaty which might have saved much for Charles. In September, for sound military reasons, he surrendered Bristol. Charles, characteristically, dismissed him from command without even seeing him. Although a reconciliation was patched up after Rupert had compelled the King to face him and obtained a court-martial which acquitted him of all charges of treachery and neglect of duty, his career as a Royalist soldier was over.

After the surrender of Oxford in 1646 Rupert was permitted to go abroad. He fought briefly for the French against the Spaniards in Flanders. Then in 1648, taking advantage of mutinous feelings in the Parliamentarian fleet, he got command of a small squadron of English ships. From 1649 to 1652 he was part Royalist admiral, part buccaneer — running supplies to the Scillies so long as they resisted, capturing English merchantmen in the Mediterranean, taking prizes off Gambia and in the Caribbean where in 1652 his brother Maurice was lost. His exploits can be overrated, and he was never a serious threat to the English Republic: Blake destroyed many of his ships in the Mediterranean. After his return to his cousin Charles II's court in France in 1652, Rupert exercised little influence in the Royalist cause. He spent most of the Interregnum in Germany, at his brother the Elector Charles Louis' court at Heidelberg, with the Emperor in Vienna, or fighting for the King of Hungary; he settled finally at Mainz, turning his energies to chemical experiments and to develop the art of the mezzotint.

Charles II invited him back to England at the Restoration and settled upon him a pension of £6,000 per annum. Rupert belonged to the generation of elder statesmen, but he had never been a statesman. His contribution to the world of Restoration England, a world very different from that of the 1630s, was inevitably that of the fighting man. He commanded at sea in the Second Dutch War (1664–7), leading the van at Southwold Bay in 1665, joining with Monck in the celebrated 'Fighting Instructions' of 1666, suffering defeat in the Four Days' Battle of 1667 and winning victory off the North Foreland in the same year. During the Third Dutch War he was appointed (1673) to the Board of Admiralty. Yet his concerns were not merely naval. He served on the Tangier Board, and, as the map of Canada shows, he was a leading figure in the early activities of the Hudson Bay Company. He was one of the founders of the Royal Society, and during this time as Governor of Windsor (from 1668) he experimented, particularly with firearms, in his own laboratory there. He continued to produce mezzotints and left to posterity some very beautiful examples of the craft. He hunted, and he played tennis with great skill. He died a bachelor, but from 1667 onwards the young actress Peg Hughes was his cherished mistress. Pepys was no doubt right in finding Rupert, with whom he clearly had an occasional brush, irascible and rather old-fashioned.

Austin Woolrych, *Battles of the English Civil War*, 1961.
P. Morrah, *Prince Rupert of the Rhine*, 1976.

WILLIAM CAVENDISH, 1st DUKE OF NEWCASTLE (1592–1676), was born at Welbeck Abbey and educated at St. John's, Cambridge. The heir to great wealth, created Earl of Newcastle in 1628, he was principally celebrated before the Civil Wars for his lavish hospitality to his sovereigns: he spent some £20,000 on entertaining Charles I in the 1630s, some of it upon the masques specially written by Ben Jonson. In 1638 he was appointed governor to the Prince of Wales. From 1642–4 he gave princely sums to raise and maintain Royalist armies in the north, and in 1643 he won much of the West Riding for Charles by his victory at Adwalton Moor. Yet he was an eccentric soldier: in Clarendon's words 'the substantial part, and fatigue of a general, he did not in any degree understand (being utterly unacquainted with war) nor could submit to'. He fought bravely on the field; but 'such articles of action were no sooner over, than he retired to his delightful company, music, or his softer pleasures, to all which he was so indulgent, and to his ease,

W.S.B.—E*

that he would not be interrupted upon what occasion soever; insomuch as he sometimes denied admission to the chiefest officers of the army ... for two days together; from whence many inconveniencies fell out'. At Marston Moor the army he had raised was shattered, his white-coated infantry refusing quarter and fighting to the last, and Newcastle, trusting little in Rupert and believing the royal cause lost, sailed away to Hamburg.

He remained in exile, mostly in Antwerp, until the Restoration, enduring a measure of poverty until he managed to raise cash through his brother who compounded for his estates. In 1645 he married, as his second wife, Margaret Lucas (1624?–74), a member of the Colchester Royalist family and a woman of literary and philosophical tastes as well as of great beauty and resolute virtue. Although he was sworn of Charles II's Privy Council in 1650, he took little part in the politics of exile. Undoubtedly this pleased the judgement of Clarendon who, though full of regard for Newcastle's dignity and courtesy, described him once as 'a most lamentable man, as fit to be a general as to be a bishop'. Most of his energies went into his passion for horsemanship. His riding-school at Antwerp achieved European fame, and in 1657 he published the first of his two remarkable books on dressage.

At the Restoration, Newcastle recovered much of his lands and in 1665 he received a dukedom. He spent little time in London, largely, it seems, because the Duchess, whose morality provoked ribaldry at Court, persuaded him that it would be more prudent to devote his time to restoring the family fortunes: in her *Life* of the Duke published in 1667 she calculated that the wars had cost him over £900,000, taking into the reckoning unrecovered lands, forced sales, woodlands and other sources of wealth plundered or destroyed, and sixteen years of unpaid rents. Nevertheless, Newcastle did not wholly neglect his public duty, for he presented his King — whom he had taught to ride a quarter of a century before — with a long political dissertation. This was highly reactionary, commending among other things the use of dragoons, the revival of the Star Chamber, the reduction of education and the diminution of the number of lawyers; and it had no practical consequences, even if Charles II ever read it. For the rest, the Duke maintained his passion for horsemanship, publishing in 1667 *A New Method and Extraordinary Invention to Dress Horses*, and constructing a racecourse at

Welbeck. Both he and the Duchess wrote verse and plays: Pepys called her play *The Humorous Lovers* 'the most silly thing that ever came upon the stage', and it is clear that the Duke's most valuable contribution to English literature was as patron rather than as author. Among those who benefited from his generosity at this time were Dryden and Shadwell.

Margaret, Duchess of Newcastle, *The Life of William Cavendish, Duke of Newcastle*, ed. C.H.Firth, 1886.
Geoffrey Trease, *Portrait of a Cavalier*, 1979.

GEORGE, BARON GORING (1608–57), Cavalier commander, son of one of Henrietta Maria's favourite courtiers, distinguished himself in the 1630s both by his devotion to gambling and women and by his bravery in fighting for the Dutch in Flanders. Wounded at the siege of Breda in 1637, he returned home and in 1639 was appointed Governor of Portsmouth. Wild and irresponsible, he had a natural military genius and could inspire men; yet he was also deeply ambitious and thoroughly unscrupulous, and thus became the subject of one of Clarendon's harshest portraits. Clarendon's recognition of the damage Goring did to the Royal cause is to be found in the judgment that he 'would, without hesitation, have broken any trust, or done any act of treachery, to have satisfied an ordinary passion or appetite; and, in truth, wanted nothing but industry (for he had wit, and courage, and understanding, and ambition, uncontrolled by any fear of God or man) to have been as eminent and successful in the highest attempt in wickedness of any man in the age he lived in, as before'.

His actions in the years 1640–2 were highly equivocal. He made Portsmouth into a base for the King, while convincing the Commons, in a speech of charm and effrontery, that he was loyal to their interests. He was deeply involved, for his own ends, in the Army Plots of 1641, yet betrayed them both to Parliament. His doubledealing persuaded Parliamentarians to think of appointing him to high command. But when fighting began in 1642 he declared for Charles; within a month he surrendered Portsmouth, and departed to Holland, where he made his peace with Henrietta Maria. Returning to England, he distinguished himself as a cavalry leader in the north until he was captured by Fairfax at Wakefield in 1643.

Exchanged in 1644, he commanded the Royalist left at Marston Moor, shattering Fairfax's cavalry, but only to be routed by Cromwell. He was already notorious for his readiness to let his men plunder, and henceforward the combined influences of drink and defeat seem to have produced a steady deterioration in him, a change the more ruinous to his cause because of the increased authority which he was given at this stage of the war. Appointed Captain of the Horse in the west of England just before Lostwithiel, he must be acquitted of Clarendon's charge of negligence in failing to prevent the escape of Parliamentarian cavalry in that battle (August 1644), and he showed his customary bravery at Newbury (October). For the rest, his influence was disastrous. He quarrelled with Rupert, intrigued against him, and disobeyed orders to join him before Naseby in 1645. In the west, where his conduct, apart from spasmodic bursts of action, was governed by a blend of laziness, drink and jealousy, he permitted the Parliamentarians to relieve Taunton early in 1645 and provoked the country folk to rise against him by allowing his men freedom to loot their homes and kill their cattle. After his appointment in May 1645 to command all the Royal forces in the west, he was heavily defeated by the Ironsides at Langport in July. Abandoning Bridgwater without a blow, he fell rapidly back to north Devon. Here, while his army dwindled swiftly in number and morale, he spent his time in debauchery and in a bitter feud with his fellow-commander Sir Richard Grenville, until in November, pleading ill-health, he left for France. He has been well described as 'the evil genius of the war in the west'. *

Next year, as the Parliamentarians overran the Royalist remnants in the west of England, Goring in the Netherlands was given the barren rank of Commander of English regiments in the Spanish service. He went to Spain in 1650 and spent the rest of his days there, taking part in the siege of Barcelona in 1652 and dying in Madrid in 1657. Goring was not a typical Royalist, and in contrast with him there must be set the figures of finer men like Rupert and Hopton. Yet the faults which he revealed in extreme — the irresponsibility, the selfishness, the readiness to quarrel — were not uncharacteristic of the Royalist leaders, and they played a substantial if imponderable part in the failure of the Royalist cause in the Civil Wars.

* Mary Coate, *Cornwall in the Great Civil War*, 1933, p.196.

RALPH, 1st BARON HOPTON (1598–1652), Royalist commander, came from Witham in Somerset and was educated in Lincoln College, Oxford. He became a professional soldier, fighting for the Elector Palatine in the Thirty Years' War, but came home to sit in the Parliaments of 1624 and 1628. Puritan in his religious outlook, Hopton, as member for Wells in the Long Parliament, voted against Strafford and for the Grand Remonstrance. It was the Militia Ordinance, with its proposal to give control of the army to Parliament, that sent him over to the King's side. Hot-tempered yet utterly honourable, Hopton was unusual among Royalist generals, for he kept his troops in order and he was not self-seeking. As Miss Coate has observed, 'like Cromwell he perceived that the two dynamic forces in war are a crusading ardour allied to a rigorous discipline', * but he was almost alone on the Royalist side in translating this perception into action. Moreover, Clarendon, who speaks well of his qualities, thought him 'rather fit for the second than for the supreme command in an army'. His role in the war was to rouse the far south-west and make what use he could of Cornish loyalty to the King. In 1643 he defeated the western Parliamentarians at Braddock Down and again at Stratton; then, moving out of Cornwall, he won a limited victory at Lansdown above Bath, where he himself was severely wounded; and later in the year the Cornish foot stormed their way into Bristol. Early in 1644 Hopton was in Sussex, holding Arundel Castle for a time, but Waller's victory at Alresford turned the tide, and Hopton went back to the west and ultimately to defeat. Quarrels in the high command and plundering by ill-disciplined troops did much to destroy the Royalists in the west during 1645, and when at the beginning of 1646 Hopton was given supreme command he could scarcely delay the end. Fairfax beat him at Torrington and drove him back to Cornwall, and he capitulated at Tresilian Bridge, near Truro, in March 1646. Hopton himself went to Scilly and then to Jersey; in 1649 he was privateering along the Cornish coast. But he fell out of favour at Charles II's exiled court, for he had no liking for dealings with Catholics and Scottish Covenanters, and he died at Bruges in 1652.

F.T.R. Edgar, *Sir Ralph Hopton: the King's Man in the West 1642–52*, 1968.

* Mary Coate, *Cornwall in the Great Civil War*, 1933, p. 73.

ROBERT DEVEREUX, 3rd EARL OF ESSEX (1591–1646), Parliamentarian general, was the son of Elizabeth's favourite, the second Earl, and grandson of her secretary Walsingham. Solid, solemn and cautious in temperament, puritanical in outlook, he resembled his grandfather, not his father. Married at fourteen to the spoiled, self-willed and lovely Frances Howard, in 1613 he underwent the shame of the divorce suit, grounded upon his alleged impotence towards her, which freed her to marry James I's favourite Somerset. The victim and the one honest figure in the whole sordid affair, it is scarcely surprising that he became an opponent of the Stuarts — though it is noteworthy that his second marriage, made when he was forty, was also a failure. In 1620 he commanded a company of volunteers in the Palatinate; and in 1625 he was Vice-Admiral in the Cadiz expedition, and in 1639 second-in-command in the Bishops' War; yet all in all, his fighting experience before the Civil War was slight. Politically, he joined the opposition in Charles I's early Parliaments, and supported the Petition of Right. Clarendon later blamed 'a weak judgment, and a little vanity, and as much of pride', rather than ambition or malice, for his decision to go against the King. No doubt Essex had been deeply seared at an impressionable age; yet this verdict does less than justice to his sense of Puritan duty. In 1641 he was adamant for Strafford's attainder, with the grim phrase, 'Stone dead hath no fellow'; and in 1642 he was one of the few peers to remain at Westminster when the King moved to establish his power at York. Appointed General of the Parliamentary army, he was defeated by Rupert in the skirmish at Powicke Bridge and forced to retreat after Edgehill, where he fought bravely. Yet he held the defences of London at Turnham Green, and in the following year, 1643, advanced to take Reading. Later he relieved Gloucester and fought his way through to London by resisting Royalists attacks at the first battle of Newbury. Nevertheless, Essex did not prove a successful commander. By circumstances as by temperament he had little power of initiative, and he had no certain authority over the other Parliamentarian generals. His most disastrous enterprise came in 1644 when, marching westwards in defiance of Parliamentary orders, he was trapped at Lostwithiel in the last days of August. Escaping himself by sea, he left nearly 6,000 men to surrender in the most notable Royalist victory of the war. His deficiencies lent substance to the demand for the Self-Denying

Ordinance in 1645, and he resigned his command just before this was enacted. He died suddenly in 1646.

EDWARD MONTAGU, VISCOUNT MANDEVILLE and 2nd EARL OF MANCHESTER (1602–71), Parliamentarian commander, came of a great Huntingdonshire family, and like the lesser Huntingdonshire squire who was three years his senior, Oliver Cromwell, went to Sidney Sussex College, Cambridge. He was given a barony in his own right, and took the courtesy title of Viscount Mandeville, when his father was created Earl of Manchester in 1626. According to Clarendon, he won court favour early through Buckingham, from whose family his first wife came. But he married five times; his second wife was a Rich, the daughter of the Puritan Earl of Warwick, and thenceforward he moved in Puritan circles unfriendly to the Crown. Austere, formal, kindly, gentle, Mandeville seems also to have had a flair for political organization, and his house in Chelsea became a centre for Pym and his supporters. The fact that he was the only peer whom Charles attempted to arrest together with the Five Members in January 1642 is a measure of his importance in the opposition. Although he had no military experience, he was given high rank in the Parliamentary army. His father died in 1642 and it was as Earl of Manchester that he became, in 1643, Major-General of the army of the Eastern Association, with Cromwell as his subordinate. His record until after Marston Moor was no bad one, though until the summer of 1644 he remained anchored to the eastern counties. But the scale of Parliament's triumph at Marston Moor transformed the future, opening up a prospect of total victory. Men like Oliver welcomed this, sensing it as realism in dealing with Charles I; but it horrified a cautious aristocrat like Manchester, who wanted a negotiated peace. As he said in a council of war that winter, 'I beseech you let's consider what we do. The King cares not how oft he fights, but it concerns us to be wary, for in fighting we venture all to nothing. If we fight him a hundred times and beat him ninety-nine, we shall be hanged — we shall lose our estates, and our posterities be undone'.

So the military opportunity created by Marston Moor was lost. Lethargy and procrastination governed Manchester's conduct, reaching a climax in the delay which allowed the Royalists to escape at the second battle of Newbury. Cromwell could not tolerate this, and in Parliament denounced Manchester's 'backwardness to all action'. Behind the clash of personalities and the opposing strategies lay the widening conflict between the Independents and the Presbyterians, with all its implications in politics, religion and social class, and here Manchester's attitude was plain. When the Self-Denying Ordinance of 1645 brought his military career to an end he returned to Parliament as a leading Presbyterian peer. He was bitterly opposed to the King's trial, he took no part in public affairs under the Republic, and he welcomed the Restoration. Charles II made him Lord Chamberlain and gave him the Garter. He died in 1671, and Burnet and Clarendon alike eulogized him, the former as 'both a virtuous and a generous man', the latter as 'of all men who had ever borne arms against the King ... the most worthy to be received into the trust and confidence in which he was placed'.

SIR THOMAS FAIRFAX (later **3rd BARON**) (1612–71), Parliamentarian commander-in-chief in the Civil War, was born at Denton-in-Wharfedale, the descendant on both sides of old-established Yorkshire families. A tall, swarthy, sensitive, rather melancholy boy, 'Black Tom' Fairfax went up to St. John's, Cambridge, in 1626, while his father Ferdinando, as M.P. for Boroughbridge, saw the opening stages of Charles I's quarrel with the Commons. The Fairfaxes were Anglicans, yet Puritan Cambridge had its influence on him, and so did the discontent which the King's support of Buckingham and the forced loan caused among the Yorkshire gentry. But Thomas Fairfax was destined by his own temperament and by the ambition of his fierce old grandfather to be a soldier, and in 1629 he joined Sir Horace Vere's company fighting for the Prince of Orange in the Netherlands. From there he went in 1631 to France where he nearly died of smallpox, and in 1632 he came back to England, to spend his next few years on the family estates in Yorkshire; in 1637 he married Vere's daughter Anne, strong-minded, possessive, and an ardent Presbyterian, and they set up home at Nunappleton in Wharfedale. When the Bishops' Wars broke out in 1639 he raised a troop of dragoons, the 'Redcaps', to fight for Charles against the Scots, and in 1640 they were in the force routed at Newburn.

In the crisis of 1641-2 the Fairfaxes, father and son, were

Sir Thomas Fairfax (later 3rd Baron)
(Artist: William Faithorne after Robert Walker)

moderates, anxious for agreement between Crown and Commons. Driven to decision, they came out for Parliament; as Fairfax later put it, 'my judgment was for Parliament, as the King's and kingdom's greatest safeguard'; his father took command of the Parliamentarian forces in Yorkshire, and he himself became General of the Yorkshire Horse. His reckless bravery quickly made his name a legend. In the confused fighting of 1643 in Yorkshire he captured Leeds and Wakefield and held the West Riding for Parliament;

defeated at Adwalton Moor, he and his father nevertheless managed
to prevent Hull from falling into Royalist hands, and late in the
year, crossing the Humber, he shared with Cromwell the brief and
brilliant cavalry victory at Winceby. The following year, 1644,
made him a soldier of national fame. After crossing into Cheshire to
relieve Nantwich, he returned to Yorkshire, stormed Selby and laid
siege to York. Challenged by the advance of Prince Rupert, he
commanded the right wing of the Parliamentarian army at Marston
Moor (July 1644). Later in the year he was critically ill for weeks
after a severe wound at the siege of Helmsley Castle. In February
1645 he was appointed Captain-General of the New Model Army, a
mark as much of his personal integrity and of his lack of political
commitment as of his military brilliance. Eventually freed from the
restraints imposed by the political Committee of Both Kingdoms,
Fairfax led the New Model to its remarkable series of victories in
1645–6, beginning with Naseby (June 1645) and Langport (July).
Between September and April he brought the Royalist west to
surrender, and in June 1646 he entered Oxford, the Royalist capital,
in triumph.

The four years of the First Civil War were the era of Fairfax's
military glory. For the complex political negotiations which followed he was ill-equipped. In the wrangles over arrears of pay and
disbandment which took up much of 1647 and which brought a split
between the army and the Presbyterian majority in the Commons, he
took the side of his men, and in August led them into London to
overawe Parliament; his concern above all was to prevent anarchy,
and thus in November, after the debates on the Agreement of the
People, he was ready to take action against the mutineers at Ware.
Yet he made no effective contribution to the negotiations with the
King. When Charles's duplicity brought about the Second Civil War
in 1648, Fairfax took the field again in full sympathy with his men,
and at Maidstone and Colchester did much to crush the Royalist
risings in the south-east. But, still a moderate at heart, he shrank
from the harsh logic of the revolution. Nominated as one of the
commissioners to try Charles, he refused to serve; there is a story that
Lady Fairfax attended the opening of the trial, and that when her
husband's name was called in the list of judges she cried out 'He has
too much wit to be here'. Equally, he seems to have resisted a
suggestion that he should lead out troops to rescue the King.

Although his personal appeal for the King's life was rejected, he remained in the service of the Republic throughout 1649, crushing the Levellers' mutiny at Burford in May. In 1650 he resigned his commission when asked to command the army to invade Presbyterian Scotland, and retired to Nunappleton, where he passed the years of the Commonwealth in private life, devoted to his family, spending his time caring for his five chestnut horses, herd of deer, and gardens, writing verse and enriching his library (which he left in his will to the Bodleian at Oxford). When fresh crisis came in 1659–60, he emerged, first as a member of Richard Cromwell's Parliament, and then, more actively to support Monck's march into England. He raised his Yorkshire friends in arms and won over some of Lambert's men for an attack on York. He declared for a free and constitutional Parliament; a member of the Commission sent to invite Charles II to return, he welcomed the Restoration — although characteristically, he was deeply angered by the disinterment and gibbeting of Cromwell's corpse.

Fairfax, who died in 1671, compels high admiration at least as much by his simple natural virtues as by his military skill. The latter, indeed, is difficult to assess with exactness; the campaigns and battles of the Civil War were confused affairs; moreover, Fairfax's own remarkable intrepidity lends colour rather than clarity to accounts of them. He was evidently an outstanding leader of troops in the heat of action, and his care for his men's well-being and discipline alike was noteworthy; the record of his battles suggests instinctive genius as a tactician, and he was a fine cavalry commander. The comparison with Cromwell is obvious but not very fruitful. The difference in their ages (Fairfax's military career effectively ended at thirty-six, whereas Oliver's did not begin until he was forty-three) makes their co-operation and mutual regard the more impressive. It was the turn in 1646–7 from war to politics, from the plain problems of fighting to the intricate ones of governing, that quickly brought the lieutenant to overshadow his commander. For Fairfax, far simpler in nature than Cromwell, was essentially unpolitical in outlook; nor was he torn by the Puritan passions which moved Oliver. He was out of his depth in the elaborate manoeuvres which followed the collapse of the Royalist forces, and in the constitution-making; his reaction to the disturbing political and social questions raised by the Levellers was entirely conven-

tional. Yet he kept men's respect and affection. Partly this fact
reflected his bravery in battle. In this he was truly heroic, as his
frequent wounds bore witness; nor, incidentally, was his courage
limited to the battlefield, for he was a delicate man, often ill,
suffering severe pain from the stone for much of his life, and from
gout and rheumatism in his later years. Partly also it sprang from his
gentleness, his courtesy, his diffidence, his mercy; once the exhilar-
ation of battle was over, Fairfax's spirit instinctively turned to
clemency for the defeated.

C. R. Markham, *Life of the Great Lord Fairfax*, 1870.
M. A. Gibb, *The Lord General*, 1938.
John Wilson, *Fairfax*, 1985.

OLIVER CROMWELL (1599–1658), was born at Huntingdon,
great-grandson of Richard Williams the nephew of Thomas Cromwell, the Tudor minister whose name he adopted. Oliver's father
Robert was a country gentleman in easy rather than wealthy
circumstances; as Oliver himself put it, 'I was by birth a gentleman,
living neither in any considerable height not yet in obscurity'. He
went to Huntingdon Grammar School, whose headmaster Thomas
Beard was a Puritan of intellectual distinction; and in 1616 to
Sidney Sussex, a Cambridge college of Puritan sympathies. But he
took no degree, for in 1617 his father died and Oliver, the only boy
among those seven Cromwell children who reached maturity, returned home to run the estate. For the next twenty-three years, until he
was forty-one, Oliver Cromwell lived a country gentleman, actively
farming at Huntingdon and at St. Ives, serving as a J.P., and
defending the rights of commoners against the Earl of Bedford's
syndicate who were draining the Fens round Ely. He spent some time
in London studying, like many of his fellow landowners, at the Inns
of Court, and in 1620 he married Elizabeth, the daughter of the city
merchant Sir John Bourchier, a profitable and completely happy
match; in 1636 he substantially increased his wealth by inheriting
from an uncle the farm of the cathedral tithes at Ely, where he went
to live. In 1628 he was a Member for Huntingdon in Charles I's third
Parliament, and saw its final scene when Eliot and others held the
Speaker in his chair while the Three Resolutions were passed; but he

took no notable part. It is certain that Cromwell himself regarded his religious development as much the most important aspect of his life in these years. He underwent at this time prolonged spiritual crisis reflected in neurotic illness and melancholy, yet he emerged with a confident Puritan faith, a faith rooted in Calvinism yet wider, more tolerant and more tender than that of many of his contemporaries who were moving in the same direction.

In 1640 his career, hitherto local, merged with that of the nation when he was elected M.P. for Cambridge in the Short and then in the Long Parliament. He was not a distinguished Parliamentarian at this time; but it was clear where his sympathies lay in that split in the ranks of the land-owning class that produced the Civil War. He spoke in favour of the 'Root and Branch' abolition of episcopacy and of the Triennial Act (1641); he was among the earliest of those who were ready to take the control of the armed forces out of the hands of the King in order to deal with the Irish rebellion; the debate on the Grand Remonstrance brought him to contemplate emigration; and it was Oliver Cromwell who first moved to put the country in a state of defence against the King's supporters in 1642. His line was a radical one, and it was natural that when hostilities broke out in the summer he, as Member for Cambridge, should take quick action to secure town and university for Parliament. Action was what Oliver required. 'At forty-three he had found his proper calling, and a force of incalculable velocity had been unloosed on the world'; so Buchan describes the turning-point of 1642.

He fought at Edgehill that October; but the experience which made this middle-aged man into a formidable soldier and the most successful cavalry commander in English history came within the single year 1643. He spent it in securing eastern England for the Parliament, fighting a series of skirmishes (some of them considerable, at Grantham, Gainsborough and Winceby), and creating and disciplining his own regiment, the 'Ironsides' as they were later to be nicknamed, men chosen for conscience as well as fighting-spirit, to stand 'for the liberty of the gospel and the laws of the land'. In January 1644 he was commissioned a Lieutenant-General, and six months later at the head of the cavalry of the Eastern Association he played a vital part in the major victory of Parliament at Marston Moor. By now clearly one of the chief figures on the Parliamentary side, he spoke strongly at Westminster this autumn both for

Oliver Cromwell c.1655
(Artist: attrib. Samuel Cooper)

religious toleration and for a more vigorous prosecution of the war.
In 1645 he was to the fore in the organization of the New Model
Army. He was appointed its Lieutenant-General under Fairfax, and
commanded its cavalry in the decisive victory at Naseby (June); and
he spent the next twelve months overcoming the remaining Royalist
forces in the west, receiving with Fairfax the surrender of Oxford in
June 1646.

The war was over, for the time being. In its course Oliver Cromwell had emerged as potentially the strongest man in England. He was popular with the victorious troops, many of whom shared his own 'Independent' religious views, hostile to the Presbyterian beliefs of the majority in the Commons; a formidable personality in the eyes of Parliamentarians, Royalists, and the Scottish allies of Parliament; a man who had grown immensely in stature, invigorated by the evidence which victories had given of 'the Lord's blessing upon the godly party principally', as he put it after Marston Moor. His only military superior, Fairfax, had little interest in politics; Oliver had much, though to him politics meant above all the needs of those whom he saw as the people of God. Yet in the confused negotiations for a settlement — between King, Parliament, Army, and Scots — of 1646-7 he had no clear line, for he was seeking one. His own beliefs and loyalty to his men led him to oppose Parliament's proposals early in 1647 to impose a Presbyterian church settlement and to disband many of the troops without arrears of pay. Yet an instinctive conservatism, a hatred of indiscipline and a deep fear of anarchy made him distrustful of the Agitators in the army, who were pressing for strong action against the Commons and a democratic settlement. In June he backed Cornet Joyce's seizure of the King from the hands of Parliament into those of the army; in July he supported his son-in-law Ireton's 'Heads of the Proposals', probably the best offer of a settlement which Charles ever received. In the fortnight of the Army Debates at Putney (28 October-11 November) on the Leveller proposals contained in 'The Agreement of the People', Cromwell and Ireton emerged as the champions of property, fearful of giving votes to men 'that have no interest but the interest of breathing'. But on the great issue of the immediate present it was the King who forced Oliver to a decision, by signing in December the 'Engagement' with the Scots. This precipitated the Second Civil War (1648). At their prayer-meeting at Windsor in April the Army resolved 'if ever the Lord brought us back again in peace, to call Charles Stuart, that man of blood, to an account for that blood he had shed, and mischief he had done to his utmost, against the Lord's cause and people in these poor nations'. Cromwell won the most remarkable of his victories at Preston, where he placed his forces between the Scots and their base, and destroyed them in a running fight southwards. The war was over

by the end of the summer. In December it was determined to put
Charles on trial, and in January 1649 he was executed. Oliver's part
and motives in these proceedings have been much controverted. It
seems clear that he shared the bitterness of the soldiers about the
Second Civil War; that he was much influenced by the keener mind
of Ireton; and that he came slowly to the conclusion that Charles
was an impossible King and, as always, acted swiftly once his mind
was made up.

From 1649 to 1653 England was ruled by the Rump, what was
left of the Commons after the wars and Pride's Purge of the
Presbyterians in December 1648. From 1653 to his death in 1658
Oliver Cromwell was Lord Protector. In the first of these periods he
was the servant of the Rump: much the greatest figure in the land by
personality as well as by his command of the army (for Fairfax,
shocked by the treatment of the King, had retired into private life),
he did more than any man to establish the Republic on a basis of
military strength. Having brought the army to his will by crushing
the Levellers at Burford, in 1649–50 he subdued much of Ireland,
massacring at Drogheda and Wexford some four thousand of those
whom he regarded as 'barbarous wretches'. In September 1650 he
defeated a powerful Scottish army at Dunbar, and exactly a year
later he crushed at Worcester Prince Charles's attempt to recover the
Crown. But in 1653, after long and vain attempts to get the Rump to
dissolve itself and so open the way to new elections, he called in a
troop of musketeers and turned the members out, crying 'It is you
have forced me to do this, for I have sought the Lord night and day,
that he would rather slay me than put upon me the doing this work'.
Thus Cromwell the soldier became Cromwell the ruler, and for the
next five years his biography is the history of England.

His objectives in this time were three: to establish and exploit the
prestige of England, to protect and fulfil the hopes of the godly, and
to found his Republican government upon consent instead of force.
In the first he was highly successful in terms of prestige; as his enemy
Clarendon said, 'his greatness at home was but a shadow of the glory
he had abroad'. He brought the First Dutch War to a satisfactory end
in 1654; in a war of Elizabethan flavour he destroyed two Spanish
treasure fleets and captured Jamaica (1655); he formed an effective
alliance with Mazarin's France, halting the persecution of the
Vaudois Protestants and sending soldiers of the New Model to help

defeat the Spaniards at the Battle of the Dunes (1658); he made trade treaties with Sweden and Portugal and secured naval bases in the Mediterranean. These were the fruits of an aggressive policy founded upon commercial interests, and they marked a turning-point in the history of English foreign policy.

But at home Cromwell passed five years of frustration; his second and third objectives contradicted one another, for the godly were a minority. There was a Puritan church settlement, Presbyterianism without coercion; many of the sectaries worshipped freely. The use of the Anglican Prayer Book was forbidden and Catholics were persecuted, and there were some savage attacks upon Quakers; yet Oliver was personally tolerant, and often the law was slackly enforced. The motive for enforcement was basically political; Royalists and Anglicans had to be prevented from recovering power. Cromwell realized the limitations of army rule, but was unable to escape from them. Without the army the godly would have been overwhelmed. So Cromwell's rule brought a series of barren political experiments — the Nominated (or Barebone's) Parliament (1653), the Instrument of Government (1653), the Humble Petition and Advice (1657). The two Protectorate Parliaments (1654–5 and 1656–8) were dissolved because they challenged the rule of Cromwell and the Army; in the interval between them he fell back upon naked force, dividing the country into eleven areas under Major-Generals. In 1657 Oliver after prolonged hesitation declined the Crown which was offered him under the Humble Petition and Advice, believing that neither the Army nor the 'people of God' would approve this solution of the dilemma. When he died on September 3rd, 1658, the anniversary of Dunbar and Worcester, there was no solution in sight.

With him died the hopes of the English Republic, for he had become its essential pillar. This is perhaps the only certain judgment that can be passed upon Oliver Cromwell. In three centuries verdicts upon him have varied greatly, beginning with Clarendon's 'brave bad man'. Carlyle gave him the rank of hero. The Victorians saw him as the champion of Parliamentary and religious liberty, and his statue outside the House of Commons is the work of a Victorian sculptor. * The twentieth century has been more interested in him as

---

* Sir Hamo Thornycroft.

the dictator who dissolved parliaments and ruled by force, and as the defender of property who crushed the Levellers, the popular movement of his age. The religious language in which he clothed his thoughts and justified his actions is scarcely to modern taste; and psychologists have found him an interesting case-history, with his hesitancies, his illnesses, his interpretation of 'God's providences'. His career is full of paradoxes. Few men are consistent, least of all those who accept political responsibility in an age of revolution; Oliver offended Royalists and Republicans, landowners and Levellers, Catholics and Presbyterians, Quakers and Episcopalians, Scots and Irish. His legacy on a long view is necessarily a mixed one. He destroyed absolute monarchy in England; he enabled the nonconformist sects to take firm root; he gave Englishmen of all political views a lasting hatred of a standing army; he gravely worsened Anglo-Irish relations; he thwarted the cause of popular democracy; he left economic power in the hands of the greater landlords and the employers. No doubt he is the classical example in English history of the great opportunist; 'no one rises so high as he who knows not whither he is going', in his own words. Yet this is scarcely satisfactory as a final verdict, accurate though it is as commentary upon Oliver's career. Behind the doubts, the mistakes, the conflicting actions, the hardness, it is impossible not to see a man of an altogether unusual force, in will-power, in ultimate sincerity of purpose, and above all in readiness to accept responsibility; impossible, too, not to accept his own claim that he did what he did 'to the interest of the people of God and this Commonwealth'.

Charles Firth, *Oliver Cromwell*, 1900.

John Buchan, *Oliver Cromwell*, 1934.

R. S. Paul, *The Lord Protector: Religion and Politics in the life of Oliver Cromwell*, 1953.

Christopher Hill, *Oliver Cromwell, 1658–1958* (Historical Association Pamphlet, G.38), 1958.

Christopher Hill, *God's Englishman: Oliver Cromwell and the English Revolution*, 1970.

Ivan Roots, ed., *Cromwell: A Profile*, 1973.

HENRY IRETON (1611–51), was born at Attenborough in Nottinghamshire. His parents were Puritan gentry; two years earlier his mother had been presented to the Archdeacon's court for refusing to be churched according to the rites of the Church of England. All the evidence we have of Henry Ireton throughout his life underlines the descriptions of him by Lucy Hutchinson (his cousin's wife) as 'a grave, serious, religious person', and by Bulstrode Whitelocke as 'a Person very active, industrious and stiff in his ways and purposes'. He went to Trinity College, Oxford, in 1626 and to the Middle Temple in 1629. Ireton can have had no difficulty in deciding where his sympathies and duty lay as the Civil War drew near and in 1642 he led a troop of horse to join the Parliamentarians under Essex before Edgehill. He met Cromwell for the first time in the fighting in the East Midlands in 1643, and henceforward Ireton's fortunes were closely linked with the career of Oliver. In 1644, after fighting at Marston Moor, he was a prominent critic of the cautious general-ship of Manchester. He commanded the left wing at Naseby (1645), was present at the surrender of Bristol, accompanied Fairfax in the western campaign of 1645–6, and was one of the commissioners for the surrender of Oxford in June 1646, the month in which he married Cromwell's daughter Bridget, then aged twenty-two.

Ireton was a brave soldier, but he seems to have been a competent rather than a distinguished commander. At Naseby, where he 'fought like a lion', he was routed by Rupert's cavalry. His im-portance for the history of his time rests not upon his military achievements but upon his part in the political manoeuvres of the period between Naseby and the execution of the King. For Ireton, although scarcely an original thinker, had a very sharp intellect. He combined a taste for constitutional law with an eye for political reality in a manner rare among the officers of the New Model; he was an effective, though perhaps long-winded, debater, and had a real aptitude for what Whitelocke called 'the business of the Pen'. His influence on the slower and far less clear mind of Cromwell was considerable; whether it was as great or as sinister as contem-poraries, both Royalists and left-wingers like Wildman and Lil-burne, alleged, is hard to assess. Throughout 1647 Ireton played a prominent part, sometimes the leading role, in the complicated negotiations which the Army leaders were conducting simul-taneously with the King, with the Presbyterian majority in the

Commons, and with the 'Agitators' who represented the rank and file. His aim at this time, like that of his military superiors Cromwell and Fairfax, was to obtain a settlement which guaranteed peace and order, secured wide religious toleration, and gave reasonable terms of disbandment to the soldiers. In the summer of 1647 he was the principal architect of what must be regarded as the wisest settlement offered to Charles I, the Heads of the Proposals. These provided for biennial parliaments meeting for 120 days, a revision of county representation in proportion to taxation, Parliamentary control of the militia for ten years, a Council of State appointed for a maximum of seven years, and the exclusion of leading Royalists from office and from Parliament for five years; there was to be religious toleration for all except papists, neither the Book of Common Prayer nor the Covenant was to be compulsory, and the bishops were to lose their coercive powers. Such terms were quite unacceptable to Charles, yet he temporized, and in the autumn Ireton, Cromwell and Fairfax were in frequent negotiation with him at Hampton Court. Against this background, an effective setting for mistrust of the generals, the Agitators of the regiments put forward in *The Case of the Army duly Stated* and *The Agreement of the People* demands for more radical constitutional change, including complete Parliamentary sovereignty and suffrage for all free-born men over the age of twenty-one. These were discussed at length in the Putney Debates (October-November 1647); and here Ireton was the most outspoken and forceful champion of political and social conservatism. To the Leveller doctrine of equality of rights he replied that 'no person hath a right to an interest or share in the disposing of the affairs of the kingdom ... that hath not a permanent fixed interest in the kingdom'. 'All the main thing that I speak for is because I would have an eye to property.' Here was a clear statement of the limitations which the leaders of the English Revolution succeeded in imposing upon it.

In November 1647 Charles escaped from Hampton Court to Carisbrooke in the Isle of Wight; from this time Ireton and, more slowly, Cromwell lost what trust they still had in him. During the Second Civil War, Ireton — like the Army as a whole — showed a harshening of spirit towards the Royalists; this was evident at Colchester in his implacable condemnation of Sir Charles Lucas and Sir George Lisle to the firing-squad on the ground that they were traitors to Parliament and entitled to no quarter. In November 1648 he wrote *The Remonstrance of the Army*, a pamphlet bitterly attacking the King and demanding his trial. Ireton was responsible for the decisive intervention of the Army, culminating in Pride's Purge. His name followed those of Bradshaw, Fairfax and Cromwell at the head of the list of commissioners for the trial, and he was not one of those who withdrew.

In the early months of the Commonwealth, Ireton was busy on committees — although he failed to win election to the Council of State. Later in 1649 he was appointed as Cromwell's second-in-command in the Irish campaign, and when Oliver returned home in 1650 Ireton became Lord Deputy. Waterford surrendered to him in that year; Limerick, after a long siege, in 1651. A month later Ireton, weakened by incessant work, died of fever. He was given a state funeral in Westminster Abbey, whence his remains were dug up to be gibbeted at the Restoration. Stern, strict, honest, never sparing himself, Ireton scarcely deserved John Lilburne's description of him as 'the cunningest of Machiavalians'; keener yet far narrower in range of mind than Cromwell, he was the subordinate whom Oliver could least afford to lose.

R. W. Ramsey, *Henry Ireton*, 1949.
Maurice Ashley, *Cromwell's Generals*, 1954, pp. 65–82.
Howard Shaw, 'Henry Ireton', *History Today*, April 1970.

SIR WILLIAM WALLER (1597;–1668), Parliamentarian Commander, son of the Lieutenant of Dover and educated at Magdalen Hall, Oxford, fought as a professional soldier for the Venetian Republic and the Queen of Bohemia. He was knighted in 1622, but was later fined for brawling at court. When the Long Parliament met in 1640 Waller sat for Andover and soon became prominent in the opposition. As a Commander in the war he took Portsmouth and was successful enough at first to be nicknamed 'William the Conqueror', but his later career was somewhat chequered. In 1643 he was soundly defeated by Hopton at Roundway Down, and although in 1644 he kept the Royalists out of Sussex and recaptured Wiltshire and Hampshire by his victory at Cheriton, he was badly mauled by the King's army at Cropredy Bridge. In this winter of

1644–5 Waller, never a very effective disciplinarian, was one of the Parliamentarian Commanders most plagued by mutinies among his troops, and his military career ended with the Self-Denying Ordinance. Thereafter he was prominent as a Presbyterian leader in the Commons, becoming a bitter foe of the army Commanders, who drove him into exile in 1647. After his return the following year he suffered at least two spells of imprisonment, and in the later 1650s he got in touch with the Royalists. But he got no reward at the Restoration. Perhaps Waller, moderate, humane, typical of many responsible Englishmen on both sides in the Civil Wars, best deserves to be remembered for some phrases in a letter he wrote to Hopton, his former companion-in-arms in Germany and now commander of the opposing Royalist forces, on the eve of the battle of Lansdown (1643): 'The great God, which is the searcher of my heart, knows with what a perfect hatred I detest this war without an enemy'.

A. H. Burne and P. Young, *The Great Civil War*, 1959.

PHILIP SKIPPON (*d.* 1660), Parliamentarian Commander, was a soldier by profession. Clarendon sourly put it that 'the man had served very long in Holland and from a common soldier had raised himself to the degree of a captain, and to the reputation of a good officer'. In fact, he was the son of a Norfolk gentleman, and had served as a volunteer with Sir Horace Vere's force, first in Germany on behalf of the Elector Palatine and then for thirteen years with the Dutch against the Spaniards. This experience was put to good use, for Skippon's principal role in the Parliamentary army was as a trainer of troops. In 1642 he was put in charge of the trained bands of the City of London, and it was these men who turned back the King's army after Edgehill and bore the brunt of the fighting at the first battle of Newbury. Appointed Major-General of infantry in the New Model, Skippon contributed greatly to the training of the army which triumphed at Naseby (1645), where he was severely wounded. Yet the battle with which his name is most closely linked was the Parliamentary defeat at Lostwithiel (1644), where he commanded the rearguard in the desperate retreat through the Cornish lanes to Fowey. Deserted by his superior, Essex, Skippon was forced to surrender, although, characteristically, he wanted the army to cut its way out. A Parliamentary captain wrote of Skippon in this campaign 'never did I see any man so patient, so humble and so truly wise and valiant in all his actions as he'.

In the Second Civil War he was in command of London. Although he declined, like Fairfax, to have anything to do with the execution of the King, he served the Commonwealth loyally in various ways — as M.P. and one of the Cromwellian lords, as Councillor of State, as the Major-General in charge of London in the scheme of 1655; and he seems to have been one of the few soldiers who wanted Oliver to take the Crown. He supported Richard Cromwell, but after his fall Skippon for the last time was reappointed Commander of the London Militia. He died some months before the Restoration. 'Stout Skippon' or 'Honest Skippon', as he was known, was a deeply religious man of no great subtlety of mind, yet of practical ability and outstanding integrity. He wrote several books of devotions for the use of soldiers: one of them was *The Christian Centurion's Observations, Advices and Resolutions*. After he was taken prisoner at Lostwithiel, the King urged him to change sides. Skippon replied that 'he was fully resolved of those Principles to which he stood to be for God and His Glory in which by God's assistance he would live and die'. The words are a commentary on the career of a man who exemplified the best sort of Puritan soldier.

C. E. Lucas Phillips, *Cromwell's Captains*, 1938.

COLONEL THOMAS PRIDE (*d.* 1658), was a man of obscure origins, perhaps the son of a drayman or brewer, who fought well for Parliament at Naseby, Bristol, Preston, Dunbar and Worcester. He was one of the officers most hostile to the Commons in 1647, and on his record he was a very appropriate choice to carry out the 'Purge' of 1648 which has immortalized his name. He signed the King's death-warrant in 1649. Although he took little part in the politics of the Republic, he seems to have been the instigator of the officers' petition which finally determined Cromwell not to take the Crown in 1657. Pride was a firm exponent of Puritan social policy. He suppressed bear-baiting and wringing the necks of the cocks. It is of greater interest to the economic historian that in 1650 he was the head of the syndicate which took over the contract for victualling the Navy. The syndicate had its ups and downs, but Pride did well enough to buy the Palace of Nonesuch, and in 1656 he was given a knighthood to dignify his rise.

JAMES, 3rd MARQUIS AND 1st DUKE OF HAMILTON (1606–49), owner of great Scottish estates, was educated at Exeter College, Oxford, and succeeded Buckingham as Master of the Horse in 1628. After leading troops very incompetently to help Gustavus Adolphus, he returned to become Charles I's Commissioner to Scotland (1638), a position which would have stretched the powers of a man far better endowed with diplomatic ability and moral force than Hamilton. Lacking the shrewdness of Argyll and the nerve of Montrose, he fell back upon intrigue and earned the contempt of all parties. He was used by Charles as the instrument of a Scottish policy which alternated between mere negation and bogus concessions. As Commissioner he entirely failed to win over the Covenanters, whose assembly continued to sit in defiance of his orders, yet his negotiations with them sowed distrust of him in the Royalist ranks. In the Bishops' Wars he took the King's side, yet in 1641 he veered towards Argyll, an alliance temporarily strengthened by the 'Incident' of 1641. In 1642 he returned to England with the King and was in his retinue when he attempted to arrest the Five Members. Back in Scotland (1643), Hamilton failed to persuade the Scots against the Solemn League and Covenant, yet on his return to court at Oxford that December he was arrested, suspect now that Montrose's policy of arming the Highlands against the Covenanters had won the King's approval. Charles kept him in prison until the Parliamentarian army liberated him from St. Michael's Mount in 1646. Nevertheless, Hamilton remained loyal to Charles, and that summer at Newcastle tried to persuade him to accept Presbyterianism as the price of Scottish backing in his negotiations with the victorious Parliament. As the Army and the Independents gained ground in England in 1647, so moderate opinion in Scotland grew more sympathetic to Charles, a trend culminating in the Second Civil War of 1648. Hamilton was the main architect of this disastrous enterprise, and it was Hamilton, slow and unimaginative as a general as he was inept and vacillating as a politician, who led over 20,000 troops to the invasion of England and to defeat by

Cromwell in the running fight round Preston. Hamilton, taken prisoner, went to the scaffold for treason two months after his King. Shallow, maladroit, consistently unsuccessful, he was nevertheless as much the victim of Charles I as of his own weaknesses.

C. V. Wedgwood's two volumes, *The King's Peace*, 1955, and *The King's War*, 1958, contain information about Hamilton.

Hilary L. Rubinstein, *Captain Luckless: James, First Duke of Hamilton, 1606–1649*, 1975.

JAMES GRAHAM, 5th EARL AND 1st MARQUIS OF MONTROSE (1612–50), most remarkable of Royalist generals in the Civil War, was born at Montrose of one of the most honourable of Scottish noble families, heir to estates in Stirling, Perth and Angus. He was educated by a tutor in Glasgow, at St. Salvator's College, St. Andrews, and by a period (1633–6) of travel in France and Italy. An attractive young man, handsome, graceful, and with keen grey eyes, he was a fine horseman and archer; he was also emotional, serious-minded and proud, unusually capable of arousing both friendship and enmity. Clarendon, writing in later years after Montrose had become a Royalist hero, noted that 'he was too apt to contemn those he did not love' and that he 'did believe somewhat to be in himself which other men were not acquainted with, which made him live more easily towards those who were, or were willing to be inferior to him, than with his superior or equals'. Such a man of such rank was bound to play a controversial as well as a prominent role in the great crisis of Scottish history which began when Laud's new Book of Public Service was introduced in 1637.

Like many of the best of Charles I's supporters, Montrose was a Royalist who had gone some distance in opposition to the King. In 1638 he was one of the first to sign the National Covenant, for he was a Scotsman proud of his country and a ruling elder of a Kirk which he believed stood for spiritual freedom. No more than other Scotsmen did he see this action as incompatible with loyalty to the Crown. He fought (and won) his first battle at the Bridge of Dee in 1639 against fellow-Scots who opposed the Covenant and held the King's commission, and in 1640 he crossed the border as an officer in Leslie's invading army and took part in the battle of Newburn. But

James Graham, 5th Earl and 1st Marquis of Montrose
(Artist: after Gerard Honthorst)

he seems to have had doubts early, doubts created by the increasing despotism of the Kirk and the revolutionary actions of its Assembly, and certainly whetted by his growing rivalry with Archibald, Earl of Argyll, who in 1639–40 led the Scottish Parliament in defiance of royal authority. In 1640 he and several other nobles signed the secret Cumbernauld Bond to resist 'the particular and indirect practising of a few' — that is, of Argyll and his followers. Not surprisingly, others had doubts of Montrose's loyalty to the Covenant, for he was in direct touch with the King. He was arrested in 1641 and kept in prison for five months without trial. The outbreak of civil war in England in 1642 and the growth of the alliance between the English Parliament and the Kirk which led in 1643 to the Solemn League and Covenant decided the issue for him. Some time in 1640–1 he had written what has come to be known as his *Discourse of Sovereignty*, a long letter in which he defended the sovereignty of the King under law and condemned the encroachments of the Kirk and the nobility; and it seems likely that it was now (1642–3) that he composed his political lyric *I'll never love Thee more* with its strange opening lines:

> My dear and only Love, I pray
> That little world of thee
> Be govern'd by no other sway
> Than purest monarchy;
> For if confusion have a part,
> Which virtuous souls abor,
> And hold a Synod in thine heart,
> I'll never love thee more.

He joined the King in 1643. The conclusion of the Solemn League and Covenant that September and the southward march of Leven's Scottish army to aid Parliament early in 1644 lent point to his desperate demand that he should be commissioned to raise the King's friends in Scotland against the Covenanters, and in March he rode out of Oxford as the King's Lieutenant-General. It seemed a hopeless enterprise. In the words of John Buchan 'he was to fling himself into the midst of a hostile country to improvise an army'. The disaster of Marston Moor at the beginning of July made his prospects even more slender. With two companions Montrose slipped through the Covenant-dominated lowlands into his own countryside in August 1644. Within twelve months he had raised an army, won six battles, destroyed the Covenanting forces and entered Glasgow in triumph.

His army consisted initially of 1,100 Irish, landed in Western Scotland in July to aid the Royalist cause; to these were added Highlanders, more numerous as his successes increased. Both elements were unorthodox, brave, savage and ill-disciplined. At Tippermuir (August 1644) he defeated an army twice the size of his own, and thence entered Perth. His next victory was at Aberdeen

(September), after which he led a large pursuing force under Argyll a dance of some two hundred miles through the mountains. In the midwinter of 1644–5 his force, now including many MacDonalds, the traditional enemies of Clan Campbell, pillaged and plundered the Campbell countryside while Argyll sheltered in his castle at Inveraray, and killed 1,500 Campbells in battle at Inverlochy (February 1645). Moving eastwards, Montrose raided Dundee despite the presence of considerable enemy forces, and then in the summer smashed three armies in succession, at Auldearn (May), Alford (June), and, after he had crossed the Forth and thus challenged the heart of Covenanting power, Kilsyth (August). Glasgow opened its gates to him, and Edinburgh hastened to set free its Royalist prisoners. The way to the south seemed to be open, and Montrose set out for the border to win back England for the King.

It was an adventure too fantastic to continue. Charles had been decisively beaten at Naseby; Parliament had less need of Scottish soldiers now, and David Leslie was moving north with some 6,000 experienced men. Montrose for his part had got few recruits from the Lowlands, and his Highlanders deserted in scores with their loot. When he met Leslie at Philiphaugh, near Selkirk (September) he had only 600 men; he was taken by surprise, and the result was a massacre rather than a battle. Montrose became a fugitive. Although he managed to raise another force in the Highlands and conduct guerrilla war for some months, Charles's own surrender to the Scots in England brought him instructions to disband his forces, and in 1646 he sailed to the continent.

There he remained until the beginning of 1650, welcomed as a hero in Paris and Vienna. Mazarin offered him high rank in the army of France, the Emperor gave him a Marshal's baton. But he was committed to the Royalist cause and fortified in his belief by the execution of Charles I. He urged Charles II against a bargain with the Covenanters, and received his commission to raise Scotland in his name. In April 1650 he landed on the Scottish mainland with a handful of Danish troops and several hundred men from Orkney. Within three weeks his army was annihilated by the Covenanters at Carbisdale. He escaped but was betrayed into his enemies' hands. Betrayed also by Charles, who had signed an agreement with Argyll and the Covenanting government without effective provision for Montrose's life and security, he was executed at the Mercat Cross in

Edinburgh in May 1650, under the attainder and outlawry decree against him in 1644. His head was placed on a spike in the Tolbooth prison, and his limbs distributed for exhibition in Glasgow, Stirling, Perth and Aberdeen.

To later generations Montrose has appeared the most attractive of all the Cavaliers, the man, as Clarendon wrote, of 'clearest spirit and honour' among the royal advisers. Even more than most supporters of the Stuarts, he was ill-served by his Kings: Charles I failed to make effective use of his gifts, Charles II left him to the mercy of his enemies. Politically naive, utterly outmanoeuvred by the more subtle Argyll in the years 1637–41, he was essentially an aristocratic man of action. More gracious and more sensitive than his fellow-nobles, and capable — as most of them were not — of total self-sacrifice to a cause, he proved to be a fine soldier and superb leader of men. He fought in extraordinary conditions, with tiny forces of wild troops in primitive country, and although these conditions throw into sharp relief the brilliance of his strategical insight and the startling flexibility of his tactics, they make comparison with Rupert or Cromwell unprofitable. What would have happened had he crossed the border with a victorious army in 1645 is therefore the wildest speculation; yet it is worth noting that his highland supporters melted away inside Scotland itself even more rapidly than their kinsmen who followed Bonnie Prince Charlie exactly one hundred years later. It is also a fact that at no time did he win much support from Lowlanders, whose opposition cannot be explained simply in terms of Presbyterian narrowness or of the personal malevolence of Argyll. To them he was a man who had let loose Irish barbarians, killed some thousands of his fellow-countrymen, and sacked Aberdeen and Dundee — a notably unromantic figure for whose summary execution there was a strong case. Nevertheless, when every reservation is made, the tale of Montrose will always retain the quality of an epic.

John Buchan, *Montrose*, 1928.
C. V. Wedgwood, *Montrose*, 1952.
E. J. Cowan, *Montrose for Covenant and King*, 1977.

ARCHIBALD CAMPBELL, 8th EARL AND 1st MARQUIS OF ARGYLL (1598–1661), Covenanting statesman, was educated

Archibald Campbell, 8th Earl and 1st Marquis of Argyll
(*Artist: after David Scougall*)

at St. Andrews and inherited his title in 1638. A wary and bitter man, harsh in mind and unprepossessing in appearance (he was short and red-haired with a cast in his eye, 'the glaed-eyed marquis'), he spent his energies until 1638 in rescuing his estates from the chaos left by his father, a ruffianly character who had been converted to Catholicism and fled from his creditors to fight in the Spanish Army. Taking part in the Glasgow Assembly of that year, Argyll, hitherto cautious about signing the Covenant, emerged as the principal figure in the national movement of the Scots against Charles I's ecclesiastical policy. His character was as complex as his career was tortuous. The hereditary chieftain of the Campbells, the largest and wealthiest of the clans, he was yet no soldier. A man of subtle and profound intellect and evasive policies, he was driven on both by ambition and by the fanatical Presbyterianism which he embraced in his fortieth year. Resolution, guile, and seriousness of purpose won him support, but never trust or affection. Like his rivals Hamilton and Montrose, he perished on the scaffold, yet the core of his cause survived. No layman in Scottish history did more for the Kirk than 'the great marquis'.

Committed to the abolition of episcopacy after 1638, he was thenceforward at the heart of the opposition to Charles. After negotiating the Treaty of Berwick (1639) he made the Scottish Parliament an effective body through the reconstruction of the Lords of the Articles. His purposes, involving greater reliance upon the middle class of the Lowlands, clashed with those of the essentially aristocratic Montrose, who was turning back from the covenanting cause to that of the Crown. In 1641 Argyll got Montrose imprisoned, and during the King's visit to Edinburgh later in the year he stage-managed an obscure plot, the Incident, to turn Scottish opinion against Charles. Although the King departed in an atmosphere of reconciliation, conferring a marquisate upon Argyll, now supreme in Scotland, it was an empty settlement. When the Civil War broke out in 1642 King and Parliament alike sought Scottish assistance, and Scottish neutrality did not last long. Common peril to their religious views brought Scots and Parliament together in the Solemn League and Covenant of 1643, negotiated on the Scottish side by Argyll. It glossed over the differences in those views by providing for 'the reformation of religion . . . according to the Word of God, and the example of the best reformed churches'.

The Solemn League led to the invasion of England by a Scottish army and thus to the decisive Parliamentarian victory of Marston Moor. But events in Scotland itself during 1644–5 scarcely added to Argyll's power. Montrose's campaign laid waste the Campbell lands while the chief of the clan sheltered in his castle at Inveraray; and at Inverlochy he slew 1,500 Campbells in a battle whose end Argyll, fleeing down the loch in his galley, did not wait to see. The eventual defeat of Montrose at Philiphaugh in 1645 did not lessen the blow to Argyll's prestige and pocket. After Charles's surrender to the Scots in 1646 Argyll tried at Newcastle to persuade him to accept the Covenant. His policy at this time was statesmanlike, pressing for the continuance in peace of the alliance achieved between the two parliaments in war: as he put it in a notable speech in the Lords that June, 'let us hold fast that union which is happily established between us, and let nothing make us again two, who are so many ways one; all of one language, in one island, all under one King, one in Religion, yea, one in Covenant'. Yet it was a policy doomed to founder on the two rocks of the King's Anglicanism and the Independency of the English Army. During 1647 the Army revolted against the Presbyterian politicians at Westminster, so the Scots were the more tempted to turn to the King. The first result of this was the Engagement of December 1647 which produced the Second Civil War. In this Argyll had no part, and he supported Cromwell against Hamilton and the Engagers.

A grimmer choice lay ahead, as the Army moved on to avenge the blood of this second war. The execution of Charles I in January 1649 appalled Scotland. Neither Covenanters nor Royalists could remain in alliance with men who were at once sectaries and regicides, and whose victim had been King of Scotland. Within a week Charles II was proclaimed King at Edinburgh, and Argyll's policy, shorn of the realism which had hitherto guided it, now was to make the young man a covenanted King, fast bound to a rigid Presbyterianism. Montrose, who envisaged a different sort of monarchy and who landed in Scotland in April 1650, had first to be dealt with: he was executed in May. Charles eventually signed the Covenant in the ship which bore him to Scotland in June. But in July Cromwell's army crossed the border, and his victory at Dunbar in September shattered Argyll's authority by destroying the Covenanters' army. Argyll, for his part, remained loyal to Charles, and put the Crown on his head at Scone in January 1651, yet his hold on the King had gone. He opposed the campaign which led to Worcester, and retired to his Highland fastnesses. Before long he made his peace with the Cromwellian regime. He played no further part in politics. At the Restoration English Presbyterians received high offices as well as mercy; but in Scotland Charles II could more easily take his revenge, and Argyll was the obvious sacrifice on personal and public grounds.

He was tried for high treason at Edinburgh in 1661, and condemned to death on the evidence of private letters written during the Commonwealth which implied approval of the Republican regime — letters written to Monck, who supplied them to the court. Like Montrose, he showed high courage on the scaffold.

John Willcock, *The Great Marquess*, 1903.

JOHN LILBURNE (1615–57), the most spectacular champion of individual freedom in the English Revolution, was probably born in Sunderland, of a well-to-do family of the lesser gentry of north-eastern England. Educated at Bishop Auckland Grammar School and the Royal Grammar School, Newcastle-upon-Tyne, he was sent to London about 1630 as apprentice to a clothier, and quickly fell under its Puritan influences. In 1636 he was taken to see John Bastwick, in prison for his tracts against the Bishops. Lilburne plunged with enthusiasm into the enterprise of getting copies of Bastwick's scurrilous *Letany* printed in Holland and smuggled into England. He was betrayed, and in 1638 haled before the Star Chamber, to face the first of a series of trials and imprisonments. From the start he displayed that blend of acumen and impudence which drove his judges to despair, and that flair for publicity and sense of an audience which made him the hero of the age with thousands of Londoners. On this occasion 'Free-born John', as he was quickly nicknamed, declined to swear the *ex officio* oath, under which he might be compelled to condemn himself or others. He was sentenced to a fine of £500, to be whipped from the Fleet prison to Westminster and there pilloried, and to be kept in prison until he conformed to the law.

He remained in prison until the meeting of the Long Parliament, when he was released on a petition presented by Oliver Cromwell. Despite the appalling conditions of the Fleet, where he was shackled and in ill health, he employed his martyrdom in two related activities which were to form parts of the pattern of his entire career. He wrote several pamphlets, on his trial and in support of the Puritan cause, and he organized petitions for his release. In 1641–2 he took part in the demonstrations and riots with which Londoners welcomed the condemnation of Strafford and the widening breach

John Lilburne
(Artist: ?Thomas Simon)

between King and Parliament. For a short time he ran a brewery, and he got married; but when the fighting began in the summer of 1642 he went off to the wars, with a captain's commission in Lord Brooke's regiment of infantry. Nearly all the Lilburnes were for Parliament; his brother Colonel Robert Lilburne had a distinguished

military career, defeating the Royalists of Northumberland in the
Second Civil War and Derby's Cavalier force at Wigan in 1651, and
signed the King's death-warrant in 1649. John fought at Edgehill
and at Brentford, where he was taken prisoner and sent to Royalist
headquarters at Oxford; here he narrowly escaped trial for treason,
but was eventually exchanged. Joining the army of the Eastern
Association, he fought as a Lieutenant-Colonel of dragoons under
Manchester at Marston Moor, and received the surrender of Tickhill
Castle. But in 1645 he declined to take the Covenant, and left the
army.

This action marked the beginning of Lilburne's courageous yet
hectic and futile political career as the leading figure among those
who from 1647 came to be called the Levellers. Hostile to the
Presbyterians, a champion of freedom of conscience and of the press,
Lilburne was in no sense a man with a political programme, still less
a political organizer. He was by temperament an individualist and a
propagandist, believing passionately in freedom, to which he and the
Levellers gave a wider political content than the Parliamentarian
leaders. In 1645 he came into collision with the Presbyterian
majority in the Commons, and was imprisoned in Newgate for two
months. His fame spread — partly at least because of the way in
which he dealt with committees who examined him, reading Magna
Carta to them and to the Sergeant-at-Arms — and crowds followed
him everywhere. His activities brought him into contact with the
abler minds of other leading radicals, William Walwyn and Richard
Overton, and he widened the scope of his pamphleteering, publishing in October *England's Birthright Justified,* which denounced such
popular grievances as monopolies, tithes and the excise, and demanded toleration, freedom of speech, annual Parliaments and the
rule of law.

Here was an outline of the Leveller programme. But in 1646
Lilburne was in trouble with the House of Lords, initially over a
libel on the Earl of Manchester. Before them he refused to kneel, he
put his fingers in his ears, and he appealed to the Commons. The
Lords despatched him to the Tower, whence he continued to
produce pamphlets, this time demanding a reform of the government of the city. In February 1647 he managed to get a Commons
committee to examine him — with the doors open to the public. By
this date Leveller ideas were gaining ground, not only in London but

also among the common soldiers of the Army, alarmed about the
arrears of their pay and about the hostility of the Presbyterians in
Parliament to Independency in religion. Lilburne turned to the Army
for support. He had hopes of the officers, and in March he wrote a
remarkable letter to Cromwell, warning him against his Parliamentary advisers in a splendid phrase ('O Cromwell, thou art led by
the nose by two unworthy covetous earthworms, Vane and St.
John') and appealing to him to resist the 'tyranny' of Parliament.
More important, he was in touch with the Agitators appointed by
the regiments. In August 1647 the Army entered London. But
Lilburne was not released from the Tower, and he took no part in the
Putney Debates of October and November on *The Case of the Army*.
He remained in prison until August 1648, and after his release he
clashed over liberty of conscience with the leaders of the Army, now
triumphant in the Second Civil War.

Lilburne opposed the trial and execution of the King. He had been
in contact with Royalist fellow-prisoners in the Tower; and he
realized that the destruction of the King did not solve his own
problems or those of the common soldiers. The way was now open
to the new and more powerful tyranny of the Army Commanders.
Characteristically, he soon appeared before the Rump with an
outspoken petition entitled *England's New Chains*. Scarcely surprisingly, the government struck back. The three chief Levellers,
Lilburne, Overton and Walwyn, were arrested in March, and when
the Leveller-mutineers were crushed at Burford in May a special
force of troops was sent to make sure Lilburne did not escape from
the Tower. There was widespread unrest this year, with rumours of
an alliance between the Levellers and the Royalists, and not until
August, after he had bitterly denounced Cromwell and the Army
leaders in *An Impeachment of High Treason*, was Lilburne put on
trial for high treason. It was an extraordinary trial, with the judges
and prisoner shouting at one another, Lilburne using every tech-
nicality and delay (at one point he sent for a chamber pot and used
it), the Guildhall packed with his supporters. The jury of Londoners
acquitted him, with immense popular rejoicing.

But it was a hollow triumph — a personal victory for Lilburne,
not for the cause for which he stood. The Leveller movement was
dead, and the remainder of Lilburne's career has the air of anti-
climax and disillusion. He started business as a soap-boiler; he got

(through Cromwell) a grant of lands in Durham; and he acted as a pleader in the law-courts for other men's cases. One of these brought disaster, for he published a pamphlet in a case against Sir Arthur Hasilrige, a leading Parliamentarian and an old enemy of the Lilburne family; the Rump took exception and banished him, in December 1651. He went in 1652 to Amsterdam and then to Bruges; hobnobbed with Royalists, notably the Duke of Buckingham; and inevitably wrote a pamphlet, *Lieutenant-Colonel John Lilburne Revived*, against the Army and Cromwell. When the Rump was turned out in 1653, he returned without official authority and was arrested. Put on trial again for breaking his banishment, he once more attracted immense popular support, and was again acquitted by the jury. But this time the government, alarmed by the popular enthusiasm, did not release him. Instead they sent him in 1654 to the remote fortress of Mount Orgueil in Jersey, where his old adversary Prynne had once been incarcerated, and there, deprived of crowds of fellow-prisoners and visitors, far away from any means of popular appeal, his spirit began to change. In October 1655 he was brought back to Dover Castle, and was converted to Quakerism, becoming dead, as he put it in a last pamphlet, *The Resurrection of John Lilburne* (1656), to 'carnal sword fightings and fleshy buslings and contests'. He was allowed free on parole a good deal; but he was now worn out by the strains and sufferings of his career, and in 1657 he died at Eltham.

Lilburne, who was the father of ten children and who lost an eye in an accident in 1645, was a remarkable man — tough, sincere, a gifted pamphleteer, a natural lawyer, a man with a vision of the needs of others. Yet he achieved nothing and he founded no lasting movement. This was partly no doubt because the Leveller movement rested on too narrow a social basis: it offered nothing to the great mass of the poor, it frightened the property-owning class, it depended too much on London craftsmen and small freeholders in economic difficulty. And the Levellers were outmanoeuvred as well as overpowered by Cromwell, Ireton and the other Army leaders. Yet the causes of Lilburne's failure lay in great part in himself. He was an individualist, with the power to defy but not to construct; far more a showman than a statesman, he performed heroically and brilliantly, yet always on issues of other men's choosing. Turbulent and impetuous, a classical case of the man who is always against the government, he roused opinion without organizing it, and his legacy is only the memory of a hero.

Pauline Gregg, *Free-Born John*, 1961.

WILLIAM WALWYN (1600–1680), was born at Newland in the Malverns, second son of a prosperous landowner and a bishop's daughter, and like Lilburne was bound apprentice in London, to a silk-dealer in Paternoster Row. He became a successful cloth-merchant, a member of the Merchant Adventurers, comfortably off, with a family even more numerous than that enjoyed by a radical tailor two centuries later, Francis Place: Walwyn is said to have had twenty children. He was widely read, unconventionally so for a man of his class, with Seneca, Lucian, Plutarch and Montaigne among his favourites. It is scarcely surprising that his religious opinions were somewhat heterodox, and he was an independent of an extreme kind, profoundly antinomian in his outlook. Walwyn's precise contribution to the Leveller movement is impossible to assess. Undoubtedly a wire-puller and perhaps an *éminence grise,* he had a clearer mind and one of finer texture than Lilburne, yet lacked the latter's zest for publicity. He was most celebrated as a pamphleteer, his first piece appearing in 1641, and it is perhaps significant that until 1646 he was mainly concerned to champion religious liberty, in such tracts as *The Power of Love* of 1643 and in his celebrated controversy with Thomas Edwards, the author of *Gangraena.* But after his meeting with Lilburne in 1646 he became more involved in secular politics, and Joseph Frank has seen him as the 'guiding hand in the organization of radical propaganda and . . . chief midwife at the birth of the Leveller party'. Certainly he was important in the Leveller pressure at the time of the Putney Debates, and in 1648 he wrote *The Bloody Project*, advocating a popular front against Presbyterians and Royalists. The Republican government in its attack on the Levellers in 1649 arrested him along with Lilburne and Overton and sent him to the Tower. Thereafter little is heard of him, apart from a pamphlet defending trial by jury in 1651. It seems likely that he made his peace with the Commonwealth and turned his energies back into trade, for he appears to have been well-established and respected at the time of his death in 1680.

Joseph Frank, *The Levellers*, 1955.

W. Schenck, *The Concern for Social Justice in the Puritan Revolution*, 1948.

A.L. Morton, *The World of the Ranks*, 1970.

RICHARD OVERTON (*fl.* 1645–63), Leveller, emerged in the 1640s from a very obscure background. He had lived in Holland, he was a Baptist of unorthodox views, and he was an unlicensed printer. By 1645 he was a notorious pamphleteer, Martin Mar-Priest, who enjoyed slinging mud at Prynne and the Presbyterians as well as at Anglicans, and the first of whose tracts, *The Arraignment of Mr. Persecution*, was a wide-ranging defence of toleration which demonstrated the cruelties of Protestants as well as of Papists. He had also written a piece called *Man's Mortalitie* which revealed a scepticism and materialism rare, or rarely expressed, in the seventeenth century; he held the Mortalist theology, that man's soul died with his body. With the arrest of Lilburne in 1646 Overton turned to politics, and for the three short years of the Leveller movement's existence he was one of its leading figures, probably its most vigorous exponent of Republicanism. His most characteristic pieces were *A Remonstrance of Many Thousand Citizens* (1646), perhaps the bext expression of the Leveller creed, and *The Hunting of the Foxes ... By Five Small Beagles* (1649), an ironical attack on the army leaders. Arrested with Lilburne and Walwyn in 1649, Overton took the engagement to the Commonwealth. He defended Lilburne in 1653, but thenceforward turned to shadier courses, offering in 1654 to become a Commonwealth spy and joining Sexby in Royalist conspiracy in 1655. Twice more he turns up, in 1659 and 1663, each time in gaol. After that no more is heard of him.

H. N. Brailsford, *The Levellers and the English Revolution*, 1961.
Joseph Frank, *The Levellers*, 1955.

THOMAS RAINSBOROUGH OR RAINBOROW (*d.* 1648), Parliamentarian soldier, the son of a naval Commander, was brought up as a sailor. The family had connections with Puritan New England and his two sisters married Winthrops from Massachusetts. After a short spell at sea in 1643 as Vice-Admiral, Rainsborough was commissioned as a Colonel and spent the remainder of the Civil Wars

serving Parliament on land. He raised a regiment under the Earl of
Manchester, officered it mainly with returned emigrants from New
England, and won a reputation by capturing Crowland Abbey.
Appointed to command a regiment in the New Model, he fought at
Naseby, Bridgwater and Bristol in 1645 and captured Woodstock in
1646. A tall man of powerful build and impulsive daring, skilled in
siege operations, he was noted for the stern discipline he imposed
on his own men and the ferocity he displayed towards the enemy;
after taking Prior's Hill Fort at Bristol, he 'immediately put to
the sword almost all in it', as Cromwell said in his report to the
Commons.

But Rainsborough's interest for the historian lies not so much in
his exploits in battle as in his part in the Putney Debates of 1647.
The leading Republican among the officers and the one field officer
with views sympathetic to those of the Levellers, he opposed
reconciliation with the King and demanded a new constitution
based apparently upon a suffrage without property qualification. He
had a flair for the cogent statement of his beliefs. The claim for
political equality has rarely been put more straightly than in his
statements, 'For really I think that the poorest he that is in England
hath a life to live, as the greatest he; and therefore, truly, Sir, I think
it's clear that every man that is to live under a government ought first
by his own consent to put himself under that government'; and 'I do
not find anything in the law of God that a lord shall choose twenty
burgesses and a gentleman but two, or a poor man shall choose
none'. Rainsborough was a hot-tempered man, and at one point in
the debates stormed at Cromwell, shouting 'one of us must not live'
and threatening to impeach him. After a reconciliation with Cromwell, Rainsborough was ordered to take up command at sea, but the
fleet mutinied, refused to have him on board, and declared for the
King (1648). So he fought on land again in the Second Civil War,
taking part in the capture of Colchester, where he was responsible
for the execution of Sir Charles Lucas and Sir George Lisle. He was
killed in the same year at the siege of Pontefract, murdered by two
Royalists who found him unarmed in his room. His funeral at the
Independent Chapel in Wapping provided a great demonstration for
the Leveller movement. 'Rainsborough, the just, the valiant, and the
true', as his epitaph called him, long remained a hero to the younger
radicals.

Hugh Ross Williamson, *Four Stuart Portraits*, 1949.

JOHN WILDMAN (1623–93), plotter, of whose origins we are
ignorant, was educated at Cambridge and studied law in London.
After 1655 he was usually known as 'Major Wildman', but his only
recorded military activity took place in 1659, when with two other
officers and three hundred volunteers he persuaded the Governor of
Windsor Castle to surrender it. His first appearance is as a Leveller in
the Putney Debates of 1647, when he helped to draft *The Case of the
Army Truly Stated* and *The Agreement of the People* and, although a
civilian, acted as a 'mouth' of the common soldiers in the discussions
with the officers. In 1648 the Commons, as alarmed as the Army
grandees by the Levellers, arrested Wildman and his friend Lilburne,
and he spent six months in prison in the Fleet. In 1649 Wildman
seems to have accepted the Republic and he gave most of his energies
from 1650 to 1655 to a highly successful series of speculations, on
his own behalf or as a commission agent, in the land market which
resulted from the sales of Royalist properties, emerging with a good
deal of property and a comfortable fortune. But when he was elected
for Scarborough in the first Protectorate Parliament (1654) and then
excluded by the government, he turned to a course of plotting which,
with intervals of imprisonment, lasted virtually for the remainder of
his life. Involved in 1654 in the plot of the three colonels and in the
scheme which led to the arrest of General Overton in Scotland, he
devised a Republican plot of his own to raise an insurrection against
the Protector in 1655, but was arrested while he was dictating a
declaration of rebellion. Cromwell treated him extremely leniently;
he was imprisoned for rather over a year and then released, very
possibly in return for agreeing to act as a spy upon the Royalists,
with whom he was by now in touch. He bought himself the
considerable estate of Becket in Berkshire and the Nonsuch Tavern in
Covent Garden, and then plunged for the next three years into a
weird tangle of conspiracies with Republicans, discontented clergymen, the Spanish rulers of the Netherlands and the exiled court of
Charles II. The main aim of these proceedings was the assassination
of Cromwell, and they came nearest to success in the 'Powder Plot'
of 1657, when a box of gunpowder was smuggled into Whitehall
Palace, at which point one of the gang betrayed the scheme. A
succession of petty plots led to the arrest of a crop of Royalists by the

Protectorate intelligence service, and sharply diminished the confidence of Hyde and the wiser Royalist chiefs in Wildman — who remained at large.

In 1659, after the fall of Richard Cromwell, Wildman was for a short time on the side of the government. A disciple of Harrington, he supported the petitions for a balanced republican scheme of government, acted as chairman of a 'Commonwealth' discussion club, and was one of a committee asked by Fleetwood to draft a new constitution. Even when the Restoration blew these gossamer projects away, Wildman contrived to remain near the centre of power, for he was for nearly a year and a half a principal figure in the government Post Office. It looks as though he set out to make it a nest of Republican intrigue; after various allegations against him, he was arrested— with Harrington and Praise-God Barebone among others — on a charge of being involved in a great conspiracy. Investigation did not produce the evidence to condemn him: Wildman was habitually cautious in speech. But in 1662 he was sent to the Scillies, beyond the reach of *habeas corpus*, and he did not leave prison until 1667. For the next twelve years, apart from a period abroad between 1670 and 1675, Wildman attached himself to Buckingham, for whom he acted as solicitor and trustee. In December 1667 Pepys recorded that someone told him that 'Wildman, the Fifth-Monarchy man, a great creature of the Duke of Buckingham's' had been nominated as one of a commission set up to examine the public accounts after the disasters of the Second Dutch War; but the Commons would not accept so notorious a character who was only two months out of gaol. Wildman was certainly not a Fifth Monarchist; his religious attitude was that of a sceptic. He supported Shaftesbury and sat for Great Bedwin in the Oxford Parliament of 1681, and during the next two years he was deeply — though as usual obscurely — involved in the events which brought the Whigs to ruin. He drafted manifestos and bought arms; it also appears that the idea of murdering the King, later worked up by the informers into the 'Rye House Plot', was originally Wildman's, though he later dropped it. Once more he was arrested (1683) and sent to the Tower. Although two small cannon were found in his cellar, there was again insufficient evidence, and he was set free.

When James II became King, Wildman was one of the small group of conspirators who prepared the way for Monmouth in

England. Yet he did so reluctantly, for he thought little of Monmouth's character, and tried to stop him coming. When the revolt failed, Wildman fled overseas, first to Germany and then to Holland. He arrived at the Hague in 1688 in time to take part in propaganda for William's invasion, writing one influential pamphlet, the *Memorial of English Protestants*. He sailed with William to England, was a prominent member of the Convention Parliament, and was appointed Postmaster-General, holding the post until he was dismissed in 1691. By this time he had got involved in a Presbyterian plot against William's authority in Scotland. Yet he may have lost his office merely because the postal service did not function very efficiently in these years — for in 1692 William III knighted him, six months before he died. He reached the age of seventy, a remarkable achievement for so habitual and so unsuccessful a plotter.

Maurice Ashley, *John Wildman*, 1947.

EDWARD SEXBY (*d.* 1658), a Suffolk man, fought in the Civil War in Cromwell's regiment of horse, and was one of the first of the Army's 'Agitators', appearing before the Commons in 1647 and opening the case for the rank and file in the Putney Debates later that year. Commissioned and appointed Governor of Portland in 1649, he commanded a regiment of foot in Scotland in 1650. A Lieutenant-Colonel in 1651, he was cashiered in that year for using too much pressure to make soldiers re-enlist. Nevertheless, from 1651–3 he was sent on a mission to Bordeaux to make trouble for the French government, then involved in the Fronde; he was in close touch with L'Ormée, the republican group in the city, and had *The Agreement of the People* translated into French for his purposes. But after his return he became a violent opponent of the Protectorate, with a variety of plans for uniting Levellers and Royalists against Cromwell. Involved in Wildman's plot of 1655, he was arrested but allowed to escape. He went to Amsterdam and employed his ready tongue and considerable self-confidence to win support from Royalist exiles for his schemes, and when their leaders began to see through his lies he turned to negotiations with the authorities in the Spanish Netherlands. In 1656 he and Wildman devised a plot in which a group of ex-soldiers headed by Miles Sindercombe were to assassinate Cromwell; this was eventually betrayed early in 1657 after gunpowder had been smuggled into Whitehall Palace, and Sindercombe poisoned himself in prison. At this time Sexby wrote with the help of the Royalist Captain Titus a notorious pamphlet in justification of assassination, *Killing No Murder*, which he dedicated ironically to Cromwell. Later in 1657 he came to England, and was arrested and sent to the Tower, where he died in 1658.

JOHN BRADSHAW (1602–59), President of the court which condemned Charles I to death, was born at Stockport and educated at the grammar school there. 'He was', as Clarendon puts it, 'a gentleman of an ancient family in Cheshire and Lancashire, but of a fortune of his own making'. Called to the bar at Gray's Inn in 1627, he prospered as a provincial barrister in Cheshire, whence he moved to London and became prominent as a prosecutor on behalf of Parliament in the Civil War years. Appointed Chief Justice of Chester in 1647, he was a competent and reasonable choice, if not a notably distinguished one, for membership of the commission set up by the Rump to try the King; and he seems to have become its president by a device not unknown to democratic bodies with smaller responsibilities, for he was elected to the post in his absence. Clarendon, a highly-prejudiced witness, says he carried out his duties 'with all the pride, impudence, and superciliousness imaginable'; he wore a steel-lined hat during the trial. Nevertheless, it is clear that he believed in the legality and in the justice of what he was doing, and when the Rump was turned out in 1653 Bradshaw is alleged to have observed, 'If this be no Parliament, then am I the King's murderer?' He was responsible for the trials of other Royalists, and in 1649 was appointed President of the Council of State of the Commonwealth, a post in which he was notorious for the length of his speeches. Bradshaw was a sincere Republican, and in 1653 he was a firm opponent of Cromwell's seizure of power, challenging him with the phrase 'Sir, we have heard what you did at the House in the morning, and before many hours all England will hear it. But, sir, you are mistaken to think that the Parliament is dissolved, for no power under heaven can dissolve them but themselves. Therefore take you notice of that.' Elected M.P. for Stafford in 1654, he declined to subscribe to the 'recognition of the government' which Cromwell imposed on all members. He retired from political life until Oliver's death, returned with the Rump in 1659, and served on the Council of State. After the Army expelled the Rump a second time he continued to attend the Council, though wasted by illness and very close to death, in protest against the violence to his beloved Commonwealth. He was buried in Westminster Abbey, and his corpse was dug up, gibbeted, and exposed after the Restoration.

C. V. Wedgwood, *The Trial of Charles I*, 1964.

JOHN LAMBERT (1619–84), ablest of Cromwell's military subordinates, was a Yorkshireman from Calton in Craven. His wife was a Lister, connected with the Fairfaxes, and Lambert joined the Parliamentarian army and became a captain in Fairfax's cavalry. His remarkably swift rise to distinction reflected his military brilliance. He fought at Marston Moor, had a regiment in the New Model, and was a Major-General at twenty-eight; he displayed high strategic insight in the early stages of the Preston campaign of 1648; he commanded the left with great courage and resilience at Dunbar (1650); in the summer of 1651 he won a crushing victory over the Scots at Inverkeithing, and pursued Hamilton's army southwards and played a vital part in the victory at Worcester. Among the Parliamentarian commanders only Fairfax and Cromwell were more gifted soldiers. Popular with his own rank and file, Lambert seems to have been less disliked by the Royalists than most of the Parliamentarian leaders. Perhaps this was because he was not very obviously a Puritan. His religious views remain unknown, he was a realist in outlook and often a cynic in speech, he spent a good deal of money on tulips, and he lived in style with his beautiful wife in Wimbledon House. He was ambitious as well as able, and he had a gift for intrigue; his portrait suggests impatience and a hint of arrogance. Many of his contemporaries did not trust him, and Oliver is alleged to have called him 'Bottomless Lambert'.

His first considerable intervention in politics came in 1647, when he helped Ireton draw up the Heads of the Proposals. By accident or design he was out of London at the time of Charles's trial — though it seems likely that he would have followed Fairfax rather than Cromwell on this question. He took the lead among the officers when in 1652 they urged reform upon the Rump, yet he had no sympathy with the radicals like Harrison. It was Lambert, essentially a conservative in outlook, who in 1653 engineered the dissolution of Barebone's Parliament and produced the first draft of the Instrument of Government, and he has thus strong claim to be the creator of the Protectorate. He served on its Council of State, he was its military Commander in the north, he seems to have been behind the scheme of 'Major Generals' created in 1655, he was until 1657 clearly its second most eminent citizen. But he opposed the proposals to make Cromwell king and the Protectorate hereditary, and this action — which it is difficult not to attribute to ambition — led to a breach and to his dismissal (on a pension of £2,000 per annum). It was, in a way, the turning-point in his career.

He accepted his enforced retirement for a time, but in Richard Cromwell's Parliament he sided openly with the Republican opponents of the Protectorate, and on Richard's overthrow regained his old commands. The Rump, recalled in May 1659, sent him to crush Sir George Booth's Royalist rising in Cheshire (August). After a quarrel between Parliament and officers over the rights and command of the Army, Lambert followed Cromwell's example and expelled the Rump (October). This action brought protests from Monck in Scotland, who crossed the border (New Year's Day 1660) to restore the authority of the civil power. Lambert's army, which had moved north to meet him, melted away as his soldiers deserted, and even his old patron Fairfax brought out the gentry of Yorkshire against him. He was captured and imprisoned in the Tower. He escaped and tried to rally the army in a last stand against the Restoration, but was recaptured, and he was one of those exempted from the Act of Indemnity of 1660. Tried in 1662, he was condemned to death but reprieved and sentenced to life imprisonment, which he spent in Guernsey up to 1670 and on St. Nicholas Island (Drake's Island) in Plymouth Sound until his death in 1684. He lived long enough to find a place in the fictitious plots of Titus Oates.

W. H. Dawson, *Cromwell's Understudy*, 1938.
M. Ashley, *Cromwell's Generals*, 1954, esp. Chapter 6.
C. E. Lucas Phillips, *Cromwell's Captains,* 1938.

EDMUND LUDLOW (1617?–92), regicide and Republican, was a Wiltshire man from Maiden Bradley, educated at Trinity

College, Oxford, and the Inner Temple. He became a member of Essex's life-guard, and fought with some distinction in the Civil War, reaching the rank of colonel. His father had been M.P. for Wiltshire and an extreme Parliamentarian; Ludlow succeeded to his seat in 1646 and outdid him in extremism. He supported the Independents, he warmly approved of Pride's Purge, and he seems to have had doubts about Cromwell at an early stage. In 1649 he signed the King's death-warrant and he became a member of the Commonwealth Council of State. For four years from 1641 he was in Ireland, serving as Lieutenant-General, and it was Ludlow who in effect completed the Cromwellian conquest. In his absence Oliver dismissed the Rump and set up the Protectorate. Ludlow's hostility was so plainly stated that he was arrested when he landed in England. He was wholly unwilling to accept the new regime. When Cromwell demanded of him 'What is it that you would have?' he answered 'That which we fought for, that the nation might be governed by its own consent'. In 1659 he helped to remove Richard Cromwell and was made a member of the Council of State. Almost alone he recognized the need for Army and Parliament to co-operate if the Republic was to survive. In 1660 he was elected to the Convention, and actually took his seat; but when it was evident that his fate would be execution, he managed to get away and take ship to France. By 1662 he had taken refuge in Vevay in Switzerland, and there he remained for a generation, writing his memoirs. The Royalists plotted against his life and managed to murder one of his fellow-refugees, John Lisle. The Revolution of 1688 stirred the old man, and he returned to England in 1689. At the instigation of Sir Edward Seymour a proclamation was issued for his arrest, and he once again escaped, making his way back to Vevay, where he died in 1692. He was a thorough-going and stubborn Republican, and his *Memoirs* are most valuable for the light they throw on the collapse of the English Republic after the death of Cromwell.

Memoirs of Edmund Ludlow, C.H. Firth, ed., 1894.
A. Worden, ed., *A Voice from the Watch Tower*, 1978.

CHARLES FLEETWOOD (1618–92), Cromwellian general, was a Northamptonshire man, educated at Emmanuel College, Cambridge, and Gray's Inn, who joined Essex's bodyguard in 1642.

He fought as a captain at the first battle of Newbury (1643), where he was wounded; commanded a regiment at Naseby; and was Lieutenant-General of Horse at Dunbar and second-in-command at Worcester. Not particularly successful on the battlefield, he was a capable military administrator to whose organization of the forces in England between Dunbar and Worcester Cromwell owed much. In 1652 he married as his second wife Cromwell's daughter Bridget, the widow of Henry Ireton.

Fleetwood proved unequal to the political responsibilities and choices which his military career and his place in Oliver's circle brought upon him. Clarendon's verdict was contemptuous: 'the character which we have always received of the man is not such as makes him equal to any notable design, or to be much relied on to-morrow for what in truth he resolved to do yesterday; however as his wit is not so great as some of the rest, so his wickedness is much less apparent than theirs'. Pious but vain and over-anxious to stand well in men's eyes, he was warned by his father-in-law against his 'natural inclination to compliance'. His irresolution found unhappy outlet in a tendency to weep in public at times of stress. He became a member of the Council of State in 1651, and in 1654 Commander-in-Chief and Lord Deputy in Ireland, where he stayed only a year, being recalled because of his sympathy towards the Anabaptists, and after an unfavourable report from his subordinate and brother-in-law Henry Cromwell. In 1655 he was Major-General in charge of the eastern counties and in 1657 a member of the new Cromwellian House of Lords, a dignity supported by his ownership at this time of the Manor of Woodstock. When Oliver decided to dismiss his last Parliament (1658) Fleetwood tried to dissuade him, only to be brushed aside with the phrase 'You are a milksop'. Throughout the crisis of his career after Oliver's death he was a potential rather than a real leader. Instrumental in removing Richard, he was appointed Commander-in-Chief in 1659; but, when the Army again 'interrupted' the Rump that October, he found himself more and more out of his depth, and at Christmas he threw his hand in, bewailing that 'God had spit in his face'. The Restoration sent him into obscurity. Fleetwood had not been a regicide, and his punishment was merely lifelong disqualification from office — which may not have been entirely unwelcome. He lived on in Stoke Newington, a follower of the eminent dissenter Dr. John Owen, until his death in 1692.

M. Ashley, *Cromwell's Generals*, 1954, esp. Chapter 11.

THOMAS HARRISON (1606–60), Cromwellian general, was the son of a prosperous butcher of Newcastle-under-Lyme. Like other students at the Inns of Court, he joined Essex's bodyguard in 1642 and fought through the Civil Wars with gallantry and distinction. A major in Fleetwood's Horse at Marston Moor, he was an officer in the New Model at Naseby, Langport and Basing House. During the Preston campaign of 1648 he commanded a regiment under Lambert and he was badly wounded at Appleby; a Major-General by 1650, he was in charge of the forces in England during Cromwell's Dunbar campaign, and in 1651 he led the pursuit of the fleeing Scots after Worcester. Harrison was prominent among those soldiers who demanded retribution upon Charles I, and even before the Second Civil War he wished to put an end to negotiations with the King. It was Harrison who guarded Charles on his last journey to London. He was a member of the court which tried him, and he signed the death sentence.

He was appointed to the Council of State in 1651. In 1653 he was Oliver's right-hand man in the expulsion of the Rump, calling in the musketeers and pulling Speaker Lenthall from his chair, and he was a leading member of the radical group of Barebone's Parliament, demanding the abolition of state control of religion. But from this point he parted company with Oliver. For Harrison was essentially a dreamer and an enthusiast: a Fifth Monarchist, he believed that the vision of Daniel was about to be fulfilled, when the saints of the Most High would possess the kingdom for ever and ever. The Protectorate of Oliver, set up under the Instrument of Government (1653), was a betrayal of the vision. Harrison lost his commission, declined to serve the Protectorate, and was twice imprisoned in Oliver's later years. He was scarcely likely, on his record, to find favour with the Rump, who disqualified him from state employment, and still less with the Stuarts. Unlike some of the surviving regicides, Harrison made no attempt to escape overseas at the Restoration. As he said at his trial in 1660, the execution of Charles I 'was not a thing done in a corner'. To him it was a sign of 'that presence of God, that was with his servants in those days'. He was hanged, drawn and quartered, dying with courage. His last words were, 'By God I have leapt over a wall, by God I have run through a troop, and by God I will go through this death, and he will make it easy to me'.

C.H. Firth, *Thomas Harrison*, 1893.
M. Ashley, *Cromwell's Generals*, 1954 esp. Chapter 5.

HENRY CROMWELL (1628–74), Oliver's fourth son, took happily and successfully to a military career, fighting under his father in Ireland in 1650 and being appointed Commander-in-Chief there in 1654. Fleetwood, the Lord Deputy went home in 1655 and henceforward Henry Cromwell was the effective ruler of Ireland, although he did not receive the title of Lord Deputy until 1657. He continued the policy of Protestant and English domination, based upon stern oppression of the Catholic majority, tempered by slightly increased consideration for the interests of the pre-Cromwellian settlers. He took little part in English affairs, was loyal to his brother Richard, and was recalled in 1659 after the latter's fall. Like Richard, he rejected proposals from the Stuarts. Ormonde and others spoke in his favour at the Restoration, and he was allowed to retire in peace to his lands in Cambridgeshire, where he lived in obscurity until he died in 1674.

R. W. Ramsey, *Henry Cromwell*, 1933.
T. C. Barnard, 'Planters and Policies in Cromwellian Ireland', *Past and Present*, November 1973.

JOHN DESBOROUGH or DISBROWE (1608–80), Cromwellian Major-General, was a Cambridgeshire landowner, trained as an attorney, who married Oliver's sister Jane in 1636 and whom Oliver appointed Quarter-Master to his troop of Horse in 1642. He was prominent in the wars, commanding cavalry at the storming of Bristol and leading the charge at Langport (1645), a Major-General at Worcester (1651). During Oliver's lifetime he served the Commonwealth loyally in various capacities — as General of the Fleet (1653), though he did not go to sea, as M.P. in the Parliaments of 1654 and 1656, as Member of the Council of State of the Protectorate. He played a leading part in the crushing of Penruddock's rising in 1655, and in the same year was one of the eleven Major-Generals set to establish order and Puritan morality: his area was the west country and he seems to have been just and even liberal in his dealings with Quakers. On the other hand he mismanaged the supplies for the disastrous expedition of Penn and Venables to Hispaniola (1655), and Venables accused him of corrupt dealings with the victuallers. A blunt, not particularly subtle man (the Royalists poked fun at him as a 'rustic'), Desborough was a firm Republican who spoke strongly and influentially against the proposal to crown his brother-in-law, threatening to quit his posts. In 1659 he was with Fleetwood and Lambert a leader of the Wallingford House group of officers which tried to turn out Richard Cromwell. Cashiered by the Rump, he was arrested soon after the Restoration on suspicion of plotting against Charles II. He escaped to Holland, returned to England at the government's order and was rearrested (1666), but released after a few months' imprisonment. In 1667 Pepys saw him walking in Tower Street, 'now no more a prisoner, and looks well'. He lived in retirement in Hackney until his death.

M. Ashley, *Cromwell's Generals*, 1954.

WILLIAM BOTELER or BUTLER (*fl.* 1640–75), who may serve as an example of Cromwell's Major-Generals, was a Northamptonshire man. The dates of his birth and death are unknown; the only fact we have about his early life is that he was educated at Oundle School. In the First Civil War he led a troop of Horse in Colonel Lydcot's regiment, with the rank of captain. When the Second Civil War broke out he was thanked by the Commons for putting down the Royalist rising in Northamptonshire. He was alleged to have demolished Royalist houses and in some to have ordered the timber to be used for building new ones elsewhere. When at a meeting of the Army Council in 1648 it was proposed to launch a campaign to 'extirpate heresy, error or whatever was opposed to sound doctrine', Boteler objected on the grounds that 'for the most part truth and light go under the name of error and heresy'. Active in his own county in suppressing seditious papers, he also put down a Leveller named Thompson at Burford. In 1650 he was a commissioner for the better propagation of the Gospels in Wales, and in 1652 he protested against any form of state-endowed church, arguing that he stood for toleration for all, not only for Christians — a position which he was later to abandon.

During the next two or three years he was variously active in ways which reveal his Puritanism. He broke up a seditious meeting of some 10,000 persons in Warwickshire who had gathered allegedly to enjoy some bear-baiting; acted as a judge for the relief of poor prisoners and sat as a member of a commission to eject scandalous ministers; and took part in presenting in London a petition for liberty of conscience (1654). When in 1655 Penruddock's Rising occurred in Wiltshire, Boteler, at that time a Major in a regiment of Horse in the south-west, was swift to join Desborough in crushing the rebels. He was urgent in demanding that justice be quickly exacted, claiming that 'Everything is lovely in its season: the same justice upon these offenders would lose much of its glory if its execution should be deferred'; he was nevertheless moderate in his treatment of them.

In 1656 Boteler was appointed as one of the Major-Generals for the counties of Northamptonshire, Bedfordshire, Huntingdon and Rutland. In David Underdown's words 'The major-generals left bitter memories. The gentry never forgot the interruption of their accustomed authority, the imprisonment of friends and neighbours, the disruption of rural sports and freedom of movement'.* Boteler seems to fit only too well into this picture. His activities were so many, his behaviour so arrogant and tactless, that he became the most execrated of Cromwell's military rulers. He called one man of quality 'Sirrah' and threatened to make him publicly proclaim Charles I a traitor or else eat his sword. He was energetic in selecting and ejecting local officials; he hunted down and punished profane and idle persons ('ranting blades' he called them); he took action against counterfeiters and watched suspiciously the behaviour of sequestered preachers. He fined one man £6 for saying 'damn' and took evident pleasure in shutting down ale-houses. Yet his bitterest opponents were the country gentry, largely because he imposed a tax of 10% on all who owned property producing £100 or more per annum. When Lord Northampton refused to pay, Boteler arrested him; Northampton appealed to Cromwell and won his case.

In 1656 Boteler entered Parliament as Member for Northampton-

*G.E. Aylmer, ed., *The Interregnum: the quest for settlement, 1640–60,* 1972, p. 176.

shire. His reported method of ensuring his election seems typical of
the man. 'The freeholders, by appointment of Major-General
Butler, were assembled on Kettering-heath; and the Sheriff having
read the writ, the Major named himself and the five following
gentlemen, Sir Gilbert Pickering [and four others]. Having first
named Sir Gilbert, he rode round the heath with a party of his own,
crying 'A Pickering, a Pickering!', and coming to the Sheriff ordered
him to set him down as duly elected. The other five were successively
returned in the same manner.' In these years Boteler grew wealthy,
buying Mansfield Park which had been confiscated from the Duke
of Newcastle. He also became less tolerant of other men's opinions,
arresting a Roman Catholic priest and trying to suppress the
Quakers, whom he had at first treated leniently: in Parliament he
took part in the savage attack on James Nayler. Although he
opposed the proposal to make Cromwell king, Boteler was probably
a member of the deputation which urged him to accept the Petition
and Advice of 1657. In 1658 he was appointed to command the
General's Regiment of Horse. But his unpopularity grew: when
Parliament met in 1659 many complaints were laid against him.
The Commons were very hostile; after a bitter debate he was
deprived of his office as J.P., and he only just avoided impeachment.

At the Restoration he narrowly escaped omission from the Act of
Oblivion. For some four years he lived as an attorney, but when the
Dutch War was beginning he was arrested and imprisoned in the
Tower. He wrote a long letter of grievances and begged for release,
promising to conform to everything except the Church of England.
He was probably released in 1667, but so ardent was he as a
conventicler that he was again arrested in 1670. That is the last we
know of him. Boteler was not one of the most important of the
Major-Generals, yet he personifies more clearly than any the less
attractive side of Cromwell's military rule. Loyal, energetic and
efficient, he was also arrogant, grasping, and merciless. His pleas for
liberty of conscience and toleration for all seem little more than
gestures to prevailing fashion; once he was given real authority, his
religious beliefs seem to have yielded to a fundamental harshness and
selfishness.

M. Ashley, *Cromwell's Generals*, 1954.
Ivan Roots, 'Swordsmen and decimators — Cromwell's major-

generals', in R.H. Parry, ed. *The English Civil War and After,
1642-58,* 1970.

ROBERT OVERTON (*c.* 1609–1668), Cromwellian general,
was a Yorkshireman from Easington who had been a student at
Gray's Inn. He fought at Marston Moor for Parliament and was in
1647 Governor of Hull. In 1650 he was with Cromwell at Dunbar,
and for the next three years he was one of the main figures of the
army of the Commonwealth in Scotland—acting as Governor of
Edinburgh, conquering Orkney and Shetland, and commanding in
western Scotland. From 1653 to 1654 he was back in his old post at
Hull, then returned to Scotland to serve under Monck. At this point
he was arrested and sent to England in connection with a mutinous
movement among a group of officers in Scotland, and he remained
in prison without trial, first in the Tower and later in Jersey, until
1659. It is not certain exactly what Overton had been doing. But he
had made it clear to Cromwell that he disapproved of the Protectorate; he had got mixed up in the obscure plottings of the Leveller
John Wildman; and he was probably a Fifth Monarchist and thus
suspect to the authorities. Parliament released Overton and reappointed him to Hull in 1659. He refused obedience to Monck and
after the Restoration he was again imprisoned on suspicion of being
involved in Fifth Monarchy conspiracy. He spent much of the
remainder of his life in prison, in the Tower, in Chepstow and
finally in Jersey once more. Overton was a scholar as well as a
soldier, a friend of Milton, sincere and utterly disinterested, yet
evidently hesitant and uncertain in political action. A correspondent
of Cromwell's wrote in Overton's defence, 'I am confident that he
had never continued so obstinate if it had not been for the imperious
spirit of his wife'.

M. Ashley, *Cromwell's Generals,* 1954.

JOHN OKEY (1606–62), was a ship's-chandler who was Colonel
of a regiment of dragoons at Naseby (the only dragoons in the New
Model) and who signed the death-warrant of Charles I. In 1649 the
University of Oxford made him a Master of Arts after he had
crushed the Leveller mutineers at Burford. He took part in Crom-

well's Scottish campaign of 1650-51, and was prominent in the storming of Dundee. In 1654 he was a member of the first Protectorate Parliament, and he was one of the Three Colonels (the others were Alured and Saunders) who put forward a petition against the Instrument of Government, asking for the summons of a full and free Parliament. As a result he was court-martialled, and although he was acquitted of treason he lost his commission. He was a member of Richard Cromwell's Parliament of 1659. In 1660 he fled abroad. Two years later he was captured at Delft through the agency of Sir George Downing (Pepys thought Downing behaved 'like a perfidious rogue'), brought home and tried as a regicide, and hanged, drawn and quartered. Okey, an Anabaptist and a diehard Republican, was a man of courage and cheerfulness, as his account of the battle of Naseby suggests.

H. G. Gibbutt, *Colonel John Okey, 1606-1662*, 1955 (Bedford-shire Historical Record Society, Vol. XXXV).

ROBERT BLAKE (1599–1657), Admiral of the Common-wealth Navy, came of a Bridgwater merchant family. He went to Oxford, first to St. Alban Hall and then to the new Somersetshire foundation of Wadham, where, it is said, he wanted to become a don. Instead he came home at his father's death in 1625 to run the family business. He sat for Bridgwater in the Short Parliament. A vigorous, cultured, intelligent man and a firm Puritan, he was soon prominent in the Parliamentarian army, defending Bristol, Lyme Regis and, in his most notable exploit (1644-5), Taunton against strong Royalist forces. Blake emerged from the wars as the most competent Parliamentarian Commander in the west. Yet the source of his enduring national reputation was still to come. In 1649, when he was fifty, the Republican Council of State appointed him 'General at Sea'. It is likely enough that he had been to sea, perhaps far afield, on the family trading vessels, but he had never held naval command before. In the eight years that remained to him he made himself the peer in naval fame of Drake and Nelson, a feat even more extraordinary than that of Cromwell as a soldier.

Clarendon, who thought Blake a man of 'a sullen nature', paid tribute to his courage, saying that he 'drew the copy of naval courage, and bold and resolute achievements'. The climax of his career at Santa Cruz illustrates this judgment. Yet Blake's career was far more than a triumph of bravery in battle, far more also than a pattern of superb seamanship. For he was the central figure, assisted by such subordinates as Penn, Lawson and Deane, in the naval revolution of the Cromwellian era, a revolution provoked by the needs and designs of the Commonwealth state and much stimulated by conflict with the Dutch in the golden age of Tromp and De Ruyter. Henceforward the Navy was a specialized fighting force with its own officers, rules and rapidly-growing traditions. It had its first Fighting Instructions, introducing the line of battle, used in the fight off the Gabbard in 1653. It was given new Articles of War, with a stern disciplinary code; improved organization ashore, naval hospitals, even better pay for seamen. The general use of the naval ensign from this time symbolized the beginning of a new era.

Blake's first contests at sea were with Prince Rupert, whom he drove off the high seas, pursuing him (1650) first to the Tagus and thence into the Mediterranean, and destroying the Royalist navy as an effective fighting force; as a consequence of this he recovered the Scillies and Jersey for Parliament in 1651. The following year brought the outbreak of the First Dutch War, with its series of large-scale naval engagements whose tactics governed the pattern of naval warfare until the days of Nelson. Blake defeated Tromp off Dover in May and De Witt off the Kentish Knock in September. But he was rash enough to challenge Tromp's fleet of twice his size off Dungeness in November and was beaten. This defeat led directly to the reorganization of English naval administration, and in March 1653 he gained his revenge upon the great Dutch admiral, winning a three-day running fight between Portland and Calais. Tromp lost seventeen warships and fifty merchantmen. Blake was wounded in this action, and the credit for the second English victory of 1653, off the Gabbard, belonged mainly to Monck, for Blake took part only in the last stage of that battle. The Dutch War ended in 1654, and in 1655 he sailed south to deal with the Barbary pirates and destroyed a fleet of their galleys beneath the batteries of Tunis. The concept of the English Mediterranean fleet was beginning to take shape, and it was further advanced by the outbreak of the Protector's war with Spain. Blake put out in 1656 to blockade Cadiz and to intercept the treasure galleons from the Plate, and he maintained a blockade of the Spanish coast through the winter of 1656–7, a feat of naval warfare hitherto unknown. Finally, in April 1657, he sank sixteen Spanish galleons and silenced the shore batteries in the enclosed bay of Santa Cruz in the Canaries, losing not a single ship and only fifty seamen; as Clarendon observed, 'the Spaniards comforted themselves with the belief that they were devils, and not men, who had destroyed them in such a manner'.

It was Blake's last voyage, for he died of fever as his flagship entered Plymouth Sound on his return. His body, after lying in state at Greenwich, was buried in Westminster Abbey. At the Restoration the Royalists dug up and scattered his remains, for Blake had been known as a strong Republican. Certainly no man save Oliver himself served the Commonwealth as effectively. Yet perhaps the best comment upon Blake's career and his role in naval history is his own observation: 'It is not for us to mind state affairs, but to keep foreigners from fooling us'.

C. D. Curtis, *Blake, Captain at Sea*, 1934.
Roger Beadon, *Robert Blake*, 1935.
Christopher Lloyd, 'Robert Blake', *History Today*, August 1957, pp. 546-51.
J. R. Powell, *Robert Blake, General at Sea*, 1972

SIR WILLIAM PENN (1621-70), Admiral, was a Bristolian, the son of a merchant, and was brought up to the sea. He served in the Parliamentarian navy, and by 1651 was commanding a squadron in pursuit of Rupert in the Mediterranean. He fought with distinction in the First Dutch War, notably in the actions of 1653 which ended with the death of Tromp, and was appointed a General of the Fleet and a Commissioner of the Admiralty. In 1654-5 he commanded the Fleet in the unhappy expedition which failed to take Hispaniola but secured Jamaica instead; like its military commander Venables, with whom he quarrelled, Penn was briefly imprisoned on his return. In disgrace, he withdrew to the estates he owned in County Cork, and it was here that his son William first came into contact with Quakerism. Restored to favour and knighted at the Restoration, he became a Commissioner of the Navy, the role in which he appears so frequently in the pages of Pepys, who first enjoyed him as 'a merry fellow and pretty good natured, and sings very loose songs' but later came to think him a dissembler and 'a very villain'. Penn served

under the Duke of York in the Second Dutch War and took part in
the action off Lowestoft in 1665. He died in 1670 and was buried in
St. Mary Redcliffe at Bristol.

JOHN THURLOE (1616–68), Cromwell's Secretary of State,
was the son of an Essex rector, trained for the law at Lincoln's Inn,
and rose in the world as steward and secretary of the Parliamentarian
leader, Oliver St. John. In 1651 Thurloe accompanied St. John to
the Hague to take part in the abortive negotiations which preceded
the First Dutch War, and in the following year he was appointed
clerk to the Council of State. In effect he became the sole Secretary
of State for nearly eight years, and all the principal civil business of
the Commonwealth, foreign and domestic, passed through his
hands. The volumes of his correspondence remain a major source for
historians of the period. He developed a devoted loyalty to Cromwell and to the Protectorate as a system of government, and
Cromwell clearly placed immense confidence in him. Yet Thurloe
was in no sense an *éminence grise*. It is significant that the index of
Firth's *Oliver Cromwell* contains only two references to Thurloe in
some 470 pages. Unambitious, thorough, ceaselessly diligent and
highly efficient, utterly reliable, Thurloe was the supreme servant of
the Cromwellian state. As M.P. first for Ely and later for Cambridge
University, he spoke in Parliament in defence of the government's
policy, yet there are few signs that he had any decisive influence in
making it. His most celebrated, and most onerous, task was as the
head of a wide-spread intelligence system whose function was to
unearth the countless Royalist plots to restore the monarchy and
assassinate Cromwell. Thurloe's spies were to be found everywhere,
in Madrid and the Hague, Dublin and the Scottish Highlands, in
country houses and Leveller meetings, even in the Royalist 'Sealed
Knot' itself, and, aided by his censorship of the postal service, they
were very successful. It is not so easy to assess the general achievement of Thurloe. There is some evidence that his office became
something of a bottleneck, slowing down the dispatch of business. A
small neat man, Thurloe was, of course, a Puritan, as the language in
which he wrote to Henry Cromwell of his father's death indicates:
'the stroke is so sore, so stupendous . . . I can do nothing but put my
mouth in the dust and say "It is the Lord"'. He was very much a
Cromwellian. He had urged Oliver to take the Crown, and he did his

best to stiffen Richard. With the end of the Protectorate he was dismissed; Monck recalled him, and he remained Secretary until just before the return of the King. His life was spared at the Restoration, in return for a detailed statement of the current diplomatic position. He remained in England under Charles II, but declined to enter his employment.

D. Underdown, *Royalist Conspiracy in England, 1649–1660*, 1960. Edmund Baker, 'John Thurloe', *History Today*, August 1958, pp. 548-55.

JOHN MILTON (1608–74), Puritan poet and pamphleteer, a Londoner born in Bread Street, Cheapside, was the son of a well-to-do scrivener who was a considerable amateur musician. Sent to St. Paul's, he showed literary promise and linguistic gifts as well as a passion for study. Thence he went in 1625 to Christ's College, Cambridge, where he wrote a number of poems in English and in Latin. *On the Morning of Christ's Nativity* was written in 1629, the year of his graduation. Nicknamed 'the lady' at Cambridge because of his fair complexion and slight build, Milton was an austere young man, strict in his Puritanism and dedicated early to using his gifts for the forwarding of the divine plan. He had intended to take orders but felt unable to do so in face of the growing Laudianism of the Church. 'Church-outed by the prelates', he turned instead to poetry as his chosen task, and in 1632 withdrew to Horton in Buckinghamshire, where his father had retired from business, and devoted himself to a strenuous course of study of the classics and ancient history in preparation for his writing. In 1632 he composed *L'Allegro* and *Il Penseroso*, neither of them published until later; in 1634 his masque *Comus* was presented at Ludlow Castle; and in 1637 he wrote *Lycidas* in memory of a Cambridge friend drowned in the Irish Sea. During 1638–9 he travelled in Italy, and when he returned to England in July 1639 it was clear that a political crisis could not be long delayed. That same month Charles sent for Wentworth from Ireland.

The crisis transformed Milton's career, turning him into a pamphleteer and, later, a civil servant; for twenty years he wrote no poetry except sonnets and Latin verses. He settled in London, taking his two nephews as resident pupils in 1640, and next year he opened

John Milton c.1629
(Artist: Unknown)

his campaign for the Puritan cause with a series of pamphlets attacking episcopacy. In 1642 he married the daughter of a Royalist magistrate of Forest Hill in Oxfordshire. After about a month she went home on a visit and declined to return to Milton; not until 1645 did she eventually do so, and then Milton supported her family, whose fortunes had been broken by the war. Shortly after her

departure Milton chose to publish a tract in defence of divorce
(1643) which caused an outcry among his fellow-Puritans. Two of
his finest pieces of prose-writing appeared in 1644 — the severe essay
Of Education and the great defence of freedom of the press,
Areopagitica, with its celebrated imperative 'Give me the liberty to
know, to utter, and to argue freely, according to conscience, above
all liberties'. The opinions expressed in *Areopagitica* were not
acceptable to the Presbyterian supporters of revolution, while for his
part Milton, as he said in 1646, believed that 'New Presbyter is but
old Priest writ large'. His Independent sympathies led him to
support the Army leaders against Parliament in the quarrel which
developed after the defeat of the Royalists in the First Civil War, and
he went on to accept the extreme Republican doctrine and the
execution of the King. This action he defended in 1649, both in *The
Tenure of Kings and Magistrates*, justifying the deposition and
punishment of tyrants, and in the *Eikonoklastes*, his notably unsuccessful reply to the *Eikon Basilike*. Milton's services and importance
to the Puritan cause were recognized by his appointment (1649) as
Latin Secretary to the Commonwealth Council of State, the post
which he held until the Restoration. By now his eyesight was failing,
and he became totally blind in 1652, the year also of his first wife's
death. The Council retained him in his post, although they provided
him with assistants (among whom was Andrew Marvell) and
reduced his salary. He married again in 1656, but his second wife
died in 1658. Towards the end of the Commonwealth he returned
to pamphleteering, with attacks on compulsion in religion and upon
tithes, and two months before Charles II was restored he wrote his
last plea for Republicanism, *The Readie and Easie Way to establish a
Free Commonwealth*.

As a defender of regicide Milton was in grave peril in 1660. He
was arrested and imprisoned, but thanks probably to the intervention of Marvell and other friends, suffered no more than a heavy
fine. With his hopes for the Puritan state destroyed, Milton turned
back to the great task he had set himself as a young man, to use
poetry to

> ... assert Eternal Providence
> and justify the ways of God to men.

Paradise Lost includes a little material written at the beginning of the Civil Wars; according to Aubrey, Milton began the body of the poem in 1658 and completed it in 1663. Not until 1667 did he find a publisher, who paid him £10 for the manuscript. *Paradise Regained* and *Samson Agonistes* followed in 1671, three years before his death. In his last years Milton, who had married a third wife, thirty years his junior, in 1663, lived in quiet retirement, taking no part in public affairs.

Aubrey, in a sympathetic description, tells us that Milton's 'harmonical and ingenious soul did lodge in a beautiful and well-proportioned body'. Not all his contemporaries were so charitable, and, indeed, Aubrey goes on to admit that 'he was much more admired abroad than at home'. There were aspects of Milton which they, as well as later generations, found somewhat repellent — the savagery of some of his invective, the harshness of the discipline visited upon his daughters and pupils, the pride which was always present in his austerity and which often ran into vanity, the narrowness of his personal relationships. And there was much that Milton was not. He was no democrat: his ideal of government seems to have been rule by an oligarchy of rich Puritans. He was not entirely consistent even in his superb championship of toleration, for he was at times willing to concede that it might be necessary in the national interest to forbid Roman Catholic worship. Yet when all qualifications are made Milton stands out as one of the dominant figures of his century. Had he died when he was thirty, *Comus*, *Lycidas* and his other early poems would have assured him immortality. He is one of the supreme political pamphleteers, not so much for his prose — which is unequal — as for the timelessness and the challenging force of the argument for social and civil freedom which is at the heart of his writing. *Paradise Lost*, an epic unparalleled in English, the finest achievement of his genius, uniting his vast classical and Renaissance learning with his extraordinarily sensitive ear and his tremendous imaginative force, was also the noblest expression of the concern of seventeenth-century Puritanism with the eternal issue of Good and Evil.

J. H. Hanford, *John Milton, Englishman*, 1950.
F. E. Hutchinson, *Milton and the English Mind*, 1947.
Christopher Hill, *Milton and the English Revolution*, 1977.

ANDREW MARVELL (1621–78), poet and politician, was born near Hull, son of the moderate Puritan master of the Hull Charterhouse, and was probably sent to Hull Grammar School. After going to Trinity College, Cambridge, he travelled abroad during the Civil War years. His most celebrated single poem, the *Horatian Ode upon Cromwell's Return from Ireland*, with its lines on the execution of Charles I, was written in 1650. From 1651 to 1653 he was tutor to Fairfax's daughter at Nunappleton in Yorkshire, and probably wrote there many of his agreeable lyrics in praise of gardens and rural life. He is always likely to be remembered for his poem *To His Coy Mistress*, with its lines,

> But at my back I always hear
> Time's winged chariot hurrying near.

After a period as tutor to Cromwell's ward, William Dutton, he became in 1657 Milton's assistant as Latin Secretary to the Council of State. From 1658 to his death in 1678 Marvell was M.P. for Hull, and looked after the needs of his constituents vigorously. A member of Harrington's Rota Club in 1659–60, Marvell defended Milton after the Restoration, standing by him at the time of his prosecution and writing the preface in his praise for the second edition of *Paradise Lost* in 1674. He grew increasingly hostile to the government in the 1670s, attacking the persecution of dissenters, inventing the nickname 'Cabal' for the group of ministers from 1673 to 1678, and denouncing the pro-French and pro-Catholic policies. His anonymous pamphlet *Account of the Growth of Popery and Arbitrary Government in England* created a sensation when it appeared in 1677, and the government offered £100 for the name of its author. As the *Horatian Ode* indicates, Marvell was more ready than many of his contemporaries to sense the values of both sides in the great conflict of the seventeenth century.

M. C. Bradbrook and M. G. Lloyd Thomas, *Andrew Marvell*, 1940.

Christopher Hill, 'Society and Andrew Marvell', *Puritanism and Revolution*, 1958.

R. L. Shaw, ed., *Andrew Marvell: Essays on the Tercentenary of his Death*, 1979.

Robert Wilcher, *Andrew Marvell: an Introductory Study*, 1986.

THOMAS HOBBES (1588–1679), political philosopher, was born at Malmesbury in Wiltshire, the son of a parson: Aubrey says 'his mother fell in labour with him on the fright of the invasion of the Spaniards'. His uncle, a prosperous glover, maintained him at Magdalen Hall, Oxford, and in 1608 he became tutor to William Cavendish, later Earl of Devonshire. He remained with the family, with short intervals, for over thirty years. During this time he took his Cavendish pupils on the grand tour and met such men as Galileo and Descartes, and for some period he was an amanuensis for Bacon. In 1640, with the prospect of civil strife, he left England for Paris, where he remained until 1652, when he came back accepting the authority of the Republican government. The year before, 1651, his masterpiece, *The Leviathan*, had been published in London. At the Restoration Hobbes had no difficulty in making his peace with Charles II, whose tutor he had been for a time in France and who enjoyed his power of repartee. Going back to the Cavendishes, he lived on until 1679, physically vigorous (he played tennis at seventy-five) and mentally alert.

John Aubrey's masterpiece is his brief life of Hobbes. It is Aubrey who tells us how Hobbes fell in love with geometry and 'was wont to draw lines on his thigh and also on the sheets, abed, and also multiply and divide'; how in writing *Leviathan* 'he walked much and contemplated, and he had in the head of his staff a pen and ink-horn, carried always a notebook in his pocket, and as soon as a notion darted, he presently entered it in his book, or else he should perhaps have lost it'; how 'he had very few books ... and was wont to say that if he had read as much as other men, he should have known no more than other men'; and how 'at night, when he was abed, and the doors made fast, and was sure nobody heard him, he sang aloud (not that he had a very good voice) but for his health's sake'. Even in Aubrey's remarkable gallery Thomas Hobbes is notably eccentric, and this quality is probably the best key to an understanding of his general relationship to seventeenth-century England. Whereas Locke became the patron saint of Whiggery, Hobbes was universally condemned, and this was because his views were idiosyncratic, acceptable neither to divine right monarchy nor to liberal republic, deplorable in the eyes of Catholic, Anglican and Puritan alike. *The Leviathan* got Hobbes, a Royalist refugee, into embarrassing difficulty, for it involved the acceptance of a *de facto*

Thomas Hobbes c.1669–70
(Artist: John Michael Wright)

sovereign, and thus drove him back to England. After the Restoration he remained politically suspect, yet his principal enemies were
the churchmen, who rightly looked upon him as an atheist.

The Leviathan is an extraordinary achievement, and by virtue of
its style and its argument the most powerful piece of political
philosophy which any Englishman has produced. Its defence of
absolutism no doubt reflects the judgment of a man who was

W.S.B.—G*

naturally timorous and whose hatred of disorder seemed to have
been confirmed by civil war. In this sense it is a book founded upon
fear. Yet it was also far more than that, in relation to its age and to
the future. For Hobbes built up his whole theory of society and the
state from a mechanistic explanation of human nature and behaviour. He threw away the ancient sanctions of political theory, the
sanctions of divinity and morality, and maintained in effect that
political society was controlled solely by expediency. Religion was
valuable merely as a means of compelling respect for secular
arguments. In the seventeenth century such startlingly modern
thinking was revolutionary and shocking, and for long afterwards it
was disreputable.

Thomas Hobbes, *The Leviathan*, 1946 ed. (Blackwell's Political
    Texts).
L. Strauss, *The Political Philosophy of Hobbes*, 1936.
C.B. Macpherson, *The Political Theory of Possessive Individualism*,
    1962.
Christopher Hill, *Puritanism and Revolution*, 1958, pp. 275–98.

JAMES HARRINGTON (1611-77), political theorist, descendant of an aristocratic family, was educated at Trinity College,
Oxford, and travelled as a young man to Rome and Venice. A
Republican by conviction, he took no active part in the Civil War and
was a personal friend of Charles I, whom he attended during his
captivity. He wrote his masterpiece, *Oceana*, in the years after the
King's execution and published it in 1656. Finding that its elaborate
and fantastic literary form prevented it from being taken as seriously
as he intended, he published several briefer and plainer expositions
of his ideas, and during the upheavals of 1659 he campaigned hard to
get his constitutional schemes adopted. But as the Commonwealth
moved towards its collapse, he had to content himself with propagating them by discussion and it was then that he formed the Rota
Club, where, as Aubrey put it, 'he had every night a meeting at the
Turke's head, in the New Pallace-yard, where was made purposely a
large ovall-table, with a passage in the middle for Miles to deliver his
coffee. About it sate his Disciples, and the Virtuosi. The Discourses
in this Kind were the most ingeniose, and smart, that ever I heard, or
expect to heare, and bandied with great eagernesse: the Arguments in

the Parliament Howse were but flatt to it.' These agreeable discussions were interrupted by the Restoration, when Harrington was
cast into prison, first into the Tower and then near Plymouth. He
was never tried, but went mad, believing that his perspiration turned
to flies and bees, and died in 1677.

Harrington attracted much attention, though he exerted limited
influence, in his own day. Later generations, not least the middle
years of the twentieth century, have found him one of the most
interesting political thinkers of English history. His ideal Commonwealth, *Oceana*, had two elements which have commended it
powerfully to our attention. It attempted to set the English Revolution, through which its author was well aware the country was
passing, in historical perspective, indicating the trend towards
Republicanism; and its analysis was drawn in essentially economic
terms, relating the form of government strictly to the distribution of
property. Only when economic and political power are in accord can
a country be stable, and the proposals he put forward in *Oceana* were
designed to produce this state of affairs, and thus secure the gains of
the Civil War. Harrington was much influenced by the Venetian
constitution which he had observed in action. He was even more
influenced by his own aristocratic background, and although he
talks much of the people, to him the people were the gentry, the
merchants and the yeomen. Servants were not to be given the
franchise, and the people were to be protected against the poor.
Nevertheless by an agrarian law the Commonwealth of *Oceana*
would have prevented too great a concentration of property in the
hands of an aristocracy; no landowner was to own land worth more
than £2,000 a year, and dowries were limited to £1,500. A secret
ballot (such as had been used in the Rota Club) was to stop landlords
controlling Parliamentary elections. The legislature would consist
of an elected senate to propose laws and an assembly to ballot,
silently, for or against their enactment. His approach to religion was
secular: there was to be a state church with paid clergy, and
toleration for all except Catholics, Jews and idolators. Other
proposals included free and compulsory education for all boys from
nine to fifteen, some compulsory military training for all but
students and apprentices, and family allowances in taxation.

The Political Works of James Harrington, J. G. A. Pocock, ed., 1975.

Charles Blitzer, *An Immortal Commonwealth: The Political Thought of James Harrington*, 1960.

Christopher Hill, *Puritanism and Revolution*, 1958, pp. 299–313.

GERRARD WINSTANLEY (1609?–after 1660), Digger and utopian writer, was born at Wigan, son of a cloth trader. We know little about his life and circumstances. Apprenticed in London, he went into trade but was hard hit by the economic troubles of the 1640s and retired into the country, living on the generosity of friends. He wrote his first pamphlet, a theological one, in 1648. In 1649–50 he was the main personality among the Diggers and wrote several pieces to justify them. The most remarkable of his writings, *The Law of Freedom*, was a utopian essay dedicated to Oliver Cromwell in 1652. We last hear of him in 1660, living in Cobham. *

The Diggers, the group who dug up the commons in Surrey, at St. George's Hill (near Walton-on-Thames) and Cobham, were few, humble and courageous. They saw their action as a symbol of the future, not as an attack on private property, and they did not touch the lands of the rich. Persecuted by the local squires and peasantry, haled before Fairfax, they survived rather over a year before being finally broken up. Winstanley deserves to be better known for his writing, for he was one of the most original thinkers among seventeenth-century radicals. A visionary, driven on like his contemporaries the first Quakers by a belief in an inner light, he appalled orthodox Calvinists by his universalist view that all men would be saved. He was a millenarian, though not one who foresaw a violent revolution. *The Law of Freedom* envisaged a community without private property, money and wage labour, and it takes its place in the pedigree of socialist thought. Its communism is the communism of the early Christians, and its classless society is closer to the dream of John Ball than to the doctrines of Karl Marx. Nevertheless, Winstanley, like Harrington, saw the origins of the upheavals of his day in social terms, and believed that political liberty must be accompanied by social equality.

G. H. Sabine, ed., *The Works of Gerrard Winstanley*, 1941.

* But see James Alsop, 'Gerrard Winstanley's later life', *Past and Present*, February 1979.

C. Hill, ed., *Winstanley: The Law of Freedom and Other Writings*, 1973.

SAMUEL HARTLIB (*c.* 1600–1670), was, in the phrase of Milton, who addressed *Of Education* to him, 'a person sent hither by some good providence from a far country to be the occasion and the incitement of great good to this island'. The 'far country' was Elbing in Polish Prussia, where Hartlib's father was a merchant, and the 'good providence' worked through the Thirty Years' War, when the Catholic capture of Elbing in 1628 drove the Protestant Hartlib into exile. He seems to have studied in Cambridge before this, falling under the influence of Baconian science. In 1628 he started a school in Chichester, which did not last long, and in 1630 he moved to London, settling in a house in Holborn for the remainder of his days. In Evelyn's words 'honest and learned, a public-spirited and ingenious person', Hartlib quickly gathered a wide circle of friends. Through his influence upon them even more than through his numerous writings, this cheerful bourgeois foreigner, of practical and fertile but not particularly original mind, has some claim to be considered the outstanding 'projector' of the central period of the English Revolution, a link between Bacon and the Royal Society, the channel where the Puritanism of the early seventeenth century merged into the scientific attitude of its later years. Individual pioneers as varied as Milton, William Petty, the agricultural reformer Weston and the Polish educational reformer Comenius, whom he persuaded to come to England in 1641, owed much to his zest for spreading information. In the 1630s Hartlib was much patronized by the political opponents of Charles I; Pym corresponded frequently with him and the wealthy Archbishop Williams, Laud's enemy, backed him. In 1646 Parliament made him an allowance. The educational changes projected but never achieved under the Commonwealth, like the development of local colleges, reflected Hartlib's influence. So did the Royal Society, for the group from which this sprang contained men directly or indirectly connected with Hartlib, like Petty, John Wilkins and Jonathan Goddard, and certainly sharing his assumptions about the relationship of scientific knowledge and social change.

Hartlib was a social reformer whose zeal ran into many directions — one of which was a lively personal charity, particularly towards

Protestant refugees. He was perhaps most widely known in his own day as a writer on agricultural reform, a phrase which included attacks on copyhold and feudal tenures, as in his *The Compleat Husband-Man* (1659). Yet he was at least as much concerned about the relief of poverty, especially that of poor children, and his *London's charity enlarged* (1650) was a detailed set of proposals. His concern extended to the Red Indians, the Jews, and the Irish, yet throughout he emphasized the central part education had to play in the hands of that 'invisible college' of all good men which would reform mankind. An internationalist in outlook as well as in background, he was deeply moved by the significance of the English events of 1640–1, and in 1641 he published *A Description of the Famous Kingdom of Macaria*, a utopian exercise in the tradition of More and Bacon. Its purpose was to reform the world. Macaria was an enlightened welfare state, based upon a science harnessed to humanity and providing a reorganized ownership of land, public education, an inheritance tax and various local services.

G. H. Turnbull, *Samuel Hartlib*, 1920.
Charles Webster, *The Great Instauration*, 1975.

PETER CHAMBERLEN (1601–83), obstetric surgeon and Leveller, belonged to a London family of barber-surgeons, four generations of whom owed their wealth and much of their reputation to their invention of a short forceps. Educated at Merchant Taylors, Emmanuel College, Cambridge, and Padua, he was a fashionable doctor of his day, physician to both Charles I and Charles II, and he went to Ireland on Cromwell's staff. He was also an enthusiastic sectary and a vigorous pamphleteer, who uniquely blended Leveller ideas on legal and social reform, Fifth Monarchist notions about a rule of the saints, and grandiose schemes of his own for solving the problem of poverty. Others of his reforming projects were directed to problems of public health: he advocated the provision of public baths, he saw hygiene as a weapon against epidemics, he wanted midwives given higher status by incorporation. Yet it is his more general social criticism that has attracted later attention. His pamphlet *The Poor Man's Advocate* (1649) was an attempt to solve the agrarian problems of the day. In it he proposed the nationalization of commons and waste land, as well as of confiscated ecclesiastical land, and the formation of a syndicate to set 20,000 poor men to work upon them. The profits of this enterprise would pay off the nation's debts as well as improve the circumstances of the poor.

DUD DUDLEY (1599–1684), ironmaster, was the illegitimate child of the fifth Baron Dudley and a collier's daughter, and, by his own account, was brought down from Balliol at the age of nineteen to run his father's ironworks at Pensnet in Worcestershire. His historical fame rests upon his claim, made at some length in his book *Metallum Martis or Iron made with Pit-Coale, Sea Coale, etc.* (1655), to have produced good quality iron with pit-coal. There is no evidence, beyond his own statement, that he succeeded, although he certainly worked under patents granted in 1621 and 1638. He does not suggest that he coked the coal, and all we know of the bellows of the seventeenth century indicates that it would be impossible at that time to make good iron with raw mineral fuel. His activities as an ironmaster were much interrupted by flood, riot, lawsuits, disputes with other ironmasters, and imprisonment for debt. During the Civil War he served as a Colonel on the Royalist side, and was appointed General of the Ordnance to Rupert; he lost his estates and was sentenced to death, but escaped execution. A new furnace at Bristol after 1651 involved him in further lawsuits, and he seems to have abandoned his ironworks shortly after the Restoration. What little evidence we have about Dudley from any other source but himself indicates a quarrelsome, litigious and unreliable man.

T. S. Ashton, *Iron and Steel in the Industrial Revolution*, 1924, pp. 10-12.

PRAISE-GOD BAREBONE OR BARBON (1596?–1679), London-born, was a leather-seller by trade, prosperous enough to become a liveryman of his Company. About 1640 he was a lay preacher to a congregation whose chapel was in his warehouse, at the Lock and Key in Fleet Street. From 1649 to 1652 (and again in 1660) he was a member of the Common Council of London. What alone distinguishes him from many another sectary of his day is that he gave his name to the Nominated or Barebone's Parliament of 1653;

in this, Cromwell's experiment in government by the godly, he was one of the four members for London. He was a consistent Republican, though out of favour during the Protectorate, and in 1660 he petitioned against the restoration of the monarchy. Twice that February Pepys records the breaking of Barebone's windows by a mob. Although he was never an advocate of violence, in 1661 he was one of many sectaries arrested after Venner's Rising, and he spent two years in the Tower. It is probable that he was the father of the economist Nicholas Barbon (d. 1689), who wrote two treatises on trade and money, and appears to have been the pioneer of fire insurance in this country.

Austin Woolrych, *Commonwealth to Protectorate*, 1982.

MARCHAMONT NEEDHAM (1620–78), was an unscrupulous journalist whose career illustrates the opportunities given to what was virtually a new occupation by the English Revolution. He came from a gentry family of Burford in Oxfordshire, was a chorister at All Souls, tried his hand at teaching at Merchant Taylors School, studied law and medicine, and then turned to journalism, editing from 1643 *Mercurius Britannicus*, whose aim was to counteract the Royalist *Mercurius Aulicus*. It was a satirical and scurrilous sheet, and its editor was a brazen liar. 'As the war progressed the duel of wits between *Aulicus* and *Britannicus*, challenging, deriding and scoring off each other week by week became an accepted and enlivening accompaniment to the conflict.' * But in 1646 Needham offended the House of Lords, who sent him to prison, and in 1647 he changed sides and produced a new sheet, the *Mercurius Pragmaticus*, even more abusive. It was in this that he called Cromwell 'the town-bull of Ely'. Not surprisingly, he was again imprisoned, and in 1649 he changed his colours again, took the Engagement, and wrote a pamphlet commending the Commonwealth as an earnest of new-found loyalty. Its line, appropriately, was that the man of sense ought to accept the new régime and avoid trouble. In 1650 he produced a third newspaper, *Mercurius Politicus*, and devoted his talents to backing the shifts and turns of Oliver's policies. He was also (1653–60) editor of the official *Public Intelligencer*. At the Restoration he lost his job and,

* C. V. Wedgwood, *The King's War*, 1958, p. 166.

backing a loser at last by writing against the return of the King, fled abroad. He was pardoned and came back to England, but henceforward earned his living by practising medicine. Yet he could not resist one or two forays into his natural profession, writing pamphlets advocating reforms in education and in medicine, and he was even employed by Danby's ministry to write against Shaftesbury.

RICHARD BUSBY (1606–95), schoolmaster, born in Lincolnshire, was educated at Westminster and at Christ Church where he became a Senior Student (i.e. a Fellow). He performed with such success in a play produced before Charles I at Oxford in 1636 that he is said to have considered a career on the stage. But he took orders instead, and in 1638 Laud appointed him Master of Westminster School. He remained there until his death fifty-seven years later, and was unquestionably the outstanding schoolmaster of the seventeenth century. His eminent pupils were very numerous. Locke, Dryden, Wren and Hooke were among them, and Busby himself at one time claimed that sixteen of the contemporary Bench of Bishops had been his pupils at Westminster. He was a remarkable man. Extremely Royalist in his views, he nevertheless retained his post throughout the Civil Wars and the Interregnum. It is one of the odder details of the English Revolution that Westminster, which lay within the shadow of the Houses of Parliament and was nominally managed by a Parliamentary committee, was left in the hands of a man who did not hide his own opinions and who made the tone of the school firmly Royalist. Dr. Busby was described by Gladstone as the founder of the Public School system. This was an exaggeration, yet Busby's Westminster, with its long hours, its classical curriculum and its monitors, was an excellent example of the traditional system from which the schools of the nineteenth century developed. Busby used his own Latin and Greek grammars as textbooks, and published expurgated editions of some classical authors. He also used the birch a good deal. Aubrey, who had liberal views on education, said that he had heard several former pupils of Busby's (one of whom was almost certainly Dryden) say that 'he hath marred by his severity more than he hath made'; and Locke, who certainly did not wish to coddle children, may well have derived his strong hostility to corporal punishment — as well as to the conventional teaching of

Richard Busby
(Artist: Unknown)

Latin, and indeed to school education as a whole — from his
experiences at the hands of Busby. On the other side, there is
evidence which suggests that Busby quite deliberately taught his
older boys to suspect the foundations of authority and to subject
them to critical examination. This was perhaps not surprising in a
Royalist schoolmaster during the 1640s and 1650s. Yet it may well
have been a salutary and significant element in the great indirect
influence which Busby undoubtedly wielded upon English life in the
later years of the seventeenth century.

L. E. Tanner, *Westminster School*, 1934.

HENRY MORE (1614–87), theologian, came from a gentry family at Grantham and was educated at Eton and Christ's College, Cambridge. Elected a Fellow of Christ's in 1639, he remained a don: a shy and saintly man who disliked controversy, he rejected several offers of deaneries and bishoprics. Brought up a Calvinist, he came to be a firm champion of the moderate Anglicanism expounded by Hooker. More is perhaps the most representative figure of the group known as the Cambridge Platonists. Tolerant and mystical rather than dogmatic, emphasizing the spiritual values of religion and the duty of man to employ reason, 'the candle of the Lord', to discern his faith, they continued in the second half of the seventeenth century the teachings of such men as Chillingworth before the wars. Their doctrines did a good deal, in their influence upon individual clergy, to make Anglicanism at once more liberal and more confident, and to prepare it for 'the Age of Reason'. More's own writings were to win the approval of such diverse men as Wesley and Coleridge.

JEREMY TAYLOR (1613–67), preacher, the son of a Cambridge barber, became a Fellow of Caius. His reputation as an exponent of Anglican orthodoxy in a university where Puritanism was strong attracted Laud's attention, and he became a Fellow of All Souls and a Chaplain to the King. The Civil War years brought difficulties upon him. For a time he found a safe retreat in Carmarthenshire, as Chaplain to the Earl of Carbery at Golden Grove, and it was here that he wrote the works that have preserved his fame — notably the pieces of devotional literature, *Holy Living* and *Holy Dying*, and his *Discourse of the Liberty of Prophesying*, a defence of toleration from the Anglican side comparable with the writing of Chillingworth. During the Republican period Taylor was imprisoned for a time. In 1658 he took a living in Ireland, and in 1661 he became Bishop of Down and Connor, dying in Ireland in 1667.

C. J. Stranks, *The Life and Writings of Jeremy Taylor*, 1952.

SIR THOMAS BROWNE (1605–82), born in London, the son of a prosperous mercer, was educated at Winchester and at Broadgate Hall (now Pembroke College), Oxford, and studied medicine at Montpellier and Padua. From 1637 onwards he was a physician at

Norwich, and he was knighted when Charles II visited the city in 1671. His writings, notably the autobiographical *Religio Medici* (published in 1642) and *Hydriotaphia, or Urn Burial* (1658), reveal through the extraordinary richness and ingenuity of their language an encyclopaedic mind and a strange blend of scepticism and credulity. Linguist, alchemist, mystic, astrologer, Browne, who seems to have been in practice a sound Anglican of liberal theological sympathies, was variously accused of atheism and of Roman Catholicism.

Basil Willey, *The Seventeenth-Century Background*, 1934.
Joan F. Bennett, *Sir Thomas Browne*, 1962.

THOMAS FULLER (1608–61), biographer, was the son of a Northamptonshire rector. Going up to Queens' College, Cambridge, he took orders, and obtained (1631) a prebend at Salisbury and (1634) the living of Broadwindsor in Dorset. He seems to have left both of these soon after 1640 and to have gone to live in London as preacher and curate of the Savoy. Kindly and sensible, Fuller preached sermons advocating peace in the early 1640s which displeased zealots on both sides of the civil strife. In 1643 he became Chaplain to the Royalist General Hopton, and from 1644–6 he was at Exeter acting as Chaplain to the infant Princess Henriette Anne. His good nature — Aubrey called him 'a pleasant facetious person and a *bonus socius*' — won him friends in both camps, like his Northamptonshire neighbours the Montagus of Boughton, who sheltered him; and during the Commonwealth he seems to have preached in several London churches. He went back to the Savoy at the Restoration, and Pepys heard him preach 'upon our forgiving of other men's trespasses, showing among other things that we are to go to law never to revenge, but only to repair, which I think a good distinction'. But he died in an epidemic in 1661. 'The great Tom Fuller', as Pepys calls him, was a character in his own day, celebrated for his feats of memory: Aubrey tells how 'he would repeat to you backwards and forwards all the signs from Ludgate to Charing Cross', and Pepys has a tale 'that he did lately to four eminently great scholars dictate together in Latin, upon different subjects of their choosing, faster than they were able to write, till they were tired'. He wrote a great deal himself, in an agreeable uncomplicated style. Both his *Holy and Profane State* (1642) and his *Church History* (1655) were widely read in his own day. His most celebrated book, *The Worthies of England* a store of diverse and amusing information upon which he had worked for many years, was first published in 1662.

Thomas Fuller, *The Worthies of England*, ed. John Freeman, 1952.
William Addison, *Worthy Dr. Fuller*, 1957.

IZAAK WALTON (1593–1683), biographer, was born at Stafford of yeoman stock, and after serving his apprenticeship in London became a prosperous ironmonger with a shop in Fleet Street. Royalist in his sympathies, he had the pattern of his life upset by the Civil Wars and gave up his business. When they were over he settled at Winchester, where after 1662 he lived in the palace of his friend Bishop Morley and where his daughter married a prebendary. Walton had two great gifts — a genius for friendship and an English style of natural, though not artless, simplicity. His five *Lives* were first published at intervals over nearly forty years: the first, that of Donne who had been his neighbour in London, came in 1640, and the last in 1678. His other celebrated work, the charming *Compleat Angler*, was written during the political troubles and published in 1653.

JOHN OWEN (1616–83), Independent theologian, of Welsh stock, son of an Oxfordshire vicar, graduated at The Queen's College, Oxford, and read widely in mathematics and philosophy as well as in theological studies. Hostile to the Laudian statutes, he left Oxford in 1637 and wrote tracts against Arminianism. In the 1640s he moved from Presbyterian to Independent views and in 1646 became minister of a congregation at Coggeshall in Essex. He was Chaplain to Cromwell during the campaigns in Ireland and in Scotland, and Preacher to the Council of State (1649–50), and in 1651 was intruded as Dean of Christ Church. From 1652 to 1658 he was Vice-Chancellor of Oxford and was the chief agent of the attempt to make the university Puritan. It was in part at least his doing that, in Clarendon's words, Oxford during the Commonwealth 'yielded a harvest of extraordinary good and sound knowledge in all parts of learning'. He was a firm disciplinarian, brisk in manner, though Anthony à Wood, a hostile witness, noted that he 'weared for the most part sweet powder in his haire, sets of points at his knees, boots, and lawn boothose tops, as the fashion then was for young men'. At national level Owen may be regarded as the outstanding ecclesiastical statesman of the Commonwealth era. He was chiefly responsible for the scheme of church settlement which was debated in the Rump and the Nominated Parliament and which eventually took shape, with modifications, in Cromwell's ordinances setting up the 'Triers' and 'Ejectors'. Owen was also prominent in opposing Cromwell's acceptance of the Crown. Ejected at the Restoration, he refused to conform; yet he had influential friends at Court and he escaped severe persecution. In 1673 he became the minister of an independent congregation in Leadenhall Street. He wrote a good deal at this time in favour of toleration and against Catholicism. His extensive doctrinal treatises were among the most distinguished produced by seventeenth-century Puritanism, and the personal influence of his teaching, for example, on men so different as Cromwell and the young William Penn, was considerable.

RICHARD BAXTER (1615–91), minister and writer, born at Rowton in Shropshire, was very largely self-taught; he endured both an inadequate grammar school at Wroxeter and a tiresome tutor. He was ordained in 1638, serving briefly as a Chaplain in the Parliamentarian forces during the Civil War, and spent the middle years of the century as minister and lecturer at Kidderminster. In 1660 he went to London and was for a short time Chaplain to Charles II, playing a leading part in the unsuccessful Savoy Conference, whose object was to include the moderate Presbyterians. He refused a bishopric and with the Act of Uniformity (1662) left the Church of England, retiring into private life at Acton. He was intermittently persecuted, and in 1685 was charged with libelling the Anglican Church in his *Paraphrase of the New Testament*, for which he was grossly abused by Jeffreys, fined and imprisoned for about eighteen months. It is not easy to assess Baxter's impact upon his own age. Contemporary opinion agreed upon his saintliness, and there can be no doubt about the success and the beauty of his pastoral work at Kidderminster. One of the most statesmanlike religious leaders of the Interregnum, he did much to promote the Voluntary Associations of Ministers from 1653 onwards, whose objects, in his own words, were to 'engage us to the most effectual practice of so much discipline as might reduce the churches to order, and satisfy ministers in administering the Sacraments, and stop the more religious people from separation, to which the unreformedness of the Church, through want of discipline, inclined them'. He was essentially a moderate in an era of deep divisions: thus he opposed not only the Royalist claims but also the rigours of the Solemn League and the policies of Cromwell. Yet his moderation and his fine qualities of mind and spirit were of no use at the Restoration, when the Savoy Conference failed. As Sir George Clark has observed, 'He had no sense of humour. He had never had any training or experience in negotiating, or in getting business through assemblies.' * Nor, indeed, was his toleration particularly comprehensive, for his scheme would have left out the sectaries and forbidden Roman Catholics to worship in public. He was a voluminous writer, mostly of popular devotional literature, moderate in tone, looking forward to the common sense of the age of Anne as well as back to the clash of principle through which he had grown to manhood; his most remarkable work is his *Saints' Everlasting Rest* of 1650. Scholar, preacher, pastor, Baxter on a long view is a recognizable spiritual ancestor of many of the central figures of later English nonconformity.

Richard Baxter's Autobiography, ed. N. H. Keeble, 1974.
William Lamont, *Richard Baxter and the Millennium*, 1979.

EDMUND CALAMY, the Elder (1600–66), Presbyterian divine, was of Huguenot origin, the son of a Guernseyman trading in Walbrook in London. He went to Pembroke Hall, Cambridge, and later took a lectureship at Bury St. Edmunds, where he showed the moderate Puritanism that was to mark his entire career. Driven from here by the Laudian Bishop Wren, he became in 1639 curate of St. Mary Aldermanbury, and in 1640 he was one of the authors, calling themselves Smectymnuus, of a tract urging a reform of episcopacy and of the liturgy. In 1643 he took the Covenant, and he was a popular preacher with the well-to-do Presbyterians of the City of London, speaking out against the Independents and the mobs of apprentices. After Oliver's death he was strongly in favour of restoring the monarchy. Pepys records him preaching a good sermon,

* G. N. Clark, *The Later Stuarts*, 1956 ed., p. 19.

before the King at Whitehall in 1660, saying 'he was very officious with his three reverences to the King, as others do'. But he declined a bishopric and was one of the nonconformist leaders at the Savoy Conference. He was ejected from his pulpit in 1662 and was sent to Newgate for a short time in 1663 for unlicensed preaching. He died in 1666, heartbroken by the effects of the Fire upon London.

HUGH PETER (1598–1660), the Puritan preacher, was born of a well-to-do mercantile family at Fowey; his paternal ancestors were Flemish Protestant refugees of the previous century, his mother a daughter of long-established Cornish gentry. In 1613 he went to Trinity College, Cambridge, as a sizar, and between then and his ordination as priest ten years later he acquired nonconformist views of a congregationalist kind, and the patronage of the Puritan Earl of Warwick. By 1628 he had a considerable notoriety in London as a converting preacher; his attacks on the popish practices of Queen Henrietta Maria got him into trouble with his bishop, leading to suspension from preaching and to flight to the Netherlands. There he spent six years, mainly as minister to the congregation of English merchants in Rotterdam. He saw service with Dutch troops against the Spaniards and also, for a month, with the army of Gustavus Adolphus in Germany, he helped to organize supplies of Puritan literature for England, and he conducted his ministry on Puritan lines, until the inquisitive arm of Archbishop Laud reached the Rotterdam church and compelled Peter in 1635 to migrate once more. This time he went to New England, succeeding Roger Williams in 1636 as minister at Salem. He played an important and constructive role in the early establishment of the Massachusetts Bay Colony; he was, for example, prominent in the foundation of Harvard College. Yet he is principally celebrated at this time for his zealous enforcement of a narrow congregationalist orthodoxy, and for his part in the condemnation and banishment of Anne Hutchinson, who had dared to accuse him and other ministers of preaching the doctrine of salvation by works.

In 1641 he returned to England as an agent of the Colony, deputed to obtain financial and other assistance. It was an hour of hope and challenge for the Puritan cause, and Peter welcomed the opportunity to 'further the reformation of the churches' in England. He was never to go back to New England; as with Oliver Cromwell, an era of revolution was to sweep him into directions of which he had not dreamed. After the outbreak of the Civil War in 1642 he became a vigorous propagandist, 'roaring it up and down' England for Parliament's sake, an extraordinary mixture of preacher, recruiting officer, pamphleteer, election agent, official reporter and counter-spy. Violent in speech, often heartless in manner, given to buffoon-ery in his sermons, something of a rabble-rouser, he was none the less effective and sincere in his devotion to the cause of 'the Saints'. As a Chaplain in the New Model Army he took part in the victorious campaigns of Naseby and Langport and from 1646 onwards he was a powerful champion of Independency, denouncing Presbyterians and Royalists alike. After the outbreak of the Second Civil War he spoke strongly in favour of bringing the King to trial; he defended Pride's Purge; and on the eve of Charles's execution he preached in St. James's Chapel on 'the terrible denunciation to the King of Babylon' (Isaiah xiv. 18–20).

As for so many Puritans, the years 1649–60 were for Peter a time of anti-climax and of some disillusionment. Before the establish-ment of the Protectorate (1653) he was a busy servant of the new Republic, sitting on committees, going to Ireland with the army of conquest, acting as Chaplain to the Council of State, disputing with John Lilburne, spreading the gospel in South Wales; and in 1654 he was appointed one of the triers who were to license clergymen. But he was not on good terms with the Protector and his government, and periodic illness and the trend of public events made him despondent in the later 1650s. When the crisis of 1660 came he tried in vain to win favour from Monck. Although Hugh Peter was not technically a 'regicide' he had clearly done more than most men to 'encompass' the death of Charles I; he symbolized 'the rule of the Saints', and he was a natural and easy target for Presbyterian hostility. He was exempted from the Act of Oblivion and Indem-nity, and executed for high treason at Charing Cross on October 16th, 1660.

Hugh Peter is in many ways an unattractive character, even if we do not accept the massive contemporary vilification and even if many worse men made their peace on handsome terms with the Restoration government. Yet he is one of special interest for two reasons. First, he was one of the numerous figures of the revolution-ary era to put forward projects of extensive social reform. In his

Good Work for a Good Magistrate, Or a short cut to great quiet
(1651), he advocated the establishment of new universities, a reform
of the poor law, a national bankruptcy law, changes in the law of
entail, municipal banks, a standard system of weights and measures,
a national land registry, a radical revision of the tax structure, and
the replanning of London. Secondly, his career as a whole — the
mercantile port-town origins, the Cambridge influence, the early
Congregationalism, the patronage of a Puritan aristocrat, the experience of the Netherlands and of Massachusetts, the gradual fusing
together of Independency and the war-effort, the eventual concentration of hostility upon the person of the King, the disunity and
despondency that came with the political problems brought by
victory — summarizes a great deal of that seventeenth-century
politico-religious movement which we call Puritanism.

R. P. Stearns, *The Strenuous Puritan*, 1954.

VAVASOR POWELL (1617–70), Welsh preacher and Fifth
Monarchist, was born at Knucklas in Radnorshire. His uncle, the
Vicar of Clun, sent him to Jesus College, Oxford, and he later
became a schoolmaster at Clun, in trouble for Puritan opinions.
After Naseby, Parliament attempted to evangelize Wales, a Royalist
stronghold, and Powell was sent as a missionary to North Wales,
where he was not very successful. In 1650, under the influence of
Thomas Harrison, the Rump passed an act for the propagation of
the gospel in Wales. Under this nearly 300 Welsh clergy were
ejected; Powell was prominent in this enterprise as one of the
'approvers' appointed to provide their successors. These were not
easy to find, and the 'approvers' used itinerant evangelists instead, of
whom Powell was the chief, travelling and preaching between 1650
and 1653 on a scale comparable with that of Howell Harris in the
next century. But Powell, like Thomas Harrison, became a Fifth
Monarchist and came out in opposition to the Protectorate. Preaching in London in December 1653 he called Oliver 'the dissemblingest
perjured villain' and told his congregation to go and pray 'Lord, wilt
Thou have Oliver Cromwell or Jesus Christ to reign over us?' He
fled to Wales, was captured and released, and continued his preaching, issuing in 1655 an attack on Cromwell called *A Word for God
against wickedness in High Places*. At the Restoration he was soon

arrested, and he spent most of the last ten years of his life in prison, refusing to swear allegiance to the monarchy. He wrote in prison a moving account of the persecution of Puritans called *The Bird in the Cage, Chirping.*

Thomas Richards, *History of the Puritan Movement in Wales*, 1920, and *Religious Developments in Wales, 1654–1662*, 1923.

GEORGE FOX (1624–90), founder of the Society of Friends (Quakers), was born in Drayton-in-the-Clay, now Fenny Drayton, Leicestershire. His father Christopher was a weaver whose neighbours knew him as 'Righteous Christer', his mother a devout and upright woman, and Fox was brought up in a Puritan household of a kind not unusual among craftsmen of the time. He had little formal education, and was apprenticed to a shoemaker. As a child he was, according to William Penn, 'religious, inward, still, solid and observing beyond his years'; and at nineteen he left home to find a faith, one of the many 'seekers' of this period of religious ferment. For four years, the Civil War years of 1643–7, he wandered, arguing with 'professors' (those who professed a religious faith), studying his Bible, sleeping under hedges and haystacks, struggling with temptations, denouncing ministers in their pulpits, crying out against idle games and feasts, and slowly gaining conviction of a direct communication with God. Whatever the remoter origins of the central Quaker doctrine of the 'Inner light', the assertion that 'every man was enlightened by the divine light of Christ', it was by experience that George Fox came to it, shedding the rigours of Calvinism and opening the way to a personal righteousness founded upon a profound mysticism. Thereafter for over forty years he was to preach this faith, at first, after his vision on Pendle Hill in Lancashire in 1652 ('and there a-top of the hill I was moved to sound the day of the Lord; and the Lord let me see a-top of the hill in what places he had a great people to be gathered'), through loosely-organized meetings of seekers. He travelled widely through England and Wales during the Commonwealth and much of Charles II's reign; he visited Scotland in 1657–8, Ireland in 1669, the American Colonies in 1671–2, and Europe in 1677 and again in 1684. In his lifetime Quakerism remained as it began, a strikingly personal and individualist faith despite the common 'testimonies' of its adherents.

George Fox
(Artist: Thomas Fairland)

Yet Fox early divined the need of organization. He established Friends' meetings in many places in the north of England in 1652–4; in 1654 some sixty Friends went southwards throughout the land as 'Publishers of Truth'; and in the later fifties the system of regular Monthly, Quarterly and Yearly Meetings, on which the Society of Friends has based its organization ever since, began to take shape under his guidance.

George Fox was a man of striking appearance, big and strong, with penetrating eyes and resonant voice, broad open face and long hair; his big white hat, long plain coat and, above all, his 'leathern breeches', soon became famous. He had need of strength and health to face the persecution which fell upon the Quakers from the first, at the hands of mobs and magistrates alike. In 1652, for example, Fox was stoned and beaten 'sore with books, fists and sticks' at Tickhill, beaten and dragged through mire, dirt and water at Ulverston, and driven into the sea with staves, clubs and fishing poles at Walney Island. Not all magistrates were unsympathetic, and one, Thomas Fell, whose widow Margaret married George Fox in 1669, made his home at Swarthmore, near Ulverston, something of a refuge for him. But most were hostile. Fox, like other Quakers, was arrested on various charges true or false, including blasphemy under the Act of 1650, heresy, holding illegal meetings, housebreaking, refusal to swear oaths, spreading writings tending to the disturbance of the peace, and raising insurrections; tried many times; and imprisoned for eight periods, amounting to nearly six years in all, in gaols ranging from Carlisle to Launceston, under Republican and Royalist government alike. Suffering did nothing to tame him, nor did persecution halt the spread of the movement. By the middle years of Charles II's reign there were perhaps 50,000 Quakers in Britain.

Fox is best studied, of course, in his *Journal*, a remarkable autobiography by any standards and in some ways unsurpassed as a piece of Protestant self-revelation. It is neither elegant nor reflective; it is certainly not modest. It is a tough, factual record interspersed with occasional passages of spiritual exhortation, the work of a man who had read little besides the Bible and one upon whose mind the beauty of the language of the Authorized Version had had surprisingly little impact. Yet in all its crudity and vigour it is immensely powerful and exciting; direct, confident, and sincere, and above all filled with the spiritual strength and vision of one of whom Penn in his introduction to the first (1694) edition of the Journal said 'as to man he was an original, being no man's copy'. It is Fox the practical mystic in action. At Lichfield in 1651 'being market day I went into the market place and went up and down in several places of it and made stands, crying, "Woe unto the bloody city of Lichfield!", and no one touched me nor laid hands upon me. As I went down the town there ran like a channel of blood down the streets, and the market place was like a pool of blood.' Before the King's Bench in 1660 'I was brought into the middle of the court; and as soon as I was come I was moved to look about and turn towards the people. And I said, "Peace be among you"; and the power of the Lord sprung over.' In 1652 'after a meeting was done in Lancaster, they brought down a distracted man in his waistcoat and another man in his waistcoat with a bundle of birchen rods bound together like besoms for them to have whipped me with them. But I was moved to speak to them in the Lord's mighty power which chained him and them, which brought him like a lamb. And I bid him throw his rods into the fire and burn them and he did so and I made him confess to the truth and the light of Christ Jesus. So the Lord's power came over all, so as we parted in love and peace.' Fox denounced 'hireling priests' in their 'steeple-houses'; held 'precious' or 'blessed' or 'mighty' meetings; argued incessantly with men of every rank; and recorded with obvious satisfaction the unhappy fate of many of those who opposed him and his teachings.

The *Journal* proper ends in 1676, by which time even Fox's physical strength had much weakened. Although he did a good deal of travelling in his later years, centred mainly upon London, much of his time and energy were devoted to developing and maintaining the growing Quaker community; partly through his share in what still remains the central executive body of the Society of Friends, the Meeting for Sufferings (established in 1675), and partly through a vast correspondence with Quakers in England, the American Colonies and Europe. He died in London in January 1690. It was a measure of his wisdom and a last sign of his achievement that his death in no sense shattered the Quaker movement.

The Journal of George Fox, ed. J. L. Nickalls, 1952.
A. Neave Brayshaw, *The Personality of George Fox*, 1933.
Sir George Newman, *Quaker Profiles*, 1946, pp. 9-30.
Vernon Noble, *The Man in Leather Breeches*, 1953.

MARGARET FELL (1614-1702), 'Mother of Quakerism', was descended from the Askews, gentry of Furness in Lancashire, and was the wife of Thomas Fell, judge, M.P. for Lancaster (from 1645) and master of Swarthmore Hall, near Ulverston. Fell was a Puritan of wide tolerance who kept open house at Swarthmore for itinerant ministers, and thither in 1652 came George Fox the Quaker. Margaret Fell was converted, and henceforth she was a leading champion of her dangerous faith, bearing witness to its teachings, petitioning both Cromwell and Charles II to abate the persecution of Quakers, and suffering at least two periods of imprisonment, one of them lasting four years. Thomas Fell was never a convert but was sympathetic to the new teaching and used his authority to protect early Quakers in the north until his death in 1658. In 1669 Margaret Fell married George Fox at the Friends' Meeting House at Broadmead in Bristol. Fox was forty-five and his wife fifty-five; of their twenty-one years of married life they spent perhaps six together, devoting themselves to the spreading of Quakerism and to the consolidation of Friends' organization. By every account Margaret Fell was a woman of immense courage and determination. Her great contribution to Quakerism was at Swarthmore, which was a centre of Quaker missionary enterprise and from which she maintained a remarkable correspondence with the early leaders of the Society of Friends. She outlived George Fox by twelve years.

Isabel Ross, *Margaret Fell, Mother of Quakerism*, 1949.

JAMES NAYLER (*c.* 1618–60), was a leading apostle of the early Quaker movement. He was of yeoman stock from Woodchurch, near Wakefield in Yorkshire, served for some eight years in the Parliamentary forces, and was a member of an Independent church. When he left the army he went back to the land. Thence, like so many in that age of religious ferment, he felt himself called to the work of God. 'I was at the plough', he told a magistrate some years later, 'meditating upon the things of God, and suddenly I heard a Voice, saying unto me "Get thee out from thy kindred and from thy father's house"'. Soon afterwards he met George Fox, and joined him in spreading the message of the Inner Light, the 'Christ within'. He was a man of attractive manner and appearance, the most persuasive of early Quaker preachers, and did much to evangelize the north of England in the early 1650s. Like his fellows, he suffered for his preaching; a mob beat him at Walney Island in 1652, and in 1653 he was imprisoned at Appleby on a charge of blasphemy (even though he converted one of the judges on the bench). But in Derbyshire in 1655 he confounded 'seven or eight priests' in a dispute, the people crying out 'A Nayler, a Nayler, hath confuted them all'. Later he moved southwards to London where at first he won many adherents to the Quaker faith.

It was at this point that what is known in Quaker history as 'the fall of Nayler' took place. He evidently became mentally unbalanced, carried away by the success of his preaching and by the flattery of some of his women followers. As George Fox put it, 'James ran out into imaginations, and a company with him'. Fox and others rebuked him, but this led only to division in the movement. Eventually on 24 October 1656, Nayler was led riding into Bristol, his followers strewing garments in the way and singing 'Holy, holy, holy, Lord God of Sabaoth'. He was arrested by the authorities and brought before the House of Commons, who debated the case for nine days. Nayler himself, sincerely enough, claimed that he had not been allowing himself to be worshipped but 'the appearance of God in him'. Lambert, who had been his commanding officer, urged leniency, and so did others, but the House resolved that Nayler was guilty of 'horrid blasphemy'; and, quite unconstitutionally, for it had no judicial powers under the Instrument of Government, and against the wishes of the Lord Protector, proceeded to pass a savage sentence. He was to be set in the pillory for two hours and then to be whipped through the streets; two days later he was again to be pilloried, his tongue was to be bored with a hot iron, and his forehead branded with the letter B; then he was to be sent to Bristol, carried through the city on horseback, facing backwards, and whipped; finally he was to be kept in solitary confinement, without pen, ink, and paper, until the Commons chose to release him. The sentence was carried out in full, despite petitions from various sources, some pointing out the dangers of making Parliament 'a court of will'; 'we are', claimed one member, 'God's executioners'. Nayler was kept in gaol until 1659, when the Rump set him free; he showed remarkable courage throughout his ordeal and an equally remarkable spirit of forgiveness after it. He was reconciled to Fox and to the Quaker movement, to which the whole episode had done a great deal of damage by causing internal divisions and much public scandal and distrust, and he ought more properly to be remembered for his evangelism and for his devotional writings — which were numerous and contain passages of great charm — than for his fall. Nayler resumed his preaching and service to Friends; but in 1660, on his way northwards, he seems to have been set upon by robbers, and he died near Huntingdon.

M. R. Brailsford, *A Quaker from Cromwell's Army*, 1927.
W. C. Braithwaite, *The Beginnings of Quakerism*, 1959 ed., esp.
  Chap. 11.

JOHN BIDDLE (1615–62), the father of English Unitarianism,
was born at Wooton-under-Edge in Gloucestershire, the son of a
tailor. A clever boy, he went from the local grammar school to
Magdalen Hall at Oxford, where he was for a time a tutor. In 1641
he became headmaster of the Crypt School, Gloucester, and he soon
fell foul of the local Presbyterians by propounding Unitarian views,
which almost all contemporaries regarded as outrageously heretical.
Biddle was summoned to London, and he was in trouble for the
remaining twenty years of his life, spending a good deal of his time in
prison. In 1647 his *Twelve Arguments* against the divinity of the
Holy Spirit was burned as blasphemous by the common hangman.
Next year the death penalty was decreed by Parliament against all
who denied the doctrine of the Trinity; characteristically, Biddle sat
down at once and wrote a pamphlet against the law. Nevertheless,
he was released from prison on surety. He suffered much from
poverty, though work as a press corrector helped him for a time. The
act of general oblivion of 1652 benefited him, but he was always in
trouble for propagating his views in speech or print. From 1655–88
he was a prisoner on the Scillies. The Restoration could scarcely
benefit a Unitarian, and in 1662 he went to prison once more, dying
there the same year. His career of persistent nonconformity, maintaining doctrines loathed both by Anglicans and by the great
majority of his fellow-Puritans, is a measure of his own heroism and
of the encouragement which the era of the English Revolution
provided for the expression even of ideas looked upon as dangerous.

H. J. McLachlan, *Socinianism in Seventeenth-Century England*,
  1951.

JOHN BUNYAN (1628–88), was born at Elstow, a village near
Bedford, where his father was a tinker, yet not a wanderer, for he had
a small freehold. Bunyan probably had some elementary schooling in
the village, and took up his father's trade, but went off to fight in the

John Bunyan c.1684–5
(Artist: Thomas Sadler)

Civil War. After his return home he underwent a long spiritual conflict, and emerged a sober Puritan instead of a gay and rather profane young man. He joined a Nonconformist community at Bedford, and soon became a noted preacher. After the Restoration, he was arrested in November 1660, and he remained in Bedford county gaol (apart from a brief release in 1666) until 1672, steadily refusing to agree not to preach publicly. Bunyan had already in 1656 started to write on religious subjects, and he continued to do so extensively in prison. The first of his greater works, *Grace Abounding to the Chief of Sinners*, was published in 1666. Released under the Declaration of Indulgence of 1672, he returned to the congregation at Bedford, and he continued to preach — in the surrounding countryside and in London as well as in Bedford itself — for the remainder of his days, unaffected by the measure of fame which came to him through *Pilgrim's Progress*, first published in 1678 and already translated into several languages before Bunyan's death in 1688. *The Life and Death of Mr. Badman* appeared in 1680, and *The Holy War* in 1682.

John Brown, *John Bunyan, His Life, Times and Work*, 1918.
O.E. Winslow, *John Bunyan*, 1961.

LUCY HUTCHINSON (1620–?), Puritan bluestocking, was born in the Tower of London, the daughter of its Lieutenant, Sir Allen Apsley. An able child of literary intelligence, she was quite unusually well educated by tutors, learning Greek and Hebrew as well as French and Latin. As a young woman she translated Lucretius into English verse, though later in life she repented of this as a sinful deed. In Trevelyan's words, her 'learning, taste, and intellect would have met the marital requirements of John Milton himself'.* Her husband John Hutchinson was a Nottinghamshire gentleman, who held the county town and its castle for Parliament during the Civil War and succeeded his father as county M.P. in 1646. Hutchinson signed the King's death warrant in 1649, but withdrew from public life when Oliver turned out the Rump. In 1660 Nottingham elected him to the Convention, but he was expelled as a regicide. He submitted to Charles II, and managed to escape execution, but he had qualms of conscience over the sufferings of his fellow regicides. As his wife, who had done her utmost to save him, said, he 'was not very well satisfied in himself for accepting the deliverance', and was happier when the government rearrested him in 1663 on suspicion of plotting. He died in prison in 1664, immortalized rather by his wife's *Memoirs of Colonel Hutchinson* than by his own deeds. The Hutchinsons were devout Baptists, and the *Memoirs* provide a vivid

---

* *England under the Stuarts*, 1949 ed., p. 9.

picture of a Puritan household when Puritanism was at its strongest and most self-conscious, as well as much detailed evidence about the conduct of the Civil War in Nottinghamshire.

LODOWICK MUGGLETON (1609–98), sectary, was the son of a farrier, born in the Bishopsgate district of London, who became a journeyman tailor. Like many others of his class, he was much moved by extreme Puritan ideas in the disturbed 1640s. Neither Presbyterianism nor the ordinary forms of independency satisfied him. Like George Fox he sought to live 'an honest and just natural life', yet the fear of hell-fire was strong with him, and he was much impressed by the Ranter John Robins, especially perhaps by the latter's claim to be able to damn his opponents to all eternity. In 1651–2 he had a series of revelations. So did his cousin, John Reeve, personal ones 'by voice of words' from Jesus Christ; the two claimed to be the 'two witnesses' of Revelation xi.3, and quickly acquired a following. Reeve died in 1658, and the sect came to be known as the 'Muggletonians'. Their beliefs were eccentric even among the sectaries of the time. God was one and eternal, with a material body larger than that of a man: he had come to earth as Jesus, and left Elijah in charge of the universe. The devil was a human being. Men were divided into the blessed and the cursed, and Muggleton had a divine commission — which he used with a will — to bless or curse to eternity. The Muggletonians neither prayed nor preached. Not surprisingly, he was several times in trouble with the authorities, both of Commonwealth and monarchy, for blasphemy, and in 1677 he was put in the pillory and had his writings publicly burned. He had a furious controversy with the Quakers, whom he denounced as 'serpents' and damned with enthusiasm in apocalyptic phraseology. Muggleton was a tough, shrewd character, who dealt firmly with schisms among his followers, condemned the sins of the flesh, enjoyed a pipe, and lived to eighty-nine.

C. E. Whiting, *Studies in English Puritanism*, 1931, chap. vi.
C. Hill, W. Lamont and B. Reay, *The World of the Muggletonians*, 1983.

JOHN ROBINS (*fl.* 1650–52), the Ranter, had been a small farmer, but sold his land and went to London when he came to believe that he had divine powers, notably that of raising the dead; he once said 'I have had nine or ten of them at my house at a time, of those that were said to be raised from the dead'. His followers deified him, and he was known as 'the Ranters' god'. He had a plan to convert the Jews by leading 144,000 men to the Holy Land, and trained his volunteers on a diet of dry bread, water, and raw vegetables; it was fatal to some. Arrested in 1651, he spent ten months in prison, in the course of which he was visited by Lodowick Muggleton and John Reeve. According to Muggleton, they used their power to pronounce eternal damnation upon him; whereupon he recanted, wrote to Cromwell, was freed from prison, returned to the country and became a farmer again.

ROGER CRAB (1621–80), the Mad Hatter, born in Buckinghamshire, became a vegetarian in 1641; served in the Parliamentarian army for seven years; set up shop as a hatter at Chesham from 1649 to 1652, thought it sin to make a profit and gave away nearly all his property to the poor; lived as a hermit at Ickenham in Middlesex, winning considerable fame as a herbal doctor and a prophet, advising his patients to abstain from meat and strong drink and cutting his own diet down to dock leaves and grass; moved in 1657 to Bethnal Green, where he joined a sect called the Philadelphians, and died there in 1680. Crab wrote an autobiography, *The English Hermit, or The Wonder of the Age* (1655), and various pamphlets, including tracts against the Quakers. Many of his ideas were representative of those of the radical fringe of the English Revolution — although he was a good deal more logical in action than most extremists. He was a teetotaller as well as a vegetarian, for economic as well as for dietetic reasons, because drink raised the price of corn, and a Leveller, claiming that 'all our proprieties are but the fruit of God's curse'. He was violently anti-clerical, condemning the Church as 'that House of the Whore's merchandise', and the clergy as 'Pimps and Pandors'. Like many Levellers, he gave up hope in the 1650s of any sudden improvement in man's state, and, while retaining his radical hostility to the social order, he took to pacifism and the belief that only through individual transformation could a new world be born.

Christopher Hill, *Puritanism and Revolution*, 1958, pp. 314–22.

JOHN PENRUDDOCK (*d.* 1655), of Compton Chamberlayne in Wiltshire, has given his name to the only Royalist rising against the government of Oliver Cromwell. Penruddock's Rising, or the Wiltshire Rebellion, of March 1655, was a small affair involving less than four hundred men and it was easily crushed. The rebels seized Salisbury; proclaimed Charles II at Blandford; completely failed to rally the support they anticipated in Dorset; and were broken by a troop of regular cavalry in three hours' fighting in South Molton. Penruddock was beheaded at Exeter after a fair trial, about fifteen others were put to death, and many more were sent to Barbados as indentured servants. Behind this hopeless episode lay a widespread Royalist conspiracy. Late in 1653 a secret group, the Sealed Knot, was formed to organize an armed restoration of the monarchy, and its plans for 1655 envisaged a major rising in Yorkshire, with simultaneous movements against the Commonwealth in Lincolnshire, Cheshire, and Shropshire, and the south-west from Hampshire to Cornwall. But the Sealed Knot was excessively cautious. The government got on the track, strengthened its own forces, and arrested many Royalists; the projects in the north and along the Welsh border fizzled out; and Penruddock's futile rising was virtually all that happened. The whole episode lowered the morale, never very high, of the more active Royalists. More important, it gave Cromwell's government the opportunity to introduce, in the autumn of 1655, the most unpopular of all its devices — the system whereby England was divided into eleven areas with a Major-General set over each, a system in effect of government by the sword.

A. H. Woolrych, *Penruddock's Rising*, 1655, Historical Association Pamphlet, G.29, 1955.

RICHARD CROMWELL(1626–1712), 'Tumbledown Dick', the third son of Oliver, was educated at Felsted School and seems to have grown into an idle young man whose main interest was in field sports. The deaths of his brothers, Robert in 1639 and Oliver in

1644, left Richard as Cromwell's eldest surviving son. He was a member of Fairfax's lifeguard, but, unlike his brother Henry, he showed no aptitude for soldiering. After his marriage his father complained that he neglected his estate and ran into debt. Although he was an M.P. in 1654 and 1656 and was put on the Committee of Trade and Navigation in 1655 he was not schooled for high place, and Oliver at one time was clearly anxious that his sons should not have greatness thrust upon them by inheritance. But the Humble Petition and Advice of 1657, with its provision that the Protector should nominate his successor, changed the situation and Richard, admitted to the Council of State and given command of a regiment, was treated as the heir-apparent. In September 1658, Oliver on his deathbed named Richard as successor, and he was publicly proclaimed Lord Protector three hours after his father died.

He held office for eight months. At first he was well received at home and abroad, and Thurloe could write 'There is not a dog that wags his tongue, so great a calm are we in', but he pointed Richard's road to failure by adding 'there are some secret murmurings in the army'. Richard firmly rejected an early proposal that a separate Commander-in-Chief should be appointed. But he wholly lacked Oliver's prestige with officers and men, the old guard of Republicans were against him, there were jealousies in the Council, and the financial difficulties of the government increased criticism. The Parliament called in January 1659 confirmed Richard as Protector but only after considerable debate. The council of the army, meeting without authority, began to plot, and in April the officers, led by Fleetwood and Desborough, carried out a coup and Richard yielded to their demand that he should dissolve Parliament. It was the end of the Protectorate and of the Cromwellian state.

Richard loyally accepted the new regime which came with the recall of the Rump in May 1659, and he declined to listen to Royalist moves to persuade him to support a restoration. But he refused for some time to leave Whitehall, for fear of the bailiffs: he claimed to have incurred £29,000 debt on behalf of the state. He was apparently still hiding from his creditors in April 1660, when he appealed to Monck for help, and shortly after this he went to Paris, where he lived for years in retirement under the name of 'John Clark', moving later to Geneva. He returned to England about 1680 and lived at Cheshunt, still using his pseudonym, 'retired, quiet and silent', as he himself described his lot, until his death in 1712. A man of honour and quiet dignity, Richard Cromwell was quite unsuited by nature or by training for the fate that came upon him. The contrast with his father, in ability, energy and experience, was too great, and led naturally to the officers' nickname of 'Queen Dick' and to Dryden's 'foolish Ishbosheth'. Yet he knew his own limitations, to his country's great gain, when at his fall he declined to be the occasion of renewed civil war, saying 'I will not have one drop of blood spilt for the preservation of my greatness'.

R. W. Ramsey, *Richard Cromwell*, 1935.
E. M. Hause, *Tumbledown Dick — The Fall of the House of Cromwell*, 1972.
Ivan Roots, 'The Short and Troublesome Reign of Richard IV', *History Today*, March 1980.

GEORGE MONCK, 1st DUKE OF ALBEMARLE (1608–70), was born at Potheridge near Torrington, of a landed family long established in Devon, connected by marriage with the Grenvilles. There is a tale that at the age of sixteen he thrashed the under-sheriff of Devon, who had arrested his father for debt (after being bribed not to do so), and he was certainly packed off on Buckingham's expedition to Cadiz under Sir Richard Grenville in 1625. This episode began a career of fighting which took him to La Rochelle in 1627–8 and to the Low Countries in the 1630s. In 1638 he returned to England a skilled soldier, distinguished by the courage which he had shown in the capture of Breda (1637) and by the seriousness with which he took his profession. He took part in the Bishops' Wars (1638–9); like Fairfax, he saw his troops routed at Newburn. In 1642 he commanded a regiment of Foot against the rebels in Ireland, and in 1643 he was one of the Royalist commanders defeated and captured by Fairfax at Nantwich. Sent to the Tower, he remained there until the end of the First Civil War, consoling himself by writing a book, *Observations upon Military and Political Affairs*, and by making love to his laundress, Mrs. Nan Ratsford, a blacksmith's daughter. From 1647 to 1649 he served Parliament as Major-General in Ulster, returning to England after making an armistice with the rebel leader Owen Roe O'Neill; this incident

George Monck, 1st Duke of Albemarle c.1665–6
(Artist: studio of Sir Peter Lely)

temporarily clouded his reputation, but not with Cromwell, under whom he fought at Dunbar (1650); and it was Monck who reduced Scotland to order by the end of 1651.

In the following year Monck, at the age of forty-four, became an Admiral, in the First Dutch War. His ignorance of nautical language was a joke; his Chaplain and first biographer, Thomas Gumble, says

W.S.B.—H*

that when the seamen, according to their terms of art, cried 'starboard and larboard', he always cried, 'Ay, boys, let us board them'. Yet he proved a successful naval commander in action, displaying his natural vigour and courage and also considerable strategical and tactical insight. His victory in the battle of the Gabbard (1653), after his fellow-admiral Richard Deane had been killed by his side, was a convincing one; and later in the same year off Scheveningen he deliberately employed the manoeuvre of 'breaking the enemy's line from to leeward' to cut the Dutch fleet in half and win the battle in which the great Dutch Admiral Van Tromp was killed. This practically ended the war, and in 1654 Monck returned to Scotland as Governor — a mark of the trust which Cromwell, now Lord Protector, placed in him. He ruled with moderation and was not unpopular. Yet the real significance of this part of his career lay in its ending; for his authority in Scotland, his army and the full treasury which he built up, gave him a central position in the crisis which gradually developed after Cromwell's death in September 1658. For six months George Monck was to be the dominant figure in England, and the use he made of his power was decisive in our history.

He accepted and supported Richard Cromwell, and when Richard departed he submitted to the recalled Rump, writing to the Speaker in June 1659 'obedience is my great principle, and I have always, and ever shall, reverence the Parliament's resolutions in civil things as infallible and sacred'. Later that summer he showed no sympathy with the Royalist intrigues which caused Sir George Booth's futile rising. What moved Monck to intervention in England was the breach between Parliament and the army commanders headed by Lambert and Fleetwood, who in October expelled the Rump. Monck purged his army of disaffected elements and prepared to march south; the unpopularity of military rule led the commanders to change their mind and recall the Rump in December; whereupon Monck, crossing the Tweed at Coldstream on New Year's Day, 1660, moved on London. The army which Lambert led north to halt him melted away in Yorkshire, with Fairfax taking the field against it. On his way Monck declared firmly against monarchy, but committed himself to nothing else; his remarkable natural taciturnity was no doubt invaluable, yet it seems likely that he had at this stage no definite policy. After his arrival in London (3 February) he submitted at first to the Rump's orders to punish the city for its defiance; but seeing how bitterly resented this action was, he turned on his masters with an ultimatum and on 21 February readmitted the members excluded by Pride's Purge twelve years earlier, a tremendously popular step which enabled Parliament to dissolve itself and opened the way to a free election. At the same time, convinced that only the return of the King would prevent anarchy, he consented at last to receive a letter from Charles II, now in Holland. 'Cautious to the end, he refused to commit anything to paper, but sent some valuable advice orally.' * The advice was the basis of the Declaration of Breda (April), itself the foundation of the Restoration settlement. The elections held later that month returned a strong Royalist majority, and Monck at last made clear to Parliament his approval of the return of the monarchy. Appropriately, it was George Monck who welcomed Charles II on the beach at Dover in May and, in effect, handed his kingdom back to him.

The great moment of his career was over. Loaded with honours and created Duke of Albemarle, he served Charles II well for ten years. Modest in his tastes, careful with his accumulated wealth, old-fashioned in his standards, he was out of place at the Restoration court; and so was the Duchess of Albemarle, the former laundress of the Tower, who had been his mistress and whom he married in 1654 after the death of her farrier husband. Little attention was paid to his political views; but in military matters he was regarded with respect. It was Monck who presided over the disbandment of the greater part of the Cromwellian Army in the months after the Restoration. He went to sea once more, against De Ruyter in the Second Dutch War (1664–7), but with little success; nor could he prevent the disaster of the Dutch attack on the fleet in the Medway, though his appointment to command did much to quell panic in London. He died in 1670 and was buried in high state in Westminster Abbey.

Charles II's government was too poor to build a monument for Monck; and later historians have tended to neglect him. In many ways he was easy to poke fun at, and to underrate. His lady, something of a scold, besides her lowly origins; his homely establishment; his slowness of speech; his total lack of brilliance; his equally

* G. Davies, *The Early Stuarts*, 1959 ed., p. 257.

total lack of political ambition — these things, in different ways, made contemporaries underestimate him. Pepys (24 October, 1667) could write: 'I know not how, the blockhead Albermarle hath strange luck to be loved, though he be (and every man must know it) the heaviest man in the world, but stout and honest to his country'. Thomas Gumble assessed him differently, saying 'his Judgement was slow but sure, he was very cogitative, and of a great natural prudence and cunning in his own affairs'. There is a measure of irony about Monck's career. Essentially a professional soldier, dedicated to his calling, he achieved little in land warfare; his campaigns in Ireland were abortive, he was defeated in his only battle in England and spent the remainder of the Civil War in the Tower, his main achievement in Scotland was as a proconsul rather than as a general. On the sea, by contrast, where he was an amateur, he may be regarded as an innovator — the founder of the *melée* school of naval warfare, anticipating Rodney by over a century. Above all, at the climax of his life, it was Monck's interpretation of the proper role of the army in the state which put an end to the Commonwealth and to military rule in England. For he believed simply and profoundly that soldiers should be the servants of civil authority, not the instruments of generals ambitious for dictatorship. 'I am engaged', he said, 'in conscience and honour to see my country freed from that intolerable slavery of a sword government, and I know that England cannot, nay, will not endure it.' Monck presided over the Restoration, ensuring that it was peaceful. By the manner in which he achieved this he achieved something which, on a long view, was much more important than the return of the Stuarts; on the morrow of the triumphs of the Cromwellian Army, the most remarkable army in English history, one of whose leading commanders he had been, he established the tradition that the British Army is non-political. No doubt George Monck owed a good deal to luck, to the realism of Charles II, to the blunders of Lambert and the other generals. But it is not easy to dispute the force of Gumble's rambling observation: 'His prudence was a Virtue Paramount in him and Mistress of all the rest, and this appeared that after the exclusion of Majesty, and put out of the Throne for many years, he restored it without one drop of blood, and made them his instruments, who had been the excluders, and having to doe with so many various interests and factions, (all striving for the Power) he managed them so well that they were all serviceable to his ends, and those children of the Serpent, with all their little Policies and cunning, could never give him the Go-by, but he out-witted them all.'

Maurice Ashley, *General Monck*, 1977.

CHARLES II (1630–85) was born to Henrietta Maria in St. James's Palace in 1630. Despite a promise in his mother's marriage treaty, he was brought up as an Anglican and not a Roman Catholic. Civil war and exile were his preparation for kingship; at the age of twelve he was present at Edgehill, at fifteen he was nominally in command of the last attempts to hold south-west England for the Crown, at sixteen he had escaped by way of Scilly and Jersey to France. He spent the next fourteen years, all his youth, in exile, coming once only to the kingdom he inherited upon his father's execution in January 1649. This visit lasted from the spring of 1650 to the autumn of 1651. In 1650 to win Scottish support he accepted a Covenant in which he did not believe and abandoned to his death Montrose, the noblest of his Scottish servants. When Cromwell had shattered the Covenanters at Dunbar in September of that year, Charles at the head of a new alliance of Scotsmen invaded England, only to see this second army destroyed twelve months later at Worcester. His escape from the battlefield into exile — with the devotion of simple peasants, the Catholic priest-holes, the hiding in the oak tree — has become a part of English legend. The bitterness of these eighteen months of 1650–1 transformed Charles, searing and hardening him, yet without diminishing that capacity for self-indulgence which was so prominent throughout his life. For nearly nine years after Worcester he and his 'court' — a faction-ridden and poverty-stricken crowd of advisers, nobles, servants and camp-followers — remained in exile, in France, the Rhineland, the Spanish Netherlands, Holland, moving as the influence of the Commonwealth government compelled them to move. The death of Oliver in 1658 gave substance to their hopes, the follies of the Rump and the soldiers made them come true. In 1660 Charles began to negotiate with the Presbyterians in England and with George Monck, and in April he issued on the latter and Hyde's advice the Declaration of Breda, promising indemnity for all except such as Parliament should exclude, 'liberty to tender consciences', a land settlement, and

Charles II
(Artist: John Michael Wright, 1660)

arrears of pay for the army, the whole to be subject to the approval of a new Parliament. Public opinion swung swiftly and strongly towards the monarchy and in May, Charles was recalled, landing at Dover and riding to London amid scenes of general popular rejoicing.

'A tall, dark man, above two yards high', as one of the placards offering reward for his capture after Worcester had proclaimed, Charles II was a man of vigorous physical appetites. He was athletic, a brisk walker, dancer, tennis-player and rider; he rode a winner at Newmarket the year before he died. He had a great many mistresses, from Lucy Walter in the later 1640s to the Duchess of Portsmouth thirty years later; the *Complete Peerage* credits (if that is the right word) him with fourteen illegitimate children. Halifax thought that 'his inclinations to love were the effects of health and a good constitution, with as little mixture of the seraphic part as ever man had'. Behind the swarthy, sensual face, the hard eyes and the bawdy tongue lay a mind which historians have tended to overrate. Experience had made him wary, cynical and unprincipled; shrewd where his father and his brother were stupid, he lacked the idealism which in some measure redeems Charles I and even James II. No doubt he was a realist, anxious to avoid 'going on his travels again'. But there never was much danger of his doing so, for Englishmen had had enough of Republicanism, and there was no real alternative to Charles II; as he himself put it to his brother James, 'they will never kill me to make you King'. There is little evidence in his reign of any consistency of policy, indeed, little desire to pursue any policy at all beyond the short term. Burnet was a harsh and censorious critic, yet it is difficult to move far from his verdict: 'He was during the active part of life given up to sloth and lewdness to such a degree, that he hated business, and could not bear the engaging in anything that gave him much trouble, or put him under any constraint. And, tho' he desired to become absolute, and to overturn both our religion and our laws, yet he would neither run the risque, nor give himself the trouble, which so great a design required.' There is no sign that his desire for religious toleration was any more sincere than his brother's in the next reign. His foreign policy consisted largely of placing England in pawn to Louis XIV, whose despotism he envied. Affable and charming though he was, there was a savage unscrupulousness below the surface. He had his full share of the Stuart disloyalty to those who served them well; and the later years of his reign saw him grow more cruel. It was Charles, not James II, who made Jeffreys Lord Chief Justice. The most adroit politician among the Stuart rulers of England, he employed his talents to limited ends.

His power was from the start more constricted than his father's had been. The Restoration settlement had to be a compromise, to win the adherence of those in place under the Commonwealth. So the clock was put back to 1641, not to 1640; Charles had no Star Chamber, nor any unparliamentary taxation. Parliament gave him revenue estimated at £1,200,000 per annum, largely dependent on customs and excise; but for ten years from 1664 the effect of the Second Dutch War on trade was disastrous, leaving royal revenue about £100,000 per annum short of the estimate. Most of the army was paid off. The land settlement benefited the profiteers as much as the faithful Royalists. As for religion, the Cavalier Parliament (1661–79) transformed 'liberty to tender consciences' into the persecuting Clarendon Code; and Charles quickly abandoned his half-hearted Declaration of Indulgence of 1662. In the main, therefore, Charles exercised his power within limits partly constitutional, partly prudential. He was master of his ministers, yet not invariably master of Parliament, and he was evidently dependent on the goodwill of the land-owning class, the principal beneficiaries of the Restoration. Unlike his brother James, Charles was not driven on by a blind faith to throw away that goodwill. His natural reaction to the novel constitutional position was — usually — to accept its implications, at least when no tactical evasion was possible. As Halifax observed, 'that Yieldingness, whatever Foundations it might lay to the Disadvantage of Posterity, was a Specifick to preserve us in Peace for his own Time'.

For the first seven years Clarendon was his chief minister. They were not very triumphant years. Besides the Plague (1665) and the Fire of London (1666) they saw the King's marriage to Catherine of Braganza (1662) and the Second Dutch War (1664-7). The marriage, a stroke of French policy, was a failure (though the cash from the dowry was useful), for Catherine, convent-bred and rather stupid, was quite out of place at the Restoration Court; moreover, she failed to produce any children. Charles quickly made it clear that she was less important than the reigning mistress, the Countess of Castlemaine, and the utmost that can be said of his later treatment of her is that it was not undignified. Clarendon, a trifle unfairly, was blamed for the deficiencies of the marriage; and — even more unfairly, for he had opposed it — for the defeats of the Dutch War, which culminated in the destruction of English warships at anchor in the Medway (1667). Charles, ready enough to see him used as a scapegoat, despite a quarter-of-a-century's devotion, dismissed him from office, and allowed him to go once more into exile.

From 1667 to 1673 Charles employed — with varying degrees of trust and for varying purposes — the group of ministers misleadingly known as the Cabal. Most of his political confidence seems to have gone to Arlington, but the central episode of this period, the Treaty of Dover (1670) was the King's own policy. The open clauses engaged England to join France in a war against the Dutch, duly undertaken in 1672. Secret clauses provided for Charles — in his own time — to declare himself a Catholic, to receive the help of French troops to convert his countrymen, and to be paid subsidies (the first was about £166,000) by Louis XIV. The reasons for so extraordinary a step remain a mystery; it seems simplest to believe that it was the money — not a large sum, but the more attractive when it came from France — he wanted. Certainly it was not religious zeal that moved him, for not until he was on his deathbed did he declare himself a Roman Catholic. In the light of this episode it is difficult to regard Charles as patriotic, save by very special pleading. Yet it is also difficult to believe that he — or Louis XIV, also, at this stage, a realist — saw the whole thing as more than a convenient bargain which gave Charles some cash and Louis an additional proof of English alliance against the Dutch. The consequence was not very satisfactory to either of them. The Third Dutch War (1672–4) was neither very successful nor popular in England, and Charles was forced to withdraw because Parliament refused to give him money to continue. As for religion, Charles in 1672 introduced another Declaration of Indulgence, granting freedom of worship to all dissenters. Parliament retaliated in 1673 with the Test Act, compelling all holders of civil or military office under the Crown to take the Anglican sacrament and to declare against transubstantiation. The Cabal lost whatever unity it had and disintegrated, with Shaftesbury, dismissed, becoming the first leader of a party opposition in English history, and Clifford, a Catholic, resigning. And the whole episode had a profound general effect. 'From about this time for many years to come it was one of the constant factors in English history that a solid body of Englishmen, who disagreed about many other things, were agreed in fearing three things which they believed to be closely allied — popery, France, and arbitrary power.' This was the great unintended result of Charles II's foreign policy.

In 1673 the King appointed Thomas Osborne, later Earl of Danby, as chief minister and proceeded — characteristically — to pursue a policy entirely contradictory to that of the Dover Treaty. After making peace with France he nearly joined in the war again on the opposite side, and in 1677 Danby arranged what might perhaps, despite its infertility, be regarded as the most important single marriage in British history, that of the Duke of York's daughter Mary, the heir presumptive, to the Protestant champion, William of Orange. Nevertheless — again characteristically — Charles kept in financial touch with France, drawing a series of subsidies from Louis XIV. Danby himself, as chief minister, had been involved in these dealings, and in 1679 the revelation of this in the Commons was an important element in his impeachment and fall from office. By this time, however, Titus Oates had invented and published (October 1678) his Popish Plot, and Charles was faced with the most serious crisis of his reign. The threat was not so much to himself: a good deal leaked out about his negotiations with Louis, but the secret terms of Dover were not published until 1682, by which time the crisis was over. It was the monarchy and the principle of hereditary succession which were threatened by the Whig proposals for 'Exclusion'.

Charles emerged triumphant, his considerable tactical skill aided by the revival of trade and by French money, by the extravagances of the opposition, and by the impossibility in seventeenth-century conditions of sustaining pressure on public opinion over a long period. He made no attempt to save Oates's Catholic victims until the Queen was threatened, when he defended her fiercely. He dissolved the Cavalier Parliament (which had sat since 1661) in February 1679 and his second the same July; he avoided meeting another until November 1680, and got rid of it in January 1681; in April 1681 he called his fourth Parliament to Oxford, away from Whig London, and dissolved it after a week, secure in the promise from Louis XIV of £400,000 in the next three years. The Whigs' nerve failed, and for the remaining four years of his reign Charles II ruled as he pleased. He refrained from calling Parliament, despite the

Triennial Act of 1641; the Rye House Plot (1683) enabled him to execute some of the Whig leaders and to persecute the Dissenters; and he attempted to safeguard the future by remodelling the town charters. Opposition was silenced, and Charles could once more saunter free from care, leaving the work of government to his brother James and to Tory loyalists.

When Charles II died in February 1685, the victim of a stroke, the monarchy seemed more secure and even more powerful than at his accession twenty-five years earlier. Appearances were delusive, as James II was to discover. Charles's pro-French and pro-Catholic policies had aroused the opposition, and he had driven it underground, not destroyed it, in the last four years of his reign. It is significant that the major constitutional results of Charles II's reign were the creation of the tradition of Parliamentary opposition and the passage of the Habeas Corpus Act. Nevertheless, the English people (not those of Scotland, where his rule was tyrannical) owed something to his laziness. The last words on Charles II must always be those of Halifax: 'Let his Royal Ashes then lie soft upon him, and cover him from harsh and unkind Censures; which though they should not be unjust can never clear themselves from being indecent'.

George Savile, Marquess of Halifax, 'A Character of King Charles II, in *Complete Works*, ed. W. Raleigh, 1912.

K. H. D. Haley, *Charles II* (Historical Association Pamphlet G63), 1966.

David Lunn, 'Charles II', *Evidence in History*, 1979.

Antonia Fraser, *King Charles II*, 1979.

CATHERINE OF BRAGANZA (1638–1705), the unlucky Queen of Charles II, was a Portuguese princess, daughter of John IV, who became the first Braganza King of Portugal in 1640. Her marriage to Charles II in 1662, a diplomatic manoeuvre backed by Louis XIV, was an event of first-class historical importance. For Portugal, it safeguarded her from the reassertion of the Spanish control which had ended in 1640 and did much to secure the Braganza dynasty on the throne, by confirming the medieval alliance with England. To England it gave Tangier, quickly dispensed with, but not before it had blunted the sensibilities of some of the soldiers who were to crush the wretched followers of Monmouth; and

Bombay, to become one of the roots of English power in India. It confirmed the trading privileges which Cromwell had extorted, and brought sugar, mahogany and port wine. More broadly, it deepened English interest in the Mediterranean and, as David Ogg put it, 'more definitely turned the directions of English policy to the wider horizons of maritime empire'. * To Charles II, it brought some £330,000 in hard cash, even though it was eighteen years before the last instalment was paid. Most important of all, the barrenness of the match helped to send Clarendon into exile in 1667, and put James II on the English throne in 1685.

To Catherine the marriage brought much unhappiness. A simple childish girl, educated in a nunnery, of whom Pepys, seeing her for the first time, said 'She hath a good, modest, and innocent look'; neither particularly beautiful (Charles's own first impression was 'her face is not so exact as to be called a beauty though her eyes are excellent good, and not anything in her face that in the last degree can shock one') nor witty; she found herself at the centre of a licentious and highly sophisticated court, and compelled to receive Charles's current mistress, Lady Castlemaine, as well as to endure her existence. There was a prolonged quarrel, profoundly embarrassing to Clarendon who was set to appease the Queen, and who has described the episode tartly yet fully. In its course Catherine's Portuguese ladies, called by Clarendon 'for the most part old and ugly and proud', were sent home. Eventually she yielded and accepted the situation meekly. She felt a passionate devotion for Charles; he for his part tolerated her on his own terms, showing warmth of feeling only at the times when she was thought to be pregnant. It was a pathetic rather than a tragic situation. According to Pepys there was gossip about the possibility of a divorce as early as 1667, and two members of the Cabal, Buckingham and Shaftesbury, proposed that the King should take this step. But Charles steadily refused, and at the time of the Popish Plot, when Oates and Bedloe produced a tale that the Queen was involved in a plot with the Catholic peers to murder him, he ignored it and stood firm in her defence. When he was dying she sent a message to beg his pardon if she had offended him in all her life, to which he answered, 'Alas, poor woman! She ask my pardon? I beg hers with all my heart'.

---

* D. Ogg, *England in the Reign of Charles II*, 1956 ed, Vol. 1, p. 187.

Whatever the tribulations of queenship, she thought well enough of England to remain in this country until 1692, when she returned to pass the remainder of her days in Portugal.

C.R. Boxer, 'The Anglo-Portuguese Marriage Treaty of 1661', *History Today*, August 1961, pp. 556–63.

HENRIETTE ANNE, DUCHESS OF ORLEANS (1644–70), 'Madame', was born in Exeter, the fifth daughter of Charles I, and baptized in its cathedral. When Queen Henrietta Maria fled to France fifteen days later she left her baby behind, and in Exeter the princess stayed until the city surrendered to the Parliamentarians in 1646. That same year her governess, Lady Dalkeith, managed to smuggle her across to France, disguised as a boy. She spent most of her life in France, where her mother had her brought up in the Roman faith, and she grew into a sweet-natured girl, vivacious yet delicate, charming rather than beautiful. Charles her brother was much attached to 'Minette', as he called her. In 1661 she married Louis XIV's brother Philip, Duke of Orleans: it was an unhappy match, for Orleans was effeminate, self-centred and jealous. 'Madame' is most celebrated for her role in the secret Treaty of Dover of 1670. Certainly she had for some time beforehand been the chief intermediary between Charles and Louis, and she took a full part in the ten days of negotiation at Dover, but it is clear that the essentials of the treaty had been settled previously by the Kings and the diplomatists. Within a month of its signature she was dead, the victim almost certainly of acute peritonitis, although there was a widespread rumour that Orleans had poisoned her.

C.H. Hartmann, *The King My Brother*, 1954.

ANNE HYDE (1637–71), first wife of James, Duke of York, was the eldest daughter of the Earl of Clarendon. Plain ('like her mother, my Lady Chancellor', according to Pepys) yet witty and lively, she caught James's fancy first in 1656 while she was a maid of honour to Mary of Orange. Though there was some sort of contract in 1659, it looks as if James wanted to get out of it after the Restoration, and Clarendon got into such a panic that he seems to have been ready to have his daughter's head cut off for being so ambitious as to let the heir-presumptive make her pregnant. But

James married her at the King's orders in September, and a child was born in October. Anne took to her new role with dignity, as well as with parvenu pride, and even won over Henrietta Maria, though her ungracious young brother-in-law Gloucester said that she always carried about with her the smell of her father's green bag. She had a hard mouth and ruled James firmly, so that Charles nicknamed him 'Tom Otter' after the henpecked husband in Ben Jonson's *Epicene*, and she retaliated to his succession of mistresses by an affair with Henry Sidney. Pepys, who knew them well, recorded that 'the Duke of York, in all things but in his amours, is led by the nose by his wife'. He also observed that 'the Duchess is not only the proudest woman in the world, but the most expenseful'. Of their eight children, two survived, the later Queens Mary and Anne. After her father Clarendon went into exile in 1667, Anne Hyde was converted to Roman Catholicism. She died of cancer of the breast at the age of thirty-four.

WILLIAM CHIFFINCH (1602?–88), held the office of Page of the Bedchamber or Closet-keeper to Charles II. In the words of *D.N.B.* he was 'employed in secret and confidential transactions'; in those of David Ogg, 'confidential agent, procurer-general, and pawnbroker-in-chief to the King'. As custodian of the backstairs he was an essential element in the machinery of Charles II's government as well as in his private life. In Halifax's words, Charles 'had backstairs to convey Informations to him, as well as for other uses', and politicians and mistresses both found Chiffinch important as barrier or channel. Pepys seems to have enjoyed a gossip and a dinner with him from time to time. No doubt others as well as Jeffreys found through him their first access to the source of power. He handled large sums of money, including at least part of Charles II's subsidies from Louis XIV. Roger North has an account of Chiffinch's ability to worm secrets out of others by outdrinking them, being himself 'a most impetuous drinker'. When Charles died, Chiffinch continued to hold his post under James II, dying in 1688 before the Revolution.

BARBARA VILLIERS, COUNTESS OF CASTLEMAINE and DUCHESS OF CLEVELAND (1641–1709), mistress of Charles II, was the 'lady of youth and beauty, with whom the King had lived in great and notorious familiarity from the time of his coming into England', as Clarendon puts it. With auburn hair, wistful blue eyes and slim figure, she was very beautiful. She was also, in Burnet's words, 'enormously vicious and ravenous', and her lovers, besides Charles and her complaisant husband, Roger Palmer, whom she married in 1659 and who was created Earl of Castlemaine in 1661, included the Earl of Chesterfield, John Churchill, Ralph Montagu, the playwright William Wycherley, and Jacob Hall the rope-dancer. *Maîtresse en titre* for the first seven years of the reign, she was forced upon Catherine of Braganza as lady-in-waiting. In some ways her authority was great, as Henry Killigrew found when in 1666 he was banished from court, and she relished her part in the campaign which got rid of Clarendon in 1667. But her political influence was small, like that of all Charles's women except the Duchess of Portsmouth. For the King, as Clarendon observed, 'did not in his nature love a busy woman, and had an aversion from speaking with any woman, or hearing them speak, of any business but to that purpose he thought them all made for'. Financially as well as sexually greedy, Castlemaine did well out of her charms, with a grant in 1669 of £4,700 a year from the revenues of the post office, rents from Irish lands, the royal estate of Nonsuch, and sundry other items. She bore Charles at least five children. The hold of this 'lewd Imperial Whore' declined at the end of the 1660s, and her creation as Duchess of Cleveland in 1670 was a sign that she was pensioned off. Yet one later episode in her career was of political consequence. After living in Paris with Ralph Montagu, English ambassador to France, she complained to Charles in 1678 that he had seduced their daughter; Montagu was dismissed, and in revenge revealed to the Commons Danby's secret negotiations with Louis, action which led to the fall of Danby and the dissolution of the Cavalier Parliament. She lived on until 1709. Her husband died in 1705, and the following year she diverted London society by marrying a former Major-General, 'Beau' Feilding. Before long he was in Newgate for maltreating her, and it was discovered that he already had a wife.

NELL GWYNNE (1650–87), mistress of Charles II, was according to one tradition born in Hereford, according to another in Drury Lane. She sold oranges at the Theatre Royal and there began as an actress in the middle 1660s. Frank and wild, 'a bold merry slut' in Pepys's phrase, she was an excellent comedienne. Pepys, who evidently had a weakness for her, thought 'pretty witty Nell' outstanding as Florimel in Dryden's *The Maiden Queen*, which he saw several times, and called her 'beyond imitation almost' in 'mad' parts, though he thought little of her in serious ones. Charles was attracted by her dark ringlets, by the legs of which she was naively vain, and by her sauciness. She bore him one son, later ennobled as the Duke of St. Alban's, in 1670 and another in 1671; and he kept his affection for her. 'The indiscreetest and wildest creature that ever was in a court' (Burnet), she was part of Charles's retinue when Parliament met at Oxford in 1681, and when the mob jostled her coach at Carfax, thinking it was that of her unpopular Catholic colleague the Duchess of Portsmouth, she delighted them by putting her head out of the window to shout 'Pray, good people, be civil; I am the Protestant whore'. Charles remembered her on his deathbed in the famous phrase 'Let not poor Nelly starve', and James paid off her debts and settled an estate near Nottingham upon her and upon the Duke of St. Alban's. When she died suddenly in 1687 Tenison preached the funeral sermon and found a good deal to say in her favour.

J.H. Wilson, *Nell Gwynne, Royal Mistress*, 1952.

LOUISE DE KEROUALLE, DUCHESS OF PORTSMOUTH (1649–1734), mistress to Charles II, came from an old Breton family and was maid of honour to Charles's sister, the Duchess of Orleans, with whom she first came to England in 1670, when the Treaty of Dover was being negotiated. Dark and beautiful with what Evelyn called her 'childish simple and baby face', she was an obvious candidate for the King's desires, and it was Buckingham who brought her back after the sudden death of the Duchess later that year. Catherine of Braganza had to accept her as a maid of honour, and by 1671 she was firmly established. In 1672 she bore Charles a son, later the Duke of Richmond; in 1674 she was created Duchess of Portsmouth; in 1675 she was given an annuity of £10,000. Evelyn in 1675 was shown her 'splendid apartment at Whitehall, luxuriously furnished, and with ten times the richness and glory beyond the Queen's'. 'Madam Carewell', as the English nicknamed her, was unpopular with Charles's subjects, for she was a

Louise de Keroualle, Duchess of Portsmouth c.1682
(Artist: Pierre Mignard)

Catholic, she was French, and she was rapacious, gaining an ample income, secured on public funds such as the post office revenues, for herself and her son, and having her Whitehall lodgings rebuilt and refurnished several times. Yet this rapacity was itself a sign that she was sure of Charles to a degree beyond that of any of her colleagues in his seraglio. For 'Fubbs', as he called Portsmouth, held a special place in his affections. Her appeal was not merely physical; as strong as ever in the last five years of his life, it reflected Portsmouth's patience, intelligence, and 'quintessential Frenchness'.* Her political significance, on the other hand, may easily be exaggerated, and certainly was by many contemporaries. Politicians, like Danby, took care to win her support. Louis XIV and his ambassadors attached considerable importance to her. She undoubtedly exercised great influence upon appointments, as, for example, when she got Sunderland made Secretary of State in 1683. But there is little real evidence that she altered the King's political decisions, and once at least, over Exclusion, he flatly rejected her advice. When Charles was taken fatally ill in 1685 it was Portsmouth who told the French ambassador Barillon to get James to find a Catholic priest; and the dying King twice commended her and Richmond to his brother's care. She spent much of James II's reign in England, and most of the remainder of her long life in France, dying there in 1734.

THOMAS VENNER (d. 1661), Fifth Monarchist and rebel, was a master cooper who emigrated to Massachusetts in the 1630s. Back in England by 1651, he got employment as a cooper in the Tower of London but, it seems, was sacked because he tried to blow it up. In the later 1650s he was head of a Fifth Monarchist church in Swan Alley, Coleman Street. The Fifth Monarchists (who were probably never more than 10,000 all told) believed that with the coming of King Jesus the elect would rule over the ungodly. A minority among them were willing to accelerate this event by violence, the more since they were particularly hostile to the rule of Oliver Cromwell, whom they readily identified with the Beast of the Book of Revelation. Venner was one of these. Briefly imprisoned in 1656, after the breakdown of talks with the Protectorate government, he attempted an armed rising in 1657 and was gaoled again until 1659. Undaunted by the Restoration — an event which indeed was irrelevant to a man of his beliefs — he tried again in 1661. With about fifty supporters he proclaimed 'King Jesus and the heads upon the gate' in the streets of London. Life Guards and other troops crushed the rebels at once. Venner, wounded nineteen times, and twelve others were executed and their heads displayed on London Bridge. But London had been in confusion, and, in the words of David Ogg, 'unfortunately from the truth that the Fifth Monarchy men were

* J.P. Kenyon, *The Stuarts*, 1958, p.135.

extremists was deduced the unwarrantable opinion that all Dissenters were politically dangerous'. * For the main historical significance of Venner's Rising of 1661 and the panic it caused lies in the
introduction of the Clarendon Code.

JAMES BUTLER, 12th EARL and 1st DUKE OF ORMONDE
(1610–88), Irish Viceroy, was born in Clerkenwell, member of the
old-established Anglo-Irish family. Educated as a Protestant and
mainly in England, he succeeded to the title in 1632, and after an
initial display of haughty independence was a loyal supporter of
Strafford in Ireland. Graceful, dignified, proud, wealthy, upright,
Ormonde served the Stuarts with splendid loyalty for over half a
century. From 1640 until he was driven out by Cromwell in 1650 he
was the effective leader of the Royalist cause in Ireland, and the
champion of Anglicanism against native Catholics and Ulster
Presbyterians alike. From 1651 until 1660 he was the adviser of the
exiled Charles II, an adviser bold but moderate after the heart of his
friend Clarendon. Given a dukedom and made Lord High Steward
at the Restoration, Ormonde was twice (1661–9 and 1677–84)
Lord Lieutenant of Ireland for Charles II. In his first term of office
he presided over the land settlement, in the second he kept Ireland
peaceful during the Popish Plot. He defended Irish interests, as for
example by his opposition to the bill forbidding the import of Irish
cattle into England, and to a remarkable extent he secured at least
the passive loyalty of the Catholic minority, aided no doubt by the
fact that almost all his near relatives were Catholics. In Restoration
England, like Clarendon, he belonged to a pre-war generation. The
fact that he was, in the words of Osmund Airy in *D.N.B.*, 'almost
the sole representative of the high-toned virtues of a nobler generation', made him enemies, and it was the opposition of Arlington
and Buckingham that brought his removal from office in 1669. His
second removal, in 1684, excusable on the score of age, came about
through pressure from James, Duke of York, on the basis of a secret
report written by his enemy Richard Talbot, later Earl of Tyrconnel.
When James was on the throne Ormonde firmly condemned his
dispensing and Catholicizing policy. He had never minced words
with his sovereigns: nearly forty years before he had replied to

* D. Ogg, *England in the Reign of Charles II*, 1956 ed., Vol. I, p. 208.

James Butler, 12th Earl and 1st Duke of Ormonde
(Artist: William Wissing)

Henrietta Maria's claim that if she had been trusted the King had now been in England, by saying that if she had never been trusted he had never been out of England. Ormonde had the manner, the authority and, to some extent, the power of an independent potentate, and his unfailing loyalty to the Stuarts was in a sense an act of condescension; for after all, the Butlers were as old as the Stuarts.

T. Carter, *The Life of James Duke of Ormonde*, 1735–6 and 1851.
Winifred Gardiner, Lady Burghclere, *Life of James Duke of Ormonde*, 2 vols., 1912.

EDWARD MONTAGU, 1st EARL OF SANDWICH (1625–72), Admiral and patron of Pepys, was the son of the member for Huntingdonshire in the Long Parliament. His father was a Royalist, but the family was divided, and Edward Montagu followed the lead of his cousin the Earl of Manchester. He was at Marston Moor and at Naseby, and he succeeded his father as the county member. In Barebone's Parliament he was prominent among the moderates, and under the Protectorate he was strongly attached to the cause of his neighbour Oliver Cromwell, whom he wanted to take the Crown. In 1656 he was appointed joint General-at-sea, although he had no naval experience. He went over to Royalism in 1659 after the fall of Richard, and brought his fleet back from the Sound in the hope of supporting Sir George Booth's rising. He arrived too late, but luckily the government was too busy coping with Lambert's activities, and Montagu was merely allowed to resign. Next year he was given joint command of the fleet with Monck, whom he detested, and purged it of Republicans and sectaries, before sailing to Holland to bring Charles II home on his flagship the *Naseby*, re-named *Royal Charles*. His reward for his services was the Earldom of Sandwich.

Sandwich had a somewhat chequered career in Charles II's reign. The picture of him which emerges even from his kinsman and protégé Pepys's *Diary* is not over-attractive. He was extravagant and much in debt, and in 1663 Pepys took it upon himself to write a 'great letter of reproof' to Sandwich about his conduct with his mistress, Mrs. Becke of Chelsea. As an Admiral he fought well at Lowestoft in 1664 under the Duke of York, breaking the Dutch line. But in 1665 he was in trouble over his handling of prize-goods, alleged to have been plundered by himself and his officers, and he was deprived of command and sent off on an embassy to Madrid. He returned to the sea in the Third Dutch War, and in 1672, having fought with great courage in the battle of Solebay, he was drowned after his ship was blown up. His body was later picked up and he was buried in Westminster Abbey.

F. R. Harns, *Edward Montagu, 1st Earl of Sandwich*, 1912.

SIR GEORGE DOWNING (1623?–84), the hard-faced business man who gave his name to Downing Street, was the son of a lawyer who had come to the Middle Temple from Salem, Massachusetts. Nephew of John Winthrop, Governor of that colony, he went with his parents to New England in 1638, and was one of the earliest graduates of Harvard College. After sailing to the West Indies, perhaps as a ship's chaplain, he came to England in the 1640s and joined the Parliamentary forces, serving, it is said, as a chaplain in Okey's regiment. By 1650 he was Scoutmaster-General of Cromwell's army in Scotland, and during the Commonwealth period he emerged as a politician, sitting in both the Cromwellian Parliaments, going on mission to Louis XIV to protest about the treatment of the Vaudois Protestants, and becoming in 1657 English resident at the Hague, where in Clarendon's words he 'would add to any imperious command of his (Cromwell's) somewhat of the bitterness of his own spirit'. His rise was no doubt aided by his marriage to a member of the Howard family; yet he was certainly a man of business capacity who quickly grasped the problems of Anglo-Dutch commercial relations at this period.

At the Restoration he dexterously changed sides, possibly easing the process by passing on to Charles information he had gleaned from his correspondence with Thurloe. He kept his post in Holland, and acquired a grant of land near Whitehall. In 1662 he arrested Okey and two other regicides while they were having a drink at Delft and sent them back to England for execution: Pepys's comment on this was 'all the world takes notice of him for a most ungrateful villain for his pains'. His contribution to Anglo-Dutch relations was unfortunate. 'Le plus grand querelleur de la diplomatie britannique', as a French dispatch called him, Downing was strongly hostile to the Dutch in commercial matters. His truculent attitude encouraged the outbreak of the Second Dutch War in 1665; and in 1671, when Charles wanted to provoke a breach with the Dutch, he again sent Downing as agent to the Hague, though this time he returned from Holland hastily and without orders, perhaps for fear of the Dutch mob, and spent a short time in the Tower as a result. At home Downing was more constructive. In 1665 he was the leading promoter of that clause in the Act for the Additional Aid, which marked the effective beginning of the process of appropriation of supply by ear-marking all money raised under the Act for the sole purpose of paying for the war; and as Secretary of the Commissioners from 1667 he was chiefly responsible for establishing a new system of book-keeping in the Treasury. As Member for Morpeth in the Parliaments of Charles II's reign he was 'a voluminous speaker' (Clarendon) on questions of trade and finance. In the last ten years before his death in 1684 he seems to have taken little part in public life.

Contemporaries disliked Downing intensely. They also thought him very wealthy, from royal bribes as well as his own investments; and no doubt the two opinions were connected. Both Clarendon and Pepys were somewhat biased, for Downing opposed Clarendon's policies and was for a time Pepys's boss. Yet both write with unusual scorn about Downing: Pepys calls him 'a niggardly fellow' and 'a mighty talker'. His public record is not attractive; a bully and a time-server, he exemplifies the worst results of the Restoration compromise. In New England a man who betrayed his trust was called 'an arrant George Downing'.

John Beresford, *The Godfather of Downing Street*, 1925.

GILBERT SHELDON (1598–1677), born at Stanton in Staffordshire, the son of a servant of the Earls of Shrewsbury, was educated at Trinity College, Oxford. In 1622 he became Fellow and in 1626 Warden of All Souls. Oxford don, royal Chaplain, friend of Edward Hyde, Sheldon was a member of Falkland's circle at Great Tew, not one of those who favoured or was favoured by Laud. When the Long Parliament met, his views were those of Hyde, with whom he kept in touch through the war years. In 1648 he was turned out of All Souls and briefly imprisoned, and during the Commonwealth he lived in retirement in his native midlands. Reinstalled at All Souls in 1659, he was appointed Bishop of London at the Restoration, and he was the dominant Anglican figure in the Savoy Conference and in the religious settlement that followed, although he did not go to Canterbury until Juxon's death in 1663. Sheldon was a subtle negotiator as well as a capable administrator. He was more responsible than any other man for the re-establishment of the Anglican Church and, more particularly, for the form that re-establishment took — with a supremacy clear and buttressed by law, yet free from the prerogative courts and from the other objectionable extremities of Laudianism. He was firm for the Act of Uniformity and for the resultant expulsion of Nonconformist clergy. An ecclesiastical statesman, courtly in manner, strong in judgment, one who in Burnet's unfavourable verdict regarded the Church as 'a matter of policy [rather] than of conscience', he was, as Burnet admits, generous and charitable, an Archbishop who stayed at Lambeth throughout the plague of 1665 while the court fled from London, and who reproved Charles II for adultery. The University of Oxford owes more to Sheldon than to most of the Archbishops who have been her sons. For he encouraged the antiquarian activities of Anthony à Wood, and he employed Wren to build at his expense the Sheldonian Theatre, opened in 1669.

V. D. Sutch, *Gilbert Sheldon, Architect of Anglican Revival, 1640–75,* 1973.

SIR MATTHEW HALE (1609–76), judge, born at Alderley in Gloucestershire, was educated at Magdalen Hall, Oxford, and trained in the law at Lincoln's Inn. He was a pupil of Noy and a protégé of Selden. Although Hale was one of Laud's counsel at his impeachment, he accepted the Parliamentarian regime and from 1654 served the Commonwealth as Chief Justice of Common Pleas. He sat in the Convention Parliament of 1660 and was appointed Chief Baron of the Exchequer, and in 1671 became Chief Justice of King's Bench. Hale was that rarity of later Sutart England, an upright judge, in integrity and in demeanour a notable contrast to such more celebrated occupants of the bench as Scroggs and Jeffreys. He defended unpopular causes both under the Commonwealth (for example, as counsel for Hamilton) and after the Restoration (when he tried to mitigate the Conventicle Act). Puritan in upbringing, plain in dress and speech, refusing to accept presents and dealing leniently with dissenters, Hale was in Baxter's phrase 'most precisely just'. An Anglican of severe cast who disliked ritual, he wished to comprehend dissenters within the Church, and was active in attempting to improve the poor law. He wrote extensively on religious and moral themes as well as on the law. In Aubrey's words, 'Matthew Hale was not only just, but wonderfully charitable and open-handed and did not sound a trumpet neither, as the hypocrites do'.

JOHN FELL (1625–86), Dean of Christ Church, born at Long-worth in Berkshire, was the son of Samuel Fell, Dean of Christ Church 1638–47. From Thame Free School he went to Christ Church, where he was elected a Student (i.e. Fellow) at the age of eleven. Ejected by the Parliamentarians in 1648, he remained a firm Royalist. Appointed Dean of the college in 1660, Fell was the dominant figure in Restoration Oxford, serving for some years as Vice-Chancellor of the University and becoming Bishop of the diocese in 1676 without giving up the deanery. Tall, vigorous, imperious and wilful, Fell kept Oxford firmly Royalist and Angli-can, attacking dissent and Romanism alike. With rather less success, he did his best to restore discipline, imposing rules for the wearing of academic dress, enforcing attendance at lectures, and taking a direct part in the examinations. He was particularly energetic, for reasons both of censorship and of scholarship, in developing the University Press, and at his own expense published Anthony à Wood's *History and Antiquities of Oxford*. His lasting memorial is to be found in the fabric of Christ Church: in his time the north side of the great quadrangle was completed and the terrace construced, and the Gothic 'Tom Tower', with Wren as architect, built over the gateway.

JOHN WILKINS (1614–72), scientist and divine, the son of an Oxford goldsmith, was born at Fawsley in Northamptonshire; his maternal grandfather was John 'Decalogue' Dod, joint-author with Robert Cleaver of the Puritan treatise on the Ten Commandments. Wilkins went to New Inn Hall and thence to Magdalen Hall, and after a short spell as Vicar of Fawsley became Chaplain to the Puritan peer Lord Saye and Sele and later to Charles Lewis, Elector Palatine. He sided with Parliament and took the Covenant. Yet his real interests were scientific. Evelyn calls him 'universally curious'. His first book — not very distinguished — was *Discovery of a New World, or Discourse On the World in the Moon* (1638), and Aubrey refers to 'Dr. Wilkins his notion of an Umbrella-like invention for retarding a ship when she drives in a storm'. He was an energetic member of Robert Boyle's 'invisible college' in London from 1645 onwards. In 1648 he was appointed Warden of Wadham, a mark of his loyalty to the Parliamentarian cause rather than of his learning. Yet it was a good appointment for the college and for Oxford.

Wilkins, moderate and humane, in Burnet's startling tribute 'the wisest clergyman I ever knew', set firm academic standards and safeguarded the university both from the anti-intellectualism of the extremer Puritans and from the worst consequences of military rule. No doubt his marriage in 1656 to Robina, the widowed sister of Cromwell, made his task easier. Meanwhile the meetings of the London philosophers were continued at Wadham, with Wilkins at their centre. Out of them, after the Restoration, grew the Royal Society: Wilkins took the chair at the meeting held in 1660 to discuss this project, and was the first secretary after the Society was chartered, so he has probably more claim than anyone else to be regarded as the principal figure in the foundation. He quickly made his peace with the Crown and with Anglicanism, and in 1668 was consecrated Bishop of Chester. That same year Pepys was busily reading Wilkins's *An Essay towards a Real Character and a Philosophical Language*, and next year he recorded — as 'foolish talk' — a rumour that Wilkins was to be made Lord Treasurer. Wilkins died in 1672. He was neither a distinguished scientist nor an outstanding scholar, but both the Royal Society and the University of Oxford owe him a great debt.

Margery Parver and E. J. Bowen, *The Beginning of the Royal Society*, 1960.

B. Shapiro, *John Wilkins: An Intellectual Biography*, 1969.

JONATHAN GODDARD (1617?–75), physician, son of a Deptford shipwright, entered Magdalen Hall, Oxford, in 1632, and in the later thirties may have been studying abroad or at Cambridge. From 1640 he was practising medicine in London, and he was elected a Fellow of the College of Physicians in 1646. Goddard was a member of that group of scientists in London, mostly connected with Gresham College, whose weekly meetings prepared the way for the Royal Society, and the mathematician John Wallis records how in 1645 they 'met sometimes at Dr. Goddard's lodging in Wood Street (or some place near) on account of his keeping an operator in his house for grinding glasses for telescopes and microscopes'. He served Oliver Cromwell as physician on both the Irish and Scottish campaigns of 1649–51 and as member of Barebone's Parliament and the Council of State. From 1651 to 1660 he was Warden of Merton

College, Oxford, and from 1655 Professor of Physic at Gresham College. After the Restoration, when he lost his Oxford post and apparently returned to his practice in London, Goddard was one of the leading figures in the establishment of the Royal Society; he was appointed to its first Council, and he was active in its experimental work on various subjects including 'the anatomy of wood'. Goddard was a prosperous doctor, famous for 'Goddard's Pills' which were supposed to revive sufferers from fainting, apoplectic seizures and 'lethargies', and which seem to have consisted mostly of ammonia. But he was not in any sense a medical pioneer like his contemporary Sydenham, nor was he a particularly distinguished scientist, although he may have been the first Englishman to make a telescope.

SIR WILLIAM PETTY (1623–87), founder-member of the Royal Society and pioneer of the use of statistics, was the son of a small clothier in Romsey, Hampshire. He learned Latin at school in Romsey; went to sea as a cabin boy at thirteen, broke his leg, and was put ashore in Normandy; became a pupil at the Jesuit College at Caen, paying his way by trade; served three years in the Navy, studied medicine in Holland, and worked as a journeyman-jeweller; acted as amanuensis for Thomas Hobbes in Paris; studied at Brasenose, and earned a living in oddments of laboratory work in Oxford and London; made a number of unprofitable inventions, including a double-writing instrument; and in 1650 became a Doctor of Physic of the University of Oxford, where he spent the better part of the next two years. Petty was one of the Fellows 'intruded' by Parliament into the governing body of Brasenose, and was shortly appointed Professor of Anatomy; he was also made Reader in Music at Gresham College in London. Public fame quickly came to him by chance through the strange affair called 'The Raising of Ann Green', in which he 'restored' a servant girl who had been hanged for abortion and coffined before life was entirely extinct. It was more important that at Oxford he was a member of the small group of scientists, including men like John Wilkins, John Wallis and Jonathan Goddard, out of which the Royal Society was later to grow, and which sometimes met at Petty's lodgings near All Souls.

Yet his stay in Oxford was short. In 1652 Petty was appointed physician to the Commonwealth Army in Ireland, and he spent many of the remaining thirty-five years of his life there. Land, not medicine, was his main concern, in this period of plantation after the Cromwellian conquest. His survey of twenty-two counties, the Down Survey, was the best for almost two centuries; in the 1660s he completed an impressive map of Ireland; a friend of Henry Cromwell, he did well for himself in the land market, owning perhaps 30,000 acres, many of them in Kerry, at his death. Acquisitive, pushing, and indiscreet, he frittered away much time and talent in financial and political feuds in Ireland. Yet it was probably his Irish experiences that directed this 'person of a stupendous invention and of as great prudence and humanity', as Aubrey calls him, into the particular form of social thinking which has made later generations interested in him.

Like many who had prospered under the Commonwealth, Petty adjusted himself comfortably to the Restoration, and was knighted in 1661. He was one of the twelve founder-members of the Royal Society, and a man of many projects. He had a passion for navigation and shipbuilding, and devised a double-bottomed boat, a controversial and not very happy experiment. But he was above all a pioneer in what we should to-day call the social sciences, interested in the application of quantitative analysis to social and economic problems. Much influenced by contemporary Dutch practice and ideas, by some of the trends of thought of the Commonwealth period, and by his friend John Graunt, he ranged not very systematically over a variety of social questions — unemployment and productivity, taxation, the penal code, land registration and planned care for the sick among them; his conclusions were usually of little value, although he sometimes produced anticipations of later approaches, as, for example, of the labour theory of value. From a later standpoint, by far his most interesting work concerned population statistics, to which he gave the name *Political Arithmetic*, writing an essay with this title in 1682 and a rather fuller work published three years after his death. Petty was one of the first men to recognize the importance of statistics in connection with such problems as taxation, employment, life insurance and the size of armed forces. His contemporaries found this short-sighted, heavy man, with his streak of vulgarity and his greed for worldly success, rather tiresome and slightly comic. The actual consequence of his work for the future can easily be overrated. Nevertheless, the pattern and direction of Petty's interests and thought provides an illuminating example of the new social and intellectual climate of late seventeenth-century England, a climate very different from that of the days of the early Stuarts.

E. Strauss, *Sir William Petty*, 1954.
Sir George Clark, *Science and Social Welfare in the Age of Newton*, 2nd ed., 1949.
K. Theodore Hoppen, 'Sir William Petty', *History Today*, February 1965, pp. 126–134.

JOHN GRAUNT (1620–74), founder of the modern study of statistics, born in London, was a haberdasher, a Puritan who became a Roman Catholic, and a man of notable integrity. Aubrey speaks of him as 'a man generally beloved' with 'an excellent working head'. Before his conversion to Catholicism he had been a member of the Common Council of London and a captain of the trained bands. Despite his trade, he was an original member of the Royal Society, and his fame rests upon his contribution to social science by the publication in 1662 of his *Observations upon the Bills of Mortality*, an attempt to draw conclusions of value to society from a study of the returns of the deaths which occurred in London. The book ran through four editions in Graunt's lifetime. From his figures Graunt drew up a 'life-table' showing the number of persons who could be expected to survive to certain ages (he reckoned that 7 per cent of Londoners lived to seventy, whereas 36 per cent died before the age of six), a type of mathematical calculation upon which modern life insurance is based.

JOHN WALLIS (1616–1703), mathematician and divine, son of a clergyman at Ashford in Kent, was educated at Felsted and at the notably Puritan college of Emmanuel, Cambridge, and was a pupil of the noted mathematician, William Oughtred. He put his mathematical ability to political use by deciphering code messages for the Parliamentarians during the Civil War, and in the 1640s he held two London livings before being appointed to the Savilian Chair of Geometry at Oxford, when its Royalist holder was ejected. During the Commonwealth he was one of the group of scientists whose meetings at Oxford foreshadowed the Royal Society, and his most celebrated work, the *Arithmetica Infinitorum*, which established his reputation, was published in 1657. A moderate in outlook and a trimmer in politics, he had no difficulty in making his peace with the monarchy in 1660 and was appointed a royal Chaplain. For the next fifty years Wallis was one of the most distinguished intellectual figures in the country. Even Aubrey, who made him the subject of one of his less kind essays, calling him 'extremely greedy' of fame, said that Wallis 'to give him due praise, hath exceedingly well deserved of the commonwealth of learning'. His *Arithmetica*, the most significant mathematical work hitherto published in England, contained the germs of the calculus and directed Newton, who read it as an undergraduate, to the binomial theorem. Like so many of his contemporaries in the Royal Society, Wallis did not limit his creative activities to one field. In particular he was interested in the practical problems of speech, and carried out experiments in the training of the deaf and dumb.

J.F. Scott, *The Mathematical Work of John Wallis*, 1938.

ROBERT BOYLE (1626–91), scientist, was born at Lismore Castle in Ireland, the seventh son and fifteenth child of the first Earl of Cork. He was sent to Eton at nine, and to a tutor in Geneva at fourteen; he travelled on the continent, and was at Florence when Galileo died; and he returned to England in 1644, living partly with his gifted sister Katharine Lady Ranelagh in London, partly on the estate he inherited at Stalbridge in Dorset. It was at Stalbridge that he began to dabble in chemistry, and in the later 1640s that he first came in touch with that circle of reformers centred on Samuel Hartlib whom he called 'the Invisible College'. In 1654 Boyle moved to Oxford, where his lodgings and laboratory were a meeting-place for such younger scientists as Petty, Wren and Hooke as well as for older men like Goddard and Wilkins. His rank and his genius made Boyle a leading figure in the foundation of the Royal Society, and he was one of its first council members, but he declined the presidency out of scruples about oath-taking. After his return to London in 1668, when he moved, laboratory, library and servants, to Lady Ranelagh's house in Pall Mall, Boyle devoted much of his time to experimental work and to his writing on 'natural philosophy'. In his own lifetime Boyle was as celebrated for his piety and his charity as for his scientific activities, studying the Bible incessantly and writing on religious and moral questions, spending much money on the diffusion of the Gospel in a range of languages from Welsh to Turkish, and helping needy scholars. He was widely esteemed by the most various of men, including Clarendon, Locke, and Newton, Aubrey, Pepys and Burnet. He died in 1691, a few days after his sister. Evelyn, who knew him well, wrote in 1696 an account which is representative. Describing him as 'tall and slender of stature, for the most part valetudinary, pale and much emaciated' and 'in his diet (as in habit) . . . extremely temperate and plain', he went on 'nor could I ever discern in him the least passion, transport, or censoriousness, whatever discourse or the times suggested. All was tranquil, easy, serious, discreet, and profitable.'

Boyle was a great scientist, of peculiar importance in the history of science in England. It is perhaps ironical that his name — almost alone among scientists of the past — is known to every English schoolboy, because of Boyle's Law, which he formulated in 1662, that the volume of a given mass of gas varies inversely with the pressure when the temperature is constant. For he was certainly not the kind of scientist whose reputation hangs upon a single discovery or upon work in a single field. Three centuries later the impressive qualities about Boyle are the range and catholicity of his mind, the width of his vision, and the generality of his influence. If, as has been claimed, 'from its foundation until the early eighteenth century the Royal Society was the chief European centre of experimental physics', * this was in large part the consequence of the contributions made to its proceedings by Robert Boyle the chemist, with his constant emphasis on experimental science and his own flow of original experiments in many fields, including pneumatics, hydrostatics, and optics. His first important publication was the appropriately-named *New Experiments Physico-Mechanical* (1660); and his 'Law' was itself an admirable example of scientific induction firmly grounded upon a series of recorded experiments. As the entries in the *Diaries* of those amateurs of science Pepys and Evelyn indicate, Boyle helped make 'natural philosophy' fashionable as well as respectable. More significantly, perhaps, it was Boyle who in his own writings and in the lead he gave to the Royal Society pioneered the proper recording of experimental procedures, thus giving labora-

* A.R. Hall, *From Galileo to Newton*, 1963, p.257.

tory science sureness and accuracy of method. At the level of personal impact, he taught Locke a great deal, and his influence upon Newton was vital both in his general contribution to the formation of Newton's outlook upon science and in his suggestions upon particular problems like those of light.

Boyle's writings were voluminous, most of them blending the detailed record of experiment with profound reflections upon the relationship of natural phenomena to divine law. Like Newton, Boyle accepted the mechanical philosophy, with its pattern of physical law and its omnipresent evidences of divine design; for neither of them was there any conflict between science and religion. The *Sceptical Chymist* of 1661, the best-known of his works, was an early work of a speculative kind, cast in the form of a dialogue, which began to lay the foundations of chemical theory and thus provided a justification for the claim that Boyle was 'The Father of Chemistry'. His later writings, using the information supplied by his experiments, show Boyle working out an organized theory of matter, based upon the 'corpuscular' view. It might be held that the supreme scientific development of the 'Age of Newton', the basis of all future advance, lay in the union, long overdue, of speculation and experiment; and that for England at least Robert Boyle did more than any other scientist — more than Newton himself — to bring this union about.

L. T. More, *The Life and Works of Robert Boyle*, 1944.
M. Boas, *Robert Boyle and Seventeenth-Century Chemistry*, 1958.
Roger Pilkington, *Robert Boyle*, 1959.

ROBERT HOOKE (1635–1703) was in ability probably second only to Newton among English scientists of the seventeenth century. The son of a clergyman of Freshwater in the Isle of Wight, he was a pupil at Westminster School under Dr. Busby, and at Oxford he found himself among that group of brilliant scientists which included John Wilkins, William Petty, Robert Boyle, and Christopher Wren, and out of which the Royal Society developed in Charles II's reign. Hooke's experimental and inventive powers particularly impressed Boyle, whose assistant he became; it was with Boyle's backing that he was in 1662 appointed Curator of Experiments for the Royal Society, and for the remaining forty-one years of his life he was the central figure in the experimental activities and discussions carried on by the society and its members. In the same year he was appointed Gresham Professor of Geometry, with rooms in Gresham College in Bishopsgate, which was the headquarters of the Royal Society until shortly after Hooke's death; and in 1677 he became one of the Society's two secretaries. By this time he was also busily engaged in surveying, town-planning and architecture, for in 1666, after the Fire of London, he was one of the Surveyors of the City, a task which involved him in fruitful collaboration with Sir Christopher Wren; he was the architect of the Monument as well as of several other buildings later destroyed. A restless little man, an energetic bachelor who preferred to walk than to take a coach or boat, he must have been one of the best-known citizens of late seventeenth-century London. John Aubrey, who knew Hooke a good deal more intimately than he knew most of the people he describes in his *Brief Lives*, speaks of him as 'but of middling stature, something crooked, pale-faced, and his face but little below, but his head is large; his eyes full and popping, and not quick; a grey eye. He has a delicate head of hair, brown, and of an excellent moist curl. He is and ever was very temperate, and moderate in diet, etc.'

Hooke had what Aubrey called a 'prodigious inventive head'. As a small boy he had made sundials, model ships and mills; for Boyle he made a highly successful air-pump; as Curator to the Royal Society he was required to produce every week for the edification and entertainment of members three or four substantial experiments; and among his inventions were the wheel barometer, a universal joint, the iris diaphragm for telescopes (nowadays in cameras) and (probably) the anchor escapement and balance spring in watches, as well as such things as a wheel-cutting machine, a new kind of glass, a wind-gauge, an improved carriage, and a compound microscope. But in Hooke's time there was no clear or valid distinction between invention, technology, and science; the studies of the Royal Society were according to its Charter 'to be applied to further promoting by the authority of experiments the sciences of natural things and of useful arts'. Nor in general were the scientists the specialists they have since become. So we find Hooke ranging over wider fields of genuinely scientific inquiry. His *Micrographia*, published in 1665 (illustrated with his own exquisite drawings), is the first treatise on microscopy, and it was Hooke who demonstrated the cellular structure of plants. In optics, Hooke challenged existing beliefs about light by his theories of refraction and colour; in chemistry, his ideas on the nature of combustion were more rational than those which triumphed for most of the eighteenth century; in geology, his early view that fossils revealed vast changes in the earth's history was unorthodox in his day. In the 1670s he spent a good deal of time investigating the theory of elasticity of materials. At intervals throughout his time with the Royal Society he turned his mind to the great basic question of late seventeenth-century science, that of the solar system, and it is clear that by 1685 he 'had a very complete picture of a mechanical system of the universe founded on universal gravitation'. *

This brings us to the relations between Hooke and Sir Isaac Newton, whom Hooke accused of plagiarism. The accusation was quite unjust; for, in simple terms, it may be said that Hooke had indeed propounded in some detail the hypothesis of universal gravity, including the 'inverse square law', but lacked the mathematical ability which Newton possessed to transform the hypothesis into a demonstrable theory. Both men were naturally irritable, suspicious, and rather vain; they quarrelled intermittently for years, and the effect of the quarrel was disastrous to Hooke's reputation after his death. Only in the twentieth century has Hooke's great ability been recognized. In the variety of his talents and the range of his scientific interests, in his experimentalism, in his enthusiasm for the application of scientific theory to the daily needs of men, he seems to us a representative figure of one of the great ages of English science.

Margaret 'Espinasse, *Robert Hooke*, 1956.
H. W. Robinson and W. Adams, *The Diary of Robert Hooke*, 1935.

ISAAC BARROW (1630–77), divine and mathematician, son of a London linen-draper, was educated at Charterhouse, Felsted and Trinity College, Cambridge. Royalist in his opinions, he left Cambridge in 1655 to travel abroad. Returning at the Restoration, he was elected Professor of Greek in 1660 and the first Lucasian

* A. R. Hall, *The Scientific Revolution*, 1500–1800, 1954, p. 266.

Professor of Mathematics in 1663. In 1669 he resigned the Lucasian chair in favour of his former pupil Isaac Newton, and turned to theology. Three years later Charles II made him Master of Trinity, and during his brief tenure he began the building of the college's splendid library, with Wren as architect. Barrow died at forty-seven. His intellectual reputation rests primarily upon his part in that great achievement of seventeenth-century Europe, the invention of the calculus. It is not unimportant that Barrow was the teacher, as well as precursor, of Newton, sensing his genius, setting him to work at Euclid and directing his attention to the problems of optics. Isaac Barrow was also a controversialist of note and a lengthy and exhaustive preacher, the style of whose published sermons much influenced Locke and the two Pitts.

P.H. Osmond, *Isaac Barrow: His Life and Times*, 1944.

SIR ISAAC NEWTON (1642–1727), greatest of English scientists, was born on a farm at Woolsthorpe Manor, seven miles from Grantham in Lincolnshire. His father was already dead, and the outward record of Newton's career is a classical example of the widow's son from a humble home who makes good by sheer intellectual ability. He went from King's School, Grantham, to Trinity College, Cambridge, as a sizar in 1661, and his outstanding qualities of mind were quickly discerned by an eminent scholar, Isaac Barrow. In 1667 he became a Minor, in 1668 a Major, Fellow of Trinity, and in 1669, at twenty-seven, he succeeded Barrow, at the latter's wish, as Lucasian Professor of Mathematics. The Royal Society elected him a Fellow in 1672. His *magnum opus*, the *Principia*, perhaps the greatest scientific work ever written, which he completed in eighteen months, was published in 1687, and won him immense prestige at once. He represented the University of Cambridge in Parliament in 1689 and in 1701–2. In 1696 he became Warden of the Mint (and Master from 1699 for the rest of his life) and carried through the most important recoinage in modern English history. From 1703 onwards he was President of the Royal Society. In 1704 his notable work on light, the *Opticks*, was published. Next year Queen Anne visited Cambridge, and conferred a knighthood on him at Trinity. In his old age Newton was recognized as one of the giants, and at his death in 1727 his body lay in state before burial in

Sir Isaac Newton c.1726
(Artist: attrib. John Vanderbank)

Westminster Abbey. His statue by Roubiliac, done some twenty years after Newton's death, stands in the place of honour in the ante-chapel of Trinity, the college also of Francis Bacon, J. J. Thomson, and Rutherford.

Yet behind this outward success lay a complex character. Newton was a withdrawn man whom his contemporaries found hard to understand. Few felt affection for him, though nearly all felt respect. He was in part the absent-minded don whom his Cambridge assistant, Humphrey Newton (another Lincolnshire man but no relation), describes, 'thinking all hours lost that was not spent in his studies', neglecting his meals and his dress, and the like. Beyond this superficial characteristic — which itself contrasts very sharply with the businesslike efficiency which Newton displayed in the affairs of the Mint — there were deeper difficulties. Temperamentally lonely, perhaps frustrated, he remained a bachelor all his days — though the sole suggestion that he ever thought of becoming anything else rests upon an old lady's gossipy recollection. Certainly he seems to have been puritanically fearful about sex: Brewster, his nineteenth-century panegyrist, relates that when his chemist friend Vigani told a coarse tale about a nun, Newton 'broke off all acquaintance with him'. He was morbidly sensitive to criticism, and his irritability led often to spitefulness. His scholarly career was punctuated by a series of unedifying controversies, each extending over several years, with Hooke, Flamsteed, the first Astronomer Royal, and Leibniz, the German philosopher. None of these men was faultless in the disputes, but neither was Newton. He was always ready to believe himself deceived or persecuted, and in 1693–4 he had a nervous breakdown in which, as his curious letters to Locke at the time show, he was clearly suffering from some form of paranoia. Yet he was a man of contrasts. He was always generous with money to others, living plainly himself. He retained throughout his life a simple and pleasing affection for Lincolnshire and Lincolnshire people. He was no time-server, and was active in opposition to James II's Catholicizing measures in Cambridge. Everything we know of him indicates that he was a man whose religious views were held with complete sincerity; these views were Arian ones which prevented him from subscribing to the Thirty-Nine Articles and thus from taking orders, a fact which was something of a barrier to earlier preferment.

The careers of seventeenth-century scientists were widely varied, as the lives of Wren and Petty show. There were no established narrow channels, for science itself was still in its infancy. Yet Newton's scientific career had a strangeness all its own. He produced a considerable proportion of the original ideas which are the essence of his legacy to mankind in the course of eighteen months which he spent alone at Woolsthorpe in 1665–7, when Cambridge was virtually closed by plague. He was then twenty-four: in his own words long afterwards, 'in those days I was in the prime of my age for invention, and minded mathematics and philosophy more than at any time since'. At the heart of these ideas was his hypothesis about the role of gravitational attraction in the universe. But he took it no further for thirteen years because of the mathematical difficulties which it raised. Instead he turned to other branches of science, in particular to optics, and this provided the subject of his first paper to the Royal Society, in 1672 when he was thirty. Newton seems to have had little sense of any need to publish the results of his investigations at any time, and the criticism and controversy which publication aroused disturbed him quite disproportionately. In 1676 he wrote of bidding adieu to science eternally 'excepting what I do for my private satisfaction', and during the next few years he had hardly any connection with the Royal Society. It was a dispute with Hooke which drove him back to the question of gravity in 1679, and to providing mathematical proof of the part played by the inverse square law in the mechanics of the heavens. He found his solution, and then seemingly forgot about it for five years, until Halley's visit to Cambridge in 1684 to ask for his opinions on the movements of the planets; and even then he could not lay his hands on it. It was Halley who persuaded him to write the *Principia*, and undertook the financial risk, as well as the labour, of seeing the book through the press. Once it was published, 'Newton's life became more full of incident, and more empty of science'. * He deliberately refrained from publishing the *Optiks*, most of which had been written before 1690, until after the death of his critic Hooke in 1703. He continued to devote long hours to study, and he left huge quantities of manuscript material at his death. But hardly any of it concerned the physical and mathematical science in which the *Principia* had revealed his pre-eminence. This was not because of any serious failure of power to handle this subject; the Queries which he added to the first Latin edition of the *Opticks* when he was sixty-four contain some remarkable insights. His interests now lay elsewhere. Some of the material — about half a million words — dealt with chemistry and alchemy, to what precise end nobody has ever been able to explain. Some of his labours were given to problems of ancient chronology. Most of the material concerned religious questions, in particular the intellectual implications of Christianity as these were revealed by exhaustive study of the Bible.

Newton the scientist was fortunate in his age. Born in the year of Galileo's death, he built upon the work of such predecessors as Kepler and Descartes (even where he proved them wrong), and he benefited from that of older contemporaries like Barrow, Wallis, and Boyle. The contemporary development of mathematical techniques, the rise of scientific societies, the widespread interest in experiment, the relevance of astronomy and mathematics to the

* A.R. Hall, *The Scientific Revolution, 1500–1800*, 1954, p.249.

practical needs of navigation, war and craftsmanship, the whole
freer intellectual climate brought about by the Puritan revolution —
all these things worked directly or indirectly to his advantage,
making his work both possible and more fruitful. Yet Newton
dominated by his own extraordinary combination of qualities — his
formidable power of concentration, his brilliant mathematical skill,
his exceptional precision in experimental work and (some would
add) his remarkable scientific foresight. So it came about that as a
young man in his twenties he grasped the principle of universal
gravitation and moved behind Kepler's Laws to the inverse square
law; worked out the prismatic theory of colours and was led to
construct the reflecting telescope, using mirrors instead of lenses;
and discovered the binomial theorem and formulated the principles
of the differential and the integral calculus. By the time of the
publication of the *Principia* he had worked out a rigorous proof of
the inverse square law. Thus in that book he stated his three Laws of
Motion and went on to explain the orbits of the planets in terms of
universal gravitation. He explained under one threory the motions
of the planets, the precession of the equinoxes, the ebb and flow of
the tides, and the orbits of comets. The *Principia* was predominantly
theoretical and mathematical, but in parts of it Newton described
his use of experimental methods. In his second book, the *Opticks*, he
provided detailed experimental proof of the prismatic theory of
light. To Newton light consisted of corpuscles travelling at high
velocity, whereas Huygens had proposed a wave theory.

The French mathematician Laplace, living a century after
Newton, wrote that 'the *Principia* is pre-eminent above any other
production of human genius'. Its implications for the range of the
human mind were vast. Starting from the basic hypothesis, confirmed by mathematical proof, that every particle of matter attracts
every other particle with a force directly proportional to their masses
and inversely as the square of the distance between them, Newton
had provided man with a new framework of thought. He had
brought all the physical phenomena of the universe, from the falling
of the apple to the movement of the planets in their orbits, into one
system, a system governed by mathematical law. This was the
achievement which provided the universality of Newton's work, gave
him primacy among the scientists of his day and justified the phrase
'the Age of Newton'. Newton's inclusion of both terrestrial and

celestial phenomena within one theory was aptly named by A.N. Whitehead 'the first physical synthesis'. In Pope's famous couplet

'Nature and Nature's Laws lay hid in Night,
God said, Let Newton be! and all was Light.'

'Light' also implied, in Newton's own words, that 'an entire liberty must be allowed in our inquiries': so prodigious a demonstration of scientific and rational truth made nonsense of intolerance. Moreover, the consequences for the development of science itself were immense. Besides providing a remarkable example of scientific method at the highest level, Newton had defined terms like mass, force, and momentum, and provided the essential foundations of theoretical physics as a mathematical science. Astronomers for the next century and a half would follow the highway which Newton had illuminated for them, and not until the end of the nineteenth century would the Newtonian system of the universe be challenged.

Newton himself appeared to take a modest view of his achievement, saying not long before he died 'I do not know what I may appear to the world; but to myself I seem to have been only like a boy, playing on the seashore, and diverting myself in now and then finding a smoother pebble or a prettier shell than ordinary, while the great ocean of truth lay all undiscovered before me'. And on one issue of fundamental importance which arose from his revolutionary discoveries he was himself entirely clear. He saw no antagonism at all between religion and science, no incompatibility between Christianity and the implications of the law of gravitation. Although he told his friend Richard Bentley in 1692 that in writing the *Principia* he 'had an eye upon such principles as might work with considering men, for the belief of a Deity', he believed firmly that it was not the scientist's task to discover final causes. Physics and theology were separate studies. Yet to Newton, God was the Final Cause, and the study of what he called 'the most beautiful system of sun, planets and comets' was the study of the divine craftsmanship. Just as in his labours in physics and mathematics he had sought, and found, the key which would unlock the mysteries of the physical universe, so in the work upon the prophecies of the Book of Daniel and of the Revelation which occupied so much of the second half of his life he was seeking the key to the mystery of God.

R. S. Westfall, *Never at Rest: A Biography of Isaac Newton*, 1980.
G. E. Christianson, *In the Presence of the Creator: Isaac Newton and His Times*, 1985.

EDMOND HALLEY (1656–1742), astronomer, was the son of a wealthy soap-boiler of Shoreditch. He was schooled at St. Paul's, and showed an early enthusiasm for astronomy: Aubrey records that 'he was very perfect in the celestial Globes in so much that I heard Mr. Moxton (the Globe-maker) say that if a star were misplaced in the Globe he would presently find it'. Thence he went to The Queen's College, Oxford, and at twenty he undertook an expedition to St. Helena to observe the southern stars. On his return in 1678 he was elected a Fellow of the Royal Society, whose assistant secretary he became from 1685 to 1693. In 1698–1700 William III put him in command of the sloop *Paramour Pink* on the first scientific survey undertaken by the Admiralty, with orders to determine the variation of the compass, and on the basis of this survey Halley drew the first chart showing lines of equal magnetic variation. In 1704 he became Savilian Professor of Geometry at Oxford, and in 1720 succeeded Flamsteed as Astonomer-Royal. A sprightly, energetic and kindly person, he lived to eighty-five, and died after drinking a glass of wine in defiance of his doctor's instructions.

Halley was a man of versatility unusual even in an age when scientists were far from narrow. He is best known for the comet to which his name has been attached. It appeared in 1682, and Halley both identified it with the one which had been recorded in 1531 and 1607 and foretold its return in the winter of 1758–9, attributing variations in its motion to the gravitational pull of Jupiter. It might be held that Halley's greatest service to science lay in his constant friendship with Isaac Newton: for it was Halley's visit to Cambridge in 1684 to discuss the inverse square law in relation to gravitation and Halley's persuasion which provoked the writing of the *Principia*, and it was Halley who met the costs of publication, prefacing the book with his own Latin ode in praise of Newton. Yet Halley was a great scientist in his own right. A gifted mathematician, he was a theoretical astronomer of distinction, notable for a new theory of terrestrial magnetism, for suggesting a connection between the earth's magnetic field and the Aurora Borealis, and for

Edmond Halley c.1721
(Artist: Richard Phillips)

drawing attention in 1716 to the opportunity which the transits of
Venus in 1761 and 1769 would present for international scientific
observation. He also helped Newton to carry out the recoinage of
1696, used a barometer to measure the height of Snowdon, studied
Romano-British antiquities, published an edition of the works of
the Greek geometer Apollonius, worked on mortality tables, and
wrote an account of the trade winds and monsoons.

Angus Armitage, *Edmond Halley*, 1966.

NEHEMIAH GREW (1641–1712), biologist, son of the headmaster of Atherstone Grammar School, graduated at Pembroke Hall, Cambridge, went on to the University of Leyden, and later practised as a doctor in Coventry and in London. His historical fame rests upon his original work in botany. Outstanding as an observer of structure, Grew may be regarded, with his Italian contemporary Malpighi, as the pioneer of plant anatomy. His major piece of writing, *The Anatomy of Plants* (first published as a whole in 1682, including his *Philosophical History of Plants* of ten years earlier) was a remarkable achievement in view of the fact that cells had first been recognized by Hooke less than twenty years before. His most significant single contribution to knowledge was his deduction that plants are reproduced sexually; he was interested also in chemical processes associated with plant life, such as, for example, pigmentation. Grew was elected a Fellow of the Royal Society in 1671 and served as one of its secretaries for several years after 1677.

JOHN RAY (1627–1705), naturalist, the son of a blacksmith at Black Notley in Essex, went to school in Braintree and thence to Cambridge. A Fellow of Trinity, lecturing in Greek and Mathematics like his contemporary and friend Isaac Barrow, he turned to the scientific study of plants during an illness. In 1658–62 he travelled over much of Britain from southern Scotland to Land's End collecting specimens and recording information, and his earliest published work (1660) was a record of the plants in Cambridgeshire, in effect the first 'county flora'. Under the Act of Uniformity of 1662, Ray, a dissenter, resigned his fellowship, yet he was fortunate in having friends willing to help him financially, and in 1663–6 a long continental tour, ending at the University of Montpellier, enabled him to accumulate what was for that time a unique knowledge of the flora and fauna of western Europe as well as a great store of material. Elected a Fellow of the Royal Society in 1667, Ray — assisted by his well-to-do friend Francis Willughby until the latter's death in 1672 — gave the remainder of his days to a systematic survey of plant and animal life and to the publication of a remarkable series of classificatory and historical volumes. A modest, unambitious, profoundly religious man who had been much influenced by the Cambridge Platonists, Ray lived at Black Notley from 1680, working with unremitting diligence and corresponding with savants and scientists throughout Europe. Perhaps the most notable of his many books were his three great folios on the *History of Plants* (the first of them appearing in 1686) and his *Synopsis of British Plants* (1690), the first scientific English flora; yet his publications also included works on animals, reptiles, and insects, as well as the books on birds and fishes which appeared under Willughby's name although they were, in fact, written by Ray. His classificatory work, based on accurate observation and identification and a complete rejection of the mythological material which had hitherto befogged botany and zoology, laid the foundations upon which Linnaeus built in the next century; although his classification was essentially artificial, based sometimes on single characters, it does in many instances result in fairly natural groupings. His experimental work was limited, yet Ray was far more than a superb cataloguer who turned natural history from a hobby into a science. He welcomed new ideas like those of Grew on sexuality in plants or of Redi on 'spontaneous generation', and in his philosophical writing, *The Wisdom of God* (1691), he discussed the adaptation of organisms to their environment and thus pointed to one of the central issues of later biological work. The greatest of the earlier English naturalists, Ray was a worthy contemporary of Isaac Newton.

C. E. Raven, *John Ray, Naturalist*, 1950.

THOMAS SYDENHAM (1624–89), physician, came from an old yet Puritan family in Dorset. He entered Magdalen Hall, Oxford, in 1642, went on to Wadham and thence to a Fellowship at All Souls in 1648, and did not finally leave Oxford until he went to practise in London in 1655. But his career was much interrupted, for he served in the Parliamentarian cavalry in the First Civil War, and fought again for the Commonwealth in 1651. Moreover, although he spent much of his time at Oxford in the study of medicine, it seems probable that he got the most valuable part of his training under the famous Huguenot doctor Barbeyrac at Montpellier. The established physicians disliked the novelty of his professional opinions and perhaps also his Puritanism, so that the College of Physicians did not grant him a Licentiate until 1663 and never elected him a Fellow. Nevertheless, Sydenham became a successful and respected practitioner. The friend of Boyle and of Locke, who collaborated with him for some years after 1667, consulted him about the famous operation on Shaftesbury, and helped him collect data on infectious diseases, Sydenham, even though he was not in close touch with the scientific movement of his time, was the best contemporary exemplar in medicine of the new spirit of rationalism. Saying that 'true practice consists in the observations of nature', he founded all his work, in diagnosis and in treatment, upon accurate and carefully-recorded clinical observation of the patient and of the disease. Such an approach has become the commonplace of modern medicine; in Sydenham's time, when doctors bound themselves to authority and dogma or to magic and quackery, it was revolutionary. Sydenham wished to classify diseases just as his contemporary John Ray was beginning to classify plants, and to this end he recorded his observations upon epidemic diseases in London over a series of years. His greatest written work, *Observationes Medicae* (first published in 1676), which came to be regarded with great respect on the continent, contained careful descriptions founded solely upon experience. It was Sydenham who first recognized hysteria as a distinct ailment; he differentiated measles from scarlet fever; and the gout from which he suffered enabled him to write an authoritative treatise on that complaint. He believed in fresh air and light diet, he was often sceptical about bleeding, he used quinine and opium. A zealous and independent physician, he is commemorated by the London district which bears his name.

G. F. Sydenham, *The History of the Sydenham Family*, ed. A. T. Cameron, 1928.

SIR CHRISTOPHER WREN (1632–1723), architect, was born at East Knoyle, in Wiltshire, the son of the rector and the nephew of Matthew Wren the Laudian bishop. When Christopher was little more than a year old his father was appointed Dean of Windsor. The Civil Wars disrupted the household, and Wren, according to Aubrey, 'a youth of prodigious inventive wit', got 'his first Instructions in Geometry and Arithmetic' from his brother-in-law, William Holder, rector of Bletchington, in Oxfordshire, in whose house the family took refuge. He was sent to Busby at Westminster, and went on to Wadham College, Oxford, when he was seventeen. Already Wren's interests were clearly scientific: he had made astronomical

Sir Christopher Wren c.1711
(Artist: Sir Godfrey Kneller)

models and a water-clock, and assisted the eminent anatomist
Charles Scarburgh in dissecting, and he quickly proved himself a
brilliant young addition to the group — including Wallis, Goddard,
Petty and Wilkins, the last of whom was the Warden of Wren's
college — who were making Oxford a centre of the new scientific
spirit during the Commonwealth period. Wren became a Fellow of
All Souls in 1653 and gave his main attention to astronomy,
investigating the rings of Saturn. The following year Evelyn dined at

All Souls and met 'that miracle of a youth, Mr. Christopher Wren'; and later he visited Dr. Wilkins who showed him 'Shadows, Dials, Perspectives, places to introduce the Species, and many other artificial, mathematical, Magical curiosities: A Way-Wiser, a Thermometer; a monstrous Magnes, Conic and other Sections, a Balance on a demie Circle, most of them of his own and that prodigious young scholar, Mr. Chr: Wren'.

In 1657 his brilliance was recognized by election at twenty-five as Professor of Anatomy at Gresham College. Four years later he returned to Oxford as Savilian Professor of Astronomy, a chair which he retained until 1673. Naturally he was one of the promoters of the Royal Society, and he wrote the preamble to its charter. We find him in the 1660s taking an original and leading part in scientific investigation, whether in his own research or in the experimental activities of the Society. He continued to work at the rings of Saturn (where Huygens forestalled him) and the satellites of Jupiter; devised a geometrical method of determining a comet's path; constructed an apparatus of suspended balls, to which Newton later referred in the *Principia*, in order to 'determine the rules of the collision and mutual rebound of hard bodies'; demanded the keeping of records of the weather and of agricultural prices; and invented an improved weather-clock and a method of grinding hyperbolical lenses. In 1662 Evelyn saw him display 'his ingenious thermometer' to the Royal Society, and in 1664 he found Wren, Boyle and Wallis at Oxford 'observing the Discus of the Sun for the passing of Mercury that day'. It was characteristic of the age as well as a tribute to his mathematical qualifications that Wren was offered early in Charles II's reign a commission to survey and direct the establishment of Tangier as a naval base. He declined the offer on the plea of health. The true reason may have been that he had already committed himself to the first of his architectural enterprises.

Wren the scientist in his early thirties was already celebrated. Wren the man, at this or any time in his life, is not easy to delineate. Both Evelyn and Aubrey knew him well, yet they tell us surprisingly little about what sort of man he was. Evelyn offers little more than the refrain which he used, for example, in 1664, 'that incomparable genius, and my worthy friend'. Aubrey reported to Anthony à Wood an instance of what sounds like characteristic kindness, saying that 'Dr. Christopher Wren, my dear friend, without my knowledge contrived an employment for me'; it was work for Ogilby the publisher, at a time when Aubrey was in great need. Wren himself left little evidence, for he seems to have disliked writing. The most valuable material comes from Hooke, who worked closely with Wren on the rebuilding of London in the 1670s and was clearly devoted to him. His celebrated tribute, 'that since the time of Archimedes there scarce ever has met in one man, in so great perfection, such a mechanical hand and so philosophical a mind' has a lapidary ring, yet in the light of Hooke's comments in his diary it was genuine. Wren was slight of build, courteous and kindly, equable in temper, reticent and hating fuss, something of a precisian, dedicated to his work, quietly yet profoundly ambitious. He was twice married — the first time at the age of thirty-seven — and twice widowed, and this may have added sadness to his gravity. He was President of the Royal Society from 1681 to 1683. Although he was thrice elected to Parliament (1685, 1689, 1701), Wren seems to have been as unpolitical as any public man could be in the second half of the seventeenth century, holding an important state appointment for fifty years during the reigns of five sovereigns. Neither Popish Plot nor Revolution, nor even the partisan feuds of Anne's reign, uprooted him. It is a tribute to his genius, perhaps also to a sense of national pride.

The career as an architect which revealed this genius began when Gilbert Sheldon, promoted to the see of London from the Wardenship of All Souls, decided to present to the University of Oxford a building to be used for the conferment of degrees and other ceremonial purposes, and invited the brilliant fellow of his college to design it. The assumptions and the technical qualifications which have since come to divide the 'professions' into separate and rigid specialisms did not exist in the seventeenth century. Christopher Wren was a distinguished experimental scientist, deeply interested in geometry, and a fine draughtsman with a flair for constructing models. It is not in the least surprising that Sheldon invited him, nor, given that Wren was naturally ambitious and willing to undertake responsibility, that he accepted. He designed a model of the new Sheldonian Theatre and displayed it in 1663, and by 1669 the building was finished. A highly original piece of work, of a type hitherto unknown in England, it stands to-day as one of the most compelling buildings in a city of much fine architecture, and it created something of a sensation in the 1660s. At about the same time as the Sheldonian, too, Wren designed for Pembroke College, Cambridge, the first wholly classical college chapel in England. Meanwhile, in the interval between the design and the completion of the Sheldonian, two things had happened which confirmed Wren in his turn to architecture and settled the pattern of his life. First, he had visited Paris (1665–6), then in the early stages of the architectural transformation wrought by Louis XIV's reign. Wren had studied new mansions within the city and country houses outside, watched the changes which were being made in the Louvre and the Tuileries, met the great Italian architect Bernini, made drawings, bought engravings, and come home deeply impressed. Secondly, the Great Fire of 1666 had gutted much of the City of London and provided an opportunity for reconstruction at once urgent and unparalleled.

Wren had in fact already been consulted by Sheldon and Sancroft about the rehabilitation of old St. Paul's, and had put forward his views in the form of a design. The matter had been discussed at a meeting held only a few days before the Fire, where John Evelyn joined Wren in proposing a new foundation 'with a noble Cupola, a form of church building not as yet known in England, but of wonderful grace'. Within a week after the Fire, Wren submitted to the authorities a plan for the reconstruction of the entire city area. Perhaps inevitably — because of the complex problem of property rights and the desperate need for speed in the re-housing — it was rejected. There was no comprehensive plan, and Wren had relatively little direct responsibility for London's new secular buildings, although he shared with Hooke the engineering work on the Fleet Canal. His opportunity lay in ecclesiastical building. Between the London Rebuilding Act of 1670 and the end of the century he built a great group of new churches in the capital — and the new St. Paul's Cathedral.

By the time Wren began this task he had been appointed (1669) Surveyor of the Royal Works, over the head of Inigo Jones's assistant, John Webb, a far more experienced man. This post, with its office and residence in Scotland Yard, carried with it the responsibility for all Crown building, and later was to enable Wren to do some of his finest work. For the present it brought him status, and was followed in 1673 by a knighthood. London's needs for materials and labour were paramount, and Wren turned first to the London churches. He provided designs for fifty-one, and fifteen were actually under construction by 1670. The detailed supervision of the work was often undertaken by the three City Surveyors, of whom Hooke was one. Although in general Wren's churches were on a 'central' pattern, emphasizing the role of the congregation in Protestant worship, their plans were remarkably varied. Many, particularly of the earlier ones, were later destroyed, especially in the Second World War; among those that have survived, or that have been faithfully restored, St. Stephen, Walbrook, and St. James, Piccadilly, provide interesting and contrasting examples. Broadly, by 1685 Wren had completed his work on the city churches, except that he later added to the London skyline a number of delightful classical steeples of a kind unique in western Europe (e.g. that of St. Bride, Fleet Street). By this date he had already begun several other buildings whose varied purposes enabled him to experiment and to show the variety of his genius. For example, in 1676–84 he built the superbly proportioned and dignified Library of Trinity College, Cambridge, and in 1681–2 he completed Wolsey's gateway at Christ Church, Oxford, by building the upper part of Tom Tower in his own version of Gothic. These were 'private' buildings — and Trinity Library he did for nothing, out of friendship for Isaac Barrow. As Surveyor he designed in these middle years of his career the austere Chelsea Hospital (1682–92) and a palace at Winchester for Charles II, almost finished when the King died in 1685 but never continued.

St. Paul's Cathedral, the most celebrated of Wren's triumphs, was begun in 1675. Wren had produced his first designs for old St. Paul's in his early thirties. The lines along which his new building was constructed were a compromise: he could not persuade the chapter to accept the sumptuously classical 'Great Model' (still to be seen in the Trophy Room at St. Paul's), but neither did he follow the basically Gothic 'Warrant' design to which royal approval was given in 1675. Instead, by his famous, and much-criticized, screen walls he gave the building the unity of classical design. The most splendid achievement of all, the great dome, a magnificent extension of the circular pattern of the classical temple, was not started until 1697, the year in which the first service was held in the new cathedral. The western towers, based fairly closely on those of Borromini at S.

Agnese in Rome, followed in the early years of the new century. By
1709 the building was structurally complete. To its making other
artists of distinction had contributed much. Among the masons
there had been Edward Pierce, the sculptor of the bust of Wren at
Oxford; among the carvers in wood and stone, Grinling Gibbons,
the brilliant young Dutchman whom Evelyn had discovered working
'in a poor solitary thatched house' and had commended to Wren.
Yet the central glory of the design and of the incomparable achievement belongs unquestionably to Wren.

He was seventy-seven when St. Paul's was finished. In the reigns
of James II and William III he had, as Royal Surveyor, designed
other fine buildings. His Whitehall extensions of 1685–8 were,
unhappily, burned down in 1698. His additions to Hampton Court,
begun in 1689, were only a modest part of a great design which
would have destroyed the Tudor palace but which was never
completed. He did the charming south front of William's palace at
Kensington. Above all in this group, he designed the lovely Painted
Hall of the Royal Naval Hospital, at Greenwich, begun in 1695 and
completed by 1702. Apart from the finishing of St. Paul's, this was
Wren's last notable building. There are indications in the 1690s,
scarcely surprising in view of his age and of the prodigious range of
his work wince the 1660s, that his vitality and resource were
diminishing. He clearly began to rely heavily upon his protégé
Nicholas Hawksmore. A new generation was arising, symbolized by
the appointment in 1702 to the post next below Wren's, the
Comptrollership of Works, of John Vanbrugh, who both as architect and as man was of very different style from Wren, who
nevertheless seems to have got on well with him. Castle Howard and
Blenheim were massive demonstrations that 'the age of Wren' was
over. There were occasional fusses about St. Paul's. In 1697 his
salary was cut by half until six months after the building should be
complete, as an inducement to speed up the pace. After it was
finished there was a row about the railings round the churchyard, in
which Wren was overruled, as he was over the far more serious
question of the appointment of James Thornhill to paint the interior
of the dome. In 1717 he objected in vain to the proposal to put a
stone balustrade round the cathedral, making the savage comment
'*ladies* think nothing well without an edging'. In 1719 he was
dismissed from the Surveyorship: the 'job' was outrageous, or-

ganized by the man who succeeded him. Wren accepted it with dignity. He lived on until he was over ninety, dying in his sleep after dinner one day in 1723.

Sir J. Summerson, *Christopher Wren*, 1953.
Margaret Whinney, *Wren*, 1971.
Kerry Downes, *The Architecture of Wren*, 1982.

EDWARD PIERCE or **PEARCE** (*d.* 1695), sculptor, was the son of an artist who had worked for Van Dyck. We know nothing of his training as a sculptor, and, indeed, he seems to have spent most of his working life as a mason. From 1663 to 1665 he was employed as mason and carver for Sir Roger Pratt, at Horseheath. After 1671 he was working in various capacities in the rebuilding of London. He was paid £50 apiece for the bronze dragons at the base of the Monument; he worked as a mason on the south side of St. Paul's; and he is said to have rebuilt St. Clement Danes from Wren's plans. He designed the Bishop's Palace at Lichfield, and his work in wood or stone, such as pulpits and staircases, may be found in a number of buildings in the midlands and southern England. In practice he can have found little time for sculpture, of which art he was the most distinguished exponent in his century. No doubt he found little demand: he was a victim of that return to foreign fashions and practitioners in the arts which was one aspect of the Restoration. He produced several statues for the Royal Exchange, some work for the City Companies, and busts of Cromwell and Milton. Perhaps his greatest as well as most appropriate achievement was the superbly sensitive bust of his master, Wren, in 1673, a piece which is outstanding among the portraits of the century.

June Seymour, 'Edward Pierce: Baroque Sculptor of London', *Guildhall Miscellany*, i (1952), p. 10.

SAMUEL BUTLER (1612–80), satirist, son of a Worcestershire farmer, went to school in Worcester and became a page to the Countess of Kent. Later he was clerk to several Puritan magistrates, one of whom, Sir Samuel Luke, is supposed to have been the original of Hudibras, the central figure of the satirical poem upon which Butler's fame rests. According to his friend Aubrey, Butler was 'of a

leonine-coloured haire, sanguinocholerique, middle sized, strong; a
severe and sound judgement, high coloured; a good fellow'. He
married a wealthy widow and at the Restoration got the post of
Secretary to the Lord President of Wales. *Hudibras*, the first part of
which was published in 1663 (the second and third followed in 1664
and 1678), greatly pleased Charles II and the courtiers by its
description of the fat and timid justice and its savage comments on
the Presbyterians whom Butler hated, those who in perhaps its most
famous couplet

> 'Compound for sins they are inclined to,
> By damning those they have no mind to.'

The King gave him £300. Yet for all the brilliance and topicality of
the poem, Butler died in poverty. Aubrey says that this was because
he refused all preferments but very good ones and 'so at last he had
none at all'.

JOHN DRYDEN (1631–1700), poet, playwright, and satirist,
was born at Aldwinkle, in Northamptonshire. Like his contemporary Locke, he was a boy at Westminster under Busby, and thence
he went to Trinity College, Cambridge. During the Republic he was
clerk to a cousin who was Cromwell's chamberlain, and in 1659 he
wrote *Heroic Stanzas* in praise of the late Lord Protector. The
Restoration found him a Royalist, hailing the King with *Astrea
Redux*, and as Charles II's reign proceeded so Dryden moved further
away from the Puritan opinions of his youth. Although he had
inherited a small estate he turned to writing for the stage as a source
of income, and produced a long series of plays of which *All for Love*
(1678) has remained the best known. But it was Dryden's narrative
poetry which established him as the greatest figure in English
literature in the second half of the seventeenth century. In 1668, the
year after the publication of *Annus Mirabilis* with its brilliant
description of the Fire of London, Charles II appointed him Poet
Laureate. No monarch was ever so well rewarded for his choice: in
1681–2 Dryden flayed Shaftesbury and the Whigs in *Absalom and
Achitophel*, the finest piece of political satire ever written in English
verse.

In 1686, with a catholicizing King upon the throne, Dryden
joined the Church of Rome, and in the following year wrote *The*

John Dryden c.1693
(Artist: Sir Godfrey Kneller)

Hind and the Panther, a defence in heroic couplets of his new faith. With the Revolution he lost the Laureateship, yet he retained both his Roman beliefs and his acknowledged supremacy over the literary world. For some years he wrote plays again. But the great achievements of the last decade of his life were his odes for music and his translations: in 1697, for example, he produced both *Alexander's*

Feast, the second of his *Odes for St. Cecilia's Day*, and his version of Vergil, the most celebrated of his translations. He died in the last year of the century, and was buried in Westminster Abbey.

Dryden was among the giants, as his own age recognized when it paid homage to him through the years in his place at Will's Coffee House. The astonishing variety of his splendid and prolific output; the consummate technique of his verse; the ease and clarity of his prose; the sensitive grasp of the issues of a changing time — these things assure his fame. It is easy to condemn Dryden as a turncoat who adjusted his opinions to the political needs of the day, and expressed them in golden words in order to secure place, pension, and applause for himself. There is evident truth in this view. The man who wrote on serious subjects for his living in Dryden's day could scarcely avoid at any rate the appearance of time-serving, and the greater the writer the worse the appearance. Yet it may be said in defence of Dryden that the change in direction of his opinions was consistent, and that he held to his Catholicism after 1688. Like many men of his time he was much moved by a fear of fanaticism and disorder. In Congreve's words Dryden 'had personal qualities to challenge both love and esteem from all who were truly acquainted with him', and among these were compassion, generosity both with money and advice, and a modesty which frequently became diffidence.

Christopher Hollis, *Dryden*, 1933.
J. M. Osborn, *John Dryden, Some Biographical Facts and Problems*, 1940.

APHRA BEHN (1640–89), the first English woman novelist, was born in Wye, Kent, the daughter of a barber. She spent some years of her childhood in Surinam, at that time an English possession, and after her return to England in 1658 married a Dutchman named Behn. Behn died before 1666, apparently leaving his widow ill provided for, and from this time forward — apart from a brief and mysterious spell as an English spy in the Netherlands — she earned her living by writing. She wrote plays, the first two of which were first performed in 1671, and novels, of which *Oroonoko* (1688) is the most celebrated, idealizing the noble savage. In general they were coarse comedy, often romantic in flavour. She seems to have been an attractive person, no doubt something of an adventuress. The *D.N.B.* credits her with the introduction of milk punch into England. She was buried in the cloister of Westminster Abbey.

George Woodcock, *The Incomparable Aphra*, 1948.
Angelina Coreau, *Reconstructing Aphra*, 1980.
Maureen Duffy, *The Passionate Shepherdess*, 1977.

JOHN AUBREY (1626–97), biographer, was born at Kington St. Michael, in Wiltshire, not far from Malmesbury, the home of the philosopher Thomas Hobbes who was his lifelong friend. He was educated at Blandford Grammar School and Trinity College, Oxford, which he entered in 1642. But his time at Oxford was interrupted, first by an outbreak of smallpox and then by the consequences of the Civil War, and this broken education, coupled with frequent ill-health in his youth, no doubt contributed to a thoroughly unsettled career. Modest, kindly, and generous, John Aubrey lived a life full of troubles, including financial difficulties which led to the ruin of the family estates and to years spent in dodging his creditors, and unhappy love affairs, one of which involved him in three years of litigation. By 1677 he had lost everything, including his books. Yet he was a man of high intelligence, and was a born antiquarian. In 1649 he revealed the megalithic remains at Avebury, hitherto ignored; in 1673 he made a tour of Surrey and collected an immense amount of topographical information. He made a similar survey of North Wiltshire, and at the command of Charles II he wrote a discourse on Stonehenge.

In 1667 he became acquainted with Antony à Wood, and for nearly a quarter of a century he supplied Wood with a mass of historical and antiquarian material. The collaboration, always difficult with a man so self-centred and spiteful as Wood, eventually broke down when Wood mutilated Aubrey's collected manuscripts. But out of it came the work which secured Aubrey's place in history, his *Brief Lives*, based upon notes collected over many years and sent in 1680 to Wood, who used them extensively in his *Athenae Oxonienses* (1691–2). Aubrey was a lifelong and passionate antiquarian, with an eye for odd detail; he was a human being with a genius for getting to know people; and he had a superb gift for the

John Aubrey
(Artist: William Faithorne)

word or phrase which conveys a portrait in a flash. He describes Sir
Walter Raleigh's enormous industry in the four words, 'He was no
Slug'; Charles Chester, an incessant talker, 'made a noise like a drum
in a room'. His lives contain a good deal of scandal, yet with the
scandal there are both shrewd judgment and a kind heart. When he
sent his 'minutes' to Wood he warned him that they 'are not fit to let
fly abroad, till about thirty years hence, for the Author and the
Persons (like Medlars) ought to be rotten first'.

Aubrey's Brief Lives, ed. Oliver Lawson Dick, 1949 (paperback,
    1962).

Anthony Powell, *John Aubrey and His Friends*, 1948.
Aubrey's Brief Lives, 1669–1696, ed. A.C.Clark, 1898.

EDWARD POCOCKE (1604–91), Oxford orientalist, born in
the city and educated at Thame Grammar School and Magdalen
Hall, became a Fellow of Corpus Christi College. He began oriental
studies as a young man, and at the age of twenty-four published an
edition of four previously unprinted epistles from the Syriac New
Testament. From 1630 to 1635 he was Chaplain to the English
Turkey merchants at Aleppo, learning Arabic and collecting manuscripts and coins, and on his return Laud had him appointed to the
Lectureship in Arabic which he had just founded at Oxford (1636).
In 1637 Pococke went again to the east, living mainly at Constantinople, and when he came back in 1641 Laud was in the Tower: he
rejected the scholarly advice, based upon successful experience,
which Pococke brought him from Grotius, to have himself smuggled
out in a box of books. Pococke himself, installed in a country living
in 1642, ran into trouble with his parishioners because of his
Laudian background, and only the intervention of Selden and others
saved his lectureship. Pococke declined the oath to the Commonwealth, but managed to continue his studies in peace, publishing his
masterpiece *Specimen historiae Arabum* in 1649. After the Restoration he lived at Christ Church as a canon and as Professor of
Hebrew, and on his death at the age of eighty-six his fine collection
of oriental manuscripts was bought for the Bodleian.

SIR WILLIAM DUGDALE (1605–86), the most celebrated of
seventeenth-century historical scholars, was born in Warwickshire,
son of a Lancashire gentleman who had been bursar of St. John's
College, Oxford. Appointed a pursuivant in 1638, he rose to become
Garter King of Arms in 1677, the year of his knighthood. An ardent
Royalist, he went with Charles I to Oxford; 'in his coat of arms with
trumpets sounding before him' summoned Banbury Castle to surrender in 1642, and appeared at Edgehill; suffered sequestration of
lands; and proclaimed Charles II at Coleshill in 1660. Yet he
allowed neither public affairs nor domestic concerns (he had nineteen children) to deflect him from the central concern of his life, the

collection of historical materials. Dugdale's three greatest achievements were the *Monasticon Anglicanum* (three volumes in 1655, 1661, and 1673), the *Antiquities of Warwickshire* (1656), and the *Baronage* (1675–6). Each of these made a unique contribution to the scholarly study of English history — the *Monasticon* in its revelation of the range and value of English monastic charters, the *Warwickshire* as a model of county history, and the *Baronage* by pioneering the study of English feudal history. Dugdale owed much to other men's work, most notably to that of Roger Dodsworth, who indeed almost certainly collected the materials of the first two volumes of the *Monasticon*, and he was not always scrupulous in acknowledging his debts. Nevertheless, his reputation must remain very high. As an editor he was unsurpassed in his age. He won the affection and respect of contemporaries by his immense industry, by his disciplined standards, and by his readiness to help younger scholars after the Restoration.

D. C. Douglas, *English Scholars*, 1951 ed., pp. 30–51.

ELIAS ASHMOLE (1617–92), antiquarian and astrologer, was born at Lichfield, educated at the grammar school there and trained to be a solicitor. He took the Royalist side in the Civil War, did a little fighting, and then got posts in the Excise at Lichfield and Worcester. He had something of a flair for profitable matrimony (he married thrice), and became an ardent antiquarian, with interests running out into botany, alchemy, and astrology; and he was apparently one of the first English Freemasons. He did well out of the Restoration, being appointed Windsor Herald and becoming a well-known London figure. In 1672 he published a considerable volume, *The Institution, Laws and Ceremonies of the Order of the Garter*. But his name has survived because of the antiquarian and ethnological collections which he inherited from his friend John Tradescant. These he offered to the University of Oxford on condition that a museum was built to house them. Twelve wagonloads of specimens were carted to Oxford, and in 1683 the Ashmolean Museum was opened (it moved to its present buildings in the nineteenth century).

SAMUEL COOPER (1609–72), miniaturist, was the nephew and pupil of John Hoskins and worked in his uncle's studio until the 1630s. About 1640 he went to live in Covent Garden, and by 1650 he had an established studio in Henrietta Street. Aubrey called him 'the Prince of Limners of this Age' and Pepys 'the great limner in little'. Mrs. Pepys sat for him and Pepys paid £30 for the portrait,

Samuel Cooper
(Artist: after a self-portrait)

even though, characteristically, he was 'not satisfied in the greatness of the resemblance'. In European eyes Cooper was the outstanding English artist of his day, achieving his greatness in a branch of painting in which England could claim supremacy. His miniatures rival those of Nicholas Hilliard in technique and in colouring, and he represented an entirely native tradition of painting. Republic and monarchy alike patronized Cooper: he produced the best portrait we have of Cromwell, and Charles II gave him a pension of £200 per annum in 1663. He was evidently a likeable and cultured man, widely travelled, something of a musician, 'good company' in Pepys's opinion, and his circle of friends included Hobbes and Petty. Less fashionable than his contemporary Lely, Cooper was the finer and surer craftsman.

Graham Reynolds, *English Portrait Miniatures*, 1952.

SIR PETER LELY (1618–80), painter, belonged to a Flanders family, although he was born at Soest in Westphalia, son of a Captain in the Brandenburg army. He studied at Haarlem and first came to England in the 1640s. Turning from landscape to the more profitable task of portraits, he painted the children of Charles I in 1647. The coming of the Republic did him no harm, nor did the Restoration. He painted Oliver Cromwell early in the Protectorate, by which time he was firmly established in upper-class favour; yet in 1661 Charles conferred a pension of £200 per annum on him, recognizing him as the successor to Van Dyck, and in 1662 he was naturalized. Until his death in 1680, just after his knighthood, Lely continued to be the leading artist in his adopted country, turning out a long succession of society portraits. Like Kneller after him, he developed a kind of studio factory, employing assistants to add details and background, and as with Kneller the result was a great quantity of mediocre work. Yet there were striking exceptions, notably perhaps when he escaped from the languid female fashions of the Restoration: the portraits of admirals which he did during the Second Dutch War (now at Greenwich) reveal Lely at his shrewd and vigorous best. In the history of English portraiture the pattern developed by Lely lasted for over a century.

R.B. Beckett, *Peter Lely*, 1951.

SAMUEL PEPYS (1633–1703), diarist and naval administrator, was a Londoner, born in the parish of St. Bride's, the fifth child of a tailor. His paternal ancestors were from Cottenham in Cambridgeshire, and he spent a year or two of the early 1640s in Huntingdon and attended the school where Oliver Cromwell had been a generation before. But he was brought back to London and went to St. Paul's School; and in 1649, a boy of strong Puritan feelings, he saw Charles I executed. Next year he went up to Magdalene College, Cambridge, graduating in 1653. In the later 1650s he took service under his cousin, Edward Montagu, that loyal Cromwellian who in 1656 was appointed joint Commander of the English fleet. In 1658 Pepys was successfully cut for the stone, and in that year too he began, in effect, his career as a civil servant by becoming a clerk to one of the Tellers of the Exchequer, George Downing. Yet the great turning-point in his life came in 1660 when, after sailing to Holland as Montagu's secretary in the fleet that brought the King home, he was appointed Clerk of the Acts to the Navy Board, and thus was launched on the course that made him the most distinguished civilian naval administrator in English history. And it was on January 1st, 1660, too, that he began to keep a diary.

The *Diary* was written in the shorthand devised by Skelton some twenty years before. Since it was first deciphered and published (in part) in the early nineteenth century it has become much the most popular of all the source-works of English history. Its value to historians lies partly in its information about the leading personalities and events of Restoration England, partly in the light it sheds on social life in Charles II's London. These things have attracted the general reader also, yet what has fascinated him at least as often has been the *Diary*'s revelation of its author in all his rich humanity. Gossip, amours, friendships, quarrels with his wife; music and sermons and plays; snobbery, delight in being in the know, patriotism, devotion to work; an endless pleasure in small things, a sense of the great occasion — all are there. As a diarist Pepys was lucky, with the Restoration, the Plague, the Fire, and the Dutch raid on the Medway to record from intimate knowledge as his framework of public events. Yet he used his luck with a superb blend of art and artlessness. Perhaps what has made the *Diary* so permanently attractive is that it was the work of a young man. He stopped writing it in his thirty-seventh year, on May 31st, 1669, because he

Samuel Pepys 1666
(Artist: John Hayls)

believed himself to be threatened with blindness. Later that same
year the death of his wife was a shattering blow.

Yet an exciting and hazardous public career, of high significance
to posterity, lay ahead of him. As Clerk of the Acts, Pepys had
already made his mark. He had begun to tackle corruption in the
dockyards; had become treasurer of the committee responsible for

Tangier; had, like his fellow-diarist Evelyn, with whom he had so little in common, stayed at his post throughout the Plague; and had in 1667–8 done his best to defend the Navy Office from Commons' criticism for the disasters of the Dutch War. Thus by 1669 he was an established public servant distinguished for zeal and shrewdness. His great achievements as a naval administrator came after 1673, when the Test Act compelled the departure of James, Duke of York, from the post of Lord High Admiral. Charles II put the Admiralty into commission and appointed Pepys as Secretary. He retained the office until 1688, apart from an interval from 1679 to 1684, and during these years he carried out or inaugurated a series of reforms. Some, like his detailed dealings with naval contracts or his development of the convoy system in the Third Dutch War, were of immediate significance; others, like his reorganization of officers' ranks and his preference for 'tarpaulins' as Commanders were the beginnings of long-term developments. All contributed to making the Admiralty an effective department of state and thus to laying the administrative foundations for the naval glories of the following centuries.

His work was not done without fierce opposition, and this did not come only from those whose jobbery Pepys ended and who disliked spending £600,000 on the thirty new ships of the line he demanded in 1677. For Pepys had long abandoned his Republican enthusiasm of 1649, and had become very much a supporter of the court; no doubt his Royalism was sharpened by James's own interest in the Navy. So it is scarcely surprising that Shaftesbuy and his followers went for Pepys as soon as he was elected M.P. for Castle Rising in 1673, accusing him of Popery, or that at the height of the Popish Plot scare in 1679 they got him dismissed from his post and sent to the Tower on a similar bogus charge. Although he was freed within a year he had been in dire peril. In James II's reign Pepys was in effect the civilian head of the Admiralty, and in the crisis of the Revolution he remained loyal to the King — although, characteristically, he did not reproach Dartmouth for his failure to challenge William's landing. Inevitably he was dismissed, and in 1689 he was again arrested and accused of passing naval information to the French. But the charge was soon dropped, and Pepys spent the remainder of his days in retirement at Clapham, publishing *Memoirs of the Navy* in 1690 and devoting some of his energies to Christ's Hospital, of which he was treasurer.

The Diary of Samuel Pepys, ed. R. C. Latham and W. Matthews,
   11 vols., 1970–83.
Arthur Bryant, Samuel Pepys: The Man in the Making, 1933;
   Samuel Pepys, The Years of Peril, 1935; Samuel Pepys, The
   Saviour of the Navy, 1938.
Richard Ollard, Pepys, 1974.

JOHN EVELYN (1620–1706), diarist, was born at Wotton
House, near Dorking in Surrey, member of a family of newly-risen
gentry who had grown rich by making gunpowder for Queen
Elizabeth. Evelyn was a Balliol man, a very cautious Royalist who
was out of England for most of the Civil War years, a sound
Anglican, and an indefatigable author. As Commissioner for the care
of sick and wounded prisoners in the Dutch Wars of Charles II's
reign he showed very real courage by staying at his post at Deptford
throughout the plague of 1665–6. His historical importance rests
very largely upon his Diary, which he kept for sixty-six years and
which has served historians as a major source, perhaps most notably
of information about politicians and about changing social customs.
It has some fine passages, not least in its account of the Fire of
London, and Evelyn was not without the seventeenth-century eye for
the 'character', as, for example, his description of Robert Boyle
shows. But, in sharp contrast to the far more humane, as well as
entertaining, diary of his friend Pepys, Evelyn's Diary tells us very
little about its writer — except in so far as this is itself a revealing
fact. In Christopher Hill's words, Evelyn's Diary is 'a carefully-
compiled semi-public document, in which we see Evelyn as he
wished posterity to see him, warts removed'. * Comparison with his
letters has led his most recent biographer to observe that 'when we
come to realize what subjects were omitted, we are forced to
conclude that he constantly bore in mind both propriety and
posterity'.† The letters also suggest that he was a snob, a prig, and
domestic tyrant, and that as a middle-aged man he used the role of
spiritual adviser to the beautiful Margaret Blagge quite unscrupulously to try to stop her marriage with Godolphin.

*History, Vol. XLII, No. 144 (Feb. 1957), p. 18.
†W. G. Hiscock, John Evelyn and His Family Circle, 1955, p. 21.

John Evelyn c.1648
(Artist: Robert Walker)

Evelyn was a virtuoso, notably well informed upon architecture, engraving, numismatics, painting, and gardens, and he wrote extensively upon these and other subjects until he was well into his eighties. One of his best-known pieces was *Fumifugium*, which was an attack upon London's smoke with constructive proposals for its abatement. Perhaps his finest achievement was *Sylva, or a discourse of Forest-trees and the propagation of timber in His Majesty's Dominions* (1664), a very succesful work of propaganda for the replanting of woodlands. Deeply devoted to trees and to gardens, Evelyn won great fame by the garden which he created at Sayes Court, the house in which he lived near the dockyard at Deptford. In the last years of his life he was busy restoring the damage caused at Wotton by the terrible storm of November 1703, which brought down 2,000 of his trees, and exhorting his grandson to continue planting in order to make it once again 'Wood-Town'.

The complete edition of the *Diary* is that by E. S. de Beer, 6 vols., 1955; the text of this edition, without the critical apparatus, is available in one volume.
Florence Higham, *John Evelyn Esquire*, 1968.

SIR HENRY MORGAN (1635–88), buccaneer, came from Llanrhymney, in Glamorgan. There are several tales to account for his presence in the West Indies: it seems most likely that he went on the expedition of Penn and Venables which captured Jamaica in 1655. He fought in the Second Dutch War (1644–7), commanding a ship in an attack on Curaçao. In 1668 he was chosen 'admiral' of the buccaneers, and his period of authority marks the climax of the power of this group of lawless seamen of all nations who ranged the waters of the Caribbean, terrorizing the inhabitants of its coasts. Under Morgan's leadership they carried out exploits of equal bravery and brutality. In 1668 his force of 400 men took and sacked Portobelo, the fortress-base of the Spanish silver fleets, and carried off a quarter of a million pieces of eight. Next year they broke into Lake Maracaibo and plundered its shores. Finally, in 1671, they captured Panama, a city of 30,000 people, killing several hundreds of its defenders for the loss of only six of their own number, and looting the country for sixty miles round. Evelyn complacently observed that 'such an action had not been done since the famous Drake'. Certainly Morgan's actions gave the *coup de grâce* to all real Spanish power in the Caribbean. Some of our information about

Morgan comes from a dubious source, *The Buccaneers of America*, an account, first published in 1678, by a Dutchman named Esquemeling, who certainly exaggerated both the heroism and the plundering. Morgan was an intrepid and ingenious leader, but he was also a mean and treacherous scoundrel who even cheated his own men out of their share of the Panama loot. In 1672 his buccaneering career ended when the British authorities in Jamaica sent him home under arrest. But he managed to win Charles II's favour, and returned to Jamaica in 1674 as Deputy Governor. Suspended from office in 1683, he seems to have spent most of his last years drinking and gambling. He was reinstated a month before his death in 1688.

C.H. Haring, *The Buccaneers in the West Indies in the Seventeenth Century*, 1910.

P.K. Kemp and Christopher Lloyd, *The Brethren of the Coast*, 1960.

SIR ROGER L'ESTRANGE (1616–1704), journalist, was born at Hunstanton, member of a well-to-do Norfolk Royalist family. He served under Rupert, and was in a Parliamentary prison for three years under sentence of death for his part in a plot to recover Lynn for the King. On his release in 1648 he at once promoted a futile Royalist rising in Kent, and then fled abroad, returning in 1653. In 1659 he was busy pamphleteering against Lambert and in favour of the monarchy, and at the Restoration he came into his own, combining the occupations of government spy and editor of a semi-official newspaper. L'Estrange, an accomplished musician and a scholar who wrote translations from the Spanish and published a very large collection of *Aesop's Fables*, a man in Pepys's words 'of fine conversation ... most courtly', was also the holder of firmly reactionary opinions, and in 1663 he wrote a pamphlet denouncing the liberty of the press. As a result he was in the same year appointed 'Surveyor of the imprimery and printing presses', and he held the office — in which he was responsible for hunting down illicit presses and pamphlets — almost continuously until the Revolution of 1688. He used his powers vigorously, employing informers and corruption and aiming particularly at Republicans and Dissenters.

One printer of a seditious pamphlet, John Twyn, was hanged, drawn and quartered on L'Estrange's evidence; and in 1670 he claimed to have suppressed over 600 pamphlets. Yet it is clear that he was in fact very unsuccessful, partly perhaps because, so it was said, he was too susceptible to female blandishments. In 1680 he ran into trouble over the Popish Plot, when a false witness was employed against him, and he fled abroad, while the London mob burned his effigy. He returned in 1681, soon recovered his authority, and did much to get Oates convicted of perjury. James II knighted him, but this did not prevent L'Estrange, characteristically, from attacking the King's proposals for religious toleration. Inevitably the Revolution brought his dismissal, and within a few years the lapse of the system of licensing of the press. His last years were unhappy ones, marked by short spells of imprisonment (he was suspected in 1696 of a share in the Assassination Plot) and by financial trouble caused by a wife addicted to gambling.

G. Kitchin, *Sir Roger L'Estrange*, 1913.

COLONEL THOMAS BLOOD (1618?–80), the adventurer, seems to have been the son of a blacksmith and was probably of Irish Presbyterian descent. He fought for Parliament in the Civil Wars, and got from Henry Cromwell a grant of Irish lands which he lost at the Restoration. In 1663 he devised a plot to seize Dublin Castle, but this was betrayed to Ormonde, the Lord-Lieutenant, and Blood became a fugitive in various disguises, among them that of a Quaker, until he escaped to Holland. Returning to Britain, he took part in a Covenanters' revolt and achieved notoriety by a daring rescue of a friend from imprisonment in Doncaster. Blood was 'not a Fifth Monarchist, but found the more militant saints congenial companions' *; it is possible that he was a government spy into the bargain. The climax of his career came in 1670–71. In 1670 he made a bold attempt to kidnap the Duke of Ormonde in St. James's Street, and carry him off to execution at Tyburn; Ormonde was rescued in time. The following year, disguised as a parson and aided by three confederates, he tried to steal the Crown Jewels from the Tower. He

* B.S. Capp, *The Fifth Monarchy Men*, 1972, p. 212.

was nearly successful, and the bare-faced effrontery of this episode seems to have won Charles II's favour. Far from being punished, Blood became popular at court and even regained some of his Irish lands. He died in 1680 after a quarrel with Buckingham.

W. C. Abbott, *Colonel Thomas Blood, Crown-Stealer*, 1911.

WILLIAM PENN (1644–1718), founder of the Quaker colony of Pennyslvania, was the son of Captain (later Admiral) Penn. Born in a house on Tower Hill, he went to school at Chigwell. When the Admiral fell into disgrace in 1655 because of the failure to capture Hispaniola, the family moved for some years to their estates in Ireland. The Restoration brought the Admiral back to favour, and William went to Christ Church. Later he was to talk of the 'hellish darkness and debauchery' of Restoration College; while there he seems to have been a Royalist and something of a dandy, yet also to have fallen under the Nonconformist spell of Dr. John Owen, who had been the Cromwellian Vice-Chancellor of the University. Penn was fined for non-attendance at chapel and sent down; he had a row with his father, who sent him to Paris. After a taste of court life and a duel he settled to study for two years (1662–4) at the Huguenot College of Saumur, where he was deeply affected by the tolerant and liberal theologian Moyse Amyraut. On his return to England he studied at Lincoln's Inn; in 1666 he went again to Ireland on business connected with the family estates, and in Ireland he was converted to Quakerism. As a boy of eleven he had been to a meeting in Cork where the preacher, Thomas Loe, had deeply moved him; now, in 1667, he heard Loe once more, and henceforward he was a Quaker.

To join a sect which was eccentric in dress and language, whose meetings were illegal and whose members were persecuted both by the law and by public opinion, was strange conduct for a gentleman born into the ruling class. The Admiral certainly thought so, but eventually recognised his son's decision before he himself died in 1670. Penn was imprisoned three times in three years: in 1670 the jury's verdict when Penn was on a charge of riot (they found him guilty of speaking in Gracechurch Street and in effect acquitted him; he had in fact been taking part in a Friends' meeting outside their meeting-house, closed under the Conventicle Act of 1670) was the occasion of Brushell's Case (1671), which established the freedom of juries. In 1672 Penn married Guli Springett in Bristol. He wrote extensively in these years, most notably, *No Cross, No Crown* (written in the Tower in 1669), a prophetic defence of Christian self-denial, and *The Great Case of Liberty of Conscience* (1671); used such influence as he had at court on behalf of his fellow Quakers; and took part on the Whig side in politics during the Exclusion Crisis (1678–81), acting as agent for Algernon Sidney in two elections. But increasingly his mind was turning towards the opportunities which the American colonies seemed to offer, both of providing a refuge where his Quaker brethren could find and practise toleration, and of establishing a 'Holy Experiment', a state living by Christian principles. In 1676 he was one of the Trustees of the colony of West New Jersey; and in 1680 he petitioned Charles II for a grant of land in America in payment of a debt of some £16,000 owing to the Admiral. The result was the colony of Pennsylvania, named after the Admiral, and founded in 1681. Penn drew up its constitution, the Frame of Government, providing for an assembly elected by all taxpayers, complete religious toleration, no oaths, and the death penalty only for wilful murder or treason. He was himself its Governor, and he was reponsible for the famous peace treaty of 1683 with the Delaware Indians. But he spent in all only four years (1682–4, 1699–1701) there. This was one of the reasons why his later relations with the colony were not easy, involving litigation and political disputes. Nevertheless, Pennsylvania prospered more rapidly than any other of the early colonies, attracting a variety of settlers — Quakers from every part of England, Welsh and Irish, Dutch and Germans. Its capital, Philadelphia, the City of Brotherly Love, grew swiftly, in schools and hospitals and culture as well as in material wealth, and before Penn died it was challenging Boston as the greatest of colonial towns. Voltaire and the other philosophers of eighteenth-century Europe were full of admiration for Pennsylvania, as a testimony to the virtues of toleration and good sense.

Some of Penn's activities in the second half of his life brought difficulties upon his colony and his fellow Quakers as well as upon himself. He had been something of a Whig under Charles II; under James II he became very much a Jacobite, a familiar figure at Court, accepting James's offers of religious freedom to Dissenters at their face value, acting as go-between to James and the Fellows of

Magdalen, and going on a mission on the King's behalf to William of Orange. He backed James's Declaration of Indulgence in 1688, no doubt in the interests of the religious and political toleration in which he believed and which he had advocated in a pamphlet (*Good Advice to the Church of England, Roman Catholick and Protestant Dissenter*) in the previous year. Macaulay, in a famous passage of his *History of England* (Vol. I, Chap. 4) savaged Penn; the attack is open to much criticism in detail, yet one phrase — 'He had no skill in reading the characters of others' — strikes home. Penn's misjudgment of James II led him into trouble after the Revolution. He was before the Council in December 1688; he was in danger of arrest in 1690-2, because he had been in communication with the exiled King, and for a time went into hiding; for two years, 1692-4, he was deprived of the governorship of Pennsylvania. He recovered public esteem in the later part of William III's reign. But there were private troubles, too; Penn had lived on a generous scale at Holland House, and ran into debt, and at one time he was a prisoner in the Fleet. Nevertheless, he continued to write; his *Essay towards the Present and Future Peace of Europe* (1693) is a fine plea for international understanding. And he remained deeply respected among Quakers, untypical though he was of them in some ways. Swift in the *Journal to Stella* tells us (1712) of what may have been his last public appearance: 'My friend Penn came there, Will Penn the Quaker, at the head of his brethren, to thank the Duke for his kindness to their people in Ireland. To see a dozen scoundrels with their hats on, and the Duke complimenting with his off, was a good sight enough.' Later in this same year Penn had a stroke. He lingered on in a second happy childhood until 1718. He lies now by the Jordans Meeting House at Chalfont St. Giles.

J. W. Graham, *William Penn*, 1916.
Catherine Owens Pease, *William Penn*, 1956.
Mary Maples Dunn, *William Penn: Politics and Conscience*, 1956.

ROBERT BARCLAY (1648-90), Quaker apologist, was born at Gordonstoun, Elgin, of a distinguished Scottish family; his mother was related to the Stuarts, his father served under Gustavus and in the Covenanting Army, and was a member of two Cromwellian Parliaments. Educated at the Scottish Theological College in Paris, a Roman Catholic institution, he became a Quaker about 1666, following his father's example. Notable for his sweet and even temper, he was in some ways like that other upper-class convert to Quakerism, William Penn — though Barclay was less courtly and less loquacious. He was associated with Penn in the setting up of a proprietary colony in East New Jersey, and was for a short time its Governor, though he never went to America. Like Penn he enjoyed the dubious distinction of court favour in the reign of James II. But there was an altogether tougher core in Barclay's mind than in that of Penn; he had imbibed Calvinism with his native air, and Quakerism had a sterner intellectual conflict to fight in Scotland. In 1672 he walked in sackcloth and ashes through the chief streets of Aberdeen as a sign from the Lord, calling upon Aberdonians to repent. But his great contribution to the Quaker cause was the publication in 1676 of his *Apologia* (in Latin, at Amsterdam), the first attempt at a systematic statement of Friends' doctrines. This work, which owed a good deal to George Keith, the Scottish Friend who later abandoned Quakerism for Anglicanism, made a valiant attempt to reconcile the Quaker belief in the Seed, the divine principle to be found in all men, with Barclay's Calvinist assumption of the innate depravity of human creatures. There was an emphasis upon spiritual passivity implied in Barclay's ideas which attracted Quaker, and other, criticism. Nevertheless, the *Apologia* remains a great landmark in the growth of Quaker exposition. Barclay himself died of fever, still a comparatively young man, at his home, Ury, in Scotland in 1690.

W. C. Braithwaite, *The Second Period of Quakerism*, 1961 ed.

WILLIAM KIFFIN (1616–1701), Baptist, was a Londoner of Welsh ancestry who was apprenticed to John Lilburne for a short time from 1629. He became a sectary in the 1630s and by 1645 was well known as a 'ringleader' of those who held unorthodox views on baptism. Kiffin was the minister of a London congregation of Baptists and was periodically in trouble either for his religious beliefs (as in 1655, when he was before the Lord Mayor for preaching against infant baptism) or for the political opinions which were thought to accompany them (as in 1660–61, when he was thrice arrested). But he was also a well-to-do cloth merchant, who made money out of contracts in the Dutch War of 1652, and this made him more acceptable to authority, so that he was, for example, able to use his influence with Clarendon to help his fellow-sectaries. Charles II once asked him for a loan of £40,000. Kiffin deemed it safer to make the king a gift of £10,000, thereby, as he observed, saving himself £30,000. Two of Kiffin's grandsons were executed for complicity in Monmouth's rebellion, and he was briefly compelled by James II to serve as a London alderman. Not surprisingly, he was one of the dissenting leaders who put no trust in James, and he successfully advised the Baptist community not to welcome the King's Declaration of Indulgence. Cautious rather than heroic, Kiffin none the less played a quietly significant role in the survival of English Nonconformity.

THOMAS, 1st LORD CLIFFORD (1630–73), member of the Cabal, belonged to a Catholic landowning family of Devon, and was educated at Exeter College, Oxford, and the Middle Temple. He was a Member for Totnes in the Convention and Cavalier Parliaments, one of the new young politicians of the Restoration. Thanks to the patronage of Arlington his rise was very rapid: a Privy Councillor in 1666, Commissioner of the Treasury in 1667, Treasurer of the Household in 1668, by which time he was clearly one of the inner circle of ministers. Direct in manner, apt to be passionate in speech, known as the 'bribemaster-general', Clifford was a vigorous champion of the Court in the Commons. Among the royal advisers he was an advocate of firm and despotic measures, and he was strongly anti-Dutch in outlook. It was therefore appropriate as well as in line with his zealous Catholicism that he should be one of the signatories of the Secret Treaty of Dover in 1670. Created a baron and appointed Lord High Treasurer in 1672, Clifford wanted Charles to defy the opposition at that time by dissolving Parliament. But the Test Act of 1673 drove him from office, and possibly also to his grave: he died in the same year, probably by his own hand. He left incomplete at his death the mansion of Ugbrooke, near Chudleigh.

C.H. Hartmann, *Clifford of the Cabal, 1630–73*, 1937.

HENRY BENNET, 1st EARL OF ARLINGTON (1618–85), member of the Cabal, born at Harlington in Middlesex, won a reputation for scholarship at Westminster and Christ Church and fought in the Royalist Army in the Civil War, suffering an injury to his nose which marked him for the rest of his days. He travelled abroad during the Commonwealth, becoming secretary to James, Duke of York, and in 1658 the exiled King's agent at Madrid. Rewarded at the Restoration by being appointed Keeper of the Privy Purse, he became in 1662 Secretary of State for the southern department. He retained this office for the next twelve years and was during this time the minister most nearly in charge of foreign affairs. When he resigned the secretaryship in 1674 he became Lord Chamberlain, a post which he held until his death in 1685, although he devoted the last few years of his life not to public affairs but to extensive re-building at his country seat of Euston in Suffolk.

Arlington was unpopular, and not merely with Clarendon whose policies he opposed and whose removal from office and from England he accomplished in 1667. Contemporaries distrusted him, much as the politicians of a century later were to distrust Shelburne, and for similar reasons. For he combined considerable ability with a deliberately smooth and supple manner. He had used what Clarendon calls his 'pleasant and agreeable humour' to win Charles's favour. He had qualities not common among Restoration politicians: he liked work and worked systematically, he was an accomplished linguist who spoke Spanish and Dutch fluently as well as French, and he had a poker face. On the other hand, what was known of his religion aroused distrust; nominally an Anglican, he was suspected of Catholic sympathies and, according to Evelyn, died in communion with Rome. He married a Dutch wife, which made his patriotism suspect. A certain formality of gait and solemnity of appearance, together with the black patch on his nose, made Arlington a butt to Buckingham and the younger men of the court.

Men thought Arlington a time-server and a selfish intriguer. In view of the lamentable failure of almost every stroke of English foreign policy in the years of his secretaryship, his buoyancy is impressive. He was a principal advocate of war with the Dutch and in 1664 supported the attack on the Smyrna fleet which led to the formal outbreak of war in 1665. His diplomacy in 1665–6 helped to give the Dutch France, Brandenburg and Denmark as allies, and to leave England isolated. This Second Dutch War ended in 1667 with the Dutch raid upon the Medway and the unprofitable Treaty of

Breda: yet it was Clarendon, the opponent of the war, not Arlington, who was exiled as its scapegoat. Turning to friendship with the Dutch, Arlington in 1668 sent Sir William Temple to negotiate the Triple Alliance with Holland and Sweden. Yet two years later he had been won over to friendship with France. He and Clifford alone of the Cabal were privy to the Catholicizing scheme of the secret Treaty of Dover (1670), which may perhaps be seen as the highwater mark of Arlington's achievement. The Third Dutch War which followed upon this treaty was even less successful than the Second, and Arlington (created an Earl in 1672) had by 1673 become pro-Dutch and an advocate of peace. He had also reversed his opinions on domestic policy; a supporter of the Declaration of Indulgence in 1672, he was by 1673 supporting the Test Act. The Commons were not convinced, and his impeachment was moved: he was 'popishly affected', he had frequently betrayed his trust, he was the 'great conduit pipe' of ill-counsel. He defended himself in a vigorous speech, and the impeachment was dropped. But after the rise to power of Danby, who did not like him, Arlington resigned his secretaryship (1674), and henceforward had no real influence upon English foreign policy.

Violet Barbour, *Henry Bennet, Earl of Arlington*, 1914.

GEORGE VILLIERS, 2nd DUKE OF BUCKINGHAM (1628–87), member of the Cabal, in Dryden's words 'Chymist, Fidler, States-Man and Buffoon', was the second son of James I's favourite, his elder brother dying in infancy. Brought up as a boy with Charles II, he spent some of the Civil War years in Italy. In 1647 he recovered his sequestrated estates, but lost them again when he rose with the Royalists in the Second Civil War. Joining Charles II's Court, he was with the King at Worcester and managed to escape to Rotterdam. At the exiled court he quarrelled incessantly with Hyde and began to intrigue with Parliament for the return of his lands. In 1657 he slipped across to England to marry Fairfax's daughter Mary, and was imprisoned by the Protectorate government. Released, in 1660 he tried to join Fairfax when the latter raised the Yorkshire gentry, but the soldiers would not have so notorious a Royalist with them.

Despite this equivocal background he returned to Charles's favour at the Restoration. He was admitted to the Privy Council in 1662;

he was prominent in the period of the Cabal; and he was employed on missions to Louis XIV (1670) and William of Orange (1673). Yet he never held high office. Clarendon, to whom Buckingham led the opposition, kept him out in the early years of the reign. After Clarendon's fall in 1667 he did for a time exercise a considerable influence over the King, and, as frequent entries in Pepys's *Diary* for 1667–8 suggest, was widely rumoured to 'rule all'. But this is extremely doubtful and certainly whatever political influence he had over Charles declined from the time of the Treaty of Dover (1670); indeed, the bogus second treaty with France in that year was devised in order to throw dust in Buckingham's eyes. He quarrelled with Arlington and the Duke of York and moved into opposition to the Crown, setting himself up as a champion of the Dissenters and a patriotic Protestant, even though he was receiving large sums of money from Louis XIV. In 1677 he was imprisoned, with three other peers, for maintaining that the Parliament which Charles had prorogued was automatically dissolved. He was released through the pleadings of Nell Gwyn. For a time he supported Shaftesbury's campaign for Exclusion, but he soon fell out with Shaftesbury and failed to support the bill in the Lords. He gradually cut adrift from the Country party and ceased by the early 1680s to take part in public life. Going to reside in Yorkshire, deeply in debt, he lived the life of a seedy country squire, and died as the result of a chill caught while digging out a fox.

Buckingham was a man of superb talents, good-looking, graceful, intelligent, witty, a musician and a playwright (his play *The Rehearsal*, a satire upon contemporary drama, was the prototype of Sheridan's *The Critic*). As Clarendon pointed out, he had the power to fascinate men: 'his quality and condescensions, the pleasantness of his humour and conversation, the extravagance and sharpness of his wit, unrestrained by any modesty or religion, drew persons of all affections and inclinations to like his company'. In view of his heredity and of his upbringing in civil war and exile, it is scarcely surprising that he had the fashionable vices of his age, and of his King; the Countess of Shrewsbury was his mistress, and he diverted Charles by mimicking Presbyterian preachers in obscene sermons. But Buckingham was too disreputable even for the Restoration. He was a bully as well as an adulterer: brutal to his wife, he murdered the Earl of Shrewsbury in a duel, relying upon the King's pardon.

Too often his wit turned into a perverse quarrelsomeness, while his political opposition was never far from treason (as when he was put in the Tower in 1667 for 'caballing' against the King) because his politics were founded upon personal antipathies and momentary whims. Dryden's famous sketch of him as Zimri in *Absalom and Achitophel*, which portrays Buckingham's fickleness, is concerned, as the poet himself said, with his 'little extravagancies' and is therefore charitable. Burnet went deeper when he said that Buckingham 'had no principles of religion, virtue, or friendship'. Anthony à Wood, not surprisingly, condemned Buckingham as 'a great favourer of fanaticks and atheists'; yet it is difficult not to attribute even this, his support of toleration, merely to a dislike of Anglican respectability. Few men of such natural gifts in our history have squandered them so trivially.

Hester W. Chapman, *Great Villiers*, 1949.

ANTHONY ASHLEY COOPER, 1st EARL OF SHAFTES-BURY (1621–83), the first party political leader in English history, was born at Wimborne St. Giles in Dorset, the heir to large estates in the south-west. He went to Exeter College, Oxford, in 1637 and was admitted to Lincoln's Inn in 1638. His election for Downton in the Long Parliament was disputed. In the First Civil War he led troops in Dorset, first for Charles and then (from 1644 on) for Parliament. His local prominence as a supporter of the Parliamentary cause, and later of the Commonwealth, led to his being chosen for the Nominated Parliament of 1653, in which he consistently supported the moderate party and sat on the Council of State. He was reappointed to the Council when Cromwell became Protector, but soon turned against him and became one of the leaders of the Republican opposition. He took his seat in the Rump at last in 1660, sided with Monck and was prominent in the Restoration. He was rewarded with a barony as Lord Ashley and with the Chancellorship of the Exchequer in 1661, and he continued to hold office despite his opposition to the Clarendon Code. In these same years he was one of the leading proprietors of the new colony of the Carolinas, and his intimate friendship with the philosopher John Locke dates also from this time. In 1670 he favoured the proposal to legitimize the Duke of Monmouth, to ensure a Protestant succession

Anthony Ashley Cooper, 1st Earl of Shaftesbury c.1672–73
(Artist: after John Greenhill)

to the throne. Kept in ignorance of the secret clauses of the Dover
Treaty, he was appointed Lord Chancellor in 1672 and created Earl
of Shaftesbury in the same year. But in 1673 he went into opposition; resentful at being duped over the Dover Treaty, whose details
were now leaking out, he was increasingly hostile to the King's pro-
French, pro-Catholic policy with its absolutist implications. He
backed the Test Act, and was dismissed from office. Henceforward

his career was spent in opposition to royal policy inside and outside
Parliament, apart from a brief and abortive period in 1679 when he
was for a few months Lord President of the Council. From 1678 he
employed Titus Oates and his Popish Plot to whip up anti-Catholic
feeling against the Government, and to back the policy, put forward
in the following year, to exclude James, Duke of York, from the
succession and replace him by the Duke of Monmouth. He and his
fellow-Whigs failed to carry Exclusion through the Lords; his
support of the lightweight Monmouth lost him much support, and
men were unwilling to push the issue to the risk of civil war. By 1681
his agitation was visibly failing, and Charles was able to turn the
tables on the Whigs at the Oxford Parliament of that year. Shaftesbury was sent to the Tower on a charge of high treason. Released
when a London jury refused to find a true bill against him, he fled to
Holland in 1682 and died at Amsterdam in the following year.

On a long view of British history, Shaftesbury was much the most
significant politician of Charles II's reign, probably the most
important between Pym and Walpole. Yet he remains a most
unattractive figure; even the Whig historians have been unable to
take the founder of the Whig party to their hearts, Macaulay talking
of his 'deliberate selfishness' and 'manifold perfidy'. Physically
small, embittered by ill-health, he had shown himself a supple and
treacherous intriguer, with something of a flair for changing sides at
the right moment; Charles II's nickname for him, 'Little Sincerity',
was peculiarly apt. As the leader of opposition after 1673 he was
brutal and unscrupulous, coolly employing the lies of Oates, the
passions of the mob and the lives of innocent Catholics as means to
his end. He had great gifts. He was a fine orator, and he had the
political leader's flair for winning men: Burnet speaks of his
'particular talent to make others trust to his judgment, and depend
on it' and points out that 'tho' by his changing sides so often it was
very visible how little he was to be depended on, yet he was to the
last much trusted by all the discontented party'. Even Dryden, in the
famous lines from *Absalom and Achitophel*, which have stained our
view of Shaftesbury ever since they were written in 1681:

> 'For close Designs and crooked Counsels fit;
> Sagacious, Bold, and Turbulent of wit'

and

'A daring Pilot in extremity;
Pleas'd with the Danger, when the Waves went high
He sought the Storms; but for a calm unfit,
Would steer too nigh the Sands, to boast his Wit.'

pays a good measure of tribute to the abilities of 'the false Achitophel'. But his powers were blighted, and at the end, when he was ageing and ill, even adoitness and nerve seem to have deserted him.

Shaftesbury belonged to that generation whose entire political life was absorbed in the English Revolution. Eras of revolution force men to choose, to commit themselves, and Shaftesbury's generation had to choose in 1640 and 1642, in 1648 and 1649, in 1653, in 1659 and 1660, and once more in the 1670s. Like nearly all his contemporaries, he trimmed and tacked a great deal; he was not the only man to change sides in the Civil Wars, and he was certainly not the only ex-Cromwellian and ex-Rumper to do well out of the Restoration. Like most men of his class he wanted the Restoration as an end to the uncertanties of military domination and to the possibilities of mob rule. Like all politicians he liked power and its use, and, if Pepys's informant who 'cries up my Lord Ashley to be almost the only man that he sees to look after business, and with the ease and mastery that he wonders at him' was right, he was more hardworking and efficient than most of Charles II's ministers. Thoroughly unscrupulous about means, he was a man of principle about ends. The promotion of trade was his constant concern — understandably, for as well as being a proprietor of Carolina he owned land in the Bahamas and Bermuda and sugar plantations in Barbados, and his English properties were in one of the main clothworking areas. So he supported the Second Dutch War (1664–7) and was ready enough to support the third (1672–4) until the full implications of Charles's policy began to emerge; and his hostility to France was at least in part based on commercial rivalry. By religion he was a deist, against a background of Puritanism, and therefore an advocate of toleration for all Protestants, opposing the Clarendon Code and supporting the King's two Declarations of Indulgence; but when it became clear that toleration was merely a mask for plans of Catholic absolutism Shaftesbury turned to the Test Act, as an essential safeguard of the liberties of all Protestant Englishmen. For the third, and most important, of Shaftesbury's principles was a belief in constitutional government rather than arbitrary despotism. Power should be based on Parliament, and Parliament must represent the men of property. This was the doctrine that his friend Locke was later (when the victory was safely won) to proclaim in his *Two Treatises on Civil Government*. He was therefore utterly opposed to the royal absolutism in alliance with France and with Popery which the Dover Treaty envisaged, and which the accession of the Catholic James II seemed likely to bring about. From this belief came the policy of Exclusion; from it too came the organization of political party and the passage in 1679 of the Habeas Corpus Act.

There is a paradox in the career and fame of Shaftesbury, and Burnet reminds us of it when he says that he 'had a wonderful faculty at opposing, and running things down; but had not the like force in building up'. Shaftesbury's political career was dedicated to opposition. The 'Country' party which became known as the Whigs and which he organized from the Green Ribbon Club in London, set up in 1675, was a strange alliance of merchants, dissenters, yeomen, city ruffians, discontented gentry and a few grandees, and its object was the negative one of preventing the Duke of York from succeeding to the throne. Its methods — rabble-raising, pope-burning processions and the like — were not notably constructive. So Shaftesbury's policy failed, and he died in exile; his friends died after the Rye House Plot; James, whom they had tried to exclude, came comfortably to the throne and was soon able to celebrate his success by beheading Monmouth, Shaftesbury's protégé. But this was not the end of the story. Rather it was the beginning, and the future belonged to Shaftesbury. For his principles triumphed in 1688. Three years of Catholic absolutism were enough to convert English opinion to them, and James was expelled for good. The way was open for constitutional government, for effective toleration, for the expansion of trade, above all for the triumph of the men of property. Moreover, in this process the Whig party, more respectable than in the days of Titus Oates and the 'brisk boys' but recognizably the lineal descendant of Shaftesbury's following, played a central and a constructive part — not least in 1714 when the great question of '79 and '88 was asked once more. Few statesmen in our history have been vindicated so swiftly and so fully.

D. Ogg, *England in the Reign of Charles II*, 2 vols., 1956 ed.

J.R. Jones, *The First Whigs*, 1961.

K.H.D. Haley, *The First Earl of Shaftesbury*, 1968.

K.H.D. Haley, 'The False Achitophel', in *History Today*, January 1967.

JOHN MAITLAND, 2nd EARL and 1st DUKE OF LAUDER-DALE (1616–82), member of the Cabal and ruler of Scotland for most of Charles II's reign, was a great nephew of Maitland of Lethington, the Scottish politician of Elizabethan days. A big, heavy, red-haired man, with a tongue too big for his mouth, which, as Burnet put it, 'made him bedew all he talked to'; broad Scots in pronunciation, rough and often passionate in manner; he had nevertheless an able mind, extraordinary memory and shrewd judgment, and was profoundly learned, in Hebrew as well as in the classical languages. His record in Charles II's reign indicates that he had few scruples and a cold heart. Pepys, supping at Lauderdale's house one night, was taken aback to hear him say 'that he had rather hear a cat mew than the best music in the world'. Brought up a Presbyterian, and equipped with a legal training, Lauderdale was a prominent Covenanter in the 1640s, a Commissioner in England for the Solemn League and Covenant (1643–6) and one of the Scottish members of the Commission of Both Kingdoms, the 'war cabinet' set up in 1644. As one of the Scottish representatives in England, he shared the responsibility for handing Charles over to Parliament in 1647.

Yet like all Scots at this time, Lauderdale had to face the dilemma created by the political intervention of the English Army and the collapse of Scottish hopes of imposing Presbyterianism upon their southern neighbours. Like many Scots, he solved it by returning to the support of the Stuarts. As events were to show, Lauderdale's return was complete and without reservations. He was one of the Commissioners who concluded with Charles I the Engagement (December 1647) which precipitated the Second Civil War. He backed the agreement with Charles II, helped to crown him at Scone in 1650, and was captured at Worcester in 1651. For the next nine years he was a prisoner in England, and when he was set free at the Restoration he made haste to demonstrate an extreme royalism.

John Maitland, 2nd Earl and 1st Duke of Lauderdale c.1664
(Artist: Samuel Cooper)

As Clarendon, the recipient of some of this obsequiousness, observed, 'He was very polite in all his discourses, called himself and
his nation a thousand traitors, and Rebells' and 'seemed not equally

delighted with any argument, as when he scornfully spake of the Covenant, upon which he brake a hundred jests'. Charles II made him Secretary of State for Scotland in 1660, and from about 1663 he was the dominant figure in the government of Scotland, becoming Lord High Commissioner in 1669. He has been called 'the crudest but most dependable tool in the Cabal' *, and Charles three times ignored an address from the Commons asking for his removal. His direct influence upon English affairs was slight, although he seems to have taken care to keep in close touch with the King, who for his part found him an amusing oddity and something of a butt in council. Lauderdale's doctrinal beliefs remained in some ways Presbyterian: his conduct, notably his deep thinking, won him a reputation as a debauchee.

The years between the Restoration and the Revolution were some of the darkest in Scottish history, the time of savage persecution of Presbyterians, and of the merciless prosecutions by the formidable Lord Advocate, 'the Bluidy' Sir George Mackenzie. Much of the responsibility for these things rested upon Lauderdale, the loyal executive of Stuart policy, whose dexterity as a manager stifled opposition in the Scottish Parliament. He had, indeed, no great enthusiasm for episcopacy himself, and for a few years after the Pentland Rising (1666) he pursued not so much a policy of moderation as a tactic of realism, attempting to win Covenanting support by a Letter of Indulgence in 1669. This was unsuccessful, and in the early 1670s he went back to persecution, with such steps as the Letters of Intercommuning (1675) which boycotted individuals by government order, and the planting of the Highland Host (1678) upon the peasantry of the south-west. The results were seen in the events of 1679 — the murder of Archbishop Sharp, and the Covenanting rebellion which Monmouth defeated at Bothwell Brig; and when Lauderdale resigned office through ill health in 1680 his policy could hardly be said to have succeeded in its aims. Nor were its wider implications and results beneficial to the Stuarts. It aroused hostility in England because the opposition in the Commons suspected that it provided a foretaste of Stuart policy in this country, and it did much to ensure the success of the appeal of William of Orange to lowland Scotland in 1689.

* D. Ogg, *England in the Reign of Charles II*, 1956 ed., Vol. I, p. 329.

D. Ogg, *England in the Reign of Charles II*, 1956 ed., Vol. II, pp. 400–20.

July Buckroyd, *Church and State in Scotland, 1660–1681*, 1980.

SIR WILLIAM TEMPLE (1628–99), diplomatist, born at Blackfriars, was educated at Bishop's Stortford School and Emmanuel College, Cambridge. His diplomatic career began in 1665 with missions to Munster and Brussels, and in 1667–8 he negotiated the Triple Alliance with Holland and Sweden. Appointed Ambassador to the Hague in 1668, Temple was in Charles II's reign the chief English protagonist of friendship with the Dutch. So during the Third Dutch War of 1672–4 he withdrew from political life, but in 1674 he was recalled to negotiate the Treaty of Westminster. Three years later came his most significant diplomatic achievement, the marriage of the Princess Mary to William III of Orange. In 1679 Temple was the principal author of a scheme to reorganize and make more efficient the Privy Council, which Charles for a short time adopted. But it broke down in face of the partisan passions of the Popish Plot period. At the Revolution, Temple remained loyal to James until William's triumph was clear; he declined office under the new regime, although his son became Secretary for War, and he spent the rest of his days in retirement.

Cautious and honourable, Temple enjoyed eminence rather than influence in the politics of his day. Moreover, he was comfortably off, and he preferred the pleasures and safety of private life. His wife, Dorothy Osborne, was a woman of ability as well as of beauty and a natural letter-writer of great charm; it took him seven years to win her, for her father was a Royalist commander and his a Parliamentarian M.P., and by the time of their marriage (1655) her beauty had been ruined by smallpox. Temple spent much time in literary pursuits and Jonathan Swift was for several years his amanuensis. He had a solid and direct prose style, and his writings on international affairs have commanded respect in the twentieth century, most notably his *Observations upon the United Provinces of the Netherlands* (1673). Ironically, he is best known for his essay on *Ancient and Modern Learning*, which accepted the *Letters of Phalaris* as genuine and laid him open to the massive attack of Bentley. He was also a horticulturist and especially a fruit-grower of distinction, both at his earlier estate of Sheen and at Moor Park, near Farnham, which he laid out in the Dutch style.

T.B. Macaulay, 'Sir William Temple' (1838) in *Critical and Historical Essays.*

SIR THOMAS OSBORNE, 1st EARL OF DANBY (1632–1712), statesman, was a Yorkshireman from Kiveton, whose father had been Vice-President of the Council of the North under Wentworth and a Royalist in the Civil War. He succeeded to the baronetcy and estates in 1647. His neighbour Buckingham was his patron in his early career. In 1665 he became M.P. for York, in 1668 joint Treasurer and in 1671 sole Treasurer of the Navy, and in 1673 Lord Treasurer. Created Earl of Danby in 1674, he was evidently chief Minister by 1675. This rapid rise resulted in part from a plausible manner, not unwelcome to the King in the days of Buckingham and Shaftesbury. Behind this, and far more important at a time of chronic monetary difficulty for the Crown, lay astute financial skill and business competence. After paying off the Navy's debts and reorganizing its accounting, Danby as Lord Treasurer set about a policy of retrenchment. He reduced the rate of interest on government loans, secured stricter control over the customs farmers and more favourable terms from the excise farmers, and increased the yield of the hereditary revenues. This policy was highly acceptable to Charles II, for, besides its material returns, which were boosted by an improvement in trade in the mid-1670s, it pointed towards the financial independence of the Crown.

Danby used the whole patronage of the Crown — honours, offices, promotions, contracts — to build up a Court party with a numerical majority, especially in the Commons. Yet his policy was not merely financial, nor were its foundations solely material. He wanted a strong monarchy based upon traditional Cavalier loyalty and uncompromising Anglicanism, and this meant firm enforcement of the penal laws against Dissenters and Catholics. Abroad he was anti-French, reversing the policy hatched at Dover in 1670. Thus the Third Dutch War came to an end in 1674, and in 1677 Danby arranged the master-stroke of his term of office, the marriage of William and Mary. Yet the very success of this policy created enemies on every hand, ranging from Louis XIV to the Country party in Parliament, men who saw a rising threat of royal absolutism. Proud, avaricious and smooth, Danby never enjoyed popularity or widespread trust. Moreover, like every minister for almost a century to come, he was at the mercy of his Sovereign. Despite his own anti-French views, he had taken part in the King's secret negotiations to secure a subsidy from Louis XIV, and in their course written to Ralph Montagu, the English ambassador in Paris, letters which in certain circumstances might be highly incriminating.

In 1678 these circumstances came about, when the Popish Plot created an atmosphere of wild anti-Catholicism and political irrationality. From the start Danby blundered in his handling of the Plot; he showed scepticism about Oates and Tonge, and allowed his opponents led by Shaftesbury to seize the tremendous weapon it offered. The unholy alliance of Louis XIV and the Country party against Danby found its opportunity in the dismissal of Ralph Montagu from his embassy in 1678. In return for a French pension, Montagu produced Danby's letters before the Commons, and the minister was impeached on a variety of charges, including one to the effect that he was a papist sympathizer and had concealed evidence about the Plot. Charles, behind whom Danby made no effort to shelter, tried to save him by dissolving Parliament and by removing him from office (1679), but the newly-elected Commons proceeded to attainder. In the upshot Danby was sent to the Tower and stayed there until 1684, hated as much by James, Duke of York and by 'high' Tories like Rochester as by the Whigs.

His career seemed over. After his release he lived largely in retirement, either in Yorkshire or in his mansion at Wimbledon. Nevertheless, as the architect of the Orange marriage of 1677, with all its implications for the safeguarding of English Protestantism, Danby could not be other than an opponent of James II's Catholicizing despotism. In 1687 he was in touch with William through the latter's agent Dykveld, and in 1688 he was one of the seven signatories of the famous invitation. Nor did he fail in action in the crisis of that autumn. It was Danby, full of schemes and energy, who brought the north of England out on William's side, outwitting James's supporters and seizing the city of York. No Whig in outlook, Danby wanted Mary to be Regent, but found himself compelled to accept the joint sovereignty. His reward was great: in 1689 he was created Marquis of Carmarthen and appointed Lord

President of the Council, and he received an imposing array of powers and dignities in the three Ridings of his native county. Moreover, from 1690 to 1694 he was once more the chief minister of the Crown, responsible for the government of England during William's frequent absences on campaign in Ireland and in Flanders. Once again his old unpopularity appeared. He quarrelled with Halifax, the Whigs denounced him, he was lampooned as 'Tom the Tyrant', and he eventually ceased to be of much use to William. Once again, in 1694, he was impeached, this time on a charge of receiving a bribe of 5,000 guineas to obtain a new charter for the East India Company, and although the impeachment came to nothing it marked the end of Danby's political greatness. He hung on to the Lord Presidency until he was dismissed in 1699, and he continued to appear in the Lords from time to time. As late as 1710 he spoke in debate, on the Sacheverell affair. He was over eighty when he died in 1712.

Danby died a Duke: in 1694 'the white Marquis' of Carmarthen, as he was called from the dead-white pallor of his face, was translated into the Duke of Leeds. This enthusiasm for outward honours suggests why men disliked him. Danby was vain, pompous, too obviously fond of money; and, like Walpole, he distrusted colleagues with ability. In a sense both parts of his career ended in failure, the first in a spell in the Tower, the second in lasting neglect. Yet his importance in English history is great, and his services to his country are often overlooked. First, in the reign of Charles II he was a minister of a new kind, illustrating, in the words of David Ogg, 'the change whereby the purse-bearer displaced confessor, favourite and lawyer'.* He was a business minister, the forerunner of Walpole, whom he anticipated in reliance on a blend of corruption and common sense. Secondly, his support of the House of Orange, in 1677 and 1688, was of decisive consequence for the liberties of Englishmen. Even James II recognized this, when in 1692 he included Danby among the few men whom he was not prepared to pardon. It would be unjust to deny him the title of patriot. Thirdly, he has a significant, though somewhat ambiguous, role in the history of political party in England. He led the 'Court' party of the 1670s as an alliance between Crown and Church, thus establishing an age-

* D. Ogg, *England in the Reign of Charles II*, 1956 ed., Vol. II, p. 527.

long 'Tory' tradition. He was a successful pioneer in the craft of political management. And it might even be held that Danby did more than anyone else to stimulate the Whig party into existence, by presenting the Commons with a profound constitutional challenge in the 1670s.

A. Browning, *Life and Letters of Sir Thomas Osborne, Earl of Danby*, 3 vols., 1944-51. (Vol. I contains the *Life*).

TITUS OATES (1648–1705), perjurer, was born at Oakham, son of a parson who had become an Anabaptist. Expelled in his first year at Merchant Taylors School, he attended two Cambridge colleges (Caius and St. John's) without attaining a degree, but he managed to get himself ordained, and in 1674 he became curate to his father, who had reverted to Anglicanism and held a living at Hastings. Before long both of them were in gaol for perjury in bringing false charges against a local schoolmaster. Titus escaped from Dover prison, spent some months as a naval Chaplain, and then became Chaplain to the Protestants in the Duke of Norfolk's household at Arundel. About this time he met Israel Tonge, a London vicar, and the two of them decided that fortune and fame were to be had by discovering and if necessary inventing Catholic, and preferably Jesuit, plots. To pick up titbits of information which would add verisimilitude to his tales, Oates haunted the coffee houses where Catholics met, and the Queen's chapel in Somerset House. Then he persuaded the Catholics that he wished to be reconciled with Rome, and in 1677 was admitted to the Jesuit college, at Valladolid in Spain. After five months he was expelled, and he left Spain claiming a bogus degree as Doctor of Divinity of Salamanca. Next he managed to gain acceptance at the English Catholic seminary at St. Omer, in the Netherlands, where he survived six months before expulsion.

In 1678 he was back in England, and he and Tonge set to work. The outcome was the celebrated 'Popish Plot' which, retailed to the magistrate Edmund Berry Godfrey and then to the Council, and heightened in its effect by the mysterious murder of Godfrey, filled London with terror in 1678-9. The details, outlined originally in forty-three articles which Oates later expanded, included the murder of the King and the entire Council, a French invasion of Ireland, a

Titus Oates c.1679
(Artist: David Loggan)

general massacre of Protestants, and the installation of the Duke of York on the throne; Oates swore that the whole project had been planned by the Jesuits at a general 'consult' at the White Horse Tavern in the Strand on 24 April 1678, at which he himself had been present. The thing was a tissue of absurdities and lies: the Jesuits had never met at the White Horse, Oates himself had been in St. Omer on that date. But it was believed by nearly everybody in a London ridden with anti-Catholic prejudice, and it brought affluence and power to its inventor. This extraordinary scoundrel, short in the neck and outrageously long of chin, with his strange nasal drawl, foul language and obscene wit, unlimited in his effrontery, quickly became the man of the hour, 'the saviour of the nation'. Lodged in Whitehall, and provided with a generous salary, cheered by the mob as he went about the town dressed in full canonicals, accompanied by special guards, and ordering arrests, he dined with the King, and was fêted by Shaftesbury and the Whig aristocrats.

A series of state trials of Catholic suspects followed, with Oates as the principal witness for the prosecution, aided by a crop of lesser informers like William Bedloe. It has been estimated that in these trials some thirty-five men were judicially murdered, beginning with the execution of Coleman, the Duke of York's secretary, in December 1678. In April 1679 Oates published his *True Narrative* of the plot. In July his career of triumph was interrupted at the trial of the Queen's doctor, Wakeman, when some of his lies were exposed and Chief Justice Scroggs directed the jury to acquit. Although Oates turned public fury against Scroggs, the pace of terror slowed. But it did not stop, and through 1680 Oates continued to flourish, his perjury culminating in the evidence upon which the House of Lords condemned the innocent Catholic Viscount Stafford in December. A quarrel with Tonge at a public dinner, at which each of them claimed to have invented the plot, did not discredit Oates, though it embarrassed his supporters, and the death of Tonge prevented further trouble from that quarter.

But in 1681 the tide turned against him. Oates's political importance lay in the fact that his activities provided an ideal background for the Whig campaign to exclude the Duke of York from the succession, and when that campaign collapsed at the Oxford Parliament (March 1681) his day was done. Charles's government was slow to act against one who had been so popular; and Shaftesbury and the Whig leaders were more important targets. But in 1682 Oates's pension was reduced and then stopped, and he was forbidden the Court. In 1684 he was arrested under the medieval law of *Scandalum Magnatum* — whereby peers could bring a criminal action against commoners for words spoken against them — and cast in damages of £100,000 for calling the Duke of York a traitor. And after York had come to the throne in 1685 Oates was tried and convicted for perjury. Jeffreys imposed a sentence of calculated barbarity, including deprivation of his clerical habit, a heavy fine, five appearances in the pillory annually, a whipping from Aldgate to Newgate on 20 May 1685 and a whipping from Newgate to Tyburn on 22 May, and — if he survived the whippings — imprisonment for life. The whippings were carried out mercilessly, yet Oates survived. He spent James II's reign in Newgate, where he contrived to write an anti-Catholic pamphlet and, if Anthony à Wood is to be believed, to get one of the prison bedmakers with child.

He was released shortly after the Revolution, and given a modest pension. There was little general sympathy for him: his character was too disgraceful, and his existence reminded too many men of their own weakness ten years earlier. In 1693 he married a well-to-do widow, and in 1698 the government gave him £500 to pay his debts. He became a Baptist preacher and employed his talents upon the congregation of Wapping Chapel. But he ran true to form to the end, for in 1701 the Baptists expelled him as 'a disorderly person and a hypocrite'. He died in 1705.

John Kenyon, *The Popish Plot*, 1972.

SIR EDMUND BERRY GODFREY (1621–78), the victim of the greatest unsolved crime of the seventeenth century, was a Kentish man, educated at Westminster and Christ Church, who became a prosperous wood and coal merchant near Charing Cross and a Justice of the Peace for Westminster. He was courageous enough to stay in London throughout the Plague, tolerant enough — though a sincere Anglican — to be noted for his moderation in enforcing the penal laws upon Nonconformists and Catholics. Burnet says that he 'lived on good terms with Papists', yet without implying any sympathy for their views. Pepys in 1669 recorded a brush between Godfrey and the King, when bailiffs at his instructions arrested one of the royal physicians for a £30 debt for firing: Charles was apparently furious, and had the bailiffs whipped and Godfrey imprisoned for some days. But there is no good reason to suppose that this isolated episode had any bearing on Godfrey's mysterious fate nine years later.

In 1678 Godfrey went to France on a holiday for his health. After his return, in September, Titus Oates laid before him the 'Popish Plot' which he had 'discovered', to set fire to London, murder the King, rouse the Irish to revolt, conquer England by French arms and massacre Protestants wholesale. He swore depositions on oath before the magistrate, and also laid a copy before the Privy Council. Godfrey warned the Catholic Coleman, the Duke of York's secretary, who was a friend of his; according to Burnet, he expressed fears for his own safety. London was thrown into a panic by Oates's revelations, and the panic was heightened when, one Saturday a fortnight later, Godfrey disappeared. The following Thursday his body was discovered in a ditch by Primrose Hill, face downwards, transfixed with his own sword. His money and jewels were untouched, his pocket book was gone. Two surgeons at the inquest gave their opinion that he had been strangled, and stabbed after death, and a verdict of 'wilful murder' was returned. Godfrey's corpse was attended to the grave by a great procession of citizens vowing vengeance, and the House of Lords set up a committee to find the murderers, who, it was almost universally assumed, were Papists. In December a Catholic silversmith, Miles Prance, was arrested, and after torture he confessed to complicity in Godfrey's murder. On his evidence, corroborated by the informer William Bedloe, three men, two of them Catholics and one Protestant, were hanged.

These men were innocent. Prance's evidence was worthless, and eventually, in 1686, he pleaded guilty to perjury, admitting that he had invented his entire tale. Bedloe was a liar almost as fertile as Oates. The mystery of Godfrey's death has remained unsolved for nearly three centuries, and has attracted much speculation. This is not surprising. The limited nature of the available evidence offers a rich variety of unprovable solutions (even suicide by hanging cannot be ruled out), and the politico-religious background of the events has stimulated controversy. One thing is certain: Sir Edmund Berry Godfrey by his death provided precisely what was needed to lend credibility to Oates's fictions, and thus to launch the Popish Plot upon its course, with all its effects in the Exclusion crisis and upon the history of political party in England.

D. Ogg, *England in the Reign of Charles II*, 1956 ed., Vol. II, pp. 564–9, 579–84.
John Dickson Carr, *The Murder of Sir Edmund Godfrey*, 1936.
John Kenyon, *The Popish Plot*, 1972.

SLINGSBY BETHEL (1617–97), born at Alne in Yorkshire, became a London merchant and spent most of the years 1637–49 in business in Hamburg. A Republican, a member of Richard Cromwell's Parliament, he was one of those mercantilists who wanted a policy of aggression against the Dutch; he clashed with Cromwell over this question, and later (1668) wrote a pamphlet against him with the title of *The World's Mistake in Oliver Cromwell*. He accepted the Restoration, prospered as a leather-seller, and became a prominent member of the Whig opposition in London. In 1680 during the Popish Plot crisis he was chosen Sheriff of London and Middlesex and, though a Dissenter, deliberately took the oaths under the Corporation Act in order to serve. Dryden paints an unattractive picture of him in *Absalom and Achitophel*; he was Shimei who

> 'Did wisely from Expensive Sins refrain,
> And never broke the Sabbath, but for Gain.'

Bethel was attacked as a Republican:

> 'His business was by Writing to persuade
> That Kings were useless, and a Clog to Trade.'

When the tide turned against the Whigs (1681–2) Bethel retreated once more to Hamburg, not returning to England until after the Revolution. His importance lies not so much in his Republicanism in itself as in the example which he provides of the London merchants' distrust of the Stuarts.

SIR WILLIAM SCROGGS (1623?–83), judge, came from Deddington, in Oxfordshire. According to Dugdale, his father was a Smithfield butcher; yet Scroggs went to Oxford, first to Oriel and then to Pembroke. He fought for the King in the Civil War, was called to the bar from Gray's Inn in 1653, and was knighted at the Restoration. Handsome and able, though brutal, foul-mouthed and a notorious debauchee, Scroggs was a successful counsel. Danby promoted him to the bench, and in 1678 he became Lord Chief Justice, just in time to preside over the Popish Plot trials. At first he accepted the tales of Oates and the informers and browbeat the defendants in his customary coarse manner. But in the trial of Wakeman, the Queen's physician, in 1679, when Oates was exposed as a liar, Scroggs instructed the jury not to believe the evidence for the prosecution, and the defendant was acquitted. Whether Scroggs's charge represented genuine devotion to justice or whether, as Roger North suggests, he sensed that royal favour was not so much on the side of the Whigs as he had supposed, the decision slowed the pace of persecution. But Scroggs himself, 'the Mouth' as he was nicknamed, was grossly assailed, by lampoons, by personal assault, by charges of encouraging Popery, and finally (1681) by impeachment. This failed, but Charles removed him from office and gave him a pension of £1,500 a year. Scroggs retired to his Essex estate and died in 1683.

GEORGE SAVILE, 1st MARQUIS OF HALIFAX (1633–95), statesman and essayist, was born at Thornhill, near Wakefield, heir to one of Yorkshire's great county families. Educated at Shrewsbury and in France and Italy, he inherited his father's baronetcy in 1644. His background was Royalist, and he sat for Pontefract in the Convention of 1660. Charles II gave him a barony in 1668 and admitted him to the Privy Council in 1672. He was a man of superb mind, urbane and witty, wealthy and incorruptible, a fine orator, one of the outstanding figures of the century: in the famous words of Dryden's *Absalom and Achitophel*:

> 'Jotham of piercing wit and pregnant thought,
> Endued by nature and by learning taught
> To move assemblies.'

But he was oddly ineffective as a politician, partly because of the strain of criticism and flippancy in him that gave frequent offence,

George Savile, 1st Marquis of Halifax
(Artist: attrib. Mary Beale)

yet more because he was a patrician intellectual who liked to be, and
could usually afford to be, aloof from decision. Independent in
judgment, a mediator by instinct, Halifax was ill-suited for political
action. The results of this were unfortunate for him. Burnet, in a
severe yet sympathetic sketch, recognizes that 'the liveliness of his
imagination was always too hard for his judgment'; but he points
out that 'with relation to the public, he went backwards and

forwards, and changed sides so often, that in conclusion no side trusted him'. So we find him in the 1660s a member of the 'Country' group, a progressive younger Royalist hostile to Clarendon; then a stern critic of the Cabal, yet also an opponent of the Test Act; next quarrelling with Danby, who had him removed from the Council after Halifax had commented that Danby's refusal of a bribe from a potential tax-farmer had been like that of 'a man, who, being asked to give another the use of his wife, declined in terms of great civility'.

In 1679 he returned as a member of 'Temple's' Privy Council. The step marked a kind of *rapprochement* with the King, with whom he had a good deal in common: his *Character of King Charles the Second*, written soon after Charles's death but not published until the next century, is much the best character study of a monarch in the English language. The agreement was clinched by an earldom. Scarcely surprisingly, Halifax, though concerned for the Protestant supremacy, did not follow Shaftesbury, with his mob politics and his support of the shallow Monmouth, in the Exclusion episode. Instead he backed the scheme for imposing limitations upon James, and, fighting almost alone, used the full powers of his oratory to defeat exclusion in the Lords in 1680. As men's tempers cooled after the crisis Halifax enjoyed more political authority than at any other time, and in 1682 he became a Marquis. But the return to England in that year of the Duke of York, who was little given to gratitude and found Halifax too clever for comfort, changed the situation. Halifax, though appointed Lord Privy Seal, in effect took up his customary role of detached critic. The politics of 'high' Tories like Rochester were no more to his taste than the proceedings of Shaftesbury's Whigs had been. He opposed the execution of the Rye House 'plotter', Russell, just as he had opposed that of the Popish 'plotter', Stafford. Significantly, it was at this time that he wrote, and circulated privately (it was not published until 1688) the most revealing of all his political pieces, *The Character of a Trimmer*, with its defence of the middle path in politics. 'Why', says Halifax in his preface, 'after we have played the fool with throwing Whig and Tory at one another, as boys do snowballs, do we grow angry at a new name, which by its true signification might do as much to put us into our wits, as the other hath done to put us out of them?'

The accession of James II in 1685 soon brought Halifax's dismissal, because of his refusal to support the repeal of the Test and

Habeas Corpus Acts. He returned to his great mansion at Rufford, more a critic than an opponent of James II's Catholic despotism. In *A Letter to a Dissenter*, not printed but circulated widely through the post, he warned Nonconformists not to be taken in by the Declaration of Indulgence of 1687: 'You are therefore to be hugged now, only that you may be the better squeezed at another time'. Sheering away from the prospect of revolution, he replied non-committally to Dykveld's inquiries in 1687, and declined to sign the invitation to William in 1688. He preserved his neutrality into the crisis itself, asking James to call a free Parliament even after the invasion, and acting as his 'ambassador' to William at Hungerford. Only after James's first attempt at flight did Halifax abandon his neutrality. He then went over wholeheartedly. He accepted William's commission to persuade James to flee a second time, and did his task harshly. He became Speaker of the Lords in the Convention, opposed the regency plan, and led the Whig peers to offer the Crown to William. In February 1689 it was Halifax who formally invited William and Mary to become King and Queen. Once again he took office as Lord Privy Seal.

Yet once again he held power for a short time only. In February 1690 he was forced to resign, ostensibly as a scapegoat for the disastrous Irish campaign of the previous autumn, in fact because he could not shake off his past. The Whigs had not forgotten his 'desertion' over exclusion; Danby, now once more becoming the leading minister, had not forgiven him. He lived on for five more years. Like most of his contemporaries of equal rank, he kept in touch with the exiled Jacobite court. He took part in the Lords' debates from time to time, as for example when in 1694 he opposed the creation of the Bank of England as a privileged corporation. And he devoted some of his energies to pamphleteering in the prose style, compounded of irony and direct statement, of which he was the finest exemplar of his time. He died in 1695 and was buried in Westminster Abbey.

The Complete Works of George Savile, Marquess of Halifax, ed. with an introduction by Walter Raleigh, 1912.
H.C. Foxcroft, *A Character of the Trimmer*, 1946.

JAMES, DUKE OF MONMOUTH (1649–85), claimant to the throne, was the eldest son of Charles II. The child of Charles's Welsh mistress Lucy Walter, he was born at The Hague and spent his childhood in exile. Until her death in 1658 his mother embarrassed Charles by claiming to be his lawful wife. Monmouth grew to manhood in the Restoration court as the spoiled favourite of Charles. At nineteen he was made Captain of the King's Life Guard and at twenty-one Captain-General of the army; in 1672–3 he served against the Dutch, and in 1678 he commanded the expeditionary force sent to Ostend against the French. Good-looking, athletic, dashing and brainless, he was a considerable libertine and popular with the London mob. Popularity stimulated his vanity, as did his victory at Bothwell Brig in 1679, when he led the force sent against the covenanting rebels and showed unusual clemency to the defeated; and it was vanity that set him at this time on the course which brought him to the scaffold six years later. A Protestant, easily led, with a claim to the throne strong enough to win support yet weak enough to compel him to be a constitutional rather than a despotic ruler, Monmouth seemed the ideal tool for Shaftesbury and the Whig extremists in the succession crisis which followed the Popish Plot revelations.

Yet his own conduct in the Exclusion campaign was certainly one of the factors which turned moderate men against his cause, for he showed himself to be indiscreet, self-willed, and politically inept. Banished in the autumn of 1679, he returned without permission almost at once. Deprived of all his offices and ordered abroad again, he refused to go. Instead he went on a series of progresses (1680–82) round England, conducting himself in half-royal state, and spreading the tale of the 'Black Box' which was alleged to contain Lucy Walter's marriage lines. Charles was sufficiently moved to sign before the Privy Council a formal statement of Monmouth's illegitimacy, and in 1682 to arrest his son for a short spell. By this time the attempt to gain exclusion by Parliamentary means was over, and some of the Whigs were turning to plans of insurrection. Monmouth's role in the so-called Rye House Plot was equivocal. He was the only member of the Whig Council of Six to escape arrest, but in 1683 he was banished from Court, and after a short-lived reconciliation with his father he fled to Holland.

He came back to England for the last time in the summer of 1685,

James, Duke of Monmouth c.1683
(Artist: after William Wissing)

landing at Lyme Regis to claim the throne from his uncle James II.
Monmouth's Rebellion was doomed before it began, as much for his
own deficiencies as for the general readiness to trust James in 1685.
After he was crowned at Taunton there came the decisive moment at
Keynsham, when he turned away from an attack on Bristol. As he
retired westwards his numbers fell away. His attempt at a surprise

attack by night at Sedgemoor failed, and he fled the battlefield, leaving his wretched peasant followers to be butchered. Captured in a ditch in the New Forest, he was executed on Tower Hill after his pitiful pleas to James for mercy had failed. James had always been jealous of him, yet he can scarcely be blamed for refusing pardon — although the effect of his decision was to clear the way for a far more dangerous claimant, William of Orange. Monmouth was a shallow lightweight, absurdly unfit for the responsibilities which chance brought upon him. The cause for which he claimed to stand, Protestantism and constitutional monarchy, was that of the future, but his death was more advantageous to it than his life. David Ogg has somewhat generously observed that Monmouth 'was the only Stuart who understood the common man'. * The real tragedy in his career was that of the hundreds of common men whom he led to death or exile in 1685.

Elizabeth D'Oyley, *James Duke of Monmouth*, 1938.
Robin Clifton, *The Last Popular Rebellion: the Western Rising of 1685*, 1984.
Ivan Roots, ed., *The Monmouth Rising*, 1986.

ROBERT FERGUSON (d. 1714) 'the Plotter', came from Aberdeenshire. A minister in his early career, of pronounced Calvinist sympathies, he was expelled from a living in Kent in 1662. Later in Charles II's reign he took to Whig politics and to plotting with Shaftesbury. He defended the 'Black Box' and Lucy Walter's claims. Involved in the Rye House affair, he escaped to Holland. In 1685 he came over with Monmouth, issuing the latter's proclamation at Lyme Regis and acting as his chaplain; and again he got safely away to Holland. Inevitably he joined William in 1689 and landed with him in Torbay. Nobody seems to have taken much notice of Ferguson on this occasion, and this fact combined with his chronic weakness for plotting to turn him into the Jacobite he remained until his death in poverty in 1714. He spent some time in prison; he wrote a *History of the Revolution*, a book which maintained that the 'Glorious Revolution' was inspired by the Vatican; and spasmodically, for example at the time of Simon Fraser's 'Scotch Plot' of

* D. Ogg, *England in the Reigns of James II and William III*, 1955, p. 148.

1703, he emerged from the Jacobite underworld on to the fringe of recorded history.

J. Ferguson, *Robert Ferguson the Plotter*, 1887.

JACK KETCH (*d.* 1686), executioner, took office probably in 1663. He seems to have been, or to have become, lamentably inefficient — although he is alleged to have gone on strike for higher fees in 1682. He bungled the beheading of Lord Russell in 1683, defending himself (in a pamphlet which he apparently wrote) on the ground that Russell 'did not dispose himself for receiving the fatal stroke in such a position as was most suitable and that he moved his body'. Two years later there was an appalling scene at Monmouth's execution, when Ketch threw down his axe after three unsuccessful blows, crying 'I can't do it'. The sheriffs compelled him to go on, and it took five blows in all and the use of a knife to sever the head. This professional ineptitude, combined with the part he took in the whipping of Titus Oates, gave him such notoriety that the executioner in 'Punchinello' came to be known as Ketch. He died in November 1686.

RICHARD CAMERON (*d.* 1680), Covenanter, was a Fifeshire man and a schoolmaster. Converted to an extreme Presbyterianism, he became a powerful preacher and leader of the zealots. In 1680, when he came back to Scotland after a period of exile in Holland, he was one of those who fixed to the cross at Sanquhar the 'Declaration' disclaiming Charles II as the King who had broken the Covenant, and declaring war on him. Later that same year Cameron and a small band of followers were hunted down and destroyed by Royal troops in Ayrshire. The name 'Cameronians' came to be attached to all extremist Covenanters, who were the particular victims of Claverhouse and his dragoons in the 'killing time' of the 1680s.

STEPHEN COLLEGE (1635?–81), the 'Protestant joiner', was a London craftsman who became an ally and instrument of the Whigs in their campaign for 'Exclusion'. A popular speaker and an anti-Popish pamphleteer, College is said to have invented 'the Protestant flail', the handy weapon with which good citizens could defend themselves against Catholic assassins. When Parliament met at Oxford in 1681 College made some rash remarks in taverns there and went about carrying pistols. In the reaction which followed the dissolution he was arrested and charged with seditious words and actions. The Old Bailey jury, empanelled by Whig sheriffs, threw out the charge, whereupon he was sent for re-trial at Oxford, this time accused of having prepared arms to wage war against the King. Some of the informers who had given false evidence in the Popish Plot trials were now employed against College, and the presence of Titus Oates as a witness on his behalf was scarcely advantageous now. College was found guilty and executed, the first of a series of Whig victims.

ARTHUR CAPEL, 1st EARL OF ESSEX (1631–83), was the son of Lord Capel who was executed in 1649 after the fall of Colchester, and was created Earl of Essex in 1661. From 1672–7 he served as Lord-Lieutenant of Ireland. Notably honest himself, he could do little to check the corruption of Irish government against the opposition of the tax-farmer Lord Ranelagh, backed by the Duchess of Portsmouth and courtiers. Yet by a blend of firmness and toleration he did something to reconcile even Papists and Presbyterians, and he was one of the least unsuccessful English Viceroys of the century. Returning to England, he went into opposition to Danby and the Court, although he served for some months in 1679 as a Commissioner of the Treasury. At first a moderate, allied with Halifax rather than with Shaftesbury, he became a champion of Exclusion, speaking strongly against the Catholic peers. Evelyn, who went to stay with him about this time (1680), described him as 'a sober, wise, judicious and pondering person, not illiterate beyond the rate of most noble-men in this age'. He was scarcely an obvious revolutionary, yet he was a suitably eminent victim for reaction, and in 1683 after the exposure of the Rye House Plot he was arrested. There is no evidence to connect him with the conspiracy, although he undoubtedly had spoken indiscreetly. Imprisoned in the Tower, he asked for a razor and cut his throat.

WILLIAM, LORD RUSSELL (1639–83), Whig martyr, son of that fifth Earl of Bedford who changed sides twice in the Civil Wars sat in Charles II's Parliaments for Tavistock and for Bedfordshire.

He was one of the pro-Protestant and anti-French M.Ps. who helped to form the 'Country Party', attacking first Buckingham and then Danby. After the Popish Plot revelations had begun, it was Russell who moved in the Commons for the withdrawal of the Duke of York from the King's presence and councils, and before long he was one of the leading supporters of Exclusion. After the Oxford Parliament of 1681, the collapse of the Whig plans for a legal change in the succession, and the death of Shaftesbury, Russell became one of the so-called 'Council of Six'. His eminence in Whig counsels made him an obvious target for royal revenge, and the obscure association of the Council of Six with the shady group who hatched what came to be known as the Rye House Plot gave the King his opportunity. In the summer of 1683 Russell and the other Whig chiefs were arrested. Charged with treason, he was condemned on hearsay evidence and beheaded in Lincoln's Inn Fields. Charles, characteristically, showed no mercy when he could afford not to do so, saying 'If I do not take his life, he will soon have mine'. High-minded, courteous, ill-advised, naive, Russell may have been guilty of treason and was certainly guilty of misprision of treason. In his death he became the proto-martyr of the Whig cause, not least because he firmly refused at his trial to abandon the belief that there are times when it is right to resist a government by force.

ALGERNON SIDNEY (1622–83), great-nephew of Sir Philip Sidney, fought for Parliament in the Civil War and was wounded at Marston Moor. He declined to take part in the trial of Charles I, and withdrew from politics after Cromwell expelled the Rump. In 1659 he returned to the Council of State. A sincere Republican, he refused to accept the Restoration, and remained in exile until 1677, engaging in a good deal of intrigue with Louis XIV and others against Charles II. After his return he was still viewed with some suspicion; his influence among opponents of the monarchy was considerable, and Louis XIV thought it worth while to include him among his pensioners. After the dissolution of the Oxford Parliament and the collapse of constitutional opposition (1681) a number of the leading Whigs turned to conspiracy against Charles II and in 1683 formed the Council of Six, of which Sidney was a member. He was among those arrested that summer in connection with the Rye House affair, and was tried before Jeffreys in November on a charge of high treason. Despite his able conduct of his own defence he was found guilty and beheaded on Tower Hill. Parts of his *Discourses Concerning Government* (published in 1696) which defended the right of rebellion were found in manuscript in his rooms and put in evidence against him. It remains uncertain whether Sidney was guilty either of the Rye House Plot or of the more general conspiracy to stage a widespread revolt of which that was a part. What is certain is that he became the most celebrated of Whig martyrs, with a reputation for a lofty and incorruptible Republicanism. The historian who a century later discovered in the French documents that Algernon Sidney had taken bribes from Louis XIV said 'I felt very near the same shock as if I had seen a son turn his back in the day of battle'.

FATHER JOHN HUDDLESTON (1608–98), was a Catholic priest, born near Preston and trained at Douai, who helped to shelter Charles II at Moseley Hall, in Staffordshire, after the battle of Worcester. He became a Benedictine, and received privileged treatment during Charles' reign, serving as Chaplain to Catherine of Braganza and being specifically exempted from the anti-Catholic measures of the Popish Plot period. When the King had his fatal stroke in 1685, the Duke of York sent for a priest; and, in Sir George Clark's words, 'old Father Huddleston, who had risked his life long before to help his King on the escape from Worcester, came quietly in by the backstairs and gave him the *viaticum* for a longer journey'*. He was, as the French Ambassador Barillon wrote, 'a man of no great acquirements', yet not so 'illiterate' as Macaulay says. In the next reign he preached in Bath Abbey when James was touching for the 'King's evil'.

David Lunn, 'Father John Huddleston and Charles II' *History Today*, April 1975.

JAMES II (1633–1701), second son and third child of Charles I and Henrietta Maria, was born at St. James's Palace and was given the title of Duke of York. His childhood was clouded, and his political opinions fixed for life, by the Civil Wars. Nearly captured

* *The Later Stuarts*, 1940 ed., p. 110.

James II with Anne Hyde, his first wife
(Artist: Sir Peter Lely)

at Edgehill, he was taken prisoner when Oxford fell in 1646, but in 1648 he escaped to Holland. Notably loyal to his brother Charles in the years of exile, he was nevertheless much influenced by Henrietta who was far less of a realist than her eldest son. From 1652 to 1655 James served in the French army under Turenne and earned a reputation as a brave cavalry commander. When the exiles were driven out of France by Mazarin's agreement with Cromwell, he took service with Spain, and in 1658 commanded the right wing against the New Model at the Battle of the Dunes.

He returned to England at the Restoration, and in several ways was a prominent figure throughout his brother's reign. Having got Clarendon's daughter, Anne Hyde, with child, he married her (1660) at Charles's orders. His mistresses were numerous, if fewer than those of Charles; they were also uglier, and Charles, whose taste was more discriminating, once said he believed his brother had his mistresses given him by his priests for penance. Until 1673 he was Lord High Admiral (an office to which he had been first appointed at the age of four-and-a-half). He had a genuine love of the sea and an aptitude for naval command, as he showed during the Dutch Wars, in the English victory off Lowestoft in 1665 (where he had Sir William Penn as his adviser) and in the drawn battle of Southwold Bay in 1672, and he cannot be blamed for the financial stringency which led to the Dutch raid up the Medway in 1667. His main contribution to the Navy lay in his readiness to support reforms like those of Pepys, and he improved the system whereby officers were trained as well as the organization of discipline.

Sometime in the 1660s James was converted to Roman Catholicism; his admission to the Roman communion seems to have become known after about 1668, and in the last fifteen years of the reign he represented the threat of Popery. What made his position peculiarly significant was the infertility of Queen Catherine. James was the heir to the kingdom. Moreover, although Anne Hyde's two surviving children, Mary and Anne, were brought up as Protestants, James's second wife, Mary of Modena, the girl of fifteen whom he married in 1672, was a Catholic. Conversion made James more moral, in quantitative terms; he was content with a single mistress thereafter. It also made him even more reactionary in outlook. All he had learned from the Civil Wars was that it was disastrous to yield to opposition, and basically he was in political outlook an extreme Royalist of 1642. As F. C. Turner has said, 'in none of his letters and in none of his reported words can there by found a hint of a liberal aim', and this attitude was fortified by conversion in the era when the champion alike of despotism and of Catholicism was his cousin Louis XIV. In the 'Grand Design' which emerged in the Treaty of Dover of 1670 it was James who wanted to use force to compel the nation to Rome.

His influence upon his far more intelligent brother was surprisingly great, although we must be careful not to exaggerate his power. Charles treated James with an odd mixture of contempt and respect: contempt for his stupidity ('la sotise de mon frere'), his lack of humour, his tiresome ardour for his faith, respect for his loyalty, his courage, above all for his readiness to work while the King idled. The Test Act of 1673 meant that James resigned the offices of state which he held, but not that his influence upon policy disappeared. This influence was probably greater in foreign policy than in domestic affairs; James's acceptance of the marriage of his elder daughter Mary to William of Orange in 1677 and the part he played in the Anglo-Dutch agreement against France in 1678 antagonized Louis XIV. When the Exclusion Crisis of 1678–81 developed, Charles fought tenaciously and subtly for his brother's right to succeed, yet he welcomed his exile first to Brussels and then to Scotland. With the reaction of the last four years of the reign (1681–5) English opinion, apart from that of the discredited Whigs, swung round violently in James's favour, and he was ruler of Scotland and the dominant figure in England. It was characteristic of his vindictiveness that he employed the medieval procedure of *Scandalum Magnatum* to secure damages against those who had spoken freely against him in the years of 'Exclusion'.

In 1685 he succeeded to the throne in a glow of popularity, with the Whigs broken, the Tory Anglicans vowing non-resistance, London tamed and the countryside enthusiastic. Monmouth's unsuccessful rising strengthened his position, increasing national loyalty and providing cogent reasons for a larger army. Within three years he had thrown away all these advantages and by the end of 1688 he was in exile in France. The reasons for this extraordinary downfall are to be found almost entirely in his own character. The Glorious Revolution would never have occurred or succeeded had James not displayed an incredible degree of folly, blindness and mismanagement. He had always been obstinate, a bad judge of men, incapable of appreciating other men's sincerely-held beliefs. Converted to a faith that most Englishmen thought wicked, he had learned nothing from his unpopularity at the time of Exclusion except the false lesson that English resistance would yield. Now, at his accession, there were signs of mental decline, of a form of paranoia which increasingly led him to ignore the general effects of his policies, and to regard criticism, or even moderation, as disloyalty. His first aim was to improve the lot of his fellow Catholics. This in itself, in the light of the last century of English history and of Louis XIV's persecution of the Huguenots by the Revocation of the Edict of Nantes at this very time, was scarcely prudent. What made it disastrous was the evidence which James seemed to provide that this first aim was merely a preliminary to the reconversion of England to

Romanism. In the process he appeared to threaten the entire constitution of the country.

Parliament, which met in 1685 both before and after Monmouth's rising, was extravagantly loyal and liberal with supply. But the Commons presented an address against the illegal employment of Catholic officers in the army, and the Lords made plain the weight of opinion against any measures which seemed likely to threaten Protestantism. James truculently prorogued Parliament: it was not dissolved until 1687, but it never met again in James's reign. He built up a standing army of some 16,000 men on Hounslow Heath to overawe London, and ignored the protests against Catholic officers. The decision of the court in the collusive action of *Godden v. Hales* (1686) legalized the use of the dispensing power to give Catholics military and civil office — and demonstrated the royal control of the Bench, aided by dismissals of judges. Ministers critical of his policy were also relieved of their posts, notably Halifax who ceased to be Lord President of the Council after he had shown himself unwilling to support the repeal of the Test Act and Habeas Corpus. He was replaced by the able and pliable Sunderland who may be regarded as the King's principal minister, even though much of his advice consisted of waiting to hear what James intended to do and then approving of it. The brutal Jeffreys became Lord Chancellor; the Jesuit Father Petre was in the inmost ring of the King's advisers; the Navy was put under the command of a Catholic. The evidences of Romanism began to spread. Catholic chapels, schools and friaries appeared in London. There was a handful of conversions among men in high place. Recusancy fines ceased to be collected. The King opposed anti-Catholic preaching — and also did his best to limit the help given to French Huguenot refugees. In 1686 he began a direct attack on the Church of England itself by instituting a body of Ecclesiastical Commissioners, headed by Jeffreys, to bring it to heel. He extended his attack to the universities, the seedground of Anglicanism, and in 1687 turned Magdalen College, Oxford, into a Catholic seminary when the Fellows refused to accept his Catholic nominee as their President. In the same year he issued his first Declaration of Indulgence as an attempt to win the support of Protestant Nonconformists, while he also began a re-modelling of local government in order to secure the election at a later date of a Parliament which would do his will. Town corporations were made less Anglican. The lists of Lords-Lieutenant and J.P.s were revised, and many were dismissed. Then James through the Lords-Lieutenant put to the J.P.s — the leading representatives of the class from which M.P.s came — three questions which in effect asked their approval of a policy of repealing the tests and the penal laws against recusants. The answers were so hostile that James abandoned for the moment any plan of recalling Parliament.

In his foreign policy James pursued a line which, despite a creditable element of independence, was eventually fatal to him. He was on good terms with William of Orange at the time of Monmouth's rising, but their relations deteriorated, partly over the question of the English regiments in the service of the States-General, partly over William's refusal to lend his support to the programme of a repeal of the tests. Towards Louis XIV, James was non-committal although he asked for cash at the start of his reign, and he paid surprisingly little heed to the advice and information which came to him from France, even in the critical summer of 1688.

The series of events leading to James's fall began with the second Declaration of Indulgence (May 1688). To put on trial for seditious libel the Seven Bishops who petitioned against its reading was perhaps the most stupid of all the King's actions, for it brought the full weight of the Church of England against him, and provided an issue round which public resistance could swiftly crystallize; the cheers which greeted their acquittal (June) heralded the failure of James's entire regime. The birth earlier in the same month of a Prince of Wales stimulated into action the growing conspiracy against James, and in July the famous invitation, signed by seven leading Englishmen, reached William of Orange. Yet not until September was James sufficiently convinced of his peril to make concessions, such as the abolition of the Ecclesiastical Commission and the restoration of the ejected Fellows of Magdalen, and then they were too late, too obviously inspired by fear, and indeed too limited, to recover the loyalty he had lost. And he rejected French help until the help was no longer available; Louis had insufficient ships at Brest to stop William in the Channel, and in September he committed his land forces to an attack in the Rhineland.

William landed in Torbay on 15 November. * The events which

---

* New style; 5th old style, and so the anniversary of the Gunpowder Plot.

followed found James a man who had lost his nerve, frequently changing his mind, broken by the desertions of his peers and generals and of his daughter Anne. He joined his army at Salisbury on 29 November, and set out back to London on 4 December; opened negotiations with William, and then decided to send his Queen and the infant prince to France and to flee his country. His failure to do even this successfully — for he was captured by Kentish fishermen as his ship was waiting for the tide off the Isle of Sheppey — was ironically characteristic of James at this stage. His second and successful departure was by compulsive courtesy of William, whose Dutch guards even guarded James for a night in his own palace. With the Duke of Berwick and a handful of servants he landed at Ambleteuse at Christmastide 1688.

James II lived on until 1701, vigorous in physical energy, senile in mind. His one considerable effort to regain his throne failed at the battle of the Boyne in Ireland (1690), whence he bolted back to France in undignified haste. Apathetic yet oddly contented, never ceasing to believe that the people of England were ready to receive him back, detached from his own troubles, the symbol of Jacobitism contributed in the last ten years of his life nothing to his cause save his mere existence. His days were spent in hunting and, increasingly, in devotional exercises. He died at St. Germain in 1701, charging his thirteen-year-old son James Edward to die rather than abandon his Roman faith. A pathetic rather than a tragic figure, James II by his follies had created the problem of Jacobitism and done no service to his fellow Catholics; and by this final legacy to the Old Pretender he ensured that Jacobitism would remain a lost cause.

F. C. Turner, *James II*, 1948.
J. P. Kenyon, *The Stuarts*, 1958, pp. 158–81.
John Miller, *James II: A Study in Kingship*, 1978.

MARY BEATRICE OF MODENA (1658–1718), second wife of James II, was the daughter of Duke Alfonso IV of Modena. She had been brought up in a convent and wanted to become a nun; at the time (1673) of the marriage, which was the work of French diplomacy, she was 'but fifteen years old, and so innocently bred that till then she had never heard of such a place as England, nor of

such a person as the Duke of York'. The marriage of the heir to the
throne to a Catholic in the year of the Test Act could not be popular,
and it contributed fuel to the explosion of the Popish Plot five years
later. Mary Beatrice acquired a reputation for haughtiness, scarcely
surprising in a girl of her background suddenly translated to a
strange land full of heretics. Gracious in manners apart from the
occasional outbursts of a furious temper, she was quick-witted
rather than intelligent. Her piety was deep and genuine, and it is
clear that the influence she gradually acquired over James strengthened rather than restrained his Catholicizing zeal. She was apt to
make scenes about his continuing attachment to Catherine Sedley
and other mistresses, yet she stood firmly and loyally by him, both in
the days of his unpopularity during the Exclusion Crisis and in the
shadows from 1688 onwards. The birth of her son James Edward in
1688, after the deaths of her five previous children, was received
with widespread scepticism which found expression in the 'warming
pan' legend; there can be no doubt whatever that the child was
genuine. At the Revolution Mary Beatrice seems to have been the
principal influence in persuading James to flee his country, and she
and the baby prince preceded him to France. In her long exile in
France she remained proud, dignified and increasingly devout, a far
more spirited figure than the apathetic James, whom she outlived by
seventeen years.

Carola Oman, *Mary of Modena*, 1963.

LOUIS DURAS, 2nd EARL OF FEVERSHAM (1640?–1719),
Commander of James II's army at Sedgemoor, was French-born, a
nephew of Turenne, and was naturalized as an Englishman in 1665.
He owed much to the patronage of James, Duke of York, receiving
military promotion and various posts at Court, including that of
Lord Chamberlain to the Queen, in the reign of Charles II. He
became Earl of Feversham in 1677, succeeding his father-in-law.
Appointed to command the army sent by James II against Monmouth's rebellion in 1685, he was in bed when the rebels un-
expectedly attacked at Sedgemoor, but his conduct of the battle was
by no means as negligible as Macaulay implies. His victory over ill-
armed peasants brought him the Garter, and also the tiny estate of

Alice Lisle. In 1688 he commanded the inglorious army of James at
Salisbury, and was later sent by the peers to bring the King back to
London after the latter's unhappy first attempt at flight. James
dispatched him with a message to William, who promptly arrested
him. He remained in England after the Revolution, protected to
some extent by the Queen-Dowager Catherine of Braganza, and was
one of the peers who voted for a regency. He seems to have been
something of a dandy, more successful as a courtier than as a general.
Burnet, kindly but not unprejudiced here, described him as an
'honest, brave and good-natured man, but weak to a degree not easy
to be conceived'.

GEORGE JEFFREYS, 1st BARON JEFFREYS OF WEM
(1648–89), the most brutal of James II's agents, was born at Acton,
near Wrexham, member of a gentry family of some distinction.
Educated at Shrewsbury, St. Paul's Westminster (under Busby),
Trinity College, Cambridge, and the Inner Temple, he was called to
the bar in 1668. He had a strong voice, great assurance, a clear mind
and a ready wit, a flair for savage cross-examination, a taste for low
company, and considerable capacity for dissipation; he employed
all these qualities in his swift rise to high legal rank, yet he owed
most to his introduction, by Chiffinch and the back stairs, to James,
Duke of York, who made him his Solicitor-General in 1677. Next
year he was appointed Recorder of the City of London. Both in
that capacity, as Judge at the Old Bailey, and as Counsel for the
prosecution before the King's Bench, he enjoyed the Popish Plot
trials, showing himself mocking and vindictive. As Roger North put
it, 'he loved to insult, and was bold without check; but that only
when his place was uppermost'. Among those he prosecuted were
Archbishop Plunket and the London joiner, College, and also
Russell after the Rye House Plot.
      In 1683 Charles II appointed Jeffreys as Lord Chief Justice. His
faults — his savage and coarse language, his bad temper, his bullying
and scoffing, his ruthless contempt for evidence — were patent, and
his knowledge of the law was limited. The price of so disgraceful an
appointment was paid by Algernon Sidney, condemned on the
flimsiest of evidence after the Rye House Plot; by Titus Oates, upon
whom Jeffreys gleefully imposed a sentence which began with a

George Jeffreys, 1st Baron Jeffreys of Wem c.1678–80
(Artist: attrib to William Claret)

whipping from Aldgate to Newgate followed after two days by another from Newgate to Tyburn, and was completed by life imprisonment with periodic exhibition in the pillory; by Richard Baxter, whose trial Jeffreys began by denouncing him as 'an old rogue, a schismatical knave, a hypocritical villain' and by singing through his nose in imitation of Puritan prayers; and by the victims of the 'Bloody Assizes', which Jeffreys held in 1685 in the west of England after Monmouth's rebellion. He began at Winchester by sentencing Lady Alice Lisle, who was over seventy, to death by burning for harbouring rebels, after some outrageous directions both on fact and on law to the jury. It is uncertain how many rebels were put to death by the 'Bloody Assizes'; perhaps 300, perhaps 120. Jeffreys made a lot of money out of selling pardons, and also out of the traffic in those sentenced to transportation. What is certain is the spirit of cruel jocularity with which he conducted the business, and the vile name he left behind him.

James II, characteristically, rewarded him. Jeffreys became Lord Chancellor and in that role defended the King's use of the dispensing power and undertook the congenial work of purging municipal charters. He was the dominant figure on the notorious Ecclesiastical Commission: not only was he its chairman, it could not meet at all without him. So he presided over the suspension of Compton and the invasion of the privileges of the universities. Nevertheless, Jeffreys was shrewd enough to sense the need for concession before the end of 1687 — and to obtain a pardon in full and legal form for himself the month before William landed in 1688. When the Royal cause collapsed Jeffreys handed over the Great Seal to James and took refuge in Wapping disguised as a seaman, but he was recognized in the *Red Cow* in Anchor and Hope Alley by a scrivener whom he had once bullied in court, and removed to the Tower, where he died in 1689. In some sense of course Jeffreys was the mirror of his age: there were other brutal prosecutors and judges in the late seventeenth century, and the rules of courts were looser and their conventions harsher than they later became. In civil matters, it must be said, he delivered quotable judgments which have found their way into the books. Moreover, he suffered greatly from the stone, and he drank a great deal of brandy. Yet when every sort of allowance is made he stands out in his own age as a man who committed many inexcusable actions and said many foul and merciless words, treating people and principles alike with contempt; and on a longer view as the most scandalous criminal judge who has ever disgraced the English Bench.

H. Montgomery Hyde, *Judge Jeffreys*, 1940.
E. W. Keeton, *Lord Chancellor Jeffreys and the Stuart Cause*, 1965.

COLONEL PERCY KIRKE (1646?–91), son of a courtier who was Gentleman of the Robes to Charles I and Groom of the Bedchamber to Charles II, was a professional soldier. Promoted Lieutenant-Colonel in 1680, he was sent the following year to Tangier, whose Governor he became in 1682; there the Governor's Regiment, raised for service at Tangier, had as its badge the Paschal Lamb. No doubt neither Kirke nor his men were softened by their service against the Moors. They returned home when Tangier was evacuated in 1684, and in 1685 Kirke fought against Monmouth's men at Sedgemoor with parts of his own and of another Tangerine regiment. What made this harsh, hard-bitten man and his 'Lambs' notorious was their summary execution of prisoners, notably in Taunton market-place. Yet Kirke was one of the officers of James II who refused to abandon his Protestantism, and it is possible that he was involved in the plot to kidnap James II when the army moved to Salisbury in the crisis of 1688. Certainly William III gave him promotion, and he was employed in the relief of Londonderry in 1689, where he distinguished himself by his dilatoriness in taking action from Lough Foyle until it was almost too late. In 1691 he went to Flanders with William's forces, and died at Brussels in that year.

ALICE LISLE (1614?–85), was the widow of John Lisle, the regicide and Cromwellian who was shot dead by an Irish Royalist in Switzerland in 1664. Living at Moyles Court, near Ringwood in Hampshire, she was well known for her dissenting views and her readiness to help the persecuted. In 1685 after Sedgemoor, she gave refuge to John Hickes, a minister who had fought for Monmouth. Arrested by Royal troops under Colonel Penruddock, whose father John Lisle had sentenced to death for leading a rising in 1655, she was tried before Jeffreys on a charge of harbouring a traitor. Despite her plea that she had merely thought Hickes was in trouble for illegal preaching, she was found guilty and sentenced to be burned alive, Jeffreys crying 'Had she been my own mother, I would have found her guilty'. The sentence was commuted to beheading, and Alice Lisle, aged over seventy, was executed at Winchester, the first victim of the Bloody Assizes.

ELIZABETH GAUNT (*d.* 1685), the last woman to be executed in England for a political offence, was the wife of a Whitechapel yeoman. An Anabaptist, she was according to Burnet a kindly woman who visited prisoners and did good works. In 1683 she sheltered a man named Burton who was outlawed after the Rye House Plot, and gave him money to escape to Amsterdam. Burton came back to England with Monmouth in 1685 and after Sedgemoor again found shelter with Mrs. Gaunt. But to save his own life he turned informer against her. She was convicted of high treason and burned to death at Tyburn. William Penn, who saw her die, wrote 'She died composedly and fearless, interpreting the cause of her death God's cause'.

HENRY HYDE, 2nd EARL OF CLARENDON (1638–1709) the eldest son of the great Clarendon, inherited the title in 1674. A devout Anglican and a friend of John Evelyn, he had his father's stiff and unbending disposition and somewhat narrow piety, but little of his ability; he was something of a mediocrity whom descent and a sense of duty brought to high place. In 1667 he defended his father vigorously against the charges which drove him into exile, and he was a bitter opponent of the Cabal, denouncing Buckingham's character with asperity. He was on good terms with James, Duke of York, who on his accession to the throne in 1685 made him Lord Privy Seal in place of the far more gifted and critical Halifax and later in the same year sent him to Ireland as Lord-Lieutenant. James knew, as he put it to the French ambassador, Barillon, that 'he could make Lord Clarendon obey him punctually'. Clarendon was intended as a respectable cloak for the King's plans to establish the Catholics in power in Ireland, and James and Sunderland used him outrageously, ignoring his complaints, undermining his authority and delivering real power into the hands of the Catholic Tyrconnel, who was formally appointed Commander-in-Chief in Ireland in 1686. It was a measure of Clarendon's weakness that he held on until he was recalled in 1687. He sincerely hoped to do something for the Irish Protestants; he needed the salary, for he was chronically in financial difficulty; above all, he was dedicated to royal authority. As he once wrote in the midst of the troubles of his viceroyalty, 'the wrath of the King is unsupportable and I am sure must crush me to nothing, who am next to nothing already, and must be altogether so without his support'.

To a man of such faith, at once sincere Anglican and sincere King-worshipper, the Revolution presented the desperate problem of loyalty. Nor was his situation simplified by the fact that his heir, Lord Cornbury, was the first officer of rank to desert James and lead his men over to William. Clarendon attacked James with peculiar, and understandable, bitterness when he met the peers in London after returning from Salisbury, and the next day went to join the invaders, believing apparently that William still could and would compel James to reign as a loyal Anglican. When events had killed this illusion, Clarendon accepted William as King *de facto*, but refused to swear the oath of allegiance, becoming the only significant lay non-juror. This refusal and his previous record compelled William to distrust him. He was involved in the first Jacobite conspiracies, of 1690, and spent two brief spells in the Tower. William showed a wise clemency to a man who was his wife's uncle, and who was an ineffectual rather than a dangerous figure, and Clarendon sensibly abandoned political activity for the remainder of his days.

Keith Feiling, *A History of the Tory Party, 1640–1714,* 1924.

LAURENCE HYDE, EARL OF ROCHESTER (1641–1711), second son of the great Clarendon, inherited much more of his father's ability than did his elder brother Henry. Arrogant, bad-tempered, domineering, said by Roger North to be too fond of the bottle and to 'swear like a cutler', he had obvious faults of personality which made him a tiresome colleague and minister, as even his patient niece Anne rapidly discovered; yet he was an able man of affairs and the most representative High Church Tory of his time, for thirty years the principal spokesman of one of the main elements of English political tradition. He began his political career as a diplomatist, on a mission to John Sobieski of Poland, and in 1678 he negotiated a treaty with the Dutch; but in the following year he was appointed a Commissioner of the Treasury, soon becoming First Lord. With Godolphin and Sunderland he formed what was nicknamed the 'Ministry of the Chits'. In 1681, the year in which he was created Earl of Rochester, he advised the summons of

Parliament to Oxford rather than to Westminster, and negotiated the notorious verbal treaty with Barillon which guaranteed Charles II French subsidies for the rest of his reign. He seems to have fallen a little from the King's favour in the last years of the 'Tory reaction' of 1681–5, even though he became Lord President of the Council (1684). His economic and efficient financial management was not to everyone's liking, and he quarrelled fiercely with Halifax.

His brother-in-law, James II, on his accession, made Rochester Lord Treasurer. But the Catholicizing policy of the new reign brought difficulties to one who was a sincere Anglican, and far less pliable in his nature than either Sunderland or Godolphin. His effective authority in office was limited, and although he went so far as to accept a place on the Ecclesiastical Commission in 1686, Sunderland was steadily hostile to him. James pressed him to accept conversion to Rome: Rochester yielded so far as to permit a disputation to be staged in his presence between two priests and two Anglican clergy; in his view the latter triumphed. Eventually in 1687 he was dismissed, obtaining a handsome pension of £4,000 per annum for ninety-nine years (or two lives) secured on the Post Office. When the Revolution came he joined his old enemy Halifax in pressing James to call a free Parliament. He had little enthusiasm for the new regime, and was one of the supporters of a Regency; yet he took the oaths of allegiance, more out of loyalty to his niece Mary than to her husband, who reciprocated his dislike. Rochester was loyal enough; he was no Jacobite, and he was readmitted to the Privy Council in 1692 at a time when William's sympathies were swinging away from the Whigs. But as the head of the High Church political party he opposed much that William stood for, at home and abroad, and looked forward to the accession of Anne, who was celebrated for her devotion to the Church. When the last election of William's reign brought a Tory majority, Rochester was appointed to Ireland (1700) as Lord-Lieutenant.

Anne's accession did not fulfil his hopes, and he displayed his principles in opposition. She quickly grew tired of his manner; he quickly grew jealous of the eminence of Marlborough. Rochester led the High Tories in favouring a limited, mainly naval war, in which England should not fight as 'a principal', while Anne accepted Marlborough's view of the necessity of continental campaigns. His partisan zeal for removing all Whigs from local offices struck at the national unity which the war required. So Rochester resigned in 1703. He continued to lead the opposition of the 'high-fliers'. In 1704 he demanded the impeachment of Marlborough, and in the following year he deeply wounded Anne both by supporting a plan to invite the heir-apparent, the Electress Sophia, to visit England and by proposing a motion in the Lords that the Church was in danger under the Queen's rule; and he was a leading critic of the Scottish Union. In 1707 he proposed that 20,000 men be withdrawn from the army in the Netherlands and sent to Spain. But the decline of the influence of the Marlboroughs brought a swing of the pendulum in Rochester's favour, and in 1710, less than a year before his sudden death, he came back to office as Lord President of the Council in the Tory ministry of that year. It was Rochester who in 1702-4 published through the Oxford University Press his father Clarendon's *History of the Rebellion and Civil Wars in England*, 'doing thereby', as G. M. Trevelyan has put it, 'a far greater service to High Tory principles than any he was ever likely to do by direct intervention in politics'.

Keith Feiling, *A History of the Tory Party, 1640–1714*, 1924.

ROBERT SPENCER, 2nd EARL OF SUNDERLAND (1641–1702), was a politician notorious for his pliancy even in an age when few men found it easy to be consistent in their political principles. Owing something in his early career to the backing of Charles II's mistress, Louise de Kéroualle, Duchess of Portsmouth, he first reached high office at the time of the Exclusion (favouring William of Orange, not Monmouth), and the King dismissed him in 1681. But he returned to favour and to office in 1682, and for the next six years was the chief figure in English government, and the leading proponent of a pro-French foreign policy. Somehow he persuaded James II to forget his support of Exclusion. As Lord President of the Council from 1685, manager of Crown patronage and of parliamentary business, and leader of the attack on the Church of England (for example, in the expulsion of the Fellows of Magdalen College, Oxford), Sunderland appeared to be the chief instrument of James's Catholic despotism; and in June 1688 he announced his own conversion to Rome. Yet he remained more realistic than his master, pressed for the summons of a Parliament in

1687–8, and advocated clemency for the Seven Bishops. When William's invasion came, Sunderland fell into utter panic, and demanded the total reversal of James's policy, whereupon the latter dismissed him; and in December, when William's success was evident, Sunderland fled to Rotterdam. He turned at once, with a blend of great dexterity and boot-licking hypocrisy, to making his peace with William and to rebuilding his career. Lady Sunderland returned to England to mobilize influence; he announced his re-conversion to Anglicanism, and wrote an anti-Catholic apologia, *The Letter to a Friend*; and although he was one of the few men exempted from the Bill of Indemnity and Act of Grace of 1689, by May of that year he felt it safe to return to England. Speaking of himself as having 'nothing to fear, little to hope for', regarded by others as 'the great apostate', he was wisely slow in attempting to re-enter public life. Not until 1691 did he take the oath in the Lords, nor until November of 1692 his seat. Yet earlier that year he was beginning to act as a confidential adviser to William III; and from 1693 to 1698, although he held no major office, he was 'the Minister behind the curtain' who organized ministries, managed Parliament and dispensed patronage. In 1698 he resigned the Lord Chamberlainship following an attack on him in the Commons, and henceforward until his death in 1702, soon after that of William III, Sunderland's role was that of the elder statesman.

It was a strange career. The eighteenth-century writer Oldmixon observed that 'Lord Sunderland had a vast genius, but his conscience was of a like extent'; in 1688 the Princess Anne had described him as 'the subtillest, workingest villain that is on the face of the earth'. Insolent and impetuous as a young man, Sunderland over the years grew into a *grand seigneur*, self-confident, suave and urbane, occasionally breaking his smooth cynicism with savage sarcasm; a modern historian has spoken of 'the sinister charm of his middle years'. He was a great deal more than a time-server. His strength lay in his quick grasp and detailed knowledge of foreign affairs, and — as three such different kings as Charles II, James II and William III all found — in his readiness to take responsibility and in his skill as a man of business; Sunderland, it has been suggested, was the first of the great 'undertakers', the intermediaries between Court and 'faction' who were essential to post-Revolution politics. No doubt he was fortunate, like others, in that William III was so little vindictive by nature; and that the political ferocities of the previous generation had died away. One of the greatest achievements of the Revolution of 1688-9 was that it was not followed by an orgy of revenge. Sunderland was a major beneficiary of this; yet it may perhaps be claimed that his own political attitude had done something to calm the violence of seventeenth-century English politics. For the rest, this highly intelligent man has a secure place in the artistic history of England, as a patron of literature, a collector of Italian paintings, and above all, the rebuilder (c. 1667–8) in elegant fashion of the Elizabethan mansion of Althorp, the Spencer family seat in Northamptonshire.

J.P. Kenyon, *Robert Spencer, Earl of Sunderland*, 1958.

FATHER EDWARD PETRE (1631–99), James II's Jesuit adviser, belonged to the Essex branch of a prominent Roman Catholic family. Born in London and educated at St. Omer, he entered the Society of Jesus in 1652 and was sent on mission to England about 1679. He spent a year in Newgate at the time of the Popish Plot, and was again in prison from 1681, when he was appointed Vice-Principal of the English Jesuits, until 1683. Petre was zealous for his faith and plausible in speech, a member of the aggressive party in the Church, and James II welcomed him at Court from the start of the reign, putting him in charge of his chapel and installing him in his own former lodgings in the Palace of Whitehall. He became an ally of Sunderland and a member of the informal inner council; in 1687 he was formally sworn of the Privy Council and he was active in the purging of the corporations and the expulsion of the Fellows of Magdalen. Petre appears to have been a vain and headstrong man who gave imprudent counsel. Yet it is easy to exaggerate his influence, and he was rather the tool of Sunderland than an *éminence grise*. His public admission to the Council probably did far more harm to the King's cause than any advice he gave. In his own person he illustrated the conflict between James II's policy and that of the Papacy, for he was not popular at Rome and Innocent XI firmly declined the royal suggestion that Petre be given a cardinal's hat. In the crisis of 1688 Petre was one of those who advised James to stay in England. He himself made a secret escape, going back to St. Omer, whose rector he became in 1693, and remained abroad for the rest of his life.

RICHARD TALBOT, EARL OF TYRCONNEL (1630–91), James II's Lord Deputy in Ireland, was the eighth son of an Irish baronet. A big, handsome, blustering, quarrelsome, rather inept man, 'lying Dick Talbot' had been left for dead at Drogheda in 1649 and made his escape in women's clothes. He had an equivocal career in the 1650s — he said he was willing to murder Cromwell but Clarendon believed he was in Oliver's pay, and when he was arrested in England in 1655 he got away surprisingly easily by making his guards drunk — and he was the companion of James, Duke of York, in his amours after the Restoration. Twice he was sent to the Tower for insulting the Duke of Ormonde, and he was again imprisoned on suspicion at the time of the Popish Plot. Tyrconnel was devoted both to Ireland and to his Catholic faith, and was the leader of those Irishmen who wished to destroy the existing settlement of Irish land, with its gross favouritism to the Protestant minority. The accession of James II in 1685 gave Tyrconnel his opportunity. As Commander of the Army in Ireland he disarmed the Protestants, filled the ranks illegally with Catholics, and undermined — with the King's approval — one of the advisers who urged James on to more extreme pro-Catholic steps in England. Appointed Lord-Deputy in 1687, he packed Irish law courts and town corporations with Catholics; and when James came to Ireland in 1689 Tyrconnel was to the fore in the Parliamentary attack on Protestant privileges and lands. He fought courageously when his cause was shattered at the Boyne, and returned to Ireland to continue the struggle in 1691, dying suddenly of apoplexy.

OBADIAH WALKER (1616–99), a Yorkshireman from Darfield, near Barnsley, James II's chief agent in his attempt to Romanize Oxford, was a Fellow of University College who after his ejection by the Parliamentarians in 1648 had travelled abroad and spent a good deal of time at Rome. Evelyn thought him 'a learned and most ingenious person' and advised a friend to put his two sons under his tuition: Walker later converted one of them to Catholicism. He was an influential figure in Oxford after his return there in 1665, and became a Master of his college in 1676. As early as 1678 an attempt was made to remove him as a suspected papist. In James's reign he came out openly in support of the King's schemes, obtaining a dispensation to keep his mastership, worshipping in a Roman chapel which he opened in the college, and encouraging the printing of propagandist books. According to Anthony à Wood, Walker, nicknamed 'Obadiah Ave-Maria', was very unpopular in Oxford: his chapel was fair game for those who wanted to cause a disturbance, like the gentleman-commoner of Christ Church 'who laughed and girn'd and shew'd a great deal of scorn', or the boy who hid a cat under his coat while mass was being sung which 'pulling by the tail, made her such an untunable noise that it put them to some disorder'. In 1688 he tried to flee abroad but was caught and put in the Tower until 1690. Deprived of his mastership, he died in London in 1699, having owed a good deal in his last years to the charity of one of his former pupils, Dr. John Radcliffe, whom he had unsuccessfully tried to convert to Rome.

WILLIAM SANCROFT (1617–93), Archbishop of Canterbury, was born of yeoman stock at Fressingfield, in Suffolk, and educated at Bury St. Edmunds Grammar School and Emmanuel College, Cambridge, of which he became a Fellow. Turned out of his fellowship in 1651, he wrote against Calvinism and against the Commonwealth, but remained in England until 1657. Returning from abroad at the Restoration, he was appointed a royal Chaplain in 1661 and Dean of St. Paul's in 1664. He held this benefice until he was elected to Canterbury in 1677, and gave much of his energy to the rebuilding of St. Paul's. As Archbishop he tried in vain to reconvert James, Duke of York, to Anglicanism, and when the latter came to the throne in 1685 Sancroft inevitably found himself in an equivocal position. He served, but only for a short time, on the Ecclesiastical Commission created in 1686, and in 1688 he was in name at least the leader of the Seven Bishops in their refusal to read the Declaration of Indulgence. After their acquittal he urged the King to retract his illegal steps, he declined to condemn William's Declaration, and he was one of those who at the eleventh hour advised James to call a free Parliament. But after James's flight Sancroft retired to his palace at Lambeth and withdrew from public action, maintaining that William was a usurper and that nobody who had taken an oath of allegiance to James could honestly swear loyalty to him. Thus he had no part in welcoming William to London, nor was he present when the Convention of 1689 declared the throne vacant. His inaction helped to make futile the project of a Regency of William and Mary in James's name, a policy which he was prepared to accept. He was deprived in 1690, and evicted from Lambeth by process of law in 1691, retiring to Fressingfield. By executing in the same year a deed conveying the exercise of his authority as Archbishop to the Non-juring Bishop Lloyd of Norwich, he did his best to perpetuate the schism in the Church of England, and to the day of his death in 1693 he continued to pray for James II as King of England, and declined to take communion with those who had sworn allegiance to William. Burnet, who disliked Sancroft, calling him a 'dry, cold man, reserved and peevish', thought he had played 'a very mean part in all the great transaction' of the Revolution; and it is easy, with Macaulay, to condemn his behaviour as ineffectual and even uncharitable. Certainly Sancroft was an embittered old man, and there were other Non-jurors, notably Ken, who declined to prolong schism. In defence of Sancroft it can be said that he was notable for his personal sanctity; that the Non-jurors, some 400 in all, included many of the most upright and learned Anglicans of the time; and that, whatever the political implications of their protest, they were contending for the spiritual independence of the Church.

HENRY COMPTON, (1632–1713), the strongest clerical opponent of James II, was born at the manor house of Compton Wynyates, in Warwickshire, the sixth son of the second Earl of Northampton. The family was pugnaciously Royalist: his father was killed fighting for the King at Hopton Heath (1643) and his brother William as a boy of eighteen defended Compton Wynyates against Parliamentarian attack; and he himself, after going to The Queen's College, Oxford (1649–52), and spending the years of the Commonwealth abroad, was commissioned as a cornet in the Royal Horse Guards. He retained a martial enthusiasm and attitude of mind, and James II was later to complain that he was 'more like a colonel than a Bishop'. But in 1666 he took holy orders. His promotion in the Church was rapid, no doubt in part because of his aristocratic rank, partly through his friendship with Danby. A Canon of Christ Church in 1669, he became Bishop of Oxford in 1674 and

Dean of the Chapel Royal and Bishop of London in 1675, and even aspired to Canterbury when Sheldon died in 1677. It is of greater historical significance that Compton was responsible for the spiritual education of the Princesses Mary and Anne. He confirmed them both (and married them both), and his influence over them was great and lasting. That influence was strongly anti-Catholic, for Compton was a vigorous Protestant.

Although Compton had opposed Exclusion, he was bound to combat James II's Catholicizing policy. In a speech to the Lords in 1685 he condemned the King's claim to dispense with the Test Act, and was dismissed from the Privy Council and the Chapel Royal as a result. Next year he declined to inhibit a London rector (John Sharp, later Archbishop of York) from preaching anti-Papal sermons. He was summoned before the Ecclesiastical Commission and suspended from the exercise of his episcopal functions. In 1687 he was in touch with William's agent, Dykveld, and in 1688 he played a leading role in persuading the Seven Bishops to draft their petition against the Declaration of Indulgence. No doubt he found ample consolation for his inability, through suspension, to join them by setting his signature to a more famous document shortly afterwards: he was the one ecclesiastic to sign the invitation to William of Orange. In the hour of revolution he played an appropriate role, safeguarding Anne's flight from London, carrying a sword and leading in person her escort of two hundred armed volunteers. He felt no crisis of conscience about accepting the new order, and in the debates on the oaths of allegiance — which five of the Seven Bishops refused — he said 'there was not nor could be made an oath to the present government that he would not take'. It was entirely suitable that it should be Compton who crowned William and Mary in the coronation service in April 1689.

Perhaps, inevitably, the remainder of Compton's life was something of an anti-climax, embittered by his double failure — in 1691 and in 1695 — to secure election to Canterbury. Although in the early years of William's reign he supported both the Toleration Act and the unsuccessful scheme for Comprehension, his sympathies narrowed as he aged. In Anne's reign he opposed Occasional Conformity and supported the cry of 'the Church in danger' in 1705 and even Sacheverell in 1710. He died in 1713. He was notably hospitable and charitable to religious refugees; and he was also a botanist of some distinction who made an important collection of rare plants, mostly from North America, in the gardens of Fulham Palace. A man of action rather than a scholar, Compton was scarcely typical of the bishops of his time, yet he expressed more vividly than any other churchman the direct and urgent interest of Anglicanism in the success of the Revolution of 1688.

Edward Carpenter, *The Protestant Bishop: the Life of Henry Compton*, 1956.

SIR JONATHAN TRELAWNY, third baronet (1650–1721), one of the Seven Bishops, was born at Pelynt, in Cornwall, son of a Royalist who had suffered sequestration and imprisonment in the Civil War, and was educated at Westminster and Christ Church. In 1685 he was prominent in calling out the Cornish militia against Monmouth, and later in that year became Bishop of Bristol. A Tory churchman like Compton, he opposed both James II's Declarations of Indulgence and stood trial as one of the Seven in 1688. It seems likely that the famous refrain of his fellow-Cornishmen,

> 'And shall Trelawny die?
> Then twenty thousand Cornishmen
> Will know the reason why'

echoed what their grandfathers had sung sixty years before when the first Trelawny baronet was sent to the Tower by the Commons for opposing Sir John Eliot. When the Revolution came, Trelawny was one of the two bishops to oppose the Regency plan, and one of the only two of the Seven who swore allegiance to the new sovereigns. In 1689 he was translated to Exeter. Under William and Anne he was a prominent High Churchman, emphatic in stressing his power and dignity and hostile to the latitudinarian opinions of most of his fellow-bishops. His importance was more political than ecclesiastical, for he had great electoral interests in Cornwall, claiming, for example, in 1702 to have returned eleven members for the government. In 1705 he deserted the 'High Tory' cause and lent his support to the Whig and moderate candidates pledged to support his fellow-Cornishman Godolphin, and he was rewarded in 1707 by promotion to the see of Winchester. In 1713, after Godolphin's death, his electoral weight was exerted on behalf of Harley's followers, and he was a firm champion of the Hanoverian Succession. More convivial than spiritual, eminent by birth and territorial power rather than by learning, Trelawny represented a type of patriotic Anglicanism which played a significant role in the great decisions of 1688 and 1714.

THOMAS KEN (1631–1711), most saintly of the Seven Bishops, was the son of a Berkhampstead attorney. Educated at Winchester and New College, and a Fellow of both, he held various livings before becoming Chaplain to Mary of Orange in 1679. Characteristically he reproached William for his 'unkind' treatment of his wife, and equally characteristically, after his return to England, he declined to allow his prebendal house at Winchester to be bespoken for Nell Gwynne during a royal visit to the city. He went as Chaplain on the Tangier expedition of 1683-4, and preached against the 'excessive liberty of swearing' in which the garrison indulged. In 1685 Charles II gave the see of Bath and Wells to 'the little black fellow that refused the lodging to poor Nelly'. Later the same year his diocese was the heart of Monmouth's rebellion, and Ken, whose loyalty was beyond doubt, interceded with James against the brutalities practised by Kirke's soldiery. Two years later he preached at court against Roman Catholicism, and in 1688 he delivered another sermon before the King in which he called for the unity of all Protestants against the claims of Rome. It is therefore not surprising to find this gentle yet courageous man one of the Seven Bishops of 1688. But after the flight of James, Ken voted for a regency and, although he was long in doubt, declined to take the oaths of allegiance to William and Mary. He was therefore deprived of his see in 1691.

He lived on for twenty years, much of the time at the home of Lord Weymouth at Longleat. The mildest, and perhaps the most statesmanlike, of the Non-jurors, Ken did not approve of perpetuating the schism by consecrating further non-juring bishops. Yet he would not yield to Anne's wish (1702) to reinstate him in his see. He accepted a pension of £200 per annum from her government, paid out of the secret service money. Ken's compassion and generosity were well known in his own day. He was an accomplished man, a musician and a poet, and we know him best through the morning and evening hymns which he wrote, 'Awake my soul and with the Sun' and 'Glory to Thee, my God, this night'.

H. A. L. Rice, *Thomas Ken: Bishop and Non-Juror*, 1958.

HENRY SIDNEY, EARL OF ROMNEY (1641–1704), supporter of William of Orange, came of a noble family whose loyalty to the Stuarts was notoriously limited: of his elder brothers, Philip, 3rd Earl of Leicester, was a prominent Cromwellian, and Algernon was a Republican executed after the Rye House Plot. Henry, the youngest of the family, was more celebrated in Charles II's reign for his looks than for his principles. He was outstandingly handsome, and known as 'a terror to husbands'. A courtier in the middle years of the reign and appointed Master of the Robes in 1677, he entered the Commons in 1679 and supported the Exclusion policy. Charles sent him as envoy to The Hague, where he won the regard of William of Orange, and from 1681 to 1685 he commanded the British regiments in Dutch service. For most of James II's reign he kept out of England, but he was in close touch with affairs at home, notably through the wife of his nephew Sunderland. Early in 1688 he returned and sounded opinion for William. His rakish indolence veiled a talent for intrigue, and Macaulay's comment on him at this point — 'Incapable, ignorant, and dissipated as he seemed to be, he understood, or rather felt, with whom it was necessary to be reserved, and with whom he might safely venture to be communicative' — may be peculiarly apt. Certainly Burnet, who was in a position to know, implied that Sidney was the prime organizer of the invitation to William, as well as one of its seven signatories.

He returned to Holland in time to take part in the invasion, but he played an undistinguished role in public affairs outside the Court during William's reign. He fought at the Boyne, and received Irish land grants, most of which were later resumed. During 1690–1 he was Secretary of State, with little influence on policy, and for a few months in 1692–3 he was a totally unsuccessful Lord-Lieutenant of Ireland. He was created Earl of Romney in 1694, and was Groom of the Stole during the last two years of William's reign, dying of smallpox in 1704.

CHARLES TALBOT, 12th EARL and only DUKE OF SHREWSBURY (1660–1718), most singular of all politicians of the days of William III and Anne, was born at Grafton, in Worcestershire, heir to great estates, a divided home and the Roman Catholic faith. He inherited the Earldom in 1667 when his father was killed in a duel by the Duke of Buckingham, Lady Shrewsbury's lover. Brought up by dreary and parsimonious relatives, he was sent in 1674 to study at Navarre College in Paris and at the military academy there, and after a brief taste of campaigning in the Netherlands came home in 1678, the year of the Popish Plot. Excluded from political life by the Parliamentary Test Act of that November, the young peer seems to have been deeply sensitive to the indignities and dangers to which prominent Catholics were exposed. In 1679, apparently under the influence of Dean (later Archbishop) Tillotson, he was converted to Anglicanism. There is no sign that he ever wavered from Protestantism for the rest of his days. Yet the fact that he had once been a Catholic, and the Catholicism of many of his Talbot relations, always encouraged hopes of his return to Rome — and strengthened Jacobite illusions about him.

Shrewsbury was a man of rare quality — deeply humane, individual in outlook, politically courageous in times of crisis, the least vindictive of men. With an able and cultured mind and a sincere charm of manner which rarely failed, he was, with his lands and wealth and rank, certain of an important part in the politics of his day. Yet he was cursed throughout life by an excessive sensitivity and by a lack of confidence which stemmed no doubt from the bitter uncertainties of his childhood. Nicknamed 'the King of Hearts', this attractive young man did not marry until he was forty-five. Politically, his self-distrust encouraged the lack of stamina which made him want to give up high office almost as soon as he was appointed. He was frequently ill, or believed himself ill; the records tell of fits, gout, spitting of blood, shortness of breath. Some of this was doubtless psychosomatic, but not all of it: a hunting accident of 1696 left a persistent legacy of chest trouble. Pride, diffidence, hypochondria, and ill-health made him always a tiresome and unreliable colleague. And in 1700, weary of politics, he left England on a belated Grand Tour and then settled in Rome for some three years. He returned early in 1706, bringing with him as his wife a witty, intelligent and somewhat eccentric Italian widow whose manners infuriated the Duchess of Marlborough and diverted English aristocratic society.

In some measure Shrewsbury's fine gifts appear wasted. He served William III, who thought better of him than of nearly all Englishmen, as Secretary of State (1689–90 and 1693–8); yet despite the dukedom conferred on him in 1694 he spent much effort trying to resign, particularly after Sir John Fenwick falsely accused him of complicity in Jacobite conspiracy. In Anne's reign, between his return in 1706 and his appointment as Lord Treasurer in 1714, he held the second-rank posts of Lord Chamberlain (1710–14) and Lord-Lieutenant of Ireland (1713–14). He did not lead, in the sense that Marlborough, Bolingbroke or Wharton led; he did not organize, as Godolphin and Harley did. Nevertheless, on three occasions in his political career his character and actions were of immense significance to his country. The first was when as a young aristocrat of Whig sympathies he was a central figure in the conspiracy which turned James II off the throne and placed William III on it. Shrewsbury was one of the Seven who signed the invitation to William; he joined William in Holland and sailed to Torbay with him; he carried to James the message which finally sent him to France; and he was from the start one of those who wanted William as King. The second occasion came in the middle years of Anne's reign when Shrewsbury, now middle-aged, a moderate rather than a Whig, the great magnate committed to neither party, joined with Harley to make it possible for Anne to get rid of the Whigs and their dependants Godolphin and Marlborough; and thus to enable the costly war of the Spanish Succession to be brought to an end. The third came in the last hours of Anne's reign when, by common consent of the dying Queen's Council, Shrewsbury was given the White Staff of the Lord Treasurer. It was a tribute to him and it was Shrewsbury who presided over the Hanoverian Succession, and thus confirmed by his actions the decision which both he and the English people had taken in 1688.

George I, who had named him as one of his Regents to govern the realm until his arrival, thought well of Shrewsbury; but the Whigs could not forgive him his activities in 1708–10. He did not long retain his offices, and he died in 1718. A patron of the arts, he built a classical mansion in Italian style for himself at Heythrop in Oxfordshire. It was burned down in later years and became the site of a Jesuit college.

A. S. Turberville, *Shrewsbury*, 1930.
Dorothy H. Somerville, *The King of Hearts*, 1962.

RICHARD LUMLEY, 1st EARL OF SCARBOROUGH (*d.* 1721), one of the seven signatories of the invitation to William of Orange, came from a family which had fought for the King in the Civil War. Brought up a Roman Catholic, he served Charles II as a soldier and in 1685 led the Sussex militia against Monmouth, who was captured by some of his men. But he disapproved of James II's policy; deprived of his regiment in 1687, he became a Protestant. He was one of the three Tories who signed the invitation to William in 1688, and he played an active part in the revolutionary movement in the north, occupying Newcastle-on-Tyne for the new regime. A Privy Councillor in the reigns of William, Anne, and George I, he was created Earl of Scarborough in 1690 and he fought at the Boyne and against the French in Flanders in the War of the League of Augsburg.

SIR JOHN MAYNARD (1602–90), Serjeant-at-Law, was a Devonian, born the son of a barrister at Tavistock and educated at Exeter College, Oxford, and the Middle Temple. He was called to the bar two years before the Petition of Right, and lived to become a Commissioner of the Great Seal after the Glorious Revolution. Thus his career spans the century of revolution as that of no other Englishman in public life. He sat for Devon constituencies in the Short and Long Parliaments, in Oliver's last Parliament, in the Convention of 1660, in Charles II's Cavalier Parliament, in James II's only Parliament, and in the Convention of 1688–9. Maynard prosecuted Strafford in 1641 and Stafford in 1680; he was a manager in the impeachment of Laud, Counsel for the Crown against Sir Henry Vane, leader in the case against Edward Coleman. Such a career required dexterity as well as longevity, professional skill as well as political sagacity. Maynard was a moderate Parliamentarian in the 1640s, critical of the Cromwellians and an opponent of the execution of Charles I. He took the Engagement to the Commonwealth, yet he defended Lilburne successfully in 1653 and was sent to the Tower because he pleaded Habeas Corpus in the Cony case of 1655. Like many shrewd men, he adjusted wisely in 1659–60; Protector's Serjeant in 1658, he became King's Serjeant, and got a knighthood into the bargain, at the Restoration. In Charles II's reign he took a moderately Whig line and made profitable use of his learning and of his oratory during the Popish Plot. At the Revolution he was on the side of the angels, seeing the victory of William as the triumph of the rule of law and achieving high office for the first time at the age of eighty-six.

GEORGE LEGGE, 1st LORD DARTMOUTH (1648–91), son of a devoted Royalist of the Civil Wars, was educated at Westminster and King's College, Cambridge, and served briefly on land and sea in the Dutch Wars. James, Duke of York, was his patron, and Legge, though a determined Protestant, stood firmly by him throughout his changing fortunes in his brother's reign. Legge was created Baron Dartmouth in 1682 and commanded the expedition sent to evacuate Tangier in 1683–4. When James came to the throne in 1685 he appointed Dartmouth Master of the Horse and Governor of the Tower. In September 1688, when the threat of William of Orange's invasion was evident, James removed the Catholic Strickland from command of the fleet and appointed Dartmouth in his place. Dartmouth's conduct thereafter, except in one respect, was ambiguous and remains controversial. It is possible, though by no means certain, that decisive action on his part could have destroyed the Revolution, either by intercepting the Dutch flotilla on its voyage, or by attacking it in Torbay and thereby awakening English hostility to the invaders. He failed to take that action, for one or more of several reasons. His own naval experience was very limited; he could not rely upon the loyalty of his captains, and there was traditional and strong anti-Catholic feeling among the seamen; both James's own instructions and those from the Navy Board encouraged him to be cautious in risking battle. The easterly winds which drove the Dutch down Channel, within sight of the English fleet, held Dartmouth at his moorings in the Downs, and even when he got out as far as Beachy Head he was driven back again to the Downs by a south-westerly gale. He eventually arrived at Torbay a fortnight after the Dutch, yet failed to engage them there; it is hard to account for this particular decision except on the hypothesis that Dartmouth believed that his captains would not obey an order to attack. Finally he took the fleet back to Spithead, where it surrendered to William five weeks after the Dutch landing. One action only of Dartmouth's was unambiguous: he firmly declined to obey the King's order to escort the infant Prince of Wales to France from Portsmouth, saying that such a step would be 'treason to the known laws of the kingdoms', and he took strict measures to ensure that the yacht which was to carry the child did not sail. Dartmouth was a man caught in the toils. His long record of personal loyalty to James and the tone of his letters to the King throughout this time forbid us to explain his inaction in terms of treachery. He did not long outlive what for him was a tragic choice of disloyalties. Relieved of his command, he took the oath of allegiance to the new sovereigns, but was soon imprisoned on a baseless charge of plotting to hand over the defences to France. In 1691 he died of apoplexy in the Tower.

M. J. Sydenham, 'The Anxieties of an Admiral', *History Today*, October 1962.

ARTHUR HERBERT, 1st EARL OF TORRINGTON (1647–1716) Admiral, came from the aristocratic Welsh Marcher family and entered the Navy at sixteen, fighting in the Dutch Wars and against Algerine pirates and taking part in the defence of Tangier against the Moors. Appointed Master of the Robes in 1684, he was elected M.P. for Dover in 1685. He was a firm Protestant, and James II dismissed him from all his posts, civil and naval, when he declined to support the repeal of the Tests. It was Herbert who, disguised as a common seaman, took the famous invitation to William of Orange in 1688. His letter to the English fleet, stressing the traditional Protestantism of the seamen, undoubtedly undermined naval loyalty to James. He was in command of the fleet which carried William to England, and in 1689 became a Commissioner of the Admiralty and Commander-in-Chief in the Channel. In that year he made contact with the enemy off Bantry Bay and fought a skirmish which brought no great credit to either side. Nevertheless, Herbert was created Earl of Torrington. There was much jealousy of him, notably on the part of his fellow Admiral, Russell, and the battle off Beachy Head in 1690 was fought against a background of muddle and mismanagement at the Admiralty. Torrington was tied by Cabinet orders which compelled him to fight the French in conditions which he considered too hazardous, notably a numerical inferiority of fifty-eight to seventy-five. In the battle the Dutch ships under his command did most of the fighting, and when Torrington called the action off and withdrew to the Thames he left the French in effective command of the Channel. He was arrested and court-martialled on a charge of 'gross misconduct': he defended himself effectively, arguing that it was his duty in all the circumstances not to fight, for the French would not invade whilst we had a fleet in being, and he was acquitted. He was never given another command. Both Burnet and Pepys wrote severely of him; but seamen like Shovell and Benbow remained loyal to him.

J. Ehrman, *The Navy in the War of William III*, 1953.

JOHN LOCKE, (1632–1704), philosopher, was a Somerset man, born at Wrington, the son of an attorney and small landowner. There was Puritanism on both sides of the family. His father fought, extremely briefly, as a Captain in the Parliamentary army in the Civil War, and his father's Colonel nominated John to a place at Westminster School, whither he went in 1647. Thus he was one of the numerous distinguished pupils of Dr. Busby, that formidable Royalist who kept his place despite the wars and taught his pupils to question the foundations of authority. A King's Scholar in 1650, John Locke went up to Christ Church, then the most notable of Oxford colleges under the headship of John Owen, in 1652. In 1658 he became a Senior Student (i.e. a Fellow) of Christ Church. In 1660, like nearly everyone else in Oxford, he welcomed the Restoration; and the evidence is, according to Maurice Cranston, that at this time John Locke was 'a man of the Right, an extreme authoritarian'.

Yet already there were portents of change. Most notably, Locke was dissatisfied with the Aristotelian logic and medieval disputations of Oxford, and had turned to an interest in science and in medicine. Here was study based upon experience, and here he would discover his approach to the principles upon which knowledge was founded. During the 1660s Locke liberalized and deepened his mind, partly by study of science and medicine under Robert Boyle, partly by his first trip abroad (a short one in 1665 to Protestant and tolerant Brandenburg), most of all by his relationship with Lord Ashley, formerly Sir Anthony Ashley Cooper, whom he first met in 1666. The following year he gave up his work as college tutor at

John Locke c.1672–6
(Artist: John Greenhill)

Christ Church, although he remained a Senior Student, and went to live at Ashley's house in London as the latter's personal physician, performing a successful operation on him soon afterwards. In this same year 1667 Locke wrote a manuscript essay on toleration which reveals a substantial widening of his views since 1660. It reflects also the fact that he had been brought by his residence with Ashley into direct contact with the political realities of Charles II's England —

for this was the year of the fall of Clarendon and the rise of Ashley to power.

London also provided other opportunities for Locke to display his intellectual strength. He became a Fellow of the Royal Society; he wrote a considerable part of a book on the rate of interest, his only economic work of consequence (it was not published until 1692); he was appointed Secretary to the Lords Proprietors of Carolina, colonial territory in which Ashley was interested, and helped to frame for it a constitution, which never came into effect. He gave some time at least to the medical care of his patron's own household: thus in 1671 we find him looking after Ashley's newborn grandson, the future third Earl of Shaftesbury. Most important of all, he wrote in 1671 the first drafts of the *Essay Concerning Human Understanding*. This, Locke's philosophical masterpiece, was not published until many years later, years in which Locke's own fortunes had been closely linked with those of his patron.

During the 1670s Locke, rather intermittently, was in some sense a political adviser to Ashley, who in 1672 was created Earl of Shaftesbury. These were the years when Shaftesbury, at first (1672–3) Lord Chancellor and ready to collaborate with Charles II, moved into opposition and became the first organizer of party in English political history. Locke's role in these developments is hard to discern and easy to exaggerate. From 1673–5 he was Secretary of the Council of Trade and Plantations; from 1675–79 he was in France, probably for his health, although it is at least interesting that these were precisely the years of secret negotiations between Louis XIV and the English opposition. He returned to England at the time of the Popish Plot and was at Shaftesbury's side during the Exclusion crisis. The year 1681, the year of the Oxford Parliament and of the collapse of the constitutional policy of exclusion, was of immense significance in the lives both of Shaftesbury and of Locke, and in the relations between them. For Shaftesbury, arrested by the government but freed by a London jury, decided to organize revolution, and Locke, himself in danger — watched by the Librarian of Christ Church, who was acting as an unpaid government spy — wrote his most celebrated work, the *Two Treatises of Government*. In form they were a refutation of the divine right philosopher Filmer's *Patriarcha*. Their central theme was a defence of the right of subjects to rebel against an arbitrary prince, and thus they were, to say the least, highly relevant to the schemes of Locke's patron. They were not in fact published until 1689, when they served to justify the 'Glorious Revolution', to provide the theoretical framework within which the political life of eighteenth-century England was conducted, and to stimulate the American colonists to revolt. Yet in their original intention the *Two Treatises* were 'not the rationalization of a revolution in need of defence but a demand for a revolution yet to be brought about'*.

Shaftesbury's revolution never came off. In 1682 he fled to Amsterdam where he died in January 1683. His body was brought home to Dorset for burial and Locke attended the funeral. He was still suspect and spied upon, and after the Rye House affair he deemed it wise to slip across to Holland that autumn. There he remained until 1689. His exile, spent mostly in Amsterdam and Rotterdam, was not disagreeable: he had numerous friends, he had taken steps to secure sufficient cash (Locke was in no way vague about money), and Holland was Protestant, tolerant, and clean. There was some peril, for James II's government, which had deprived him of his Studentship at Christ Church, attempted to have him extradited, and for a time he hid under the pseudonym of Dr. van der Linden, but the Dutch authorities declined to hand him over. Certainly his exile was fruitful in writing. These were the years of his letters to English friends which later (1693) were published as *Thoughts concerning Education*, in some ways perhaps the most notable work any Englishman has ever written on the subject, and certainly one which is perennially refreshing in its individual humanity and freedom from humbug. In 1686 he wrote his *Letter on Toleration*, first published in Latin at Gouda in 1689, a sane and moderate attempt to define the proper limits of both governmental and ecclesiastical interference with freedom of conscience: it won him widespread fame in a Europe overshadowed by Louis XIV's Revocation of the Edict of Nantes. Above all, in the same year he completed the book on which his eminence as a philosopher rests, the *Essay concerning Human Understanding*, whose object was 'to take a survey of our own understandings, examine our own powers, and see to what things they were adapted'. His approach to these

* Peter Laslett, 'The English Revolution and Locke's *Two Treatises of Government*', *Cambridge Historical Journal*, Vol. XII, No. 1, 1956.

problems in the *Essay*, above all his theory of knowledge with its foundation of empiricism, established him as one of the great creative philosophers of modern history.

Naturally Locke rejoiced in the Revolution of 1688, which both represented the triumph of his ideas and opened for him the way of return to his native country. 1689 was indeed *annus mirabilis* for John Locke. Not only did he come home in the convoy that brought Queen Mary to England, where he took up residence in London and accepted a minor government post. He also had in the press in that one year all three of his greatest works, the *Two Treatises,* the *Essay concerning Human Understanding*, and the *Letter on Toleration*, These publications firmly established his reputation in educated circles in the English-speaking world and in Europe. From 1691 Locke lived for most of the time at the country house of Otes in Essex, the home of Sir Francis and Lady Masham, a bachelor savant with his 4,000 books, his telescope, meteorological instruments and botanical specimens, rather fussy, yet as always courteous, humane, and modest. He indulged in literary controversy, notably in connection with his *The Reasonableness of Christianity*, which he published — anonymously — in 1695 and which, for all his formal Anglicanism, was remarkably Unitarian in flavour. In 1696 he was appointed a Commissioner for Trade: the pay was good, but the work in London was arduous, especially for an ageing asthmatic, and he resigned in 1700. He died at Otes in 1704, and lies buried in the churchyard of High Laver nearby. Locke is one of the giants of the seventeenth century, for, like Bacon and Newton, he asked new questions and created a new arena of thought.

Maurice Cranston, *John Locke*, 1957.

WILLIAM III (1650–1702), 'The Deliverer' of 1688, was born at The Hague, the only child of William II of Orange and Mary, eldest daughter of Charles I. His father died before he was born and his mother when he was barely ten; his childhood was unhappy, disputed between his mother and his paternal grandmother; his future in the Netherlands uncertain, for Cromwell at the end of the First Dutch War (1652–4) compelled the Dutch Republican government to promise to exclude him from high office. In 1670 he paid his

William III
(Artist: attrib. Thomas Murray)

first visit to England shortly after his host Charles II had negotiated the Treaty of Dover which provided for the dismemberment of the United Provinces. Out of the war which followed came, when he was twenty-one, the leadership of his people and his life's work. The French invasion of the provinces in 1672 brought the downfall of the Republican government; William of Orange, called to be Stadt-holder of Holland and Captain-General of the Dutch forces, led the nation in halting the French as his ancestor William the Silent had halted the Spaniards a century earlier. Henceforward he believed it his mission to prevent Louis XIV establishing hegemony over all Europe, a belief in destiny which fitted well with his Calvinism, as with the motto of the House of Orange, *Je maintiendrai*. It was a cold, hard passion, in a man who grew up taciturn, cautious, obstinate and occasionally ruthless. He wished above all to defeat the French on the battlefield, yet for all his personal bravery he was a mediocre general. The war continued until 1678, when the Dutch politicians against his wishes signed the Treaty of Nymegen, which William thought a defeat and which opened the way to a series of French diplomatic gains, notably in the Rhineland.

A year before the treaty William had taken the step which in the long run was to prove decisive in the conflict between Louis XIV and his foes. He married Mary, the eldest daughter of James II and heir-presumptive to the throne. Outwardly the marriage, blighted by lack of children, was not strikingly happy. William's behaviour was often surly, and he had his mistresses, yet they were neither so numerous nor so publicly flaunted as those of his two uncles. Nevertheless, Mary shared his resolution and responsibility, and his grief on her death in 1694 was intense and sincere. William's interest in events in Britain was profound during the years of uneasy peace with Louis which followed Nymegen; Whig refugees after the collapse of the Exclusion scheme kept him informed, and he took care to employ his own agents, especially during the growing crisis of James's reign. After the execution of Monmouth in 1685 he was the one hope of the English opposition, while for his part England was vital to all schemes against Louis, provided the mere threat of intervention there did not bring out France against the Dutch. William trod this tight-rope delicately. Although he proceeded cautiously, from some time in 1687 he was preparing invasion, and when in 1688, following the birth of the Prince James Edward,

Admiral Herbert brought the famous invitation, he was ready to come as fast as circumstances would permit. Aided by James II's folly in refusing to ask for French help and by Louis's blunders in keeping his fleet in the Mediterranean and in marching his army to the upper Rhineland, he sailed in November, after a false start in October, and landed at Brixham on the anniversary of Gunpowder Plot, with the largest army that had ever invaded England. In the events that followed before James fled to France William showed great wisdom. He treated the invasion as a professional military operation until it was clear that there would be no armed resistance, he carefully refrained from taking any political decisions beyond such immediately practical ones as were needed to ensure law and order, and he took the calculated risk of allowing his father-in-law to escape.

By the end of 1688 he was in possession. But the Revolution had barely begun. He had been invited to save the Protestant religion, not to take the throne. To us to-day it seems inevitable that he should have become King, yet this was by no means apparent to contemporaries, especially to the Tories, and not until late February 1689, when he had made it clear that he would not be his 'wife's gentleman usher', did he and Mary accept the throne. Neither by temperament nor in view of the needs of the European situation (war with Louis broke out in 1689) did William want a throne whose powers were seriously restricted. Although the Revolution Settlement made possible the limited monarchy of later years, it left the prerogative in 1689 much what it had been since 1660. Use would be the test, and in domestic affairs at least William's use of the prerogative was astonishingly restrained. In some ways too he imposed his own character on the settlement. It was free from bloodshed and vindictiveness; there were few scapegoats, and those only for a short time; the mild treatment of Sunderland is the supreme example of this. The Toleration Act of 1689 reflected William's views and virtues as well as those of the Whigs. There were times when in the face of the disagreements among Englishmen and the obvious doubts many of them had about the durability of the settlement, he despaired, and as early as 1689 he threatened to return to Holland. Yet it was fundamentally clear that he was essential, and events drove the point home. His victory at the Boyne in 1690, with all its consequences in securing Ireland and sending

James back to France, was decisive in confirming the events of 1688–9.

For William what mattered above all else was that England was committed to hostility to Louis XIV, to the War of the League of Augsburg (1689–97). It was not a successful war, apart from the Boyne and the naval battle of La Hogue (1692), which redeemed the defeat off Beachy Head (1690). William, whose generalship did not improve with time, was defeated at Steenkirk (1692) and Neerwinden (1693), and for most of the war the allied army in the Netherlands was tied down in endless sieges. The expedition to Brest (1694) failed in circumstances of treachery. Namur, indeed, was taken in 1695, but this simply offset its loss in 1692. When peace was made at Ryswick in 1697 its terms suggested that it was merely a truce — although Louis did indeed recognize William as King of England. Contemporaries thought it a disastrous war, and a costly one; and they would have been surprised to learn that later historians would acclaim its financial legacies, the Bank of England and the National Debt, as the greatest achievements of William's reign. Not the least of their grievances was William's readiness to employ foreign generals like Ginkel and Ruvigny. So in 1698 the Commons cut the army down to 7,000 men and sent home the Dutch Guards, the latter step being a deliberate insult which provoked William to the point of writing a speech of abdication.

The main reason why William employed Dutchmen was that he could not trust Englishmen. The fundamental problem of the reign, certainly of William's relationship with the English ruling class, was that of loyalty. Few politicians refrained from keeping in touch with James II at St. Germain. The facts that this was inevitable in view of the insecurity of the Revolution settlement through most of William's reign and that William knew it to be inevitable did not reduce the tensions which resulted. From the circumstances of the Revolution, as well as from their earlier background, the Tories were less sympathetic to William than the Whigs, and, on the whole, more likely to take their Jacobitism seriously; the Whigs for their part were more interested in reducing the royal prerogative and therefore the less acceptable to any King on that account. Somers was the one orthodox Whig in whom William had much confidence. Of other politicians Shrewsbury and Sunderland, neither of them strong partisans, seem to have appealed to him most; but Shrewsbury was neurotic, Sunderland's record was too dark for even William to be able to give him high office, and Somers was extremely unpopular in the last years of the reign. What made the situation worse was William's prolonged absences abroad during the war years, and the unexpected death of Mary in 1694 added to the practical difficulties. Yet it also, on a longer view, compelled Englishmen to commit themselves more fully to William himself. The discovery of the Assassination Plot of 1696 stimulated loyalty, and led to the declaration of that year, that he was the 'rightful and lawful King'. Thereafter it was possible to regard his throne as secure — even though the problem of loyalty was never completely solved, and even though serious quarrels between William and his English subjects lay ahead.

For William of Orange had little flair for popularity, even if London crowds were ready enough at times to cheer him. Aloof, withdrawn, fiercely self-controlled, he suffered from asthma and thus escaped as much as he could from the smoke of London to the country air of Kensington or Hampton Court, or to the hunting which was his only pastime. His few intimate friends were Dutchmen like Bentinck and Keppel. He was never easy to get on with, for he expected his servants to practise the same selfless devotion to his cause as he himself showed. Tough in the way that only the man who is never wholly fit can be tough, he drove his ministers to the utmost, and few of them were equal to it. His qualities were austere ones for an age in which English courtiers had had little chance of experiencing them: he had no time for flatterers, he was loyal to his word, he was ready to take advice, he was a man of direct, not of deceitful, intelligence. Hence, as David Ogg has put it, 'he never aroused their contempt and eventually he won their respect'.

The last years of his reign, after Ryswick, were largely devoted to an attempt to solve the problem of the Spanish Succession on lines which did not allow Louis XIV to overturn the balance of power in Europe. The problem was little understood in England, and William conducted the diplomacy which led to the two Partition Treaties (1698 and 1699) in secret, not consulting English opinion until 1700. This brought an outcry. The Irish estates which he had so lavishly granted to his Dutch friends were taken away from them. The Act of Settlement (1701), made necessary by the death in 1700 of Princess Anne's only surviving child, the Duke of Gloucester, contained, as well as its provision for the Hanoverian Succession, clauses which were clearly shafts aimed at William, like those which prohibited future monarchs leaving the country without Parliamentary permission or granting lands or office to foreigners. The gulf between William III and his English people seemed wider than ever it had been. But Louis XIV did much to close it, not so much by his acceptance of Charles II's will in November 1700 as by his blunders of 1701 — his invasion of the Spanish Netherlands and occupation of the Dutch Barrier fortresses, and his grant of the monopoly of Spanish-American trade to a French company. By the autumn much English opinion had swung round to support William's belief that war with Louis XIV must be renewed, and in September the Treaty of the Grand Alliance was signed. Within weeks Louis's final blunder, the recognition of the Old Pretender as James III, united the great mass of English opinion, Tory as well as Whig, squires and merchants alike, behind William in opposition to the arrogant attempt to dominate Europe and to place a Popish prince on the English throne. But by the time the actual fighting in the War of the Spanish Succession began in the spring of 1702, William III was dead; thrown when his horse stumbled, it is said over a molehill, in Hampton Court park, he was too frail and tired to recover from the shock.

'The little gentleman in black velvet' had, as G. M. Trevelyan observed, done his work too late to help either the Jacobites or Louis XIV. William had committed England to the final struggle with Louis XIV. Characteristically, he had overcome his deep distrust of Marlborough and nominated him as his successor in the conduct of the war; characteristically also he had, as his last piece of political advice to Englishmen, commended the project of a legislative union with Scotland. For William III, by far the ablest occupant of the English throne since the days of the Tudors, was distinguished by political judgment of a very high order. He was in some ways fortunate; both James II and Louis XIV aided him by crass blunders. But, as we have seen, he was ill served by English politicians, and his personal achievement, whether in retaining the throne or in carrying out the Revolution and in establishing the Settlement, was immense. His capacity for devotion to a cause no doubt contributed to this achievement. So did his profound belief in toleration and humanity, so too his essential and recognizable honesty of purpose. Yet the central element was a cautious, unhurried, wide-ranging judgment. He never won English hearts; as much perhaps because he was an European statesman as because he was a reserved and truculent man. To no one King does England owe so much, in constitutional evolution and international advance alike.

D. Ogg, *William III*, 1956.
Stephen Baxter, *William III*, 1966.
J. R. Western, *Monarchy and Revolution*, 1972.

MARY II (1662-94) was the elder daughter of James, Duke of York, and Anne Hyde. Brought up a Protestant at Charles II's insistence, despite the conversion of both her parents to Romanism, she was married to William of Orange in 1677. In 1678 she had two miscarriages, and thereafter remained childless. Sincerely as well as dutifully accepting her husband's attitude to her father's policy on the English throne after 1685, she joined him in condemning the Declaration of Indulgence and supporting the Seven Bishops. Mary accepted the Revolution and the deposition of her father as necessary to the security of Protestantism. Nor had she any doubts that William must rule as King, and she turned down Danby's plan that she should be sole sovereign with the words 'I shall take it extreme unkindly, if any, under pretence of their care for me, should set up a divided interest between me and the Prince'. As Queen she played no significant part in the making of political decisions. Yet as Regent during William's frequent absences she was a calm and dignified head of state, not least in the crises of 1690 and 1692. She died of smallpox in 1694.

Few women in English history have been so important as Mary II, who made possible the curious form taken by the English Revolution of 1688-9, and also made her highly unpopular husband acceptable to the English people, in particular to the moderate Tory leaders. Yet her importance lay in her mere existence rather than in her qualities, with one significant exception — her devotion to Protestantism. Owing much to those two very different yet practical divines Compton, her childhood tutor, and Burnet, her adviser at The Hague, she firmly resisted her father's efforts to win her to Rome. In her way Mary was as much a symbol of Protestantism as the last English woman who had been Queen of England before her,

Mary II
(Artist: after William Wissing)

Elizabeth I. With something of the primness of her grandfather
Clarendon, almost morbidly conscientious about her own conduct,
Mary found in a practical religion, appropriate to the temper of the
late seventeenth century, the way of expressing a deep natural
kindliness. She was a patron of the movement which led to the
S.P.C.K., and she originated the project of Greenwich Hospital

which William carried out as a memorial to her. Her graciousness and sincerity made her popular both in the Holland she grew to love and in the England which she came to dislike.

A precocious and lively child who grew into a sensitive and intelligent woman, she suffered bitterly in her personal life as a result of her public role. She had been her father's favourite child, and the prolonged crisis of 1688–90, ending only with the Boyne, was a torment to Mary, prevented by her duty to William from showing any sign of her sorrow for her father. James, characteristically, solemnly cursed and disowned her. Her sister Anne, self-centred and unimaginative and in this period dominated by Sarah Churchill, disliked William intensely, and the disgrace of Marlborough in the 1690s led to a complete break between her and Mary which was never healed. Nor were Mary's relations with William easy. The evidence suggests that she had had no wish to marry and that the barren match which was of such decisive importance in British and European history and by which she sacrificed so much came near to shipwreck. There was his attachment to Elizabeth Villiers; probably more important, there was the difficulty, felt by all who knew him, of understanding William's whole complex and awkward personality. Yet Mary came to love him with 'a passion that cannot but end with my life', triumphing by her almost puritanical sense of duty and her capacity for affection. Moreover, it seems certain that the outward signs of disharmony, of which Jacobite gossip made the most, reflected William's temperamental reserve and boorishness rather than any deeper failure. His grief at her death was frightening to observers. Its intensity, in this strange man in whom public and private feelings were so inextricably blended, may not improperly be regarded as a measure of his adopted country's debt to the most honest and attractive of Stuart monarchs.

Hester W. Chapman, *Mary II, Queen of England*, 1953.

WILLIAM, BENTINCK, 1st EARL OF PORTLAND (1649?–1709), friend and adviser of William III, came from a noble Dutch family. As page of honour and then as Gentleman of the Bedchamber, he first won William's trust and friendship during the dark days of the early 1670s. In 1675 he nursed William through smallpox and then nearly died of the disease himself. By the time of

the invasion of England, Bentinck had served William loyally in the Netherlands for nearly twenty years, and it is scarcely surprising that the King rewarded him liberally with English lands and honours, making him Earl of Portland, first Gentleman of the Bedchamber and Groom of the Stole. Bentinck fought at the Boyne and at Landen, where he was wounded. Yet his main contribution to public affairs in England was as a diplomatist. He had already shown his skill in 1688 by negotiating the neutrality of the German princes during the invasion; his informal discussions with Marshal Boufflers laid the foundations of the Treaty of Ryswick; and he was the chief architect of both the Partition Treaties. Patriotic to his adopted country, utterly loyal to its sovereign, Bentinck became intensely unpopular in England. In part this was the result of his own characteristics: he was a blunt man who had a gift for making enemies and who, though quite incorruptible, liked wealth. Yet in the main it reflected popular recognition of the hard facts that William trusted no Englishman and that few English politicians deserved his trust. Towards the end of the reign Bentinck took offence at William's favouritism towards the handsome young Dutchman Arnoud van Keppel, created Earl of Albemarle in 1696, and showed his jealousy by bouts of sullenness and by resigning (1699) his offices at Court. Yet there was no open quarrel, nor any decline of Bentinck's loyalty, and there was a reconciliation on William's deathbed. Under Anne, Bentinck inevitably disappeared from favour, yet he remained in England until his death in 1709.

JOHN GRAHAM, OF CLAVERHOUSE, 1st VISCOUNT DUNDEE (1649–89), member of a younger branch of the same noble family as the Marquis of Montrose, was educated at the University of St. Andrews, and after a career abroad as a soldier of fortune returned to Scotland to become the leading figure in the merciless subjugation of the Covenanters in the south-west in 'the killing time' of 1679–88. Defeated by the Covenanters at Drumclog Moss (1679), he took part in Monmouth's victory over them at Bothwell Brig some three weeks later, and opposed Monmouth's policy of clemency. Pious, stern and blood-thirsty, Claverhouse was no more 'romantic' than the men and women his dragoons hunted down over the moors of Galloway. His policy was one of disciplined terror, with little heed to legal niceties; ringleaders were summarily executed, lesser folk thrust into prison by the hundred. It was temporarily successful; James Renwick, executed in 1688, was the last of the 'Cameronian martyrs'. In many ways the episode provided a precise parallel to the contemporary outrages of Louis XIV against the Huguenots.

Claverhouse's opinions and actions commended him to James II, whose pro-Catholic policy he supported. He was with the King at Salisbury in the crisis of 1688 and was one of those who wanted him to stake all in a final stand. Allowed to return to Scotland, he sat for a time in the Convention which met in Edinburgh in March 1689, and then made his escape from the city with a troop of horsemen to rouse the Highlands against William. In July his army of clansmen ambushed Hugh Mackay's government force in the Pass of Killie-crankie. Claverhouse's wild and barefooted highlanders armed with claymores shattered their opponents, but Claverhouse was killed in the course of the victory. His death did not mean the end of Highland resistance to William, for that was brought about by the victory of William Cleland's peasant army at Dunkeld a month later; yet it certainly deprived Scottish Jacobitism of its most dangerous leader.

C. S. Terry, *John Graham of Claverhouse, Viscount Dundee, 1648–89*, 1905.

GEORGE WALKER, (1645?–90), the son of a Yorkshireman who became Chancellor of the diocese of Armagh in Ireland, was educated at Glasgow University and later ordained. Parson at Donaghmore in Tyrone from 1674, he raised a Protestant force at Dungannon in the crisis of 1688 and became joint-Governor of Londonderry during its siege of 103 days in 1689, and the central figure in its resistance. He was hailed as a hero when he visited England afterwards. Returning to Ireland, he was killed at the Battle of the Boyne.

T. B. Macaulay, *History of England* (first pub. 1848, many eds.), Chap. 12.

GODERT DE GINKEL, 1st EARL OF ATHLONE (1630–1703), born at Utrecht, was already an experienced soldier when he came to England as one of William's Commanders in 1688. One of the handful of Dutchmen to whom England owed much at this time, Ginkel was responsible for the reduction of Ireland. He fought with distinction at the Boyne (1690); left in charge in 1691 after William's return to England, he captured the stronghold of Athlone, defeated the main Irish force at Aughrim, and finished the war by taking Limerick. Ginkel gave the Irish reasonable terms of surrender and was in no way responsible for the later breach of the treaty by the English government. Returning to England in triumph, he was rewarded with the Earldom of Athlone (1692) and a large grant of Irish lands, of which, like other Dutch grantees, he was later deprived by Act of Parliament. He joined William's forces in Flanders and was his companion-in-arms throughout the War of the League of Augsburg, fighting at Steinkirk (1692), Landen (1693), and at the recapture of Namur (1695). When the War of the Spanish Succession broke out, Athlone, now over seventy, expected the supreme command in the Netherlands, and was offended when it was given to the relatively inexperienced Marlborough. The campaign of 1702 led him to recognize Marlborough's ability in handsome terms, saying 'The success of this campaign is solely due to this incomparable chief, since I confess that I, serving as second in command, opposed in all circumstances his opinions and proposals'. He died in 1703.

DANIEL FINCH, 2nd EARL OF NOTTINGHAM (1647–1730), was the son of a Lord Chancellor and member of a family eminent in the law throughout the seventeenth century. He was educated at Westminster under Busby and at Christ Church, Oxford. In Charles II's reign he opposed 'Exclusion' and served as a Commissioner of the Admiralty in the 'Tory reaction' (1681–4). Throughout his political career he was regarded as a 'High Tory', and he was certainly an outstanding lay champion in politics of 'High' churchmanship during the reigns of William III and Anne. Yet it is more difficult and even more misleading to attach labels to Nottingham than to his contemporaries, though for quite different reasons. Whereas they had few principles, he had strong and independent ones. Tall, melancholy and formal in manner and pessimistic in outlook ('Dismal' was his nickname), old-fashioned in eloquence and in dress, extremely hard-working, the father of twenty-one children, Nottingham was shrewd as well as honest, deeply patriotic but exceptionally angular. As Sir Keith Feiling has put it, 'he liked office but was an indigestible colleague'.

He played an important role in the Revolution — for the Church of England, a vital one. As a devout Anglican he had opposed James II's Catholicizing policy, but he could not bring himself to desert his King, until James had deserted his kingdom; and he was one of the three Commissioners sent by the Peers to negotiate with William at Hungerford. After James's flight Nottingham was one of that middle group who pressed unsuccessfully for a regency. His greatest contribution to the revolutionary settlement lay in the Toleration Act, safeguarding the political supremacy of Anglicanism at the price of freedom of worship for most Nonconformists. His further plan of comprehension, to enlarge the scope of the Church of England to admit the Presbyterians and some other Nonconformists, proved unacceptable. His own appointment to office as Secretary of State (1689–93) was an additional guarantee to Anglicans that the Church would come to no harm in the new regime. In William's eyes, Nottingham had the merit of being one of the few English politicians who did not keep contact with James II.

Nottingham became Secretary of State once more for the first two years of Anne's reign. The Methuen Treaty with Portugal (1703) embodied his policy: indeed, it is characteristic of his independence of outlook that, whereas most Tories were hostile to the Whig policy of 'No peace without Spain', he wished to make Spain rather than Flanders the main area of British military effort. Out of office from 1704, in the rest of the reign he was very clearly the champion of the High Church — trying and failing to get a bill against Occasional Conformity through in 1704 by 'tacking' it to a vote of supply, trying again and succeeding in 1711, with the support of the Whigs (now in opposition), condemning the Act of Union with Scotland in 1707 on sectarian grounds. But in 1714 he refused to support the Schism Act, which forbade all but Anglicans to teach in schools, on the ground that this was a 'barbarous' law which deprived parents of 'the natural right of educating their own children'. And he consistently refused to have any truck with Jacobitism. A leader of the Hanover Tories, he was one of the eighteen men whom George I named as Regents to rule Great Britain until he should arrive from Hanover; and he was appointed Lord

President of the Council by the new King, holding office until he was dismissed in 1716, because he urged lenient treatment for the Peers involved in the Jacobite rebellion of 1715. He was now aged nearly seventy, and, although he lived on until 1730, his dismissal marked the end of a political career which, in the context of the times through which he lived, was conscientious, honourable and remarkably consistent.

Henry Horwitz, *Revolution Politics: the career of Daniel Finch, 2nd Earl of Nottingham*, 1968.

SIR EDWARD SEYMOUR (1633–1708) (baronet in 1685), a prominent member of every House of Commons from the Restoration to the middle years of Anne's reign, was 'descended', as an unanimous testimony of the Commons put it in 1701, 'from ancestors who have been successful in commanding armies and fleets of this kingdom and from a Protector of the realm'. A grandee with his family mansion of Berry Pomeroy, near Totnes, in Devon, proud of his lineage and insolent in speech (Sir Keith Feiling notes the story of Seymour as Speaker of the Commons telling Colonel Birch that it was indecent for him to brush his beard without a looking-glass), Seymour was by temperament a loyalist and thus became 'High Tory' in outlook in the reigns of William and Anne. Yet he was above all a 'country' politician, electoral master of a 'Western Empire' which included seats in Cornwall and Devon, and the natural leader of the west country M.P.s of his day. Seymour had no doubts about the supremacy of the landed interest. He once said 'I am one of those that welcome all propositions that have a tendency to ease Lands', and in Anne's reign he walked out of the Commons when a tax on malt was proposed. Ambitious, vain, insular, full of prejudices, against 'fanatics', Popery, the Dutch and the Scots, Seymour was not an easy colleague, nor was his financial integrity above reproach, as the attack on him in 1694 indicated; his patriotism was far from selfless. But he was a man of ability and courage whose beliefs and prejudices reflected much that was generally accepted by Englishmen of his day.

M.P. for Hindon in 1661, he led the Commons in demanding the impeachment of Clarendon (1667). Twice chosen as Speaker in Charles II's reign, a country gentleman interrupting the succession of lawyers who had established a monopoly of the office, he was rejected the second time (1679) by the King. Strongly anti-Catholic, he was, nevertheless, hostile to Exclusion, one of the relatively few M.P.s of the years 1678-81 who were; characteristically his opposition rested not on theories of hereditary right but upon the practical difficulties of enforcing the policy, and he was a leading advocate of 'limitations' or a 'regency'. He enjoyed royal favour at the crisis of Exclusion, but lost it in the last years of Charles's reign — perhaps because he did not get the office to which he felt entitled, yet perhaps also because he read the signs of approaching Catholicism.

Certainly in James's reign his attitude was clear from start to finish. He once claimed 'My family were instrumental in the Reformation, and not any have been pointed out for Popery', and almost alone he upset the brief honeymoon of the first session of James's only Parliament by a violent attack on the government for its intrigue and corruption in the elections, in which Seymour's west country influence had been somewhat diminished. In the course of this he stressed the need for M.P.s 'attached to the laws of England' at a time when 'there is already talk about the repeal of the Test Act and the Habeas Corpus Act, the one a bulwark against the establishment of Popery at the expense of Protestantism, the other the firmest foundation of English liberties'. Thus Seymour had nailed his colours to the mast at once, and it is not surprising to find him leading west country opposition to James's pressure on the J.P.s in 1687. When William landed next year at Torbay and advanced to Exeter, it was appropriate that Seymour should be one of the first leading Englishmen to join him, and characteristic that he should do so in a carriage drawn by seven horses. His reason for rebellion was the need to defend Protestantism, and thus it was not necessarily illogical of him to oppose the offer of the Crown to William. He took the oaths to William and Mary, and demonstrated his loyalty to the Revolution by never dabbling in Jacobitism.

There were still nearly twenty years of his political career ahead, years spent partly in jealousy and sheer obstreperousness, partly in the maintenance of high-flying Toryism of an independent kind. He held office as a Treasury Commissioner from 1691 to 1694; lost his seat at Exeter in the Whiggish election of 1695, regained it in the Tory swing of 1698, and thenceforward for the rest of William's reign pursued a savage vendetta against the Whigs. Nevertheless, it was in keeping with his general attitude that it should be Seymour who in the last months of William's reign moved in the Commons for no peace with France while Louis XIV continued to recognize the Old Pretender as James III. Under Anne he held office as Comptroller of the Household from 1702–4. His views on the conduct of the war were Tory ones, opposed to the costly land campaigns in the Netherlands, and they did not please Marlborough, who wrote to Sarah in June 1703 'We are bound not to wish for anybody's death, but should Sir Edward Seymour die it would be no great loss to the Queen nor the nation'. Seymour for his part thought Marlborough should be impeached. Inevitably with the development of the war Seymour was dismissed, in 1704. He died in 1708, in some ways much more a prototype of later 'Toryism' than either Harley or St. John.

Keith Feiling, *A History of the Tory Party, 1640–1714*, 1924.

THOMAS, 1st MARQUIS OF WHARTON (1648–1715), Whig politician, was the son of a wealthy Presbyterian Peer who had fought on the Parliamentarian side in the Civil War and increased his wealth in the process. Brought up under a Puritan regime of discipline and hard work, he reacted full-bloodedly to the easier moral air of the Restoration, rapidly acquiring what Macaulay called 'the dissoluteness of the emancipated precisian'. A sceptic distinguished by the ribaldry of his conversation even in the reign of Charles II, a notorious rake and an unblushing liar, a jockey whose horses were remarkably successful at Newmarket, a brilliant swordsman who fought and won many duels, Thomas Wharton in his private life was scarcely a creditable — though by no means unique — offspring of the Puritan Revolution. But he drew his public principles also from that Revolution, and to these he adhered with a consistency unparalleled in his generation. Consequently, in the light of a career which began with Exclusion and finished with the Hanoverian Succession, he may be considered the most significant Whig politician between Shaftesbury and Walpole.

Entering the Commons in the year of the Test Act, he remained an M.P. until he inherited his father's title in 1696, sitting first for the Wharton borough of Wendover and then as one of the county

Thomas, 1st Marquis of Wharton c.1710
(Artist: Sir Godfrey Kneller)

members. Buckinghamshire was Hampden country and Nonconformist country too, and Tom Wharton was strongly for Exclusion.
He kept clear of the Rye House Plot (though his house was searched)
and of Monmouth's desperate venture; he was an intrepid duellist,
but a cautious revolutionary who disliked backing losers. Outspoken in opposition to James's policy in the Parliament of 1685,

Wharton was one of the leading younger men in the conspiracy which prepared the way for William's invasion. He may even have drafted the famous invitation signed by the seven grandees, and certainly he was one of the first group of important Englishmen to join William at Exeter. And he made one other contribution to the enterprise of 1688. Wharton was the author of *Lilliburlero*, the Revolution song which was said to have 'whistled James out of three kingdoms'.

A member of the committee which drafted the Bill of Rights, Wharton was Comptroller of the Household from 1689 to 1702, a post which made him in practice the principal link between William and the Commons. Although his loyalty to the Revolution was complete and he never 'insured' at St. Germain, his relations with William III were not easy, partly because his tough hard cynicism made little appeal to William, partly also because he did not share the King's readiness to find political virtue in men who were not Whigs. In these years, and to rather less extent in Anne's reign, Wharton's principal activity may be regarded as that of a party organizer. He seems to have arranged the meetings of the Whig Junto in each reign, and to have managed the Whig voting in the Commons while he was a member of the lower House. As for electioneering and borough-mongering, Wharton was at once a pioneer and an acknowledged expert, particularly, of course, on and near the Wharton properties in Buckinghamshire, Westmoreland and Yorkshire.

Anne, who disapproved of his morals as well as of his partisan politics, dismissed him from office on her accession, and not until 1708, when he became Lord-Lieutenant of Ireland, would she accept him again. In the interval he was involved in the franchise case of *Ashby v. White* (Ashby was a Whig cobbler in Wharton's own borough of Aylesbury), and, to greater national advantage, in promoting the Union with Scotland, which brought him an Earldom. After the fall of the Whigs in 1710 Wharton was prominent in opposition to the Treaty of Utrecht and to such Tory measures as the Schism Act. He lived long enough to see the Hanoverians safely installed, and died a Marquis in 1715. By his persistent maintenance of the principles of the Glorious Revolution, 'Liberty and Property', 'Honest Tom' Wharton had prepared the way for the Whig supremacy of the eighteenth century.

John Carswell, *The Old Cause*, 1954, pp. 25–127.

JOHN, BARON SOMERS (1651–1716), lawyer and Whig, born at Whiteladies, near Worcester, the son of an attorney, was educated at Worcester Cathedral School, Trinity College, Oxford, and the Middle Temple, and called to the bar in 1676. His first big case, which opened his way to political as well as legal eminence, was the Trial of the Seven Bishops (1688), in which as junior counsel for the defence he put the constitutional argument against James with lucid force; and he seems to have been the leading draftsman of the Declaration of Right. William III rewarded Somers' services by making him Solicitor-General (1689), Attorney-General (1692), Lord Keeper (1693) and finally Lord Chancellor (1697). Throughout the period from the Revolution to the death of Anne, Somers was a consistent and energetic Whig, becoming one of the five Lords of the Whig Junto. Able, cautious, and eloquent, Somers was one of the few Englishmen to whom William III gave his confidence; it was Somers who persuaded the King not to return to Holland after the Commons voted in 1698 to disband the Dutch guards. Yet his intimacy with the King increased Tory rancour against him, and in 1700 William dismissed him from office because of the Commons' lack of trust. In 1701 the Tory majority in the Commons proposed his impeachment, mainly on the ground that in 1698 he had affixed the Great Seal to a blank commission authorizing unnamed plenipotentiaries to sign the Partition Treaty of that year, but the Lords declined to proceed.

In Anne's reign Somers was long out of favour: the Queen was prejudiced, and in 1702 declined to have him sworn of her Council. No doubt it was prudence which led him in 1703 to make insincere offers of service at St. Germain; like Marlborough, he was ready to insure. Meanwhile with Wharton he led the Whigs in the Lords, and he played a prominent and statesmanlike part in forming and passing both the Regency Act (1706) and the Act of Union with Scotland (1707). After the Whig triumph of 1708 Anne accepted him as Lord President of the Council and his courteous and grave manner soon led her to revise her opinion of him. As a member of the ministry Somers was a leading advocate of the policy of 'No peace without Spain' which prolonged the war with Louis XIV. He fell with his colleagues in 1710, not before he had indulged in intrigue to secure his own succession to Godolphin's place as Treasurer, and he did not reappear at the Privy Council until the day before Anne's death in 1714. Like all the Whigs, Somers welcomed the Hanoverian Succession, but George I did not name him among the Lords Justices who were to rule until his own arrival. Somers died in 1716. Macaulay described him as 'the greatest man among the members of the Junto, and, in some respects, the greatest man of that age'. This may be a Whiggish verdict. Nevertheless, he was unquestionably a man of outstanding mind who won his way by ability into the topmost ranks of the Whig aristocracy, a superb lawyer, a great constructive statesman, and a judicious patron of such writers as Addison and the historiographers Rymer and Madox.

W.L. Sachse, *Lord Somers: A Political Portrait*, 1975.

CHARLES MONTAGU, 1st EARL OF HALIFAX (1661–1715), the statesman responsible for the foundation of the National Debt and the Bank of England, was born at Horton, in Northamptonshire, of a cadet branch of a family already prominent in seventeenth-century England, and was educated at Westminster and Trinity College, Cambridge, of which he became a Fellow. A clever and witty young man, he wrote with Matthew Prior in 1687 *The Town and Country Mouse*, a successful burlesque of John Dryden's recently-published *The Hind and the Panther*. Elected M.P. for Malden in 1689, he was an able debater and rose very swiftly to eminence, becoming a Commissioner of the Treasury in 1691 and Chancellor of the Exchequer in 1694. He held these offices until 1699, and he was in that time the main figure responsible for a series of financial reforms as important as any in our history. These measures, adopted initially to finance William's War of the League of Augsburg (1689–97), made it possible in the next reign for Godolphin to pay for Marlborough's war; and they provided the structure within which British public finance has been conducted ever since. They included the creation of the National Debt arising from the long-term loan of 1693; the establishment in 1694 of the Bank of England, itself the product of another loan; the beginning of the system of a general fund, consolidating the national finances; the great re-coinage of 1696, carried through in co-operation with the new Master of the Mint, Montagu's old Trinity friend Sir Isaac

Newton, and paid for by the imposition of the window tax; and the first issue of Exchequer bills. Not the least important feature of these measures was that for the first time they gave the man who lent to the state a real sense of confidence, secured on assets more stable than the whim of a monarch. Thereby perhaps Montagu did more than any other man to estblish the Revolution Settlement.

Montagu, who sat in the Commons until he got his peerage in 1700, was an adroit Parliamentarian, and has been described by David Ogg as 'our first real cabinet minister, because he headed a great department, and had to defend his conduct of that department in the Commons'. In 1698 he was responsible for the setting-up of the 'new' East India Company. He was a Whig leader, a member of the Junto of five, and was one of those let into the secret of the Partition Treaty of 1699. In the anti-Whig reaction of the last years of William's reign this, together with the grants of Irish land which he received, provided an excuse for his impeachment in 1701; the Lords dismissed the charges.

The writer of the *D.N.B.* article on Halifax observes in a crushing sentence that 'his ambition was great, his vanity excessive, and his arrogance unbounded'. There is some evidence that success went to his head. It seems likely that personal qualities account for the fact that he held no great office in Anne's reign, even in the years of Whig supremacy, although he was one of their leaders in the Lords' debates. He was one of the English Commissioners appointed to negotiate the Union with Scotland, and in 1706 he went on a Whig diplomatic mission to see the Electress Sophia in Hanover. In 1714 he was one of the Regents named by George I to administer the kingdom, and he was at the Treasury again for a few months before his death in 1715. A man of taste, Halifax was not unimportant as a patron of literature; for all Swift's hard comment that what Halifax gave to literary men was 'good words and good dinners', it is clear that he did much more than this for Addison.

D. Ogg, *England in the Reigns of James II and William III*, 1955 Chap. 14.

EDWARD RUSSELL, EARL OF ORFORD (1653–1727), Admiral, a member of the great Whig family, was commissioned in Charles II's navy. The persecution of the Whigs in the early 1680s drove him to support William of Orange, with whom he kept in touch during James II's reign. In 1688 he was one of the seven signatories of the famous invitation, and after the Revolution he was in the inner circle of Whig leaders, the Junto. When Torrington was defeated off Beachy Head in 1690 and withdrew to the Thames, it was Russell who was sent to arrest and supersede him. Two years later he defeated the French fleet off Barfleur in the battle of La Hogue. The victory saved Britain from invasion and broke French naval strength for the remainder of the war. Much of the credit for the destruction of the French warships belongs to Rooke, and Russell was strongly, though probably unjustly, criticized at home for his failure to follow up his success by landing on the enemy coast. The government, predominantly Tory at the time, dismissed him, but he was recalled to employment in 1694, serving both as First Lord and at sea. In 1694–5 he commanded the first major English fleet to winter abroad when, most reluctantly and at William's insistence, he remained in the Mediterranean. Created Earl of Orford in 1697, he was dismissed from office in 1699, and later unsuccessfully impeached for his part in the Partition Treaty. An obstinate and truculent man, Orford was the least effective of the Junto in Anne's reign, though he was briefly First Lord again in 1709–10. George I recognized his Whiggery rather than his esteem by appointing him one of the Lords Justices in 1714.

J. Ehrman, *The Navy in the War of William III*, 1953.

WILLIAM BLATHWAYT (1649?–1717), provides an early example of the higher civil servant, at an age when there was no clear distinction between politics and administration. He belonged to that group of 'new men' of the late seventeenth century whose most celebrated representative was Samuel Pepys, permanent or semi-permanent officials whose posts depended on personal or political favour or upon investment yet who exercised some influence upon policy. William III called Blathwayt a 'dull' man of 'good method'; he was efficient and industrious, he organized well, he was willing to accept responsibility up to a point; he evaded the higher and more hazardous posts, declining the Secretaryship of State in 1695 and also an ambassadorship at Ryswick in 1697; he was well paid, with an annual income at the peak of his career of about £4,000 from salaries, quite apart from perquisites. Considerable and important work, daily contact with the great, a satisfying measure of power without much ultimate responsibility, a very comfortable income, and, for the age, a substantial degree of security — here is a recognizable prototype.

Blathwayt held several offices simultaneously: he was a pluralist but a hard-working one, in no sense a sinecurist. His most important posts were as (1675) Secretary to the Lords of Trade and Plantations; (1681-3) chief clerk in the office of Secretary of State; (1683-1704) Secretary at War; (1686) a clerk of the Privy Council; (1696-1706) a Commissioner of Trade. He weathered the political storms of his time with remarkably little trouble, but his life was not without its political excitements and embarrassments. As a clerk to the council he heard James II denounce the Fellows of Magdalen, and saw the Seven Bishops present their petition; this last occasion made him a Crown witness at the trial. Yet the most significant part of his career came after the Revolution when as Secretary at War he went with William III to Flanders in the campaigning season each summer, and thereby became the Acting Secretary of State for part of the year — the chief of a sort of mobile foreign office, dealing with all correspondence on foreign affairs and becoming the effective head of the diplomatic service each summer. The limits of his constitutional authority were carefully regarded; Blathwayt issued 'directions', not 'instructions', which were the official and formal prerogative of the Secretary of State. And William kept all major decisions in his own hands. Blathwayt's influence, nevertheless, was considerable, in terms of correspondence, patronage, and access to the King.

Blathwayt was also an M.P. for some twenty years, representing Bath for most of them, and in the final stages of his career he was a firm Whig, speaking against Harley in the Commons. He retired from public life in 1710 to the elegant mansion he had earlier built for himself at Dyrham Park, in Gloucestershire, and there he died in 1717. Substantially more than a clerk yet a great deal less than a responsible minister, he illustrated an important stage in the evolution of the machinery of English government.

G.A. Jacobsen, *William Blathwayt: a late seventeenth-century administrator*, 1932.

R. A. Preston, 'William Blathwayt and the Evolution of a Royal Personal Secretariat', *History*, New Series, Vol. XXXIV, pp. 28–43.

GILBERT BURNET, (1643–1715), historian and Bishop, was a burly, hearty Scotsman who married three wealthy wives. Charitable, tolerant, avidly hard-working, he had immense self-confidence and little tact. Perhaps the most impressive illustration of the former is to be found in the remarkable letter which Burnet wrote to Charles II in 1680, concluding with the splendid passage 'And now, Sir, permit me to tell you that all the distrust your people have of you, all the necessities you are under, all the indignation of heaven that is upon you, and appears in the defeating of all your counsels, flow from this, that you have not feared nor served God, but have given yourself up to so many sinful pleasures'. As for his tactlessness, there is a story that when the Whigs were comparing the shabby treatment of the Duke of Marlborough with that of the great Belisarius at Byzantium, the Duchess asked who Belisarius was and why he had lost favour; Burnet answered that one reason was that he had a 'brimstone of a wife'. His contemporaries found Burnet slightly comic, and the Tories among them, like Swift, disliked him strongly. But he was a man of real distinction of mind, learned, courageous, notably unmalicious, who, even if he was not as important as he assumed, played a significant and unusual part in the life of his day.

Born at Edinburgh, the son of a Scottish advocate who was anti-episcopalian yet refused to take the Covenant, Burnet was a precocious, widely-read boy who was educated at Marischal College, Aberdeen. In the early 1660s he travelled to England, Holland and France; while in Scotland he struck up a friendship with Lauderdale and opposed the repressive anti-Presbyterian policy of Archbishop Sharp and Rothes. From 1665 to 1672, when Lauderdale was in power and pursuing a moderate policy, Burnet, first as minister of Saltoun parish and then as Professor at the University of Glasgow, was one of the few Scotsmen whose aim was to reconcile Presbyterians and Episcopalians. Despite his youth he was offered, but refused, two bishoprics. But in 1672, when Lauderdale returned to the policy of persecution, Burnet quarrelled with him, and departed to England where his abilities won him favour at court and an

Gilbert Burnet c.1689–91
(Artist: after John Riley)

appointment as a royal Chaplain. Characteristically, he took Charles to task about his private life. In 1675 he became Chaplain of the Rolls Chapel.

In the Popish Plot period Burnet, essentially a humane and moderate man, spoke out against the persecution of Catholics. Yet he was firmly against Catholic claims, as his *History of the Reformation*, published at this time, and his attempts to reconvert

James, Duke of York, made clear. His political views became increasingly Whiggish; he was friendly with the Whig leaders implicated in the Rye House Plot (1683) and attended Russell to the scaffold. In 1684, after preaching on 5 November a two-hour sermon against popery, he was deprived of his Rolls chaplaincy, and went abroad. He travelled through France, Italy (where he met, and got on well with, Pope Innocent XI), the Rhineland and Switzerland, coming finally to Holland, where he became an adviser to William of Orange, while James II in England initiated his prosecution on a charge of treason. Burnet was largely responsible for the instructions to Dykveld in 1687. He landed at Brixham with William, and on the latter's arrival in London he preached at St. Paul's to the text 'It is the Lord's doing and it is marvellous in our eyes'.

Appointed Bishop of Salisbury, Burnet supported the Toleration Act and the abortive scheme of comprehension. He appears to have had considerable influence upon Queen Mary. A good bishop, he had a strong sense of pastoral care and did his utmost to raise the standard of clergy in his diocese. Yet he was involved in much controversy. His kindly tolerance both of Non-jurors and of Presbyterians made him enemies as well as friends, and his *Exposition of the 39 Articles of the Church of England* (1698), a statement of latitudinarian views, caused a first-class storm between the two houses of Convocation. In Anne's reign he spoke vigorously for Occasional Conformity and against Sacheverell, for the Union with Scotland and against the Peace proposals of 1711. Yet his greatest achievement was a non-controversial one. It was Burnet who had pressed William to transfer the proceeds of the first-fruits and tenths, annexed by the Crown at the Reformation and now being enjoyed by such inappropriate beneficiaries as a son of Nell Gwynne, to a fund to relieve clergymen in poor benefices, and who persuaded his successor to do so in 1704 — thus establishing Queen Anne's Bounty.

His *History of My Own Time*, published after his death (the first volume in 1723, the second in 1734), is an invaluable source of material about the years 1660–89. Often inaccurate, prejudiced, not particularly elegant in style (Horace Walpole talks of Burnet's 'rough chisel'), its value lies in the sheer blunt force of its narrative and in its detailed information about the personalities of the period.

Burnet conceived it originally in the form of memoirs and though he
re-cast and re-wrote extensively, the work has the intimate and
urgent flavour of the memoirs of a man of strong opinions who liked
to be at the centre of affairs. And his learning, his travels, his broad
common sense and essential liberality of mind, his reflection on the
purpose of historical writing, made his work far more than a
partisan apologia for early Whiggery.

T. E. S. Clarke and H. C. Foxcroft, *Life of Gilbert Burnet*, 1907.
Mary Delorue, 'Gilbert Burnet', *History Today*, September 1979.

JOHN TILLOTSON, (1630–94), Archbishop of Canterbury,
was the son of a well-to-do Halifax clothworker who was at one
time a prominent member of a Puritan congregation. Educated at
Clare, Cambridge, where he was elected a Fellow in 1651, he
departed from the Calvinism of his early years under the influence of
the writings of Chillingworth. Appointed lecturer at the church of
St. Lawrence Jewry and preacher at Lincoln's Inn (1665), Tillotson
won an immense reputation in Charles II's reign as a preacher, plain
and direct in style, stressing man's moral duty and emphasizing the
place of reason in religion. He was a vigorous opponent, in pamphlet
and pulpit, of the claims of Rome, as for example in a famous
sermon before the Commons on the anniversary of Gunpowder Plot
in 1678. Dean of Canterbury from 1672, after the Revolution he
was appointed Dean of St. Paul's. Appropriately for a man who had
appeared on the nonconforming side at the Savoy Conference,
Tillotson was a supporter of the Toleration Act of 1689 and was
energetic in promoting the abortive scheme of comprehension of the
same year. In 1691, when Sancroft was deprived, Tillotson became
Archbishop of Canterbury. His tenure was brief, for he died in 1694,
yet the appointment of a churchman of latitudinarian views to the
primacy was a significant milestone in the history of religion in
England. His practical religion — reasonable, charitable, temperate,
lacking the heat and passion of the previous generation but not yet
sunk in the complacency of the next — represented the strongest
element in the Anglicanism of his time.

THOMAS TENISON, (1636–1715), Archbishop of Canterbury, was born at Cottenham, in Cambridgeshire, the son of a

Norfolk rector. Educated at Corpus Christi College, Cambridge, of which he became a Fellow, he was ordained in 1659. From 1680 to 1691 he was Rector of St. Martin's in the Fields. Here he won a reputation as preacher and pamphleteer. Moreover, in Burnet's words, 'Whitehall lying within that parish, he stood as in the front of the battle all King James's reign'. For Tenison was strongly anti-Catholic, and enjoyed a vigorous controversy with the Jesuits. In 1688 he was a prominent supporter of the Seven Bishops, and he was well-informed about the projected invasion of that year: his close friend Evelyn recorded under 10 August that 'Dr. Tenison now told me there would suddenly be some great thing discovered'. His promotion after the Revolution was rapid, for he was Bishop of Lincoln in 1691 and he succeeded Tillotson at Canterbury in 1694. He owed advancement undoubtedly to his latitudinarian views and to his moderation towards Dissenters, reflecting an outlook with which William III was in close accord. Politically he was a Whig, and his appointment sharpened the divisions which already existed between a bench of Bishops who were mainly 'Low Church' and the 'High Church' majority of the lesser clergy. Moreover, the confidence of William meant the hostility of Anne, who took advice on ecclesiastical questions from Sharp of York rather than from Tenison. It was one of the ironies of the reign of a Queen whose main interest was the Church of England that she was on bad terms with the Archbishop of Canterbury — and he outlived her. Tenison compounded his disfavour by opposing the Occasional Conformity Bill and by keeping in steady contact with Hanover. He was an active supporter of the Scottish Union of 1707, defending it by arguments showing a broad clarity towards Presbyterianism. He was at the head of the list of Lords Justices appointed by the Hanoverian successor in 1714, and lived long enough to see George I installed in 1715. As in doctrine, so in the range of his social concern Tenison foreshadowed the eighteenth century. While he was at St. Martin's he opened the first public library in London; he endowed a school: he played a central part in the foundation of the Society for the Propagation of the Gospel in Foreign Parts (1701); and he was also prominent in the movement in Anne's reign for the reformation of manners.

E. F. Carpenter, *Thomas Tenison, Archbishop of Canterbury*, 1948.

SIR JOHN HOLT (1642–1710), judge, was born at Thame, the son of a barrister, and educated at Abingdon Grammar School, Winchester, and Oriel College, Oxford. From Gray's Inn he was called to the bar in 1663, and he had a notable career as a counsel, appearing for the Catholic Peers during the Popish Plot as well as for Lord Russell after the Rye House Plot. Holt was appointed Recorder of London in 1686 but resigned next year when he declined to obey what he regarded as James II's illegal command to sentence deserters from the army to death in peace time. A man of Whig views, he approved of the Revolution, and in 1689 he was appointed Chief Justice of the King's Bench, a post which he held until the end of his life. Holt probably did more than any other single man to liberalize English justice in the years after the Glorious Revolution, and thus to secure for posterity one of the principal benefits of that event. The contrast between his conduct of trials and that of such recent judges as Scroggs and Jeffreys was profound, even if the immediate changes in legal procedure were relatively few. Where they had bullied the defendant and hectored witnesses, he was eminently fair in his attitude and excluded irrelevant evidence which might damage the accused. His cast of mind was liberal: he disapproved of standing armies, disliked informers, and was sceptic about witches. As his judgment in *Smith v. Browne and Others* showed, he believed that no Negro could be held in slavery on English soil. In the extra-ordinary case of Charles Knollys, who committed murder and claimed to be called to the Lords as Earl of Banbury so that he could be tried by his peers Holt firmly defended the independence of the bench when the Lords summoned the judges to appear and explain their verdict, saying 'I am not to be arraigned for what I do judicially'. The celebrated electoral case of *Ashby v. White*, in which a Whig cobbler of Aylesbury claimed that he had been deprived of his right to vote by the Tory Mayor White, came before Holt in Anne's reign, and Holt held for Ashby on the ground that a vote was a property right. By these and other decisions Holt exercised a lasting influence upon the development of English law.

SIR JOHN FENWICK (1645?–97), Jacobite conspirator, was a professional soldier and member of a distinguished Northumberland family who had been M.P. for that county. From 1688 onwards he plotted persistently against William and he was briefly imprisoned in 1689. An insolent swaggerer, he deliberately insulted Queen Mary in Hyde Park, and William bore him an unusual hostility. He was deeply involved in the Assassination Plot of 1696; his task was to lead a revolt after the murder of the King. Upon the discovery of the plot Fenwick went into hiding, and when he was captured made, in the hope of pardon, a confession which alleged that Godolphin, Marlborough, Shrewsbury and other leading men were implicated. He also bribed the two informers who were the two principal witnesses against him to leave the country. One did; but the other took Fenwick's money and stayed to give evidence. The Commons condemned his confession as false and scandalous, and the Whigs, infuriated by his revelations — which contained little truth — brought in a Bill of Attainder against him. Despite strong feelings that such a step was unjust and unwarrantable, it was carried by narrow majorities in both houses. Fenwick was beheaded on Tower Hill in 1697, the last victim of attainder in English history.

SIR JOSIAH CHILD (1630–99), merchant-prince, was the son of a London merchant. He laid the foundations of his fortune at Portsmouth, in brewing and in providing stores for the Navy, became mayor of the town in 1658, and continued to amass money after the Restoration. After trying in vain in 1668 he got the Navy victualling contract in 1672. Child was the type of businessman, ambitious and dictatorial, for whom money and power go together. Evelyn's description of him as 'most sordidly avaricious' tells only half the truth. Pepys noted in his *Diary* the Duke of York's hostility to the proposal that Child should become a Commissioner of the Admiralty: for Child was both a parvenu and, at this stage, a Whig. But it was to be the East India Company which, so far as possible, satisfied Josiah Child's ambition and gave him his place in history. He first became a stockholder in 1671 and a director in 1674, and in 1681 he was chosen Governor of the Company. For nearly all the next ten years he was either Governor or Deputy Governor (each office could be held for two years only in succession), and for the rest of his life he was the dominant figure in the Company, exercising a despotic and disliked authority. In the 1680s things were difficult for the Company, and Child secured royal favour by presenting the King with 10,000 guineas annually from 1681 to 1688. He had evidently abandoned Whiggery; indeed, he supported James II too warmly, and fell out of favour in 1689. Although he retained his hold on the Company, his autocracy was one of the factors which led to the foundation of the rival New East India Company in 1698. Socially, Child prospered. He bought the estate of Wanstead Abbey in 1673, became a baronet in 1678, and married his daughter to the heir of the Duke of Beaufort in 1682. In economic matters Child, beneath a superficial liberalism, was a man of mercantilist ideas. His *New Discourse of Trade*, probably the most widely-read of all seventeenth-century economic writings, advocated the reduction of the legal interest rate, yet accepted the need to check the export of bullion and to restrict the import of foreign manufactures.

W. Letwin, *Sir Josiah Child, Merchant Economist*, 1959.

SIR JOHN BANKS (1627–99), financier, was the son of a prosperous Maidstone business man. His own entry into public affairs came when in 1652 he joined a syndicate formed to victual the Navy; by the time of his death nearly half a century later he had done much to finance the wars of Cromwell and Charles II against the Dutch and of William III against the French, and in the process made himself one of the wealthiest men in England. He had also married (1654) the daughter of a wealthy London merchant and alderman and secured the future by a substantial financial settlement; built up a group of landed estates in Kent and bought himself a fine house in Lincoln's Inn Fields; served as a member of two Parliaments during the Protectorate, and of eight more under the later Stuarts; been first a Director and then Governor of the wealthiest corporation in the land, the East India Company; married (1678) his eldest daughter to the Lord Chancellor's son and thus linked his fortunes with the powerful political clan of the Finches; and been on friendly terms not only with men of Pepys' standing but also with James Duke of York and with Shaftesbury.

Banks was a parvenu, in Evelyn's words of 1678 'a merchant of small beginnings, [who] by usurie, etc., amassed an estate of 100,000 pounds'; twenty years later it was almost £200,000. The wealth came from many diverse sources — naval contracts for canvas and saltpetre; trade with the Levant, the East Indies and New England in cloth and lead, pepper and diamonds; the sale of grain,

hops, fat cattle, timber and fruit from his Kentish lands, as well as
the rents from them; investments; and above all from the profits of
loans, to numerous private individuals as well as to government.
Banks swiftly perceived the virtues of liquidity: his ability to supply
cash showed itself shortly after the Restoration when — a man still
in his middle thirties — he took over the repayment of a royal debt
of £2,700 (and seems to have made 63% profit in six months, with a
baronetcy into the bargain). The times favoured him, for the second
half of the seventeenth century brought not only a great expansion of
European overseas trade and colonisation, but also the urgent need
of the Crown to foot the bills of great European wars against the
Dutch and the French.

Banks had the qualities to seize the opportunity, with rich success.
A skilful financial manipulator and supple bargainer, never willing
to let his money lie idle, always with an eye to the main chance
(measured in interest and discount); endlessly industrious, precise
and methodical in his accounts; he took pains also to cultivate
influential company, whether at Court, the Admiralty or the Royal
Society. Moreover, quintessentially the business man, Banks rode
out the political and religious storms of Republic and Restoration,
Exclusion and Revolution, remarkably comfortably. Never a fanatical Puritan, he moved easily into a moderate Anglicanism. His
politics were far from ardent. In the Commons he served on
numerous committees, mostly on economic matters, but seems never
once in his twenty-six years as an M.P. to have made a speech to the
Commons in full session. He opposed Exclusion, despite his friendship with Shaftesbury; as a Deputy-Lieutenant of Kent he said 'no'
to two of James II's 'Three Questions' in 1688 and took a moderate
Tory line against him at the Revolution; but followed Nottingham
and the other Finches against offering the throne to William and
Mary. This did not stop him from making a series of large loans to
William's government throughout the 1690s.

Sir John Banks scarcely sounds an attractive man, and his portrait,
attributed to Lely, suggests some insensitivity and a hir.: of arrogance. Successful financiers are not always popular. The Whigs did
not like Banks, and the Kent country gentry were ready to condemn
him in terms like those used in 1667 as a 'newly made baronet from a
father that had been a shopman'. Yet two comments may fairly be
made about his career. One is that, as Professor Coleman puts it, he

'obviously preferred profits to power'*. In this he contrasts sharply
with his more notorious contemporary Sir Josiah Child. Secondly,
whatever his motives, Banks' financial expertise was unquestionably
advantageous to his country. It was an aspect of patriotism as well as
of the wish for political stability which marked his entire career, and
one peculiarly appropriate to the age of growing moderation and
compromise through which he lived.

D.C. Coleman, *Sir John Banks*, 1963.

WILLIAM PATERSON, (1658–1719), company-promoter, was
a Scot from Dumfriesshire who came to England as a boy, prospered
in trade, especially with the West Indies, and by the 1690s was well
known in the City of London. An odd mixture of shrewdness and
folly, Paterson belonged to the race of 'projectors' who flourished in
the later seventeenth century and for whom the trade boom of the
early 1690s provided scope and temptation. He is associated in
British history with two ventures of this period, and it was characteristic of this imaginative and unlucky man that he withdrew early
from the highly successful Bank of England and persevered to the end
in the disastrous Darien scheme. Paterson is generally called 'the
founder of the Bank of England', and he was indeed the leading
figure of the mercantile group who put forward and negotiated with
Charles Montagu, Chancellor of the Exchequer, the scheme on the
lines of which the Bank was created. But he failed to pay up all his
subscription, quarrelled with his fellow-directors over policy, and
resigned in 1695. By this time he was becoming heavily involved in
the development of the Company of Scotland Trading to Africa and
the Indies, the so-called Darien Company, whose creation was
authorized by an Act of the Scottish Estates that May. Paterson had
a well-warranted confidence in the economic prospects of Scotland.
Unhappily, misled by his own successes in the Caribbean and by the
superficial merits of the site of Darien, set between two oceans, he
gave his energies — and much of his own cash — to sending his
fellow-countrymen down a road which was a ghastly dead end. The
withdrawal of the English half of the capital and his own impeachment by the Westminster Parliament in 1695 increased his

* D.C. Coleman, *Sir John Banks*, 1963, p.195.

resentment against a country which he believed had undervalued his own financial acumen, and whetted his enthusiasm to found a Scottish colony in Panama. He himself went to Darien; fever made him desperately ill and killed his wife, but neither this experience nor the expulsion of the colonists by Spain convinced him of the folly of the enterprise. Like most Scots, he blamed William III and the English. He was wise enough in Anne's reign to support the Act of Union (1707), realizing its advantages for Scottish economic development. Yet even here Paterson was unlucky, for it was some years before he got his share of the 'Equivalent' which England paid to solace the investors in the Darien Company.

G. P. Insh, *The Company of Scotland Trading to Africa and the Indies*, (1932).
John Prebble, *The Darien Disaster* (1970).

GREGORY KING (1648–1712), statistician, was born at Lichfield, the son of a mathematician who sent him to school at the age of two and taught him to read the Psalter at three. From Lichfield Grammar School he went as clerk to the antiquary Sir William Dugdale, then Norroy King-of-Arms, and later he was employed by several of the Staffordshire nobility. Going to London in 1672, he worked for John Ogilby the printer, etching plates, making maps and helping to edit Ogilby's Road-Book. He appears also to have acted as a surveyor in planning streets in the Soho district. From 1677, when he was appointed Rouge Dragon Pursuivant, he made his living as a herald, becoming Registrar of the College of Arms in 1684. He was dismissed in 1694 as a result of quarrelling with the Earl Marshal over the arrangements for the funeral of Queen Mary, and thereafter seems to have been employed in the Treasury. King was a man of great ability and wide culture, distinguished in his own day. Yet what has made him of interest to later generations, and of high significance to historians, was the pioneering statistical work he produced in 1696, although it was not published until the beginning of the nineteenth century — his *Natural and Political Observations upon the State and Condition of England*. This was the first careful calculation of the population of England and Wales. Using the Hearth Tax returns, King reckoned 5,500,000 in 1688 — a pretty accurate figure (except for a big over-estimate of those more than sixty years of age). Furthermore, he surveyed the distribution of population according to income among the various classes from peers to paupers, and thus provided a range of valuable material about English society at the time of the Glorious Revolution.

JOHN BELLERS, (1654–1725), Quaker, philanthropist and economic writer, inherited through marriage the manor of Coln St. Aldwyn, in Gloucestershire. Belonging to the second generation of Friends, he symbolizes the early stages of the turn of Quakerism from enthusiasm to good works. He has been called 'the first of the long line of great Quaker philanthropists and the pioneer of modern Christian Socialism', and his most celebrated scheme was his *Proposals for Raising a Colledge of Industry* (1695), which was to maintain the sick and infirm and educate children; such an institution was set up by London Quakers, though on a much less ambitious scale than Bellers had envisaged. He was an early champion of prison reform, wanted hospitals founded to train medical students, and advocated a nationally-planned medical service based on a system of insurance. Bellers had sympathy with the street children and young hooligans of the London of his day, the so-called 'Black Guard', recognizing, as he put it, how much was 'owing to birth and education that hath made the difference between them and us', and he petitioned the Lord Mayor on their behalf, observing that he would be confronted with them on the Day of Judgment. More widely, he wanted to see the establishment of a European state system, involving annual congresses, and the creation of a supreme court to settle international disputes. There was a refreshing tang about some of his observations: as, for example, 'Mohammedans are men and beating out their brains to put sense into them is a great mistake', or 'What is prayed for of God above, men must be instrumental to accomplish here below, there being few, if any, who believe He will make His angels visible to do it'. His economic writings, like his social and international docrines, were well in advance of their time; and his anticipation of the labour theory of value interested Karl Marx as well as Robert Owen. But his influence in his lifetime was restricted to his own community.

W. C. Braithwaite, *The Second Period of Quakerism*, 1961 ed.

ANTHONY À WOOD (1632–95), the Oxford antiquary, was born in a house opposite Merton College, the house where he lived all his days. Educated at New College School, Thame Grammar School, and Merton, where he was admitted as an undergraduate in 1647, Wood inherited a modest independent income, sufficient to enable him to devote his life to the collection of materials for the history of Oxford and, in particular, of the University and its members. Two volumes were published in his lifetime — the *Historia et Antiquitates Universitatis Oxoniensis* (1691–2). He left also at his death many other papers, including a good deal of autobiographical material; and the whole collection has been of great value to historians, not least in providing a view of Oxford during the revolutionary years of the seventeenth century. Wood was an unattractive character — peevish, spiteful and quarrelsome, living alone in a couple of attics, growing more bitter as the years increased his deafness, morbidly interested in mortality and illness. His dealings with the kindly Aubrey, who supplied him with an immense quantity of information, do him little credit. He was extremely unpopular in Oxford and was at one time suspected of being a Papist. In 1693 he was at the instance of the second Earl of Clarendon accused of libelling the first Earl, Charles II's minister, in *Athenae Oxonienses*, and the book was publicly burned. Yet the savagery which made his contemporaries hate him gives a tang to his account of Restoration Oxford and a sharp individuality to his comments on events and persons. A gossip and an abusive one, educated, shrewd, utterly reactionary, Wood had the diarist's eye for detail and flair for the pithy phrase. He died in 1695, having set his papers in order and supervised the digging of his grave in Merton.

The Life and Times of Anthony à Wood, ed. Llewelyn Powis, 1961, is an abridgment of the five volumes edited by Andrew Clark, 1891–1900.

JOHN RADCLIFFE (1652?–1714), physician and benefactor of Oxford, was a Yorkshireman, the son of a Wakefield attorney whose Puritan sympathies seem to have secured him the post of Governor of the local House of Correction. Educated at Wakefield Grammar School and University College, Oxford, he was elected a Fellow of Lincoln in 1669. Turning to the study of medicine, he began to practise in Oxford in 1675, and moved to London in 1684, settling first in a house next door to Kneller in Covent Garden and later in Bloomsbury Square. Radcliffe seems to have been a highly successful doctor from the start, and at the height of his career in London was said to be making £7,000 per annum. His success certainly did not rest upon profound knowledge. It came rather from a flair for diagnosis and a contempt for many of the orthodox remedies of his day. Like Sydenham he advocated fresh air, he disliked the custom of bleeding patients, and he recommended his 'bitter', a tincture which, it was claimed, 'corrects all irregularities of the Head and Stomach by hard drinking or otherwise'. Moreover, he won royal patronage quickly, becoming Physician to the Princess Anne in 1686 and to William III after the Revolution. Consciously a 'character', Radcliffe was arrogant, rude, and outspoken, particularly in his cups. He lost his appointment with Anne in 1694 when he told a messenger who interrupted a drinking-party to summon him to the princess that 'her Highness's distemper was nothing but the vapours'. He sat in the Commons as a High Tory and his political sympathies were Jacobite: he had been a pupil of Obadiah Walker, the Master of University College and James II's chief agent in the attempted Romanization of Oxford, and befriended him after his downfall. On his death in 1714 he left £140,000, and Oxford was his principal legatee, gaining in particular the Radcliffe Camera as an addition to the Bodleian Library, and the Radcliffe Infirmary.

C. R. Hone, *The Life of Dr. John Radcliffe*, 1950.

CELIA FIENNES (1662–1741), was the daughter of Colonel Nathaniel Fiennes, the unlucky Parliamentarian Commander who surrendered Bristol to Prince Rupert in 1643, and the grand-daughter of 'Old Subtlety', the Puritan Viscount Saye and Sele, one of Charles I's leading opponents. During the reigns of James II and William III, riding on horseback and accompanied by a servant or two, she travelled extensively throughout England and into both Scotland and Wales; and she has left a full and lively record of her tours and travels in her *Journeys*, an account most of which was probably written in 1702. As a first-hand description of late seventeenth-century England it is quite invaluable, for Celia Fiennes was a woman of abundant vitality and assured social status who had a passion for facts and a breathless zest for writing them down. Dissenting and Whig by family background, she moved confidently in the world of trade and industry as well as among the landed gentry; perhaps prim in manner, she was clearly vigorous and persistent in her interests and questions, and the directness of her style is merely strengthened by a paucity of punctuation and by spelling which is weird even by the standards of her time. She ranged easily and agreeably from 'spaws' to coalmines, from holy wells to Westminster Hall, from the 'very strong' ale of Yorkshire to the 'clouted cream' of Cornwall. She took in her stride mansions like Chatsworth, Lowther and Mount Edgcumbe, the paper mills of Canterbury and the dockyards of Plymouth, highwaymen, bad inns, appalling roads, local superstitions, parliamentary elections and the Lord Mayor's Show. She is commemorated by a memorial inscription in the church of Newton Toney, near Salisbury, the village in whose manor house she was born.

Christopher Morris (ed.), *The Journeys of Celia Fiennes*, rev. ed., 1972.

WILLIAM DAMPIER (1651–1715), buccaneer and writer, came from farming stock at East Coker, near Yeovil, learned some arithmetic and Latin at school, and was put to sea at seventeen with a Weymouth trader. In the next five years he sailed to Newfoundland and the East Indies and fought in the Third Dutch War. Then in 1674 he spent a year on a Jamaica plantation belonging to the squire of East Coker, and after a spell of logwood-cutting in Campeche, where he began to keep a diary, he drifted into buccaneering. He was one of the gang of five hundred who in 1679–81 took Portobelo and looted the Isthmus and the coasts of Peru and Chile. In 1682–3 he was in Virginia, and he spent the next eight years on a series of privateering and piratical voyages that took him to Cape Verde and Sierra Leone, across the 'South Seas' and round the Horn, to the East Indies, the Philippines and the coasts of Australia. Marooned on the Nicobar Islands, he got to Sumatra, and by 1691 he was back in England, bringing with him a Malay boy who soon died of smallpox, and a journal which he had carried about with him in hollow bamboos. We know little of what Dampier did during the next six years, but in 1697 he published *A New Voyage Round the*

World, the record of his adventures. This brought him fame. Pepys had him to dinner with Evelyn, and Hans Sloane got Thomas Murray to paint the portrait now in the National Portrait Gallery. Besides its agreeable style and charm as an adventure story, the book revealed Dampier as a discerning and scientific observer of natural phenomena. Together with his *Discourse of Winds* (1699), which examined in particular the wind-system of the Pacific, it did much to stimulate informed interest in the southern oceans during the eighteenth century.

Success also brought responsibility to Dampier, and this was unfortunate. Evelyn had noted that 'he seemed a (more) modest man, than one would imagine, by the relation of the crew he had sorted with'. Dampier was a tough, skilled seaman, but he was no disciplinarian or leader of men. In 1699 he was sent in command of H.M.S. *Roebuck* on a voyage of exploration, in which he sailed along the western shores of Australia and, striking north around New Guinea, discovered Dampier Strait and the New Britain archipelago. But the *Roebuck* was wrecked off Ascension Island, and when Dampier got home in 1702 he was court-martialled for his unjust treatment of his lieutenant, and declared 'not fit to be employed as a commander of H.M. ships'. This verdict did not prevent him being sent out again in 1703 in command of the privateer *St. George*, whose travels were dismally unsuccessful, with mutinies, desertions, an almost total lack of prizes, and the imprisonment of Dampier in the Dutch East Indies. He got home in 1707 poorer in cash and repute, and he never commanded at sea again, although he served as pilot on Woodes Rogers' successful privateering expedition of 1708–11. Dampier died in London in 1715, by his writings as much as by his voyages the forerunner of Cook.

Dampier's Voyages, ed. John Masefield (1906) and Sir Albert Gray (1927).
Clennell Wilkinson, *William Dampier*, 1929.
Christopher Lloyd, *William Dampier*, 1966.

WILLIAM KIDD (*c.* 1645–1701), pirate, was born at Greenock, son of a covenanting minister. He went to sea as a boy, settled in the American colonies, and commanded a privateer in William III's war against the French, receiving £150 reward from New York City in 1691. He was recommended in 1695 to the Governor of Massachusetts, who gave him a special commission, drawn under the Great Seal, to seize and hang pirates in the eastern seas, and in 1696 Kidd set sail in the *Adventure*, first to New York and thence to the coast of Madagascar. By 1698 there were stories that Kidd himself had turned pirate, and when he returned to Boston in the summer of 1699 he was arrested. The main complaint against him involved a French vessel, the *Queda Merchant*, alleged to have been carrying £70,000 treasure. Kidd's version threw blame on his own mutinous crew. In 1700 he and his companions were sent to England for trial. It was Kidd's misfortune that his case became involved in the contemporary political attack on Somers, who as Lord Keeper had issued the original commission, and the trial was notably prejudiced. Eventually Kidd was condemned on a charge of murdering one of his crew by hitting him over the head with a bucket, and hanged at Wapping Old Stairs in 1701. Some of the treasure was recovered, and part of it was spent by the Commissioners of Greenwich Hospital on buying the Queen's House, the lovely building by Inigo Jones which now forms part of the National Maritime Museum at Greenwich.

G. Brooks, ed., *The Trial of Captain Kidd*, 1930.

HENRY PURCELL (1659?–95), musician, was probably born at Westminster of a Shropshire family. His father became a gentleman of the Chapel Royal in 1660, and Purcell himself was a chorister there. He was appointed composer-in-ordinary to the King in 1677 and organist of Westminster Abbey in 1679. By this time he had already written a number of anthems, including possibly 'They that go down to the sea in ships'. Certainly in his early twenties Purcell was already active in the full range of his very varied compositions, writing fantasias for stringed instruments, odes and 'welcome songs', and musical dramas. In 1682 he was appointed organist of the Chapel Royal, and in 1683 his first printed composition, a group of sonatas, appeared, as well as the first of his 'Odes for St. Cecilia's Day'. For the coronation of James II in 1685 he wrote the anthem 'My heart is inditing'. The years 1688–90 saw the writing and production of the opera *Dido and Aeneas*, and in 1691

Henry Purcell c.1695
(Artist: John Closterman)

came *King Arthur*. For the funeral of Queen Mary, early in 1695, he wrote 'Thou knowest, Lord'. Purcell himself died later that same year. He was still only in his middle thirties, and his output had been immense, including seventy-nine anthems and other sacred works, over fifty dramatic pieces and thirty-two odes, as well as numerous fantasias, sonatas, harpsichord pieces, and songs of various kinds. Purcell was both a gifted singer and an erudite musician much influenced by French and Italian work. In vocal and choral music he has remained unrivalled by any Englishman: the death-song of Dido — 'Dido's Lament', a splendid example of a ground bass — revealed his extraordinary mastery of song, while his use of choruses had substantial influence upon Handel. His work as a whole illustrates the curious balance which late seventeeth-century England struck between the sacred and the secular. In some ways he began a new age, for while his anthems maintained the tradition of Byrd and Gibbons, his dramatic and operatic work pointed to the future. Purcell's achievement was a peak from which there was a sudden descent, for no English composer of comparable genius was to appear for two hundred years.

A.K.Holland, *Henry Purcell*, 1948.
Curtis Price, *Henry Purcell and the London Stage*, 1984.

WILLIAM CONGREVE (1670–1729), playwright, born at Bardsey, near Leeds, went as a child to Ireland where his father was an army officer, and was educated, like Swift, at Kilkenny Grammar School and Trinity College, Dublin. He studied law at the Middle Temple, produced some mediocre verse and a bad novel, helped Dryden with his succession of classical translations, and, between 1693 and 1700, wrote the series of comedies of manners upon which his reputation rests. *Love for Love*, the most popular of his plays, was first produced in 1695. Congreve, the most notable of the 'Restoration dramatists', wrote all his plays in the reign of William III. Although he lived nearly thirty years longer, he produced no drama after *The Way of the World* (1700). His plays were denounced for their immorality by Jeremy Collier and by the Society for the Reformation of Manners, and his brittle cynicism went rather out of fashion in Anne's reign. Congreve was a successful sinecurist, drawing money from licensing hackney coaches and wine, and, after 1714, from the secretaryship for Jamaica. A member of the Kit-Cat Club, he was also on friendly terms both with Swift and with Pope.

J.C.Hodges, *William Congreve: The Man*, 1941.

QUEEN ANNE (1665–1714), was born in St. James's Palace, the second daughter of James, Duke of York, and his first wife, Anne Hyde. As befitted the grand-daughter of Clarendon, she was brought

Queen Anne
(Artist: studio of John Closterman)

up in the Anglican faith. She was a plain girl; her looks came from
the Hydes, not from her paternal grandmother, Henrietta Maria. In
1683 she married Prince George of Denmark. Five years later, under
the guidance of John Churchill, later Duke of Marlborough, and his
wife Sarah, for many years Anne's intimate friend, she deserted her
father in the Revolution and joined William of Orange and his wife,

her sister Mary. The Declaration of Rights of 1688 made her the heir-presumptive to the throne. The lack of issue of William and Mary and the death of the latter in 1694 ensured her succession, confirmed under the Act of Settlement (1701), when William died in 1702.

There is a sharp and poignant contrast between the glories of Anne's reign and the pathetic, limited qualities of the Queen herself. Unintelligent, narrow, conventional, with the uncharitableness and ingratitude of the Stuarts, more distinguished for her appetite than for her conversation, Anne could never have been a great queen. Like Victoria, she had a strong sense of duty and a genuine piety. But she entirely lacked the relentless determination and, more serious, the robust constitution of Queen Victoria. Behind the high political problem of the English succession in the early eighteenth century lies the endless personal frustration and pain of Anne, to whom eighteen pregnancies had given only five children born alive — and from whom all five had been taken young, the last, the Duke of Gloucester, dying at the age of ten in 1700. When she ascended the throne Anne was a chronic invalid. To physical pain there was joined a nagging unease of conscience, over her treatment of her father in 1688 and afterwards over her unhealed quarrel with her sister Mary, and over her exclusion from the throne of her half-brother the Old Pretender. The death of her well-loved husband in 1708 was a cruel blow; the break with Sarah in 1710 was another, for all the immediate relief it doubtless brought.

These sources of personal unhappiness had political significance, for monarchy was still essentially personal. In effect they increased her inevitable dependence upon her ministers, making possible both the domination exercised by 'Mr. and Mrs. Freeman' (the Marlboroughs) over 'poor dear unfortunate Mrs. Morley' up to 1710 and the success of Harley's employment of Mrs. Masham to bring that domination to an end. It is difficult to detect the independent mind or hand of Anne in any of the major decisions of her reign, like the commitment to 'No peace without Spain', or the Scottish Union, or the Utrecht settlement. Nor is it possible to credit Anne herself with deep prescience or great authority in changing her ministers before holding a general election in which the new ministers were triumphant, as she did four times. She liked to make her right to choose her ministers a reality, and in detail her preferences might be decisive; but there were very firm practical limits to her power, as was shown in February 1708 when at Harley's instigation she tried to remove Godolphin and had after a week to get rid of Harley instead. She was hostile to and suspicious of party — like most important contemporaries, including many partisans. In 1708 she wrote to Marlborough: 'The parties are such bugbears that I dare not venture to write my mind freely of either of them without a cypher, for fear of any accident. I pray God keep me out of the hands of both of them.' Yet in practice she found herself in the hands of the Whigs between 1708 and 1710, and of the Tories from 1710 to 1714.

Anne was not negligible. She could be very obstinate, as for example when she persevered for two months in 1702 to have Prince George made allied Commander-in-Chief. Her prejudices, or wishes, on certain subjects had to be respected, and she would never have the heir to the throne, the Electress Sophia of Hanover, in England. In particular she had strong, though not always clear, High Church views and a high regard for the religious functions of the monarchy. She 'touched' for the 'king's evil'; she founded (1704) Queen Anne's bounty to add to the stipends of ill-paid clergymen; she concerned herself very directly and thoughtfully with high ecclesiastical appointments. By no means all of these went to High Churchmen, for she seems genuinely to have tried to choose on merit. During the Sacheverell Trial she did not disguise her sympathies for the doctor, but she never promoted him even to a deanery, nor (for rather different reasons) would she give Swift a bishopric.

Firmly patriotic, Anne presided with pride and personal satisfaction over the long roll of Marlborough's victories up to 1709. But when the rift came she acted characteristically, dismissing Godolphin in 1710 by a written message with no word of thanks, and Marlborough in 1711 by a letter 'so very offensive that the Duke flung it into the fire'. In the last years of her reign her ill-health increased, and at Christmas 1713 she recovered, but it was clear that she would not live long. The Tory leaders, Oxford and Bolingbroke, were quarrelling, and eventually Anne yielded to the latter's pressure, exerted through Mrs. Masham, and dismissed Oxford. There was a scene at the Council, with violent accusations in front of the ailing Queen. That was on 27 July. Two days later Anne was taken seriously ill; on the 30th, when it was clear that she was dying, she gave the White Staff of the Treasureship to the neutral Protestant Shrewsbury, thus ensuring the Hanoverian Succession. She died at Kensington Palace in the early morning of 1 August, the last of the Stuart rulers of England.

J. P. Kenyon, *The Stuarts*, 1958, pp. 205-27.
David Green, *Queen Anne*, 1970.
Edward Gregg, *Queen Anne*, 1980.

PRINCE GEORGE OF DENMARK (1653–1708), Queen Anne's consort, was a notably undistinguished person who found appropriate place in the unkind rhyme composed about the royal family shortly after the Revolution:

> 'King William thinks all,
> Queen Mary talks all,
> Prince George drinks all,
> And Princess Anne eats all.'

He married Anne in 1683, and they were a devoted couple for the remainder of their days. A heavy eater as well as drinker, dull and unimaginative, he played a very minor role in English political life. He had been a competent soldier as a young man, and Anne tried hard in 1702 to have him appointed Commander-in-Chief of the allied armies fighting Louis XIV, but the allies would not stomach him; instead he became and remained till his death, Lord High Admiral, an office in which he was effectively dominated by Marlborough's brother, Admiral George Churchill. A parliamentary grant of £100,000 per annum for life was made to him. His vote was useful in the Lords: thus in 1702, even though he was himself a Lutheran, he did as he was told and voted for the Occasional Conformity Bill. For the rest, whether from prudence, idleness, or stupidity, he kept out of politics and did not seek after popularity. This was probably very fortunate indeed at that stage in the evolution of the monarchy. He was a patron of science and was on friendly terms with Newton. A kindly man, liked by his servants, perhaps not quite so absurd as he has been made out to be, he died in 1708, deeply mourned by Anne.

JOHN CHURCHILL, DUKE OF MARLBOROUGH (1650–1722), was a Devonian, probably born at Great Trill in the parish of Axminster, son of a country gentleman, Winston Churchill, who impoverished his family by fighting on the Cavalier side in the Civil Wars. Educated at St. Paul's School and, more effectively, at the Court of Charles II, he became at the age of sixteen a page to James, Duke of York, whose mistress was Churchill's sister Arabella. Churchill's own liaison with Charles II's mistress Barbara Villiers, Duchess of Cleveland, did no harm to his prospects, and, indeed, provided him with large sums of money. Yet the two most important results of his career at court were military apprenticeship and matrimony. As a soldier he served at Tangier and in the Third Dutch War (1672–4), commanding a regiment in Flanders under the celebrated Turenne. For his wife he chose in 1678 Sarah Jennings, a beautiful Maid of Honour; it was a marriage of love, not of convenience. The Duke of York remained his patron throughout Charles's reign. So Churchill went with him into exile during the climax of the Exclusion controversy; so too he enjoyed royal favour in the years 1681–5, and Sarah became Lady of the Bedchamber to the Princess Anne.

With James on the throne (1685–8) Churchill's wealth and esteem increased. He was made a baron at the coronation, and he played a decisive role in the defeat of Monmouth at Sedgemoor. He took no part in the King's Romanizing policy, yet remained on the fringe of the conspiracy against him. Like the Princess Anne, now much under the Churchills' influence, he was a known Anglican. When the crisis came in 1688 he deserted the royal army at Salisbury, a step which did much to make the Revolution bloodless. For a time he enjoyed favour in the new regime. Created Earl of Marlborough, he fought in Flanders (1689) and captured Cork and Kinsale in a swift campaign in Ireland (1690). But William did not trust him, more because of the Churchill influence over Anne, the probable successor to the throne, than because of the contacts which he, like most other leading Englishmen, had with the exiled James II. In 1692 he was dismissed and was for a short time in the Tower. Yet after the Treaty of Ryswick (1697) brought a lull in the wars, William, aware of his military skill as well as of the authority he held over Anne, selected Marlborough as his successor in the great conflict with France. In 1701 Marlborough was named Commander-

John Churchill, Duke of Marlborough
(Artist: Unknown)

in-Chief. In the same year he negotiated the Grand Alliance against Louis XIV, thereby establishing himself as a European figure; and in 1702 the death of William brought Anne to the throne and Marlborough to the chief place in the English state.

Anne reigned for twelve years. For the first six of them, Marlborough was supreme: Commander-in-Chief in what has come to be called 'Marlborough's War', the War of the Spanish Succession, and dominant in counsel at home, exercising his authority through the friend whom he installed as Lord Treasurer, Godolphin. His supremacy rested on two foundations. The less important of these was Sarah's hold upon Anne's affection and confidence; the more, his unparalleled military skill, bringing the great triumphs of Blenheim (1704), Ramillies (1706), and Oudenarde (1708). Yet he was, in the eyes of Europeans, statesman as well as general, the supreme diplomatist who held the alliance against France together and determined its objectives. Only Louis XIV himself was a greater figure in western Europe, and his power was evidently waning before the battle strokes of 'Malbrouck'. His victorious career brought him great rewards. Captain-General, Master General of the Ordnance, a Duke in 1702, a Prince of the Holy Roman Empire in 1705, he received, after Blenheim, the gift of the royal manor of Woodstock and the construction of a palace upon it at national expense.

Within three years of Oudenarde his authority had disintegrated. Between 1707 and 1710 Sarah was ousted from Anne's favour by Harley's creature, Mrs. Masham. This mattered less than changes in the balance of English politics which forced Marlborough into dependence upon the Whigs whom Anne disliked and against whom public opinion turned by 1710; and a great deal less than the growing unpopularity of a war which grew steadily more costly and showed no signs of ending. The policy of 'No peace without Spain', to which first Marlborough and then the Whigs had committed themselves, led to the breakdown of peace negotiations in 1709 and again in 1710. His fourth victory, Malplaquet (1709), was a Pyrrhic one, with the allied losses half as great again as those of the French. And in that same year, in what G. M. Trevelyan called 'one of the very few imprudent acts of his life', he deeply offended the Queen and played into the hands of his opponents by asking, in vain, to be made Captain-General for life.

The dismissal of Godolphin in the summer of 1710 was a turning point in the career of Marlborough, for the new ministry treated him with scant respect. They dismissed Sarah from all her offices at court early in 1711, and they retained the Duke as Commander-in-Chief partly out of regard for the views of their Austrian and Dutch allies, partly in order not to relax pressure on the French while the peace negotiations, which they had reopened, were conducted. For his part he refrained from resigning, it seems, in order that the building of

Blenheim Palace at public expense should continue. In 1711 he won his last victories — the victories which he himself considered his most skilful — in the passage of the *Ne Plus Ultra* lines and the capture of Bouchain, leaving the road to Paris virtually clear. But on 31 December Anne dismissed him by letter.

In 1712 he left England for the Low Countries. He did not return until the summer of 1714, landing just after Anne's death. The Hanoverians restored him at once to his post of Commander-in-Chief, and he guided the campaign against the Fifteen from his armchair, but he never again exercised political authority. Two paralytic strokes in 1716 did much to incapacitate him, yet he lived on until 1722. He was buried in Westminster Abbey. Blenheim Palace, where his body now lies, was not completed until 1727.

Marlborough the soldier stands clear to our vision. No British general of the front rank has been so successful, and Cromwell and Wellington alone challenge comparison. Blenheim was his most celebrated battle, as it was certainly the most decisive in its consequences for all Europe; and perhaps the most celebrated thing about Blenheim was the decision to march to the Danube, an act of daring and surprise which illustrates one of the qualities which made him an outstanding Commander. The many others including the ceaseless attention to detail which did more than anything else to win the affection of his men for 'Corporal John'; the readiness, rare in his age and very rare in relation to the wars of William III's day, to seek battle and victory; and the recognition, founded no doubt on his youthful experiences in Charles II's Dutch Wars, of the place of sea-power in English military campaigns. At Blenheim and at Ramillies he conducted battles which were to a great extent planned and based upon prepared positions; at Oudenarde, with equal success, a much less orthodox affair, with troops fitted into a changing pattern of action. He trained his infantry in disciplined fire, he used cavalry (as Gustavus had used them) for shock rather than fire; above all, perhaps, he devoted care and time to the use and management of his artillery.

Marlborough the man has always been a controversial figure. Macaulay, the most celebrated historian to denounce him, relied unwittingly on inadequate and inaccurate documents; and for his character-judgments, elsewhere as here, he rested on the solid Victorian verities in a way which we reject. Given the standards of

his day, we are not likely to condemn Marlborough for accepting his
sister's lover as his patron, or even for investing some of the money
he got from his own mistress. His contemporaries found him
unusually cautious about money for a man of his rank and were
ready to condemn him as avaricious. It is impossible to deny this
charge, yet we may be ready to pardon him by pointing to the
relative poverty of his early upbringing. Behind his almost unfailing
courtesy and graciousness of manner there often lay, no doubt, a
measure of prudence and of calculation. Marlborough was a self-
made man in a way that was not common among the leading men of
his generation, and he could not easily be imprudent. Nor is it
possible to ignore, in this and other ways, the influence of Sarah
upon him. Devoted to her though he was — and this devotion is one
of his most attractive characteristics — he could scarcely avoid
becoming a patient man.

The most serious charges against Marlborough concern his political activities. His desertion of James in 1688 can be justified, and
even praised unless we are prepared either to accept the complete
validity of the Tory doctrine of non-resistance or to condemn nearly
a whole generation of Protestants with him. Even its calculated
timing can be defended on the ground that it did much to prevent
civil war. His prolonged dealings with the Jacobites can, similarly,
be excused on the plea that many of his contemporaries in the
uncertainties of the age also indulged in them; and it is clear that the
Camaret letter, in which he was believed to have warned the French
of the attack on Brest (1694), may well have been a Jacobite
fabrication. Yet the excuses are thin and the record humiliating
when set alongside the conduct of such a man as Wharton, for
example. Perhaps Berwick's hard-headed judgment was right when,
advising James the Old Pretender to grant the pardon which
Marlborough had stooped to ask in the last months of Anne's reign,
he said 'one may give to those sort of people as good as they bring,
that is words for words, for I see nothing else in all Marlborough
says, and, indeed, he has never behaved himself otherwise'.

It may be that the most serious political criticisms which can be
levied against Marlborough concern his loyal rather than his disloyal
conduct. In its crude form the charge made by the Tories against
him, that he continued the war to maintain himself in power, is
scarcely warranted. But his insistence on the doctrine of 'No peace

without Spain', coupled with his reluctance to release troops from Flanders to serve in the Peninsula; his virtual surrender of political power to the Whigs; his inability to recognize the substance in the growing demand for peace after 1708 — these things indicate a limited statesmanship, and suggest that the man most dazzled by his victories was Marlborough himself. He was the last serving soldier who was at the same time a central figure in British political life, and he was a political failure. In the last analysis Marlborough's fame rests solely upon his achievements upon the battlefield. By them he did more than any other man to break the power of Louis XIV — the work that William III had chosen him to do.

C. T. Atkinson, *Marlborough*, 1921.
W. S. Churchill, *Marlborough: his Life and Times*, 4 vols., 1933-8.
D. G. Chandler, *Marlborough as military commander*, 1973.

SARAH, DUCHESS OF MARLBOROUGH (1660-1744), the daughter of a Hertfordshire landowner named Jennings, was eighteen when she married John Churchill. When the Princess Anne married in 1683 she appointed Sarah, who had been an attendant upon her in Mary of Modena's household, a Lady of her Bedchamber. For over thirty years the careers of 'Mr. and Mrs. Freeman' and 'Mrs. Morley' were interlinked, with great consequences for British history. Sarah was the central link. Marlborough's greatness rests upon his own genius, but his power always in part hung upon his wife's place as royal favourite, and most of all in the first years of Anne's reign before Blenheim had sanctioned his authority. Sarah Churchill had wit, beauty, and character, and was devoted to her husband. She did not dominate his politics: he never followed her Whig partisanship even when he was driven after 1708 to depend upon Whig support of his war. Instead she put at his service her domination of Anne. Masterful, vigorous, shrewd, a brilliant talker, it was Sarah who organized Anne's flight from her father in 1688, and it was to Sarah that Anne remained loyal in William's reign, sacrificing the affection of her sister Mary.

When Anne came to the throne in 1702 Sarah was richly rewarded. Groom of the Stole, Mistress of the Robes, Keeper of the Privy Purse, she was supreme at court. Yet, if Swift is to be trusted, trouble between the two women began early in the reign. In

Sarah, Duchess of Marlborough c.1700
(Artist: after Sir George Kneller)

Professor Kenyon's words, 'qualities that had stimulated an active, discontented young princess only jarred on an ailing, prematurely-aged queen'*. Sarah in middle age grew more imperious, worse-tempered, more the bully than the confidante. The death of her only surviving son from smallpox at seventeen and the prolonged absences of her husband no doubt played their part in hardening her.

* J.P. Kenyon, *The Stuarts*, 1958, pp. 215-16.

W.S.B.—N*

Bickerings grew into quarrels, and it was ironically unfortunate that Anne should turn for relief from hectoring to a woman whose post at court had come through Sarah's patronage, Abigail Masham. From 1707, when Sarah bitterly reproached Anne about her friendship with Abigail, the storms grew, intensified by the policy of Harley. Often enough they were over petty things, like the row of 1709 over the rebuilding of part of Sarah's rooms in St. James' Palace, but behind the trivialities lay great issues — Marlborough's career, the fate of the Whig ministry, and the continuation of the Spanish Succession War. The end of the long friendship came in the painful scene of April 1710, when Sarah forced her way into the royal presence and broke down in hysterical tears while the Queen remained impassive. She was dismissed from all her offices early in 1711. Characteristically, she took away all she could from her palace rooms, even the locks.

The Marlboroughs lived in exile for the last two years of Anne's reign, returning only when the Queen lay dying. Two years later the Duke had a stroke. He lived on, a semi-invalid, until 1722. Sarah outlived him by twenty-two years, certainly one of the most remarkable of the subjects of the early Hanoverians. She completed the great palace of Blenheim at Woodstock. She quarrelled incessantly — with her daughters, with her son-in-law Sunderland, with Walpole, with Vanbrugh, with the Duke's quartermaster-general Cadogan. In Leslie Stephen's words in *D.N.B.*, 'her pugnacity was boundless, and though wrong-headed she was far too shrewd to be contemptible'. Spiteful, vulgar, indefatigable, almost heroic, she published in 1742 a defence of her 'conduct' at court which aroused a considerable controversy. In her will she left £20,000 to the Earl of Chesterfield and £10,000 to William Pitt.

David Green, *Sarah Duchess of Marlborough*, 1967.

SIDNEY, 1ST EARL OF GODOLPHIN (1645-1712), the principal minister of Anne's reign, was a younger son of a leading Cornish landed family. The Godolphins were mainly Royalist in the Civil War; his uncle Sidney, the poet, had been killed in a skirmish at Chagford in 1643; and he himself began his court and political career by becoming a page of honour to Charles II. In 1668 he was elected M.P. for Helston, the town near which Godolphin Manor

still stands, and in the 1670s he played a minor role in several
diplomatic missions, one of which in 1678 brought him close
acquaintance with William of Orange. In the following year he was
appointed one of the Commissioners of the Treasury. It was an
office he was to hold for much of the remainder of his life (he was a
Commissioner 1679–84, 1684–9, 1690–7, 1700–1; and Lord
Treasurer 1702–10), at once the source of his usefulness to successive
monarchs and thus of his political authority, and the clue to an
understanding of his political outlook. He rode out the storms of
1679–81, even though at one stage he committed himself to
Exclusion; in the last years of Charles II he was the least important
of the 'Chits' who conducted the business of government. He
survived James II's reign without compromising himself too deeply,
a courtier who in his office of Lord Chamberlain to the Queen
conducted her to the door of her chapel to attend Mass but refrained
from accompanying her inside. He took some care to maintain
contact with the Prince of Orange, and in 1688 was one of the three
Commissioners whom James sent to treat with the invader. After
James had fled he served William; his experience at the Treasury
commended him, and so did his moderation as a neutral magnate
not too deeply committed to the politics of either Whigs or Tories.
Like nearly all William's servants, however, he kept in touch with
the exiled court at St. Germain; and this was temporarily his
undoing, for the revelations of Sir John Fenwick after the Assassination Plot (1696) implicated him and he was forced out of office. He
was back again, briefly, before William's death.

It was in Anne's reign that Godolphin's career reached its climax.
He had long been friendly with John Churchill, and in 1698 the links
were strengthened by the marriage of his only son Francis to
Churchill's daughter Henrietta. This association, something of a
political liability under William, led Godolphin to the summit of
power upon the accession of Anne (1702), when Churchill (Earl of
Marlborough since 1701) and his wife Sarah dominated the mind of
the Queen. Godolphin — Mr. Montgomery in the correspondence
of Sarah and Anne — became Lord Treasurer, and held office until
1710. What may fairly be called the Marlborough-Godolphin
Ministry won great triumphs in the War of the Spanish Succession;
Godolphin's role was so to manage Parliament and patronage that
financial and political support for the war was always available,

even though the Land Tax went up to 4s. in the £. He was more
responsible than any other statesman for the outstanding legislative
achievement of the reign, the Act of Union with Scotland (1707);
and his reorganization of the East India Company (1708) was also a
notable piece of compromise. Yet his power was never really secure.
He broke with the High Tories, who wanted a limited war rather
than Marlborough's large-scale land campaigns; driven into dependence upon the Whigs, he committed himself to their more foolish
policies like the trial of Dr. Sacheverell (1710). Especially after
1708, the rising costs and seeming endlessness of the war made the
ministry unpopular. Above all, Godolphin lost the Queen's support.
He had upset her as early as 1706 by forcing her to give office to
Whig politicians; his suggestions about episcopal appointments
were tactless; and the quarrel between Anne and Sarah could scarcely
fail to damage him. He was not a European figure and so could be
dispensed with more easily than the Duke. So in August 1710 Anne
dismissed him by letter, commanding him to break his staff of
office. With that ingratitude which was common to the Stuart
rulers, she offered no word of thanks for his eight years of service,
and the pension she promised was never paid. Two years later Sarah
wrote on the first leaf of her Bible 'The 15th of September 1712 at
two in the morning the Earl of Godolphin dyed at the Duke of
Marlborough's hous in St. Albans, who was the best man that ever
lived'.

The most celebrated comment on Godolphin is that of Charles II:
'never in the way, never out of it'. Historians, reflecting as Charles
could not on the later and more significant years of Godolphin's
career, have tended to regard him as essentially a smooth and
accommodating time-server. Macaulay was particularly severe upon
him, commenting at one point 'no part of his life warrants us in
ascribing his conduct to any exalted motive'. It is true that he did not
play a notably heroic part in the era of the 'Glorious Revolution'.
Yet that revolution owes much of its character and its glory to the
fact that its participants abstained from heroics. Godolphin, like
William III, helped to lower the temperature of English politics in
the late seventeenth century. He does not seem to have been
particularly popular, even though his chief interests outside politics
were gaming and racehorses. His fame rests firmly upon his eight
years as chief minister under Anne, when contemporaries called him

'prime minister'. But it is difficult to use that phrase of him in anything like its modern sense, nor did he ever possess the personal authority of Walpole a generation later. The constitutional role of 'the clockwork Godolphin' (Sir George Clark's phrase) in an age when royal power was still real, the cabinet embryonic and parties a novelty, is hard to define. Nominally a moderate Tory, he was in fact non-party, saving the Queen, in the words of her plea of 1705, from 'the power of the merciless men of both parties'; and viewing the task of government, especially in relation to the war with Louis XIV, from a standpoint resembling that of the senior civil servant more than that of the party politician of to-day.

G. M. Trevelyan, *England under Queen Anne*, 3 vols., 1930–4.
Sir Tresham Lever, *Godolphin, His Life and Times*, 1952.
A. L. Rowse, 'The Godolphin-Marlborough Duumvirate', *History Today*, March 1976.

ADMIRAL SIR GEORGE ROOKE (1650–1709), the captor of Gibraltar, had fought at Beachy Head and La Hogue; he had been Commander-in-Chief both in the Mediterranean and in the Channel; and in 1700 he had been in command of a fleet supporting Charles XII of Sweden against the Danes in the Sound. Loyal, honest, cantankerous, Rooke was a capable rather than an imaginative admiral. He has been described as 'a sluggish, wary man whose imagination had no room for great designs' *; he was certainly very hostile to the policy of British naval control of the Mediterranean. In 1702 he had put to sea, with a force of soldiers under Ormonde, to take Cadiz. The expedition had been a fiasco, redeemed only by the chance discovery on the way home that a Spanish treasure-fleet, guarded by fifteen French ships of the line, was sheltering in Vigo Bay. Rooke's force sailed up the narrow inlet and destroyed the warships, although most of the treasure seems to have been removed before the battle. Two years later, in 1704, Rooke entered the Mediterranean with the object of combining with the Duke of Savoy's army in an attack upon Toulon. This proved impossible. Nor did the landing of 1,600 marines near Barcelona, then under French control, provoke the Catalans to rise in revolt. The marines

* W. S. Churchill, *Marlborough*, 1967 ed., Vol. II, p. 84.

were re-embarked, and the fleet sailed off in search of other prey. At a council of war Gibraltar was decided upon, perhaps because Byng, whom Rooke disliked, spoke against it. It was not a new idea, but the Rock in 1704 was remarkably ill-fortified, and it fell comparatively easily. British possession was challenged within less than a month, by a French fleet under Admiral Toulouse, and in a battle off Malaga, Rooke's force drove off the French, who made no further challenge for control of the Mediterranean during the war. 1704 was a year of decisive victories. Blenheim had been fought in the interval between the taking of Gibraltar and the action off Malaga. George Rooke, who had been a Tory M.P. since 1698, was acclaimed when he got home as a victor at least equal to Marlborough, whom the Whigs had adopted as their own. This flattered the Admiral a good deal.

ADMIRAL SIR CLOWDISLEY SHOVELL (1650–1707), from Cockthorpe in Norfolk, was perhaps the most noteworthy British Admiral of the period between Blake and Anson. Legend says that he began his career as a cabin-boy, and there was a family tradition of him swimming under fire with dispatches in his mouth. His most distinguished fighting achievements were at Barfleur, where he broke the French line of battle in 1692, and in the Mediterranean during the early years of Anne's reign. He took part with Rooke in the capture of Gibraltar and the battle off Malaga (1704), and commanded the naval forces which assisted Peterborough to capture Barcelona (1705). But returning to England after the unsuccessful attack on Toulon in 1707, Shovell's flagship *The Association* was wrecked with three others of his fleet on the Western Rocks of the Scilly Isles. Nearly two thousand men were lost, and Shovell was one of them: cast ashore alive but unconscious, he was murdered, so the story goes, by a woman for the sake of his emerald ring. Buried first in the sands of Porth Hellick, his body was later taken to Westminster Abbey, where it lies beneath a monument which, as Addison pointed out, is peculiarly inappropriate to a man who seems to have been very much a blunt and rough sea-captain.

Peterborough, Commander of the land forces at Barcelona in 1705, described Shovell at the time as 'brave if I may say to a fault ... and thinks that whatever is directed first must be begun, and when begun must be carried on what accidents soever occur, or whatsoever improbabilities come in the way'. Five years later Prince Eugene, leading the allied armies attacking Toulon, underlined this comment when he wrote of the two British Admirals Shovell and Norris that 'they refuse to listen to facts, and adhere obstinately to their opinion that for good or ill everything must be staked on the siege of Toulon. Yet the pure impossibility of this is clearly before their eyes.' Shovell was, for whatever reason, an unlucky Commander, whose achievements in battle were limited. His importance in the history of the British Navy rests more upon the standards of discipline and skill which the evidence shows him exacting from his officers. In this sense Shovell was one of those who laid essential foundations for the naval triumphs of the middle years of the eighteenth century.

CHARLES MORDAUNT, 3rd EARL OF PETERBOROUGH

(1658–1735), the hero of Barcelona, was the son of a Cavalier conspirator, Viscount Mordaunt, and served in the Navy as a boy. As a young man in the 1680s he was an outspoken member of the Whig opposition; he left for Holland in 1686 and accompanied William of Orange throughout the enterprise of 1688. Created Earl of Monmouth in 1689, he was for a short time First Commissioner of the Treasury. Vain, boastful, dishonest, reckless, above all fickle and unstable in opinions and purposes, he was 'a skeleton in outward figure' (Swift), a man of wit and charm, courage and high talents, who infuriated everyone with whom he had dealings. His thoroughly disreputable attempt to incriminate Shrewsbury and Marlborough in the Fenwick conspiracy (1696) landed him in the Tower. Inheritance of the Earldom of Peterborough (1697) did something to restore his credit, but not until the War of the Spanish Succession did he achieve the celebrity to which he believed himself entitled. In 1705 he was appointed, with Admiral Sir Clowdisley Shovell, joint Commander of the expedition sent to win Spain for the Archduke Charles, and in an assault in which he showed reckless personal gallantry his forces captured Barcelona, the strongest fortress in the country. He followed this up by overrunning the province of Valencia, and thereby committing his country to the Carlist cause and the ruinous doctrine of 'No peace without Spain'. These activities, related to the public in the exaggerated *An Account of the Earl of Peterborough's conduct in Spain*, by Dr. John Freind

(1707), made him a national hero. This was the limit of his achievements. His quarrelsomeness, levity and capacity for mischief made him impossible to work with; in September 1706 Marlborough was writing 'I do not think much ceremony ought to be used in removing him from a place where he has hazarded the loss of the whole country', and in 1707 he was recalled. A long series of official inquiries into his conduct did little except enable the Tories to use him as a propagandist counterweight to Marlborough: Swift in particular lauded his generalship in his political pamphlets. But when the Tories came to power from 1710 they employed him as a diplomatist rather than as a soldier, and then for motives clearly stated by Queen Anne when she wrote to Harley, 'I think he should be sent somewhere, for I fear if he comes home while the parliament is sitting he will be very troublesome'. Peterborough's official career ended with the coming of the Hanoverians in 1714. His capacity for mischief did not. His activities included dabbling in European politics, in which he claimed to have caused the fall of Alberoni, who called him 'a most pretentious fool and consummate blackguard'; thrashing an Italian tenor for insolent behaviour to the singer Anastasia Robinson, whom he eventually married; and writing his memoirs, which so shocked his widow after his death that she burned the manuscript at once. He lived on, a patron of letters and a friend of Swift, Pope and Gay, travelling abroad a good deal, until he died at Lisbon in 1735.

For the Spanish campaign, see G. M. Trevelyan, *England under Queen Anne: Ramillies and the Union with Scotland*, 1932, Chaps. 4 and 7.

JOHN, BARON CUTTS (1661–1707), soldier, was born at Arkesden of an old Essex family and educated at Catharine Hall, Cambridge. Handsome, conceited and witty, a writer of verse, celebrated by his friend Steele as 'Honest Cynthio', he was a soldier of fantastic courage, nicknamed 'Salamander' for his recklessness under fire. As a young man he had been a friend of Monmouth, and his Whiggish views helped to win him the enmity of Swift, who called him 'as brave and brainless as the sword he wears'. He began his soldiering against the Turks and in 1686 won European fame at the siege of Buda. Two years later he came to England as an officer in

William's invading army. He fought through the battles of William's reign — at the Boyne (after which he was rewarded with an Irish peerage) and Limerick, at Steinkirk and Brest and at Namur, where he led the assault. In 1701 he went with Marlborough to Holland, and in 1702 displayed even more than his customary intrepidity at the siege of Venloo. Marlborough left him in command of the English forces in Holland when he went home that winter, and in 1704 he held high command at Blenheim. But many campaigns and frequent wounds had shattered his health, and in 1705 he was appointed to Ireland, where he died suddenly in 1707.

JAMES, DUKE OF BERWICK (1670–1734), Marshal of France, was the natural son of James II and Arabella Churchill, the elder sister of John Churchill, later Duke of Marlborough. He appears to have inherited Churchill rather than Stuart qualities, for he became a distinguished soldier and a shrewd judge of political reality. Born and brought up in France as a Roman Catholic, he was given the title of Duke of Berwick in 1687. As a soldier he fought against the Turks in Hungary and against William III in Ireland and in Flanders, before taking command in 1705 of the French army in Spain. In 1706 he recaptured Madrid for King Philip, and in 1707 won at Almanza the decisive battle of the Spanish campaign, the victory which determined the ultimate failure of the British cause in the peninsula. The High Tories toasted him as 'the brave English general who had defeated the French' — for the 'British' commander in the battle was the French Huguenot Ruvigny, Earl of Galway. His other campaigns for Louis XIV included the reduction of the Camisard rebels of the Cévennes and the capture of Nice in 1705, and the subjugation of Barcelona and its Catalan defenders in 1714. In the later years of Anne's reign Berwick was deeply involved in the Jacobite plans for the succession, and his letters show a sense of the possible unusual among the Jacobites. Berwick was also one of the channels through which Marlborough maintained his Jacobite links, and he grew rather contemptuous of his uncle's attention to political insurance. After the deaths of Anne in 1714 and Louis XIV in 1715 he was a supporter of the Anglo-French *rapprochement* pursued by Orleans. He was killed in battle at Philipsbourg in 1734.

Sir C. Petrie, *The Marshal Duke of Berwick*, 1953.

ROBERT HARLEY(1661–1724), politician and bibliophile, came from Brampton Bryan in Herefordshire. His father and grandfather had both fought for Parliament in the Civil War, and he was like Defoe a pupil of the Dissenting Academies, brought up under Presbyterian tutors. Entering Parliament after the Revolution, he was member for Tregoney (1689–90) and New Radnor (1690–1711), quickly making a name for himself as a moderate of mainly Tory views, proposing the unsuccessful land bank of 1696 and the reductions in the army after the Treaty of Ryswick. By the beginning of Anne's reign he was the most influential member of the Commons, and was Speaker from 1702–5. From 1704–8 he was Secretary of State, the third in the ruling 'Triumvirate' with Godolphin and Marlborough; but from 1707 he was employing Mrs. Masham to undermine their influence with Anne, and in 1708 they forced his resignation. In 1710 he returned to office as Chancellor of the Exchequer and head of a predominantly Tory government, becoming Earl of Oxford and Lord Treasurer in 1711, the year also when he was stabbed by Antoine de Guiscard. His supremacy did not last long. He fell out with St. John, his health deteriorated, he drank more heavily, and in July 1714 Anne dismissed him. Five days later she was dead. Harley spent some time in the Tower under the Hanoverian regime, but his impeachment failed for lack of evidence, and he passed his final years in peace, making occasional appearances in the Lords.

Harley is a puzzling figure. A small man with a dry voice, slovenly in speech and writing, uninspiring in presence, rather lazy, with no flair for publicizing himself, he had no obvious source of personal strength. He was always an intriguer enjoying secretiveness and double dealing, whisperings and the use of the backstairs, deserving his nickname of 'Robin the Trickster'. His cabinet colleague Lord Cowper tells us in his diary of Harley's tendency 'to love tricks even when not necessary, but from an inward satisfaction he took in applauding his own cunning', and adds the comment 'if any man was ever born under a necessity of being a knave, he was'. No doubt his intrigues paid political dividends; certainly the most celebrated of them, the use of Mrs. Masham at Court, achieved its purpose. But Harley had other qualities which served him well. He had a well stocked and cultivated mind. He had equanimity and plenty of courage, as he showed both in 1707 when Greg, one of his clerks,

Robert Harley, 1st Earl of Oxford c. 1714
(Artist: Sir Godfrey Kneller)

was caught passing information to the French and it was widely believed that Harley himself would be charged with treason, and in 1711 when Guiscard stabbed him with a penknife. Behind his laziness there was wisdom and a dislike of going to extremes, a quality of high value at this stage of English political life. He had the power to wait — unlike St. John. He shared with those two other architects of parliamentary majorities, Shaftesbury and Walpole, the ability to weigh men, to discern their motives and their price. And he was prepared to recognize the existence and needs of public opinion outside Westminster and London, as his employment of Daniel Defoe and others both as reporters and as journalists shows.

Yet even if we admit that Harley was more than Macaulay's 'dull, puzzleheaded man', it remains difficult to assess his achievement. This is partly because he has been overshadowed by the magnificence of Marlborough and the flashiness of Bolingbroke, yet mainly because of the nature of his policies. Harley was essentially a moderate, following the middle of the road by temperament as well as by design. To see him as the Revolution Whig who ended as the Tory leader, the builder of a Tory party, is not merely to exaggerate the meaning of party labels at that time. It is also to misconstrue the purposes of Harley. In 1705, writing to Godolphin on the problem of maintaining a government, he said 'The foundation is, persons and parties are to come to the Queen, and not the Queen to them'. In 1710, after Anne had dismissed Godolphin, in a letter to the Duke of Newcastle he used the sentence 'As soon as the Queen has shewn strength and ability to give the law to both sides, then will moderation be truly shewn in the exercise of power without regard to parties only'. He tried, as Godolphin and Marlborough tried in the early years of the reign, to secure a government in which the Queen was served by the best men irrespective of party. He failed as they had failed; and whereas they were in 1708 driven to dependence on the Whigs (discarding the moderate Harley in the process), he from 1710 was driven into increasing dependence on the high fliers among the Tories. This state of affairs suited St. John at the time, and was the underlying reason — more important than Harley's ill-health, excessive drinking, late hours and torpor — why he eventually, though too late, triumphed over his rival. It is ironic that when Bolingbroke came a quarter of a century later to write his political testament in *The Patriot King*, the doctrines he preached were those of Harley.

The substance of Harley's positive achievements lay principally in measures upon which moderate men could agree. It was characteristic that he should be the first to move the proposals which became the Act of Settlement (1701), and that he should be a leading champion of the Union with Scotland (1707): as Sir Keith Feiling has observed, 'on no single public question were Harley's exertions so great, or his record so consistent, as on the Union'. He was the principal figure behind the foundation of the South Sea Company (1711); whatever fate overtook this later, it was in its beginning a sound and defensible project. On the fundamental problem of British government in Anne's reign, the succession, Harley's views remain in doubt. Outwardly committed to Hanover, he was during 1713–14 in constant touch with the Jacobites in France and he kept the contact in later years. No more than Bolingbroke did he have any clear-cut design in 1714, and it is difficult to see in his dealings with the Pretender anything more than the insurance which so cautious a politician would naturally take out in the circumstances. Unlike Bolingbroke, he took the risk of staying to stand trial.

On one matter at least his reputation is not in doubt. He had a true passion for books and manuscripts, and over the years he built up a remarkable collection ranging from early classics and Saxon charters to comparatively modern books. His son Edward added substantially to it, and after his death many of the manuscripts were sold to the British Museum to form the Harleian Collection.

Angus McInnes, *Robert Harley, Puritan Politician*, 1970.
Sheila Biddle, *Bolingbroke and Harley*, 1975.

HENRY ST. JOHN, 1st VISCOUNT BOLINGBROKE (1678–1751), Tory politician, born at Battersea, son of a Whig rake and grandson of a Puritan Admiral, was educated at Eton, where Robert Walpole was his contemporary. He entered the Commons as member for Wootton Bassett in 1701, and no politician in our history has risen so swiftly to eminence merely by his own abilities. Within twelve months he was a leader of the 'high-flying' Tories, and from 1704–8 he was Secretary at War. St. John dazzled many of his contemporaries by his grace and eloquence, his wit and resource, and at this stage he was ready to learn from Harley in the Commons and from Marlborough, for whom he showed a genuine hero-worship in the years of Blenheim and Ramillies. But his views, alike of principles and of men, were never fixed. In 1710 he joined Harley in the task of destroying Marlborough and of ending the Spanish Succession War. Created Viscount Bolingbroke in 1712, he was the chief English architect of the Treaty of Utrecht in 1713. He was already on bad terms with Harley, now Earl of Oxford, and in 1714 he became the head of the ministry by persuading Anne to dismiss the older man. It was too late. In the famous words of his letter to Swift, 'The Earl of Oxford was removed on Tuesday; the Queen died on Sunday. What a world is this and how does fortune banter us!'

George I dismissed Bolingbroke from the secretaryship even before he landed in England. Facing the certainty of impeachment, Bolingbroke fled to France, and in 1715 became Secretary of State to the Old Pretender, who in his turn dismissed him in 1716. Seven years later, by dint of supplicating English politicians and of bribing George I's mistress, the Duchess of Kendal, he was allowed to return to England but not to resume his seat in the Lords. His house at Dawley became for some ten years the centre of opposition, an opposition stimulated by his writings in *The Craftsman* from 1726 onwards. Completely failing to break Walpole, Bolingbroke gave up the struggle and withdrew to France in 1736. He devoted the remaining fifteen years of his life to writing, his most celebrated piece being his political essay, *The Idea of a Patriot King*.

Bolingbroke has one substantial political achievement to his credit, the Treaty of Utrecht. He recognized that the country needed peace, and he initiated and carried through the negotiations to obtain it. Yet even this was marred by the methods he used, above all by the 'Restraining Orders' to Ormonde and by the desertion of the Catalans; and his secret negotiations with the French and Britain's cavalier treatment, to put it in modern terms, of her allies contributed powerfully to the legend of 'perfidious Albion'. Bolingbroke himself paid the penalty of these methods, for they convinced the Elector of Hanover that he was a Jacobite and could not be trusted. The treaty apart, Bolingbroke's career was that of an unscrupulous politician whose lack of principle was not even excused by success. He used Marlborough and Harley to promote his own rise to power and turned against them when they had served his purpose. A freethinker and a notorious profligate who treated his first wife with harsh infidelity, he used his gifts to play up to the prejudices of the Anglican High Tories, and then abandoned them to the political wilderness by his flight to the Pretender in 1715. The real criticism of his conduct at the death of Anne lies not so much in the folly of his flirtation with Jacobitism as in the complete absence of preparation for a foreseeable crisis. The brilliant realist had no plan ready. Just before Anne's death he had even invited the Whig chiefs to dinner and sounded their support. When the crisis came his nerve failed completely, and he fled disguised as a valet.

He soon despaired of Jacobitism, for he was never allowed real power at St. Germain. But his rash action overshadowed the remainder of his career. Besides keeping him out of the political fighting-line, it left him always vulnerable, and in particular it gravely weakened his efforts to destroy Walpole. He claimed after his return to be above party, to wish to set the nation free from the Whigs and from the 'Robinocracy'. But his only way of doing this was to fuse the various opponents of Walpole into another party, and in this he did not succeed, despite his victory over the Excise Bill in 1733. In practice there was nothing to suggest that the opposition was more than factious. Moreover, Walpole was a far shrewder politician than Marlborough and far tougher than the ageing Harley. So Bolingbroke's second political career was less successful than his first.

His reputation has depended as much upon his writings as upon his political practice, and with even less real justification. *The Idea of a Patriot King*, with its doctrine of the abolition of party and its emphasis upon service to an idealized crown above all faction, was not original, nor was it notably influential. It is no longer possible to maintain that George III as Prince of Wales was brought up on it. The cult of Bolingbroke — of a highly-idealized Bolingbroke — was the creation of a nineteenth-century Tory, Disraeli. Further, his teachings were fundamentally out of touch with the political and constitutional evolution of his time. As a political philosopher Bolingbroke was shallow. It is unfair to maintain that he was also bogus, merely because the principles he developed in his writings were different from the practice which he followed when he was in Parliament; the conditions of the 1730s were very different from those of Anne's reign. Nevertheless, the contrast between the two is extraordinarily sharp. We may perhaps defend the earlier Bolingbroke as a superb political tactician, or the later one by saying with Keith Feiling that he 'Harleysized, that is to say modernized, the whole basis of Tory thought' *. Both lines of defence are generous. He has remained something of an enigma to historians, yet it seems impossible to escape the truth of the much-quoted words of Swift's friend, Erasmus Lewis, when he wrote 'His character is too bad to carry the great ensigns; for the man of Mercury's bottom is too narrow, his faults are of the first magnitude'.

Jeffrey Hart, *Viscount Bolingbroke, Tory Humanist*, 1965.
H. T. Dickinson, *Bolingbroke*, 1970.
Sheila Biddle, *Bolingbroke and Harley*, 1975.

ABIGAIL MASHAM [nee HILL] (*d.* 1734), was a distant relative of Sarah, Duchess of Marlborough, who crowned many kindnesses to her and to her brother Jack by obtaining for her the post of Woman of the Bedchamber to Queen Anne. She may also have been related to Robert Harley, who used her to break the long-standing and intimate friendship between the Queen and the Marlboroughs. A plain red-nosed woman, Abigail Masham was determined, even-tempered, patient and of Tory opinions. Trevelyan calls her 'mean-souled', 'an adventuress, a listener at keyholes'. Even without these qualities she would no doubt have provided something of a relief to the Queen from the outbursts and hectorings of Sarah; with them, she was an excellent tool for a politician anxious to end the domination of Marlborough. In 1707 she married Samuel Masham, Groom of the Bedchamber to Prince George. By the November of that year Sarah, only too well aware of what was happening, was writing of 'the black ingratitude of Mrs. Masham, a woman that I took out of a garret and saved from starving'. Within two years more, Abigail, in command of 'the back way into the Queen's closet', had almost achieved her design, assisted by the stormy anger of the woman she was supplanting. In January 1710 there was a political crisis brought about by Anne's offer, without consulting Marlborough, of a regiment to Jack Hill.

*Keith Feiling, *History of the Tory party, 1640–1714*, 1959 ed., p. 482.

The Duke threatened to resign unless Abigail was dismissed. The dispute was patched up: Abigail kept her post, Jack did not get his. Yet the end of the Marlborough's power was within sight. In April came the last meeting of Sarah and the Queen, and four months later Anne dismissed Godolphin, the other pillar of the Duke's power at court.

It is arguable that the effect of Abigail Masham's intrigues may easily be overrated, and that the unpopularity of the war at this stage would have brought Godolphin and the Marlboroughs down before long. To Harley, the prime mover in the affair, Abigail Masham was as much a political fact at this stage of British political development as the unsatisfactory nature of Marlborough's victory at Malplaquet. But Harley, like Sarah, was himself to suffer from Abigail's lack of gratitude. When in 1711 the gulf between Harley and St. John began to grow, she began to turn to St. John, who was adroit enough to win her support by backing, against Harley's wishes, the unsuccessful Quebec expedition of that year, whose military commander was Jack Hill. In 1712 her husband, thanks to Harley, became Lord Masham, one of the dozen Peers created to get 'peace without Spain' through the Lords. Yet in the rivalry of the last years of Anne's reign Abigail, characteristically, employed her malice, her talents for intrigue, and her influence over her mistress against Harley. There were rumours that she was profitably involved in dubious transactions in the South Sea Company, rumours only scotched by Anne's prorogation of her last Parliament. For her, as for St. John, success came too slowly this time. The death of Anne in 1714 threw Abigail Masham into the obscurity of private life.

DR. HENRY SACHEVERELL, (1674?–1724), was the grandson of a Nonconformist minister ejected in 1662. A Fellow of Magdalen, Oxford, he became notorious as a rabble-rousing preacher of High Church opinions. Impressive in appearance but superficial in mind, intemperate in language, with a flair for slightly pompous Billingsgate, 'the Doctor' was an unattractive and foolish character, the mouthpiece of the 'high-flying' Tories of Oxford. In 1702 he had celebrated the accession of Queen Anne by a sermon on the alliance of throne and altar. In it he provided a Tory catchword by hanging out 'the bloody flag of defiance' against Dissenters, and he denounced occasional conformists, those 'insidious persons who can creep to our altars' with the purpose of undermining them. In 1709, on the anniversary of William III's landing in Torbay, Sacheverell delivered before the Lord Mayor of London at St. Paul's a sermon on the text. 'In perils among false brethren'. It was printed and sold 40,000 copies. In effect it was an inflammatory attack both upon the Glorious Revolution and upon the predominantly Whig government of the day. Sacheverell defended non-resistance, assailed toleration as well as occasional conformity, condemned the dissenting academies for teaching 'all the hellish principles of Fanaticism, Regicide, and Anarchy', and denounced Lord Treasurer Godolphin as the 'wily Volpone' who had betrayed his party. The Lords condemned the sermon as a seditious libel, and the government decided to impeach its author. This decision was a political blunder, and opened the way to the fall of the government. Public opinion, tired of the expensive and apparently endless war, was ready to take up any cause against Godolphin and the Whigs, and Sacheverell and 'the Church in danger' were — for the time being — an excellent one.

The impeachment opened in February 1710. Westminster Hall was packed; like the early stages of Warren Hastings' trial, that of Sacheverell was an event of the London season, with Whig and Tory ladies going at seven in the morning to secure their seats. The doctor himself travelled to and fro in a glass coach, with a retinue armed with bludgeons and drawn swords and a vast mob roaring for 'High Church and Sacheverell'. Queen Anne's sympathies were as evident as those of the crowds, and her Chaplains supported Sacheverell as he faced his opponents. The Whig accusers of Sacheverell had little difficulty in demonstrating that the Revolution was an act of just resistance, and his Tory champions, not daring to deny this, were driven to considerable sophistry in order to square Sacheverell's words with the events of 1688. The doctor himself ingeniously maintained that there had in fact been no resistance in that year, for William of Orange had himself proclaimed that he did not come to conquer England. Whatever the merits of these arguments, the votes of the Peers revealed how the political tide was flowing in 1710. By sixty-nine to fifty-two they found him guilty; by a majority of six votes only they suspended him from preaching for three years, in effect the lightest possible sentence.

Sacheverell was, briefly, a national hero. A Tory admirer had presented him with a living in Shropshire, and his journey thither was a triumphal progress, with banquets and peals of bells, the local gentry providing guards of honour as he passed through the country- side and the towns welcoming him with speeches. Five months later, in August 1710, Anne dismissed Godolphin. In October a general election was held in which 'Sacheverell' was a password to victory. The Tories and High Churchmen, backed by the Queen, won a handsome triumph, and in the four years of power which followed they placed on the statute book two of the doctor's favourite measures, the Occasional Conformity Act (1711) and the Schism Act (1714), the latter aimed at closing down dissenting academies. Sacheverell himself meanwhile was presented (1713) to a London living, St. Andrew's, Holborn. But this was the limit of his promotion. If ever a man had, in purely political terms, earned a bishopric, it was Sacheverell. Yet none came his way, even though he courted St. John with some care, and Anne's death in 1714 extinguished his hopes and well as those of more eminent men. There were some, like the Oxford Jacobite Thomas Hearne, who thought that Sacheverell ought at the least, if he really believed what he preached, to have become a Non-juror; Hearne considered him 'conceited, ignorant, imprudent'. He died in 1724, it is said from the results of an accident.

Geoffrey Holmes, *The Trial of Dr. Sacheverell*, 1973.

MATTHEW PRIOR (1664–1721), diplomatist and poet, the talented son of a joiner at Wimborne, in Dorset, went to London as a boy and was educated at Westminster and St. John's College, Cambridge, by the patronage of the Earl of Dorset. In 1687 he joined Charles Montagu in writing *The Town and Country Mouse*, a successful parody of Dryden's *The Hind and the Panther*. He became a diplomatist in the reign of William III, going to Holland and France, where he was Portland's secretary, and taking part in the negotiations at Ryswick in 1697. In 1701 he was elected M.P. for East Grinstead. A witty companionable man, Mat Prior enjoyed the friendship of Marlborough as well as that of Montagu (now Earl of Halifax), and got a minor post as Commissioner of Trade. But a reshuffle of the government in 1706 deprived him of it, caused him financial hardship, and drove him into the ranks of the Tories, even though he was essentially a man of moderate opinions. In 1711 St. John, anxious to bring the War of the Spanish Succession to an end, sent Prior to France to open peace talks. He showed himself an adroit and tough negotiator — though the Mayor of Dover upset the plans for secrecy by detaining him as a suspected French spy. Prior accompanied St. John to Paris when the formal negotiations started in 1712 and played a vital role in the Utrecht settlement, although the Queen did not think his birth good enough for a post of the first rank. Prior was not a Jacobite and and did not involve himself in the project, which the French were pushing, to put the Old Pretender on the throne after Anne's death. Nevertheless, the Whigs imprisoned him for some time in 1715–17. After his release a subscription edition of his poems brought him a large sum, and with this and a gift of £4,000 from Lord Harley he bought an estate in Essex, where he lived until his death in 1721. As a writer Prior is most distinguished for his witty epigrams and short familiar poems, like the charming *To a Child of Quality*.

L.G. Wickham Legg, *Matthew Prior*, 1921.

SOPHIA, DOWAGER ELECTRESS OF HANOVER (1630–1714), who almost became Queen Sophy of Great Britain, was the youngest daughter of James I's daughter, Elizabeth, and Frederick the Elector Palatine. In 1649 it was rumoured that she would marry Charles II, but nothing came of it; instead she married Ernest Augustus, first Elector of Hanover. By the time of the Glorious Revolution she was the last surviving grandchild of James I, and the nearest Protestant heir to the English throne after Mary, Anne and their descendants, and the proposal to fix the succession upon her and upon the Hanoverian line was discussed at that time. In 1701, after the deaths of Mary and of Anne's children, Sophia was named in the Act of Settlement as the heir. She was a clever, witty and lively old woman, broad in her interests, international in outlook, a friend of the philosopher Leibniz; abler and less parochial than her son George, she much enjoyed her position as heir-apparent and had no hesitation about playing English politicians off against each other. Knowing that the Whigs on the whole were firmly tied to the Hanoverians anyway, she was ready to be cool to them and to encourage the Tories. She welcomed the project of a visit to England

which English politicians out of office canvassed from time to time
in order to embarrass the government; Anne regarded it with horror
and contrived to prevent it. Although Sophia was thirty-five years
Anne's senior, she died, aged eight-four, only some three months
before her in 1714.

A. W. Ward, *The Electress Sophia and the Hanoverian Succession*,
   1909.

JAMES FRANCIS EDWARD STUART (1688–1766), Prince
of Wales, Chevalier de St. George, the Old Pretender, was born to
Mary of Modena and James II in St. James's Palace. Few men of
rank in modern English history have had a more infelicitous
inheritance. Popularly believed to be an imposter smuggled into the
palace in a warming-pan, certainly when less than six months old
smuggled out of the country where he had been born heir to the
throne, James Edward was in Macaulay's words 'the most unfortunate of princes, destined to seventy-seven years of exile and
wandering, of vain projects, of honours more galling than insults,
and of hopes such as make the heart sick'. By his own virtues and
weaknesses alike he contributed substantially to his misfortunes. His
devotion to Catholicism almost certainly cost him the succession in
1714, yet his tame and flabby personality did nothing to encourage
his supporters to lay down their lives, or would-be sympathizers to
risk their property, for him.

Proclaimed King of England by Louis XIV in 1701, with his
father's deathbed injunction to die rather than abandon Romanism
sounding in his ears, he began his political career at thirteen, a
helpless tool of his country's enemy. In the futile Jacobite 'invasion'
of 1708 he fell ill with measles at Dunkirk, and then sailed all round
Scotland and Ireland and back to Dunkirk without landing, showing great courage when the French flagship which was carrying him
was bombarded by the pursuing Admiral Byng. He fought at
Oudenarde and at Malplaquet; driven from France by the Treaty of
Utrecht, he took refuge in Lorraine. In the Fifteen he arrived on a
French ship at Peterhead too late to be of effective help, yet not too
late to discourage his supporters by his 'heavy' countenance, his lack
of vitality, and his sedate comment that 'for myself it is no new thing
to be unfortunate'. After six weeks in Scotland he took ship at

Montrose to escape Argyll's pursuing forces, and returned to Lorraine.

His court was riddled with faction, intrigue, and spies; and Bolingbroke, for a short time its ablest member and the Pretender's secretary, was dismissed in 1716. By way of Avignon and Rome he went to Madrid, whence Alberoni organized the futile Jacobite expedition of 1719, and thence back to Rome, where he settled for the long remainder of his days. In that same year he married the Polish princess Maria Clementina Sobieski, who in 1724 deserted him and went into a nunnery. The Pope rewarded him for his loyalty to his faith by giving him a pension. Gray, visiting Rome in 1740, left a gloomy description of him as 'a thin, ill-made man, extremely tall and awkward, of a most unpromising countenance, a good deal resembling King James the Second, and has extremely the air and look of an idiot, particularly when he laughs or prays. The first he does not often, the latter continually.' He showed little enthusiasm for the Forty-Five, saying sensibly but unheroically to Charles Edward 'Be careful, my boy, for I would not lose you for all the crowns in the world'. He died in 1766 and was buried in St. Peter's.

Sir Charles Petrie, *The Jacobite Movement, the first phase, 1698–1716*, 1948, and *The Jacobite Movement, the second phrase, 1716–1807*, 1950.

J.P. Kenyon, 'The Birth of the Old Pretender', *History Today*, June 1963.

JONATHAN SWIFT (1677–1745), political journalist and satirist, was born in Dublin of English parents and sent to school in Kilkenny. Then he went on to Trinity College, Dublin, where his career was distinguished by his neglect of all studies save history and poetry, so that he eventually only obtained a degree *speciali gratia*. In 1689 he joined Sir William Temple's household, and he spent much of the 1690s with Temple, either at Sheen or at Moor Park, writing *A Tale of a Tub* and *The Battle of the Books* at this time (although they were not published until 1704). Ordained in Ireland in 1694, he held a small prebend there in 1695–6; in 1699 he obtained the living of Laracor, a hamlet near Dublin, and in 1700 a stall in St. Patrick's Cathedral in Dublin. Ambitious, conscious of his literary powers, morose and bitter even as a young man, Swift

Jonathan Swift c.1718
(Artist: Charles Jervas)

was never content with Ireland, and during the first half of Anne's reign he spent a good deal of time in England, hoping always for preferment and making the friendship of writers like Addison and Steele and of patrons like Halifax. Politically he tended to call himself a Whig, but the Whigs disappointed him, particularly by failing to give him the post of Queen's Secretary in Vienna in 1708.

The power and fame Swift needed were to come through his pen, yet his writings of these years — although they revealed his ferocious strength — were not entirely discreet. Queen Anne did not approve of *A Tale of a Tub*. *The Argument to Prove that the Abolishing of Christianity may . . . be attended with Some Inconveniences* (1708) was perhaps too ironic, while his pamphlet of that same year against the abolition of the sacramental test for offices in Ireland was certainly too honest.

Swift's chance came in 1710, with the change of ministry, for Harley was shrewd enough to see his political possibilities. Within a few months this obscure and sour Irish clergyman was sharing the secrets of the Tory government and dining à trois with Harley and St. John. In 1711 he was a leading member of the Tory 'Brothers' Club' formed to rival the Whig Kit-Cat. For the better part of four years Swift was a major figure in English political life, and he did more than any man to make this period a golden age of political journalism. In 1710–11 he denounced the Whigs with peculiar savagery in the Tory journal *The Examiner*, and in 1711 he demonstrated his crushing controversial powers in *The Conduct of the Allies*, one of the greatest of all political pamphlets. It sold 11,000 copies in a month and, by shattering the Whig argument for 'No peace without Spain', won English public opinion to accept St. John's policy and thus, in Trevelyan's words, 'materially helped to obtain peace for Europe on the only possible terms'*.

In 1713 Anne made Swift Dean of St. Patrick's Cathedral in Dublin. It was not what he wanted; as he said, 'all that the Court or Ministry did for me was to let me choose my station in the country where I am banished'. And banishment came suddenly upon him. In 1713–14 he did his best, in vain, to patch up the widening quarrel between the two Tory leaders. He was quite unaware of the negotiations of St. John with the French for the restoration of the Old Pretender, and in his last pamphlet for the Tories, *The Public Spirit of the Whigs* (March 1714), he answered Steele's pamphlet alleging that the Protestant succession was in danger. Four months later Anne died, the Tory ministry was dismissed, and Swift's day of power in English politics was done.

He returned to Ireland and apart from two visits to England spent

---

*G. M. Trevelyan, *England under Queen Anne*, Vol. III, 1934, p. 192.

the remainder of his days there. No minister in the years of Whig supremacy was likely to give him employment or preferment in England. In Lord Orrery's opinion, he made a virtue out of this necessity: 'his chief aim was to be removed into England; but when he found himself entirely disappointed, he turned his thoughts to opposition, and became the patron of Ireland'. In 1724 he wrote the *Drapier's Letters* in successful opposition to Walpole's project of 'Wood's Halfpence', and for a time he was the hero of all Ireland. Two years later the most famous of all his works, *Gulliver's Travels*, was published. As Dean of St. Patrick's he was a bitter opponent of the Non-conformists and a generous donor to charity. From about 1738 he was increasingly ill, and in his last years out of his mind. He died in 1745 and was buried in St. Patrick's with his own inscription, *'ubi saeva indignatio ulterius cor lacerare nequit'*, carved on his tomb.

'Swift shares with Bunyan and Defoe the distinction of having given pleasure to a greater number of people in the last two hundred years than any other English author' *. If this statement is true, the irony of such a distinction would have pleased Swift, who so commonly appeared bitter and misanthropic. A frustrated man, whose relations with Stella and 'Vanessa' remain baffling under any kind of analysis; a brooding man who was always ready to impute malice and ingratitude, and whose hatreds — of Whigs and Jacobites, of Low Churchmen, Dissenters and free-thinkers, of Marlborough and Wharton, of the Scots and the Dutch — were corrosive of truth and decency in his language; deeply susceptible to flattery, for all his harshness; yielding to a self-pity unworthy of his magnificent abilities — Swift, at best, remains an unattractive figure. Part of the truth no doubt lies in his remark in a letter of 1725 that 'principally I hate and detest that animal called man; although I heartily love John, Peter, Thomas and so forth'. Both the *Journal to Stella* and *Gulliver's Travels* throw shadow as well as light, and his political career is oddly incidental to any understanding of the man. Yet of two things there can be no doubt. Swift was a man of superb force of mind, a fit peer of Newton and Bentley; and as controversialist and journalist he has no superior in modern English history.

---

* John Hayward, *Swift: Gulliver's Travels and Selected Writings*, 1934, p. xiii.

J. Middleton Murry, *Swift*, 1954.

Michael Foot, *The Pen and the Sword*, 1957.

J. A. Downie, *Jonathan Swift, Political Writer*, 1984.

DANIEL DEFOE (1660–1731), journalist, government agent and novelist, the son of a London butcher, was intended for the Nonconformist ministry and educated at a Dissenting Academy at Newington. But he went into trade instead and after his apprenticeship set up business as a hose-factor in 1685. That same year he fought for Monmouth, and managed to escape punishment; and in 1688 he joined William III's army. In 1692 his business failed for £17,000. From 1694 he had a minor government post as accountant to the Commissioners of the Glass Duty, until the duty was abolished in 1699. Before that date he had gone into business again, managing a brick and tile works at Tilbury. He had already written pamphlets supporting the revolutionary settlement, the Protestant cause, and toleration, and a book, *The Essay on Projects* (1698), which contained enlightened views on trade and education. Yet he was little known until his verse satire, *The True-Born Englishman*, appeared in 1701, defending the King and his Dutch friends against English insularity. It showed Defoe's power of making people laugh, sold 80,000 copies, and won him the favour of William III. But in 1702, after Anne had come to the throne, Defoe's flair for irony got him into trouble. His pamphlet, *The Shortest Way with the Dissenters*, parodied the violence of Anglican extremists by taking it to its logical conclusion and advising the extermination of the Nonconformists. The High Churchmen were obtuse enough to believe in it at first, and furious when they discovered the hoax. Defoe was sentenced to be pilloried and imprisoned; and his business failed again, not suprisingly. But the London crowd cheered him in the pillory, and the ministers Godolphin and Harley got him released from gaol in 1703, for he was a man whose lively pen could be useful.

Defoe's work as government agent in Anne's reign was intimately linked with the career and policies of Harley, a man like himself of dissenting origins, secretive temperament and moderate opinions. While Harley was in office from 1704 to 1708 and again after 1710 Defoe went up and down the country on his behalf, often in the guise of a merchant, testing public opinion about the war, noting the political activities of local justices, and exhorting his fellow Dissenters to support the government. From 1706 he spent a good deal of time in Edinburgh, reporting Scottish opinions on the Union and persuading Presbyterian ministers to accept it. Over the same period he was writing his paper the *Review,* which appeared three times a week. Presumably financed by the government, primarily political in tone, with plentiful comment and little news, nevertheless, like everything Defoe wrote, it had an independent flavour, and set a tradition for the English press by its advocacy of social reforms. Defoe also turned out a stream of pamphlets, and found time to write a substantial *History of the Union* (with Scotland). When Harley broke with Godolphin and the Whigs and lost office in 1708, Defoe continued to work for the government, and his *Review,* for example, backed the prosecution of Sacheverell. When the Tories returned to power after 1710 it was Harley's moderate Toryism that Defoe supported, not St. John and the high-fliers, and his influence waned as Swift's star rose in these last years of Anne's reign. Defoe always distrusted extremists, and he was no Jacobite, although he wrote in favour of the Treaty of Utrecht. Indeed, he was in trouble in 1713 for a use of irony similar to that of 1702; he wrote three so-called 'Hanover' pamphlets against the Jacobites, the first of which was taken seriously as Jacobite propaganda, and the Whigs, who had not forgiven him for following Harley again after 1710, seized the chance to have him briefly imprisoned. Harley got him pardoned.

The fall of Harley in 1714 and the death of Anne a week later brought another twist to Defoe's fortunes. The *Review* had already ended in 1713; the Whigs imprisoned him for a short time as an associate of Harley; and in 1715 he was again in prison on a charge of criminal libel against the Earl of Anglesey. He saved himself by coming to terms with the government. For the next ten years he was once more a government agent, this time in a very odd role — that of editor, in the pay and interest of George I's ministers, of the leading Jacobite paper, *Mist's Weekly Journal,* with the aim of toning down its policy and leading its readers to acceptance of the Hanoverians. He continued to write pamphlets, and it has been calculated that in 1715–18 he produced eighty-six. Far more important, he turned also to the occupation that has immortalized him for posterity, the writing of novels. In 1719, at the age of fifty-nine, he produced his first. It was *Robinson Crusoe* and it became a classic at once. In 1720 he wrote *Captain Singleton*, in 1722 *Moll Flanders* as well as the fictional *Journal of the Plague Year*, in 1724 *Roxana*. In 1724 too he wrote the first volume of his *Tour through the Whole Island of Britain*, a factual account which is more informative than any other book about the economic and social state of Britain in the early eighteenth century. The remaining volumes followed in 1725–6, and Defoe continued to write, mostly about trade, until for some reason which nobody has ever satisfactorily explained he disappeared from his haunts and died in hiding in 1731. The author of *Robinson Crusoe* and *Moll Flanders* was one of the most extraordinary men of his time. Distrusted, equivocal in his political partisanship, never quite on terms with his contemporaries, always a Dissenter and usually an outsider, Daniel Defoe was nevertheless in Trevelyan's phrase 'one of the first who saw the old world through a pair of sharp modern eyes'*.

J.R. Sutherland, *Daniel Defoe*, 1950.
G.D.H. Cole, *Persons and Periods*, 1938.
Peter Earle, *The World of Defoe*, 1976.

JACOB TONSON (1656?–1736), described in the *D.N.B.* as 'son of a London chirurgeon', was a successful publisher in a golden period of English literature, the Augustan Age when the greatest men of letters and the leading politicians were interlinked as never before or since. Apprenticed as a stationer in 1670, he started his own business at the Judge's Head in Chancery Lane in 1677; took a nephew into partnership in 1699; and retired about 1720 to an estate at Ledbury in Herefordshire. A genial yet shrewd business man, he made substantial profits early in his career as a result of buying the copyright of *Paradise Lost*. Among the contemporaries whose work he published were Dryden, Addison, Steele and Pope. His relations with authors were not invariably happy, and Dryden has left a sour description of Tonson

> 'With leering looks, bull-faced and freckled-fair;
> With two left legs, and Judas-coloured hair,
> And frowsy pores that taint the ambient air.'

*G.M. Trevelyan, *England under Queen Anne*, Vol. I, 1936, ed., p. 2.

Yet the gain was mutual: as the dramatist Wycherley put it to Pope, 'you will make Jacob's ladder raise you to immortality'. Contracts for state publishing added to Tonson's profits. Historians have reason to be grateful to him for reprinting Rymer's *Foedera*; so has the Cambridge University Press, whose first printed book (1698) was the opening volume, on *Horace*, of a series of quarto classics published by Tonson. Nor was his business flair confined to publishing: for he seems to have done well out of the investment in the South Sea Company, and even out of John Law's Mississippi Scheme.

Business, and literary men, provided one side of Jacob Tonson's career; the other — not separate from the first — came from politics. Towards the end of William III's reign a group of leading Whigs used to meet informally at an eating-house in Shire Lane near Temple Bar kept by one Christopher Cat, noted for his mutton pies. When Cat moved to the Fountain Tavern in the Strand (? 1698), the 'Kit–Cat Club' moved with him, with Tonson in effect as its secretary. He was thus a central figure in the creation of perhaps the most famous political club in English history, whose members included Somers and Wharton and the young Robert Walpole, Addison and Steele, Congreve and Vanbrugh. About 1703 they moved to the Kit–Cat room in Tonson's country house of Barn Elms, near Putney (which Vanbrugh had designed). The club is immortalised in the series of Kit–Cat portraits painted by Kneller for Tonson, now in the National Portrait Gallery. Thus Jacob Tonson the publisher — whom Pope, about 1731, described as 'full of matter, secret history and wit and spirit, at almost four-score' — played a role at once central and unusual in that critical generation of British history which followed the 'Glorious Revolution'.

D.N.B., Jacob Tonson.
John Carswell, *The Old Cause*, 1954 (especially Chapter VI).

SIR RICHARD STEELE (1672–1729), journalist and Whig, was an Irishman from Dublin, the son of a well-to-do attorney. He was educated at Charterhouse, with Addison as his contemporary, and at Merton College, Oxford. After serving in the Life Guards and living a somewhat dissipated life he turned to writing plays, and in 1707 Harley gave him the post of official gazetteer. In 1709 he started the *Tatler*, published every other weekday, and ran it with Addison's help until 1711; and during 1711–12 he and Addison produced the *Spectator*. Their aim, in which they attained a real measure of success, was to civilize public taste, to make the middle class in particular more moral and more polite — 'to enliven morality with wit, and to temper wit with morality'. Hence came, for example, Steele's famous attack upon duelling. These two papers were very largely non-political. But Steele was an ardent Whig and also used his pen on behalf of Godolphin's ministry, which rewarded him with a second official post, in the Stamp Office. When the Whig's were turned out in 1710 Steele lost his gazetteership, yet not until 1713 did he resign his second office, become an M.P., and attack the Harley–St. John ministry over the question of the French delay in dismantling the fortifications of Dunkirk. In 1714 he wrote *The Crisis*, a pamphlet in which he declared that the Protestant succession was in peril under the Tory ministry, and this caused his expulsion from the Commons. The accession of George I brought Steele into favour. He was knighted in 1715 and obtained a number of government posts. In 1718 he quarrelled with Addison when the Whig groups in Parliament split over the Peerage Bill. His last play, *The Conscious Lovers*, was produced at Drury Lane in 1722.

G. A. Aitken, *Sir Richard Steele*, 1889.
W. Connely, *Sir Richard Steele*, 1934.

JOSEPH ADDISON (1672–1719), essayist and politician, born at Milston, near Amesbury in Wiltshire, the son of an Anglican divine, was educated at Charterhouse and at The Queen's and Magdalen Colleges, Oxford, where he showed himself an elegant scholar in Latin verse. His political views were Whig, and through the patronage of Somers and Charles Montagu he obtained a pension of £300 a year to enable him to travel on the continent in preparation for a diplomatic career. He was abroad from 1699 to 1703, and his first service to the Whigs on his return was to write at Godolphin's instance his poem *The Campaign* (1705), in praise of Marlborough's victory at Blenheim. In 1706 he was rewarded with an under-secretaryship of state, in 1708 Whig interest put him in as M.P. for Lostwithiel, and next year he went to Ireland as Chief Secretary under Wharton, the new Lord-Lieutenant. So shy that he failed miserably as a speaker in the Commons, something of a prig and prone to jealously, Addison was nevertheless by this time a popular figure in literary circles in London, and he began his career as an essayist by his contributions to Richard Steele's *Tatler* in 1709. Godolphin's ministry fell in 1710 and Addison lost his secretary-ship. In the election that October Addison's efforts in his short-lived political journal, *The Whig Examiner*, did not save his party from rout, although he himself was returned for Malmesbury without a contest.

'In a fortunate hour he turned for awhile from the service of party to that of mankind' *. The first number of the *Spectator*, produced by Steele and Addison together, appeared in March 1711. It came out daily and ran until the end of 1712. Addison wrote nearly half the pieces in it, and all the best ones. Witty, decorous and urbane, the effective creator of Sir Roger de Coverley, he at once established himself as one of the most elegant of essayists, and over the succeeding years he did much to civilize as well as entertain thousands of middle-class readers, many of whom were women. His descriptions of English country life, under the most good-natured of squires, have coloured the work of social historians of Anne's reign ever since; and in much of what he wrote — as for example in his acceptance of the Newtonian universe, expressed in the famous *Hymn*, 'The spacious firmament on high', published in the *Spectator* in 1712 — he reflected with conscious fidelity the outlook of the intelligent educated man of his age. After the *Spectator* its successor, the *Guardian* of 1713, was dull, no doubt because Addison con-tributed little to it. This was the year of the production of his tragedy *Cato*, which received an immense welcome at Drury Lane. In 1714, when Steele had turned to politics, Addison added another volume to the *Spectator*. But the accession of George I and the recall of the Whigs brought Addison himself back to politics, for a short time as Irish Secretary once more and then as a Lord Commissioner of trade, and in 1715–16 he wrote a successful political newspaper, the *Freeholder*. He married in 1716 the imperious Countess Dow-ager of Warwick, and the last years of his life were clouded by domestic disagreements as well as by ill-health and a quarrel with Steele. He died in 1719 at the age of forty-seven.

*G. M. Trevelyan, *England under Queen Anne*, Vol. III, 1934, p.101.

P. Smithers, *Joseph Addison*, 1954.

B. Dobrée, *Essays in Biography*, 1925.

T. B. Macaulay, 'The Life and Writings of Addison', in *Critical and Historical Essays*, 1843.

RICHARD BENTLEY (1662–1742), the greatest classical scholar of his time, was the son of a yeoman from Oulton, in the West Riding of Yorkshire, and was educated at Wakefield Grammar School, whence he went up to St. John's College, Cambridge, in 1676. An appointment in 1682 as tutor to the son of Stillingfleet, then Dean of St. Paul's, gave him access to an excellent private library, and until 1689 he lived in Stillingfleet's house, applying his enormous industry and strong mind to the acquisition of a store of classical and biblical erudition. The first published piece of work which revealed the outstanding force of his mind was his *Letter to John Mill* (1691). In 1692 he was appointed Keeper of the Royal Libraries, and his room in St. James's Palace became the regular meeting-place of as eminent a group of men as have ever met together in our history, with Locke, Newton and Wren among them. At the end of that decade he became involved in the contemporary controversy about the respective merits of the ancients and the moderns. A young Oxford man, Charles Boyle, published an edition of the *Letters of Phalaris*, a Greek tyrant of 600 B.C., in the preface to which he criticized Bentley for discourtesy about the loan of a manuscript from the Royal Library. Bentley after some delay replied to Boyle, demonstrating conclusively that the *Letters* were spurious and that Boyle's edition was a very bad one. Boyle and a number of Oxford dons produced a superficial and witty reply, aimed at Bentley's arrogance. To this Bentley's answer (1699) was the *Dissertation on the Letters of Phalaris*, crushing, shrewd, luminous, a brilliant masterpiece of classical erudition which showed its author's remarkable range of philological and historical learning and established his place as a dominant figure in the contemporary restoration of classical studies.

In the following year Bentley was appointed by the Crown as Master of Trinity College, Cambridge, and this office he held until his death forty-two years later. Bentley was a formidable and overbearing man; the Fellows of Trinity quickly suspected him of

Richard Bentley c.1710
(Artist: after Sir James Thornhill)

intruding upon their rights, and so the years of Bentley's mastership were a period of prolonged strife within the college, strife which was stimulated by litigation and insult. At one point he was deprived of the mastership, but he contrived to evade expulsion, waiting until the fortunes of the conflict turned once more to his favour. Meanwhile he managed both to raise the intellectual standards of the college and to publish a considerable output of classical scholarship, most of it textual criticism, written in a style at once lucid and pungent. If later ages have come to regard much of his detailed work, for example, in his edition of Horace, as more ingenious than convincing, his intellectual stature remains undiminished. Bentley was a giant entirely comparable with Newton and Wren, a great European figure as few Englishmen of his time were.

R. J. White, *Dr. Bentley: A Study in Academic Scarlet*, 1965.

GEORGE HICKES (1642–1715), divine and scholar, was one of two Yorkshire brothers who travelled very different spiritual roads. He became the most active of the Non-Jurors; his brother John was the Nonconformist minister executed after Monmouth's rebellion in 1685 and for whose harbouring Alice Lisle was put to death. Born on a farm near Thirsk, George Hickes went to Northallerton Grammar School and thence to St. John's College, Oxford. He was for some years a Fellow of Lincoln and later Chaplain to Lauderdale, and in 1683 he was elected Dean of Worcester. He was an outspoken Anglican opponent of James II's Declaration of Indulgence. But he accepted the implications of the doctrine of non-resistance; he declined the oaths to William and Mary, and was therefore deprived of his deanery in 1690. Unlike other eminent Non-Jurors, such as Ken, Hickes was ready to prolong the schism indefinitely, and he was a leading figure in their negotiations with James II. Yet Hickes was at the same time devoting himself to sustained and laborious scholarship. In the words of Professor Douglas, 'the investigations which were later to produce the most elaborate treatise of historical philology that was ever devoted to the Anglo-Saxon language, were carried on by a political refugee busy with the constant preparation of pamphlets, and risking his neck in negotiations with a deposed prince'. The great treatise was the *Thesaurus* of the northern tongues, published in 1703–5, which opened the way to the linguistic and more especially to the historical study of Anglo-Saxon times.

D. C. Douglas, *English Scholars*, 1951 ed., pp. 77-97.

ELIZABETH ELSTOB (1683–1756), 'the Saxon nymph', was the daughter of a Newcastle-on-Tyne merchant and the sister of William Elstob, divine, antiquary, and Fellow of University College, Oxford. She learned eight languages, despite a guardian who told her (at the age of eight) that 'surely one tongue was enough for a woman', and she became an Anglo-Saxon scholar. In 1709 she published an edition of Aelfric's *Homily on the Nativity of Saint Gregory*, and in 1715 an Anglo-Saxon grammar called *Rudiments of Grammar for the English Tongue* and intended for those 'whose education hath not allowed them an Acquaintance with the Grammars of other languages'. Until 1715 she lived with her brother, and his death in that year left her in poverty. For many years she ran a school at Evesham, not very successfully despite some financial aid from Queen Caroline, and in 1758 she became governess to the Duchess of Portland's children. No doubt Elizabeth Elstob was not a great Anglo-Saxon scholar; but it was a phenomenon that she should be one at all. As Professor David Douglas has put it, she must 'be regarded as a pioneer in the plea that historical scholarship should not be confined to men'*.

SIR JOHN VANBRUGH (1664–1726), playwright and architect, was a Londoner, the son of a rich sugar-baker, with Flemish blood from his refugee grandfather. Brought up to be a gentleman, Vanbrugh was commissioned in the Earl of Huntingdon's regiment at twenty-two. From 1690 to 1692 he was imprisoned in France as a suspected spy, for some of the time in the Bastille, where he whiled away the hours writing plays. After a very short spell as a captain in the Marines, he devoted his considerable wit and his somewhat intermittent energies to writing for the theatre. He produced ten plays in all during his life. The first was *The Relapse* (1696), the best-known *The Provok'd Wife* (1697), the most convincing *The Confederacy* (1705) which he adapted from the French. As a playwright Vanbrugh was fluent, readable, uneven and, by the standards of Restoration comedy, conventional in theme, tone and situation.

He became an architect quite suddenly, by designing the great Yorkshire mansion of Castle Howard for the Earl of Carlisle in

* *English Scholars*, 1660–1730, 1951 ed., p. 75. The whole passage is a scholarly commentary on Elizabeth Elstob's work.

Sir John Vanbrugh c.1704–10
(Artist: Sir George Kneller)

1699. He had had no sort of professional training, and therefore his appointment in 1702 as Comptroller of Works, involving the dismissal from that post of William Talman, the architect of Chatsworth, was a scandalous 'job' — though not quite as scandalous as Vanbrugh's further appointment, in 1704, as Clarencieux

King of Arms, despite his complete contempt for heraldry. This succession of episodes, all contrived by his patron Carlisle, forms a curious beginning for a distinguished architectural career. He began building Castle Howard in 1701, and four years later he got an even more splendid commission, for Marlborough's palace of Blenheim. In 1705 also he built the Opera House in the Haymarket, and managed it for two years: it failed lamentably, partly at least because the acoustics were bad. In 1707 he began to remodel Kimbolton Castle, and in 1710 he designed King's Weston House near Bristol.

His later career was not without vicissitudes. Vanbrugh's politics were notoriously Whig. He was a founder-member of the Kit-Cat Club, and there were those, like Marlborough's Jacobite friend the Earl of Ailesbury, who believed that it was his Whig views that had made him architect of Blenheim. When the Whig ministers were turned out after 1710 Vanbrugh was in difficulty. Funds for Blenheim were cut off, and in 1712 he was dismissed from his comptrollership. But George I's accession in 1714 restored the Whigs. Vanbrugh not only recovered his office; he got a knighthood, and in 1716 took over from Wren as Surveyor at Greenwich, where he built an extraordinary dormitory block alongside his predecessor's hall. During the remaining years of his life he built three more mansions, Eastbury, Seaton Delaval, and Grimsthorpe. Blenheim Palace itself was completed a year before his death in 1726, but not by Vanbrugh. He had become involved in a prolonged row with the Duchess of Marlborough, who eventually forbade him to appear at Blenheim at all and only paid her debts to him after Walpole had intervened.

Blenheim, at once castle and palace, was Vanbrugh's masterpiece, the most staggering achievement of the so-called 'English Baroque' style of which he was the most brilliant exponent. Yet Blenheim contains some of the work of Hawksmore, to whose professional expertise he owed much. Seaton Delaval, that unforgettable Northumbrian house, with its Tudor flavour and octagonal towers, its air of fantasy and impression of movement, is perhaps Vanbrugh's best memorial.

L. Whistler, *Sir John Vanbrugh, Architect and Dramatist*, 1938, and *The Imagination of Vanbrugh*, 1954.

NICHOLAS HAWKSMORE or HAWKSMOOR (1661–1736), architect, born in Nottinghamshire, went to London at eighteen and was employed by Sir Christopher Wren as a domestic clerk. At twenty-one he was helping Wren at Chelsea Hospital, and for the next quarter of a century, until Wren's retirement in 1718, Hawksmore occupied a variety of subordinate posts, such as Clerk of the Works or Deputy Surveyor, at the various 'Royal Works', including Greenwich, Kensington and Hampton Court. Moreover, he acted as amanuensis for Wren at St. Paul's from 1691 onwards, and in 1692, under the latter's nominal supervision, constructed the Writing School at Christ's Hospital, a building which in its feeling for mass reveals a very different hand from Wren's. From 1699 Hawksmore was closely associated with Sir John Vanbrugh, in such buildings as Castle Howard and Blenheim, the latter of which he finished; and from 1707 he was also building independently. Dismissed from his posts at the Royal Works in 1718, he became Deputy Comptroller under Vanbrugh not long before the latter died in 1726. Hawksmore himself died ten years later after a long professional career. The debt of Vanbrugh to this modest man of humble origins who was always subordinate to him was great, and in some of the work it is very difficult to disentangle their respective contributions. It has been suggested that it is 'to Vanbrugh that we chiefly owe the daring novelties of composition [of such houses as Castle Howard and Blenheim]; but that it was Hawksmore who discovered the mode of expression appropriate to these adventures' *. Certainly Hawksmore's own legacy to posterity was a splendid one, including as it did the six churches he built in the city of London after 1712, with Christ Church, Spitalfields, as perhaps the most distinguished; and at Oxford the chapel and hall of The Queen's College and much of the north quadrangle of All Souls.

H. S. Goodhart-Rendel, *Nicholas Hawksmoor*, 1924.
Kerry Downes, *Hawksmoor*, 1959.

SIR GODFREY KNELLER (1646?–1723), portrait-painter, was born at Lubeck, son of the city surveyor, and studied in Holland and Italy. Coming to England in 1675, he quickly became fashion-

* Sir John Summerson, *Architecture in Britain, 1530–1830*, 1953, p. 175.

able, and few artists have had so successful a career in this country. He painted Charles II and James II and was appointed court painter to William III. Naturalized in 1683, he was knighted in 1691 and made a baronet in 1715. Kneller was an arrogant man with a high opinion of his own powers. Like Lely, he made art into an organized industry: his studio was a painting factory, with specialist assistants who each added a particular item, like a wig or draperies, to the basic portrait done by the master himself, and who turned out the numerous copies of Kneller's royal portraits. Inevitably much of his considerable output was mechanical and uninspired. Nevertheless, Kneller had the sharp eye of the great portrait-painter, as he showed, for example, in the famous series of forty-two paintings of the Whigs in the Kit-Cat Club, of which those of Vanbrugh and Wharton are representative. Whatever the artist's judgment upon Kneller's attitude to his sitters, for the historian at least he provides unusually valuable documentary evidence.

M. Whinney and O. Millar, *English Art*, 1625–1714, 1957.

JANE WENHAM (*d.* 1730), of Hertfordshire, was the last woman to be convicted for witchcraft in England. At her trial (1712) the jury found her guilty despite the directions of the judge, Sir John Powell, who commented upon one of the charges that there was no law against flying. She was condemned to death but pardoned. The case provoked a number of pamphlets, on both sides. The Age of Reason brought the abolition of the death penalty for witchcraft in 1736.

EDWARD LLOYD (*d.* 1713), was keeping a coffee-house in Tower Street, London, in 1688, and he moved to larger premises in Lombard Street in 1692. Four years later he began to publish every three weeks a paper called *Lloyd's News*, which contained a good deal of special information about shipping as well as more general news from home and abroad. This lasted only a few months, being apparently brought to an end because of a protest from the House of Lords over an erroneous item, and it was not revived for nearly forty years, when it took the form of *Lloyd's List*, devoted to material about shipping. Little is known of Edward Lloyd; but by the time of his death in 1713 his coffee house was already prospering, as the

Tatler and *Spectator* showed, and was firmly established as a centre of marine insurance.

SIR AMBROSE CROWLEY (1658–1713), ironmaster, was born at Stourbridge, son of a Quaker nailer and blacksmith who built up a prosperous business as an ironmonger (i.e. a wholesale trader in iron goods) and in 1673 sent him as apprentice to a London merchant in the same line of trade. By 1684 he had established his own business with its headquarters in London and with a factory for the manufacture of nails in Sunderland, where he employed foreign workmen from Liège. It seems possible that it was Crowley who originated the modern usage of the word 'factory'. In 1691 he moved the factory to Winlaton, near Newcastle-upon-Tyne, and soon extended its activity to various kinds of ironware. A strong personality with boundless self-confidence, Crowley had laid the foundations of success. The French Wars between 1689 and 1713 gave him the opportunity to expand. From about 1693 he obtained contracts to supply the Navy, first with sheathing nails and then with every kind of iron goods. He developed his business with bold and shrewd judgment, creating a second works, including slitting and rolling mills, at Winlaton, transferring his headquarters to Greenwich, and buying out competitors. With a chain of warehouses in the midlands and at the naval bases along the Thames Estuary, Ambrose Crowley had built up by 1707, the year of his knighthood, the greatest industrial organization of his day. When he died in 1713, a few weeks after being elected M.P. for Andover, he was worth well over £100,000. Besides its sheer scale, Crowley's business was in several ways remarkable. Although his trading interests link him more closely with the great merchants of the seventeenth century than with the industrialists of the eighteenth, the integrated structure of his enterprise and his deliberate concentration upon a national rather than a regional market anticipated the later age. He provided his factories with a written constitution, the *Law Book of the Crowley Iron Works* (a copy of which is in the British Museum), which defined the functions of his staff and the modes of production. It also gave expression to Crowley's genuine and unusual concern for the well-being, moral even more than physical, of his employees: they were provided with a scheme of compulsory insurance, a school, a welfare code and a system of arbitration. Most significant of all, there can be little doubt that Crowley owed a great measure of his success simply to his honesty. Hard, loud-voiced, autocratic, terrifyingly efficient, Crowley was neither a popular nor an attractive man, yet his contemporaries had immense regard for his integrity. He seems to have dropped his connection with the Quakers when he went to London; he was married in church and active in parish business. But he followed throughout his career the Quaker precept of complete honesty in all business dealings.

M. W. Flinn, *Men of Iron: The Crowleys in the Early Iron Industry*, 1962.

ABRAHAM DARBY (1678–1717), discoverer of the process of smelting iron with coke, was born near Dudley, where his father and his grandfather had been yeomen who combined farming with the making of nails and locks. Apprenticed to a manufacturer of malt-mills in Birmingham, in 1699 he became a partner in a brass-works at Baptist Mills, Bristol. Anxious to extend the works to include iron casting, he visited Holland in 1704 and brought skilled workmen back with him; and in 1707 in conjunction with his assistant John Thomas he took out a patent for 'Casting Iron-Bellied Pots, and other Iron-bellied ware in Sand only, without Loam or Clay'. Presumably this opened prospects of expansion, for soon Darby withdrew from the Baptist Mills concern and took a lease of an iron furnace at Coalbrookdale in Shropshire. So began one of the most celebrated of pioneering industries in British history, and it was here at some time before 1711 that Darby, aided by the peculiarly suitable clod coal of the district, hit upon the process of smelting iron with coke. Yet it was a generation before this revolutionary technique became widely known: partly because it was some time before the process became reliable and its product acceptable to the forge-masters, partly perhaps because the Darbys were Quakers, with little liking for self-advertisement. In his own lifetime Abraham Darby saw no revolution in the iron industry as a consequence of his discovery. His immediate achievement was the substantial foundation of a dynasty of Quaker ironmasters based upon Coalbrookdale. The firm grew rapidly, and at the time of his early death in 1717 was about to open a new furnace at Dolgelley.

Arthur Raistrick, *Dynasty of Ironfounders: the Darbys and Coal-brookdale*, 1953, pp. 17-46.

THOMAS NEWCOMEN (1663–1729), was a blacksmith or ironmonger of Dartmouth. He was a skilled craftsman and no scientist, yet it is of considerable interest that in the 1680s he was corresponding with Robert Hooke about atmospheric engines and about the steam-pump invented by the Huguenot refugee, Dr. Papin, a friend of Hooke. His invention of the atmospheric engine was in essence simply an improvement upon the 'fire engine' patented (1698) by another Devonian, Thomas Savery, the military engineer. The Newcomen engine, made in 1705, was a reciprocating engine intended to drive pumps for draining mines. It used steam-power to create a vacuum upon which the pressure of the atmosphere would act and so move the heavy beam connected with the pumping rods. It was widely used during the eighteenth century, in the coalpits of the north and midlands as well as in the tin-mines of Cornwall, and also as an indirect source of power by driving water-wheels for ironworks. Its weakness, seriously felt in Cornwall if not on the coalfields, was its inordinate consumption of fuel, and this led in the later years of the eighteenth century to its transformation by Cornish engineers such as the Trevithicks and its replacement by James Watt's steam-engine.

L. T. C. Rolt, *Thomas Newcomen: the pre-history of the steam-engine*, 1963.
L. T. C. Rolt and J. S. Allen, *The Steam Engine of Thomas New-comen*, 1977.

GLOSSARY

(Biographies of those named in bold type will be found on the pages indicated.)

Agitators. Representatives chosen by the rank and file of the New Model Army in 1647 to discuss problems of pay with the officers and with Parliament.

Agreement of the People. The proposals of the Levellers for a new constitution, first propounded in 1647: their main item was a substantial extension of the franchise, falling short, however, of manhood suffrage. (See **Lilburne**, p. 157–8.)

Antinomianism. The belief that the customary moral code is not binding on Christians, because faith alone is sufficient for salvation; held in the seventeenth century only by a tiny minority on the Puritan left.

Apology of the Commons. Presented by the Commons to James I in 1604, stating their views of their rights and privileges.

Arminians. The word (derived from the Dutch theologian Jacob Arminius, hostile to Calvinism) used c.1600–50 to describe those Anglican who wished to reintroduce Catholic ceremonies into the Church of England. (See **Andrewes**, p. 35, and **Laud**, p. 74–9.)

Attainder. An Act of Parliament condemning a man to death, usually for treason. (See **Strafford**, p. 72 and **Fenwick**, p. 389.)

Authorized Version. The English translation of the Bible made as a result of the Hampton Court Conference of 1604; first published in 1611.

Baptists. A Puritan sect which took firm shape during the seventeenth century; its members rejected infant baptism.

Barebone's Parliament. See **Nominated Assembly**, below.

Book of Sports. A declaration in favour of certain lawful sports, issued by James I in 1618 and reissued by Charles I in 1633. This expressed royal approval of such activities as morris dancing after divine service on Sundays, and became an object of zealous opposition from Puritans of sabbatarian opinions.

Calvinism. The version of Protestantism expounded by John Calvin, upon whom most seventeenth-century English Puritanism was based; its most celebrated features were the doctrine of predestination, and the abolition of episcopacy in church government.

Cameronians. (See **Cameron**, p. 321.)

Clarendon Code. The series of statutes in the early years of Charles II's reign which imposed various disabilities on Dissenters. The Corporation Act (1661) excluded them from town government, the Act of Uniformity (1662) deprived them of church livings and schoolmasterships; the Conventicle Act (1664) restricted their meetings, the Five Mile Act (1665) attempted to prevent their ministers from living in towns.

Conventicles. Meetings of Protestant Dissenters for religious purposes.

Copernican Astronomy. The astronomy propounded by the Polish scientist Copernicus, which regarded the sun as the centre of the universe, in contrast to the earlier Ptolemaic astronomy which placed the earth at the centre.

Country Party. That loosely-organized group of M.P.s led by Shaftesbury who opposed the Court Party led by Danby in Charles II's reign. See **Whig**, below.

Court of Wards. Established by statute in 1540 to safeguard the Crown's financial interests in the royal wards and the administration of their lands, marriages, etc.

Court Party. That group of M.P.s who wished to defend the authority of the Crown in Charles II's reign. See **Tory**, below.

Covenanters. Those Scottish Presbyterians, ministers and laity, who remained loyal to the National Covenant against episcopacy, first sworn in 1638. See **National Covenant**, below.

Customs Farmers. The customs, i.e. taxes on imports and exports, were normally collected not by government officials but by the tax-farmers, who in return for a lump sum had acquired the right to collect and who expected to clear a good profit on the transaction.

Declarations of Indulgence. The declarations made by Charles II (in 1662 and 1672) and by James II (1687 and 1688), on the strength of the royal prerogative, relaxing the penal laws against Catholics and Dissenters.

Diggers. (See **Winstanley**, p. 190.)

Dissenters. The term used in the later seventeenth century, after the Restoration, to describe those Protestants who declined to worship according to Anglican rites. They dissented from, or refused to conform to, the Church of England; from the eighteenth century onwards they were usually called Nonconformists.

Distraint of Knighthood. The name given to the legal process whereby Charles I in the 1630s compelled all those who owned land worth £40 per annum to become knights (and to pay fees for the privilege) or to pay a substantial fine.

Divine Right of Kings. The doctrine, devised in the Middle Ages as a counterblast to Papal claims, which maintained that Kings were of divine appointment and responsible only to God for their conduct. (See **James I**, p. 4.)

Eastern Association. The group of eastern counties (Norfolk, Suffolk, Cambs., Essex and Herts., and later Hunts. and Lincs.) which joined to create an army for Parliament in the early stages of the Civil War.

Ecclesiastical Commission. A court on the lines of **High Commission** (*q.v.*) set up by James II in 1686 as a means of coercing those clergy who resisted his Catholicizing policy.

Engagement. (1) The treaty made by Charles I with the Scots in 1647, which led to the Second Civil War. (2) The oath of loyalty to the Republican Commonwealth, required of all men over eighteen in 1650.

Exclusion. The proposal to exclude James, Duke of York, from the succession to the throne on the ground that he was a Roman Catholic: hence the 'Exclusion Crisis' of 1678–81.

Fifth Monarchists. Those Puritan extremists who believed that the prophecies of Daniel were about to be fulfilled: the Fourth Monarchy, that of Rome which had become Antichrist, was shortly to be overthrown, and the Fifth, the reign of King Jesus, would begin. (See **Venner**, p. 236.)

Five Members. The five members of the Commons whom Charles I tried to arrest in January 1642. They were **Pym**, p. 107, **Hampden**, p. 109, **Hesilrige**, p. 111, **Holles**, p. 112 and **William Strode**, p. 107. (See also **Lenthall**, p. 112.)

Forced Loan. The demand for a compulsory loan, made by Charles I without Parliamentary sanction in 1626 and repeated in 1637, concentrated opposition to him in the early stages of his reign.

Forest Fines were imposed by Charles I in the 1630s for encroachments made by landowners upon royal forest land during past centuries and for breaches of laws long obsolete.

Friends. See **Quakers**, below.

Gentry. An imprecise term usually meaning relatively well-to-do landowners, next below the peerage in social standing; they were the group from which J.P.s, for example, were drawn, but their incomes varied widely.

Grand Remonstrance. The statement of parliamentarian grievances against Charles I, and proposals for reform, debated in November 1641. (See **Pym**, p. 106, and **Hampden**, p. 110.)

Habeas Corpus. A writ issued to the gaoler requiring him to show cause before a judge on a named date why a particular prisoner should not be set free: given statutory backing in criminal cases in 1679, it became the most important single legal safeguard of individual liberty.

Heads of the Proposals. (See **Ireton**, p. 142.)

High Commission. An ecclesiastical prerogative court established c.1580 and much used in Elizabeth's reign as a means of crushing Puritanism.

Humble Petition and Advice. The constitution of 1657 under which Oliver Cromwell was offered the Crown; it set up a second chamber.

Impeachment. Trial by the House of Lords on charges brought by the House of Commons.

Impositions. Non-parliamentary taxes on imports levied by James I's government, and declared legal by the judges in Bate's Case (1606) on the ground that the King had authority to regulate foreign trade.

Independents. A general name applied to Puritans of radical and often individualist doctrinal opinions; in the 1640s it came to have a political usage, meaning the more radical and extreme opponents of the King.

Instrument of Government. The republican constitution of December 1653 under which Oliver Cromwell became Lord Protector.

Ironsides. The name ('Old Ironsides') first applied to Oliver Cromwell by Prince Rupert and later used of his regiment of Puritans.

Jacobites. Those who remained loyal to James II (*Jacobus*, Latin = James) after the Revolution of 1688, and to James Edward, the Old Pretender, after his father's death in 1701.

Junto (or Junta). The group of grandees who guided the policies of the Whigs in the reigns of William III and Anne: its principal members were **Somers, p. 377, Montagu, p. 379,** and **Wharton, p. 376.**

Kirk. The Presbyterian Church in Scotland.

Latitudinarians. Those divines who in the late seventeenth century held liberal doctrinal views and favoured toleration. (See **Tillotson, p. 386** and **Tenison, p. 387.**)

Levellers. The democratic political movement which arose in the later 1640s demanding a wider franchise and many social reforms. (See **Lilburne, p. 157,** and **Walwyn, p. 160.**)

Limitations. The scheme put forward c.1679 as an alternative to Exclusion, whereby James, Duke of York was to succeed to the throne but with limited powers.

Major-Generals. The officers appointed by Cromwell in 1655–6 to control the militia and to administer Puritan social policy.

Monopolies. The practice, indulged in both by Elizabeth I and by the first two Stuarts, of giving or selling to courtiers or others the sole right to manufacture or sell certain articles or commodities.

National Covenant. Sworn by the Scots in 1638, to defend their Presbyterian Church against episcopacy.

New Model Army. The new army raised by Parliament in 1645 under the command of Fairfax.

Nineteen Propositions. The demands put by Parliament to Charles I in 1642 just before the outbreak of civil war. Their main features included parliamentary control of the Church, the army, the King's council, and the education of his children. Charles rejected them.

Nominated Assembly. (= **Barebone's Parliament** or **Parliament of Saints**). Set up in 1653, consisting of godly members nominated by the Council of Officers, some of them having been chosen by local Puritan congregations.

Nonconformists. See **Dissenters**, above.

Non-Jurors. Those clergy who declined to swear the oath of allegiance to William and Mary after the Revolution of 1688, and who were deprived of their benefices.

Non-Resistance. The doctrine of non-resistance to the Crown was preached by many Anglican divines after the Restoration: the monarch was divinely appointed, and therefore rebellion was a sin.

Occasional Conformity. The practice, indulged in by many Dissenters in the reigns of William III and Anne, of receiving the Anglican sacrament once a year in order to qualify for civil office.

Pilgrim Fathers. The group of Puritans who sailed to North America from Plymouth in the *Mayflower* in 1620.

Popish Plot. (See Oates, p. 308.)

Prerogative. The recognized, yet ill-defined, powers of the King, above and beyond those which he could use through Parliament.

Prerogative Courts. Courts, e.g. Star Chamber and High Commission, which were in effect offshoots of the King's Council; they were quicker and cheaper in procedure and more subject to royal control than the Common Law courts.

Presbyterian. Strictly, one who accepted Calvinist teachings about church government, with rule by synods of lay elders and ministers replacing bishops, as, for example, in the Church of Scotland. But the English Presbyterians in the seventeenth century were not as rigid as the Scots. In the 1640s the word came to have a political usage, meaning a conservative and moderate Puritan opponent of the Crown.

Protestation of the Commons. A protest in 1621 stating that the Commons' privileges and freedom of discussion, especially of foreign policy, were of right; the King solemnly tore from the journal of the House the pages on which it was recorded.

Puritan. A word of diverse and changing meaning in the seventeenth century, it indicates (1) one who, while remaining within the Church of England, was deeply hostile to the changes, e.g. in church government and in ritual, introduced by Laud and other Arminians; (2) one who broke away from the Church and joined or formed one of the sects; (3) especially *c.* 1630-60, a political opponent of royal government.

Quaker. Member of the sect known as the Society of Friends which came into being in the 1650s; Quakers had no ministers or formal liturgy and rejected tithes, oaths and war. (See **George Fox**, p. 205.)

Recusants. Those who refused (*recuso*, Latin = I refuse) to attend Church of England services; the great majority of them in the early seventeenth century were Roman Catholics.

Root and Branch. The name given to the Puritan proposals for the radical reform of the Church — notably for the abolition of episcopacy — originally put forward in a London petition to the Long Parliament in 1640.

Rump. The name given to what was left of the Long Parliament after Pride's Purge (1648).

Sectaries. Puritans who belonged to one of the many sects which sprang up in the middle years of the seventeenth century. The word usually denotes extremism, and excludes such conservative Puritans as the Presbyterians.

Self-denying Ordinance. Passed by Parliament in 1645, to remove M.P.s from military command and thus get rid of lukewarm commanders. (See **Manchester**, p. 130.)

Seven Bishops. The bishops whom James II had tried for seditious libel in 1688, and whose acquittal was a signal for revolution. They were **Sancroft** (Canterbury), p. 343, **Ken** (Bath and Wells), p. 347, **Trelawny** (Bristol), p. 346, Lake (Chichester), Lloyd (St. Asaph), Turner (Ely), and White (Peterborough).

Ship Money. A non-parliamentary tax traditionally imposed on the coastal counties in lieu of providing ships for naval service; extended to inland counties by Charles I in 1635.

Solemn League and Covenant. The treaty between the English Parliament and the Scots in 1643.

Spanish Marriage Project. James I's plan to marry his heir to a Spanish princess and thus bring peace between Catholics and Protestants.

Star Chamber. The most famous of the prerogative courts, it was in fact the King's Council sitting as a court, originally in a room in the palace at Westminster which, in the words of Sir Thomas Smith (1565) 'is called the Star Chamber, either because it is full of windows or because at the first all the roof thereof was decked with images of stars gilded'.

Tonnage and Poundage. Long-established customs duties, per tun of wine imported and per pound's worth of merchandise imported or exported, traditionally granted to the Crown at the beginning of each reign; in 1625 it was for the first time only granted for one year, which much offended Charles I.

Tory. A word meaning an Irish bandit, employed by the enemies of the Court in Charles II's reign to describe its supporters at the time of the Exclusion crisis; it became a party name for those politicians who supported the claims of the Crown and of the Church of England.

Train or Trained Bands. The traditional local militia, based on the duty of every man to serve when the country was invaded; embodied locally by both sides in the Civil War, they proved of little military worth, except those of London, who provided a highly important reserve for Parliament.

Unitarians. Those Dissenters who declined to accept the doctrine of the Trinity; they emerged as a separate sect during the Commonwealth period. Members of other dissenting groups, e.g. many English Presbyterians, held Unitarian views.

Whig. An abbreviation of Whigamore, meaning a Scottish Presbyterian rebel; employed by courtiers at the time of the Exclusion crisis as a term of abuse to describe their opponents, the Country Party; became a party name for those politicians who wished to limit royal power, supported toleration for Dissenters, and won a strong following among the merchants.

INDEX

Burnet, Gilbert, Bishop – *contd.*
315; on Sancroft, 344
Burton, Henry, 78, 95
Busby, Richard, 195-6, 250, 263, 271, 354, 370
Butler, Samuel, 270-1

Calamy, Edward, the Elder, 201-2
Cameron, Richard, 321
Carew, Thomas, 86
Carr, Robert, Earl of Somerset, 6, 12, 14-15, 15-16, 36
Cary, Lucius: *see* Falkland, 2nd Viscount
Castlemaine, Barbara Villiers, Countess of, 226, 230, 232-3, 405
Catesby, Robert, 12-13
Catherine of Braganza, Queen Consort, 102, 226, 228, 229-31, 233, 234, 324, 332
Cavendish, William: *see* Newcastle, 1st Duke of
Cecil, Robert, Earl of Salisbury, 4, 10-12, 14, 15, 23, 26, 80
Chamberlain, Peter, 192-3
Charles I, 5, 51-7, 57, 60, 62, 63, 82, 87, 109, 111, 112-13, 117, 118, 123, 130, 132, 171, 188, 192; and Buckingham, 17-20; and Eliot, 67; and Wentworth, 68, 70, 71, 72, 73, 74; and Laud, 74, 76; and Van Dyck, 85, 86; and Hyde, 100; and Pym, 105-7; and Rupert, 119, 121, 122; and Cromwell, 134-8; and Ireton, 141, 142; in Scotland, 147, 148, 149, 150
Charles II, 60, 112, 117, 122, 124, 130, 154, 186, 192, 198, 223-9, 237, 240, 271, 279, 282, 288, 292, 304, 312, 323, 324, 332, 338, 339, 347, 348, 360, 373, 382, 449; as Prince of Wales, 86, 87, 138; and Clarendon, 100, 102; and Montrose, 150; and Monck, 221-2; and Catherine of Braganza, 229-30; and 'Minette', 321; and mistresses, 232-6; and Buckingham, 295; and Shaftesbury, 298; and Lauderdale, 301-3; and Danby, 305-6; and Monmouth, 318; and Godolphin, 412-13
Charles Louis, Elector of Palatine, 8, 122, 243

Chiffinch, William, 232, 332
Child, Sir Josiah, 388-9
Chillingworth, William, 97, 99, 197, 385
Churchill, Arabella, 405, 419
Churchill, John; *see* Marlborough
Clarendon, Edward Hyde, 1st Earl of, 60, 61, 97, 100-3, 112, 114, 117, 126, 127, 128, 144, 164, 170, 177, 179, 223, 226-7, 230, 231, 237, 241, 249, 293, 295, 342, 400; on George Villiers, 17; on Bancroft, 33; on Pembroke, 40; on Ben Johnson, 42; on Charles I, 51; on Laud, 77; on Portland, 79; on Cottington, 81; on Falkland, 98; on Pym, 107; on Hampden, 109; on Newcastle, 123, 124; on Goring, 125; on Manchester, 130; on Cromwell, 138, 139; on Montrose, 147, 151; on Bradshaw, 166; on John Owen, 199; on Castlemaine, 223; on Downing, 240, 241; on Buckingham, 295; on Lauderdale, 303
Clarendon, Henry Hyde, 2nd Earl of, 336-7, 394
Clifford, Thomas, 1st Lord, 227, 292, 294
Coke, Sir Edward, 21-6, 28, 70, 92
Coleman, Edward, 310, 312, 351
College, Stephen, 321, 332
Compton, Henry, Bishop, 334, 334-6, 365
Congreve, William, 273, 400
Cooper, Samuel, 278-9
Cottington, Francis, Baron, 80-1
Cotton, Sir Robert, 37-9
Crab, Roger, 215-6
Cranfield, Lionel, Earl of Middlesex, 17, 20, 31-2, 33, 65
Crashaw, Richard, 91
Cromwell, Henry, 170, 172, 246, 287
Cromwell, Oliver, 56, 81, 95, 107, 112, 113, 115, 117, 118, 119-20, 126, 127, 129, 132, 134-40, 142, 145, 147, 151, 154, 162, 163, 166, 167, 169, 172, 180, 190, 192, 194, 200, 202, 204, 239, 270, 280, 296, 313, 258; and Vane, 116; and Manchester, 129; and Fairfax, 133; and Ireton, 141-2; and Lilburne, 155, 157, 158; and Lambert, 167; and